SVIATOSLAV RICHTER
NOTEBOOKS AND CONVERSATIONS

5/VIII **Вагнер**

„Гибель Богов"

дир. W. Furtwängler
Зигфрид – Ludwig Suthaus
Брингильда – Martha Mödl
Гунтер – Alfred Poell
Хаген – Josef Greindl
Гутруна – Sena Yurinac
Вальтрауда – Margarete Klose
Альберих – ~~Hans~~ Alois Pernerstorfer
I норна – Margrete Klose
II норна Hilde Rössel-Majdan
III норна – Sena Yurinac
Воглинда – Sena Yurinac
Вельгунда – Magda Gabory
Флосхильда – Hilde Rössel-Majdan

слушали:
Ирина Антокова, Наташа Меллер, Галина Писаренко
Вера Прохорова, Эльвира Орлова, Наталия Журавлева
Татьяна Зеленина, Юрий Ярославцев
Виктор Маланичев, Михаил Никешичев
Новомир Писаренко, Виктор Зеленин
С. Р.

перевод либретто
Н. Журавлёв

...по обору придут черны сны пройдут. Зато
...енем заре провещает светлый день и
впервые слышите тему новой брунгил...
...ную и женственную. Появление счастливы...
...и их разговор перед отъездом Зигфрида.
...из самых вдохновенно-радостных момен...
...Затем вы уже на Рейне (тема котор...
...сем рядом «темой грозящих богов»), вы слы...
...пение дочерей Рейна в варианте оканчи...
...щем «Золото Рейна» и потом, «клич мен...
...всё более ударение ... ... лад.
...прибыли в Geidhöhle, вернее к их жилищу и
...звека здесь ... проходную весть к зл...
...дыслал Альбериха. Но— идали рок ...
...строе приближение Зигфрида в ...
...нем Гранг. Официальное знакомство; —
...рика с чашей волшебного напитка (перем...
...водится с Хагеном ... — ... Действие ве...
...водится быстро ... уже Зигфрид ...
...вать брунгильд... дел Гунтера, Хаген один
...знавшим ... Брунгильда любится кольце...
...вот ... полет Валькирий и это Вальтра...
...рассказываем про Вотанов Вальгаллу...
...бда не отдаёт как но не слушает отчаянн...
...со Вальтрауты, та уезжает, очень крич...
...слышен рок Зигфрид, но это же, он а Гунтер...
...им-невидимка ... завладевает I. Действ...
...говор Хагена с Альберихом, «Себе клянусь я
...орит Хаген. Затем ... ... и наконец знам...
...де «Весыле Хагена» по поводу приезда Гунтера...
...ищет бодой. Кульминации братья— когда Бри...
...ова узнаёт Зигфрида уже кольцо на его ру...
...ство ... закалили ... Хаген, бр-д и ...
...ана музыка ... ... вот отъ Рейн во...
...все и дочери ... ... Рейна хохочущ...
...гордым по кольцу он им ... Затем
...ска расколдованного Зигфрида, смерть и тра...
...и марш. Гунтер в беспокойстве. Зигфрид...
...ают. Хаген ... Гунтера но ...

Sviatoslav Richter
Notebooks and Conversations
BRUNO MONSAINGEON

Translated by Stewart Spencer

Princeton University Press
Princeton and Oxford

Published in the United States by Princeton University Press,
41 William Street, Princeton, New Jersey 08540

First published in 1998 by Editions Van de Velde/Actes Sud/Arte Editions, France
This English translation first published in 2001
by Faber and Faber Limited
3 Queen Square, London WC1N 3AU

This work is published with a subsidy from
the French Ministry of Culture – Centre national du livre

Third printing, and first paperback printing, 2002
Paperback ISBN 0-691-09549-3

The cloth edition of this book has been cataloged as follows

Library of Congress Catalog Card Number 00-111970
ISBN 0-691-07438-0

This book has been composed in Sabon

www.pupress.princeton.edu

Photoset by Agnesi Text, Hadleigh, Suffolk
Printed in England by Clays Ltd, St Ives plc

3 5 7 9 10 8 6 4

Contents

Introduction

'Maestro wants Bruno to do his biography.'

'Did he say so himself?'

'Yes, I was in his room a few moments ago and he asked me to look out for you and pass on this message: he wants Bruno to do his biography.'

'But what does he mean: "do" his biography?'

I was talking to a remarkable woman by the name of Milena Borromeo. She had already devoted many years of her life to Richter, having originally worked for an Italian concert agency that had organized his tours of the peninsula. She had been assigned to him because she spoke not only Italian and French but also Russian. Maestro – she never used the definite article but treated the word almost as though it were a proper name – had then asked her to take sole charge of him, with the result that she had become his agent, impresario, assistant, housekeeper and nanny. A saint, always present whatever happened, travelling with him, organizing his life for him and keeping him constant company, undemanding and warm-hearted.

I had gone to see her early in 1995 in order to talk to her about a dream that had obsessed me for ages: it was to make a film about Sviatoslav Richter. I knew that until then no one had managed to persuade him to take part in such a project, but on the other hand I had succeeded in cracking some other equally tough nuts, and it seemed to me terrible to think that an artist as powerfully expressive as Richter – a pianist universally recognized as one of the greatest in history – might die without revealing some of his thoughts about music or first telling the world something about his various activities and his turbulent existence in general, an existence about which people knew either next to nothing or, worse, rumours that were neither verified nor verifiable.

I had succeeded in gaining access to all the great musicians who had ever meant anything to me, those who, since my childhood, had helped to give meaning to my life. I had already met 'Maestro', but did not have the first idea how to tackle him on the subject of a film. I knew that he had become increasingly withdrawn and cut off from the world and that he hated cameras and everything to do with films, even though he was passionate about the cinema and had an impressive knowledge of the medium. If only I could manage to enter his world and gain acceptance, there was no doubt that I could make considerable progress with him, if necessary shoot some Pasolinian scenes and use methods that would not be unworthy of him. It would be enough to create a sense of complicity between us, and to this I was prepared to devote all the time that I needed. If Milena were to speak to him and obtain his permission to see me, might I not then manage to tame him?

Milena had been wonderful and had said that she was convinced of the need to make a film about Richter, but she had discouraged me: 'Many similar projects have already been put to him, but they all came to nothing. He didn't even look at them. He's there in the next room, he's just had an operation on his leg and doesn't even know if he'll ever play the piano again. A film about him? Don't count on it. He's living in another world.'

I made no attempt to delude myself but left copies of two of the films that I had recently made, one on David Oistrakh, the other on Dietrich Fischer-Dieskau.

Then nothing. Summer was drawing nearer – it was still 1995 – and I felt mentally exhausted. Within the space of four years I had completed four major projects, into each of which I had poured all my energies: *L'inconnu de Santa Barbara*, a film about the young French violinist Gilles Apap; *Artist of the People?*, a documentary about David Oistrakh that had been a good ten years in the making; *The Violin of the Century*, an intimate portrait of a miraculous man, Yehudi Menuhin, that was also the culmination of a close friendship dating back to my youth; and, finally, *Autumn Journey*, a retrospective of the magical career of Dietrich Fischer-Dieskau.

I had made these four films one after the other, and they had involved such a degree of emotional investment that I now felt a very real need to recharge my batteries before throwing myself into my next project. For the time being, I refused to be a slave to deadlines: I would take time off to write and think things over, but with no particular aim. I would be free. In early September I was due to leave for a short concert tour in Latin America. I cancelled it.

Lassitude, laziness, premonition? I really could not be bothered to work out what I was feeling.

It was at the beginning of September, at the very time when I should have been on the other side of the world, that the real adventure began in the form of a totally unexpected phone call from the publisher Francis Van de Velde, who in the early 1980s had published a short book that I had written on Nadia Boulanger. Francis had long been a friend of Richter and of the latter's companion, the great soprano Nina Dorliac.

'Nina tells me that Richter has written a kind of ship's diary, notebooks in which he jots down his musical impressions; he's prepared to hand them over to you and work through them with you with a view to having them published. The manuscript is said to run to hundreds of pages.'

'What would my role be?' I asked. 'To read, translate, choose which passages to publish, beat the notes into shape? Could I really work with Richter?'

I was stunned. For us to work together on a literary project of this kind, we would have to meet, and I might then be able to take advantage of the situation and interest him in a film project.

A few days later, Milena, Francis and I met at the Hôtel Majestic, where Richter had been living the life of a hermit for the last few months. We all had only a vague notion of what we were up to.

'Maestro wants Bruno to do his biography,' Milena repeated.

'But what does he mean: "do" his biography? I'm not a biographer. I make films. I'm not about to "do" the biography of someone I've met ten times at most. I need to see him.'

'He won't see anyone.'

'Then what does he want?'

'He wants Bruno to do . . .'

'That doesn't mean anything.'

'Yes it does. Maestro has been complaining about the rumours that are circulating about him, he wants to put the record straight and for you to do his biography.'

'How can I put the record straight if I don't meet him? And what sort of a biography would it be? Written? Filmed? What? I need to see him.'

'He won't see anyone.'

It was all getting more and more confusing. But my first thought was: why had he chosen me? I had in fact seen quite a lot of Richter twenty years earlier, at Tours and in Paris. On one occasion he had even come to my home to practise on my piano for a recital that he was giving with Zoltán Kocsis. It had been a memorable occasion for me, though for rather embarrassing reasons: it was a beautiful June day, the windows had been open, and a neighbour had come and complained about the noise. The rehearsal had been abandoned and we had all had a good laugh.

But did he know me? Whenever we met, he spoke and smiled and was utterly charming, but I did not have the impression that he knew anything about my work and what I was trying to achieve. And so, for me, it was as though he did not know me. At best, I was a name, a face among so many others.

Then, in 1981, a curious thing happened. For a whole month I had effectively been living in another world. Glenn Gould and I were about to complete the editing of our film on the Goldberg Variations in an underground studio somewhere outside Toronto. In the state of intense excitement in which we found ourselves, it was impossible to tear ourselves away from a project that we had come to regard as our child. There was always a comma to be inserted, a subtle point to be honed, an edit that needed attention. When the editing process was finished, we spent a whole night watching the film, but this time as spectators. Suddenly, in the middle of the night, Glenn turned to me: 'You know Richter. Are you in touch with him?'

'Er . . . '

'A musician like him, such a tremendous pianist and he doesn't know how to make a recording. He has no recording philosophy and allows records to be released that are a betrayal of his abilities and in no way represent him. He really must learn the specific art of recording. I'd like to make a recording with him in which I'd be his producer.'

'Glenn, are you serious?'

'I'm damned serious. He could play whatever repertory he liked, even Rachmaninov, on my own piano if he wanted. Put it to him.'

Three weeks later, at the Fêtes Musicales de Touraine, I raised the matter with Richter, first of all explaining that I had just finished a film about the Goldberg Variations with Glenn Gould.

'Did he play the repeats?'

'Yes, the first repeats in the canonic variations.'

'What! Not *all* of them? But I spoke to him about it in Moscow in 1957, after his concert. Such a musician, such a tremendous pianist . . . The work is too complicated; without the repeats no one can follow it. And in any case, that's how it's written.'

'But, Maestro, that's not what's at issue. Don't you think his proposal is worth considering?'

'Where and when?'

'In America, of course.'

'I never go to America.' He then reflected for a moment, before adding: 'Tell Glenn Gould that I accept, but on condition that he agrees to give a recital at my festival in Tours.'

He said this with a smile in his voice, knowing perfectly well that Gould refused to perform in public. And that was the end of the matter.

I thought about this incident even as I was talking to Milena. It was a crazy situation. For years I had been trying to make contact with Richter, and now here I was in the entrance hall of his hotel, and he was refusing to see me while begging me to write about him for reasons that I did not really understand. It was all so vague that I needed to stop and give serious thought to the matter in an attempt to bring some clarity to the situation. It was in order to find a way out of the impasse in which we now found ourselves that I suggested drafting ten or so pages on some of the questions that I believed were important to Richter. I could only write out the text in long hand as I had no Cyrillic typewriter, and my hand-writing was in any case difficult to decipher.

'All the better, he hates anything typed. He always thinks it's mere paperwork.'

I returned home and sat up all the next night working on these dozen pages. By dawn, I still had to write the conclusion, which I did not find at all easy.

It so happened that since *perestroĭka* Proust's works had started to appear in Russian, with the result that on each of my visits to Moscow I had gradually been able to acquire copies of all the volumes of *A la recherche du temps perdu*, with the exception of the final part, *Le temps retrouvé*, which had not yet appeared and, indeed, has still not appeared. I recalled the episode with Berma, the actress modelled on Rachel or Sarah Bernhardt, in which Proust addresses the whole problem of interpretation: by playing Phèdre, did Berma make a new masterpiece out of an existing masterpiece, a masterpiece of interpretation? I quoted this episode by way of a coda, adding: 'What does Maestro think? In other words, can an interpreter be a genius? Can interpretation be seen as an act of genius?' I then faxed my twelve pages to Richter at his hotel.

The same morning I was woken by a phone call from Milena: 'Maestro wants to see you at once.'

The invisible obstacle over which I had been stumbling for years had developed a crack. He wanted to see me, and to see me at once.

Armed with a tape recorder placed at my disposal by Idéale Audience, the production company that was interested in making a film about Richter and to whom I had obviously already spoken, I found myself a few hours later in the salon of the Maestro's modest apartment at the Hôtel Majestic. On the music stand of his digital piano, a Yamaha Clavinova, there was a sheet of paper on which he had written some instructions, a sort of *aide-mémoire* intended for his own private use. (In spite of the totally unpredictable nature of the life that he had chosen to lead, he was always extremely meticulous and well ordered.) While I was waiting, I read what he had written: 'Clean your teeth properly morning and night, read a little Proust or Thomas Mann every day . . . '

The door opened. Richter appeared, looking much older, but imposing, magnificent, smiling, although a little sombre. He held out his hand: '*Privyet!*' ('Hello' in Russian.) We had not seen each other for ten or twelve years, yet he said 'hello' as though we had had a meal together only the previous evening. Then he added: 'Do you remember the day I came to your house?' It was almost twenty years earlier, and in two words he made me realize that he knew me better than I thought and that I was not, as I feared, someone whose face he had seen without knowing who I was.

'Can one now get Proust in Russian in Moscow?' he asked. (He had not been back to Moscow for over two years.)

'Yes,' I said. 'Everything apart from *Le temps retrouvé*.'

'*Le temps retrouvé* is the only volume of *A la recherche* that I don't know. Shall I die without having read it?' He groaned.

Why had I bought Proust in Russian in Moscow? What had inspired me to quote the passage about Berma? This was a sore point with Richter, raising what was a key question for him, the very real problem of interpretation. What is an interpreter? What can he add to an existing work? Or, rather, should he not add anything at all? In Richter's eyes, the interpreter did not exist or rather he was merely a mirror that reflected the score, the fanatically exact and scrupulous reader of the score. It was a fanciful vision, of course, as the force of Richter's personality was such that he was one of the few pianists whom one could identify from the very first note. Gould and Richter.

But this was how we made contact, with the result that during the next two and a half months I saw Richter virtually every day. Even so, nothing had been agreed between us. He remained holed up in his hotel, ill and depressed. When I placed a modest microphone between us, he screwed up his face in disgust as though it were some barbaric and threatening instrument, but it was sufficient for me to place a bunch of white flowers in front of the microphone and conceal it from his sight and the matter was arranged to his satisfaction. Even before the tape recorder had been switched on, he had already declared: 'Nothing interests me any more. It's up to you.'

In circumstances like these, it is difficult to draft a shooting script or even anything that might resemble one. But at least there was now a certain complicity between us. And our conversations took place on a daily basis, unless he cancelled them, generally half an hour before my arrival. On each occasion they lasted a good two hours and sometimes took the form of quite staggering confessions, invariably told in a tone of touching spontaneity.

At the same time, in the wings and in collusion with Nina Dorliac, we were drawing up a plan of campaign. What we were currently doing clearly left Richter cold, at least for the present, although I thought I detected a growing involvement on his part. We were gathering material for a book: that at least was the implication and, indeed, was fairly clear. But as far as a film was concerned, this was to remain a no-go area for some time to come. While recording our conversations, I regretted the absence of a camera capable of capturing a face of such overwhelming sadness but that was also often comical and, above all, infinitely expressive. It was a thousand pities that, at least for the moment, the gentleness of his voice and the originality of what he had to say were immortalized only in sound. Moreover, it was often not the actual content of what he was saying that was so fascinating, but the poetry of his silences or the gestures that accompanied them. Only a camera could have captured these.

Nina Dorliac was won over by the idea of a film and even suggested that we film Richter in secret, without his knowledge. This seemed to her to be paramount. But imagine what might happen: there would be a screen behind which would be a camera and its operator, with a hole pierced in the screen for the lens. It only needed some object to be dropped and Richter would discover the trick and realize that he had been filmed without his knowledge. This seemed to me quite monstrous.

No, we had to be available to start filming at any given moment, no matter where we were, depending on Richter's frame of mind and the point that our relations had reached. An extremely flexible plan was drawn up by Idéale Audience, capable of dealing with every eventuality, and it was left to me to find a suitable occasion for broaching the question with Richter.

In the meantime, we continued our daily sessions. Maestro seemed to enjoy them. His physical and, in consequence, his mental health improved spectacularly. He had even started to play the piano again, after a break of more than six months. (His last concert had been in Lübeck the previous March.) One day in late October he went off to explore Paris, walking all the way from the Avenue Kléber to the Madeleine and back. He was away for three hours. When he got back, he was clearly pleased to see me and happy to talk, and the result was a particularly rewarding session in the course of which he went over to the piano and played me some excerpts from the overture to *Carmen* ('Is it really in A major what I'm playing? To me, it sounds to be in B major') and a prelude that he had written in his youth and presented to Heinrich Neuhaus on his arrival at the Moscow Conservatory in 1937. He spoke to me about his deteriorating hearing, about the sounds that obsessed and assailed his brain both day and night and about the reasons why he now always performed with a score, even though he knew by heart virtually every piece of Western music written during the last two hundred years. In its tone and contents, everything he confided in me was profoundly moving in its candour. At the end of the afternoon, he asked if I would be returning the next day.

'Of course.'

Then, with that characteristic and melancholic pout of his: 'It's not really very interesting, is it, what I'm telling you?'

'But Maestro . . . '

For nearly two months I had been looking for an opportunity to tell him, unambiguously, that I wanted to make a film of him. And on this

particular day he was so happy that I added: 'Not only is it very interesting, but it would be even better if it were filmed.' I had jumped in at
the deep end. It was as though a blinding light had suddenly set me free.

His reaction was incredible: '*Da nyet potom.*' Literally, 'Yes, no, later . . .'
Effectively, it meant 'We'll see.'

This was the first time that I had mentioned it, and I could hardly have
expected a better response than 'We'll see'.

At that very moment Nina came into the room. Realizing what we
were discussing and believing that this was a good time to back me up
and force him to take a decision, she insisted: 'Look, Slava, Bruno will
come with a friend and very little equipment, it'll be nothing.' It was like
talking to a child as you lift him into the dentist's chair, increasing his
fears while thinking that you are reassuring him by telling him that he
will feel nothing. The hapless Richter felt caught in a trap.

'No! No!' he groaned. He thought there was a kind of conspiracy
between Nina and me. I understood his exasperation. Faced with so violent
a reaction, Nina had gone very quiet. I felt an immense confusion, but
Richter himself, his expression impenetrable, at least confirmed that he
wanted to see me the next day.

The next morning I received the inevitable phone call from Milena
Borromeo: 'Maestro is still angry from last night. Nothing against you
personally, but he feels tired and won't see you today. I'll call you again
tomorrow.'

The next day brought with it a further cancellation, then silence. I had
clearly spoken out of turn. Yet I had had no choice but to reveal my hand:
the idea had to be mooted at some stage. Whether or not I had spoken
too hastily, or whether Nina's intervention had been ill-timed, we should
have left him time to allow the idea to germinate. No one could put
pressure on Richter. I thought I would never see him again.

The following week, I was on the very point of leaving for England –
throughout the whole of that autumn I had kept on only a single engage-
ment that would prevent me from seeing Richter: the London première of
my recent film about Menuhin, which would be shown in the presence of
the Queen, with a gala dinner at Buckingham Palace – when, after five
days of silence, Milena rang me again: 'Maestro wants to see you today.'

'Milena, I've been waiting for you to call for five days. I'm on the point
of leaving for England.'

'Maestro wants to see you.'

'I can't cancel, my film is to be shown to the Queen.'

'You promise to call us as soon as you get back?'

Two days later, I had scarcely opened the door when the phone rang. It was Milena: 'What! You're in Paris and you haven't called us? Maestro would like to see you.'

Minutes later, I was at his hotel, where I found him in a delightful, even mischievous mood. He wanted to read me 'something'. He opened one of his notebooks – the notebooks that were originally to have been the object of our collaboration but which I had still not seen, even though he continued to note down his impressions in them – and read me his comments on my film about Dietrich Fischer-Dieskau. The next day there was exactly the same little game, only this time it was my film about David Oistrakh, which he ended up by praising.

During these five days of apparent silence, he had evidently taken the trouble to watch these films, and I could interpret his desire to read me the notes he had made only as an indirect and discreet way of letting me know that he approved of them and that he was implicitly agreeing to take part in a similar adventure centred upon himself.

However, the main question preoccupying the minds of everyone connected with Richter throughout this whole autumn was whether to confirm or cancel a lengthy series of concerts that he was due to give in Japan between October and the following January. The early weeks of the tour had, of course, already been cancelled as he had not touched a piano for six months and felt so badly prepared. Moreover, the prospect of a visit to Japan – a country he loved but which he already knew – held out little appeal. 'I want to discover new places,' he told me. 'And I no longer have the strength to go to Japan by road.' And he described what he saw as his ideal tour: 'Six weeks driving slowly round the Île-de-France or a part of Italy; a concert every other evening announced by the local constable, in this or that tiny village with no more than a pretty little church or a school.'

No, he had no wish to return to Japan, with all the constraints of a tight schedule that were unavoidable in so highly organized a country. But to have sat around in Paris for the last six months was no more acceptable to as restless a spirit as Richter the wanderer, a man who was nomadic by nature, and by the end of October he had resigned himself to going to Japan, on certain conditions, the first of which was self-evident: for a month before his first concert, he would have to be given time to get back to the piano. The second could have been thought up only by Richter himself: he would go to Japan under a general anaesthetic; he would be put to sleep in his hotel in Paris, an ambulance would take him to the airport and he would wake up in his hotel in Tokyo. This demand seemed eminently reasonable to him, but it failed to impress the doctors who were consulted.

He left, unanaesthetized, on 15 November. 'Come what may, I shan't give any concerts for a month and I'll play only simple things: Chopin studies and the concertos of Schumann and Tchaikovsky,' he declared by way of saying goodbye.

A month later, he was back in Europe, without having played a note. He was unwell. I met him in Italy, in a small town on the Ligurian coast, where we recorded a few more scraps of conversation. He had taken to his bed and would get up only in the evening to take us out to supper at an extremely elegant hotel inside the ramparts of the old town. Then he came back to Paris to be properly looked after. He was the very image of suffering – suffering both mental and physical. For the coming spring, we needed to get him out of these gloomy hotel rooms. He did not want to go to Moscow, even though he had a flat there that he had not seen for three years, and so we found him a house in an attractive country setting near Auvers-sur-Oise. It was here that he spent the spring, a stay interrupted by brief periods of hospitalization which, although necessary, merely added to his depression. There was neither a piano nor any music, no books to read, no walks to go on, only a more or less permanent state of torpor. Was it really still Richter? The great Richter, energetic, indestructible and insatiably curious? One evening, on our return from a moving visit to Van Gogh's house, where, in spite of his exhaustion, he had insisted on climbing the three flights of stairs to the painter's pitiful room – an act of homage, at the end of his life, on the part of one great artist to another – he told me for the first time that he had known such a state of deep depression in the past but that on this occasion he was convinced that his weak heart would not allow him to emerge from it alive.

But summer came and, with it, another journey, this time to Germany, where he was to spend time in a cardiology unit. The prospect of a car journey with several stops *en route* invigorated him. Valenciennes, Mons, Aachen . . . Even the mere mention of the itinerary made him more lively, and when I questioned the delights of a night in Valenciennes, he let me feel the sharp end of his tongue: 'Valenciennes! Amazing! The town of Zola and his cycle of twenty novels!' And he proceeded to quote from memory, in their chronological order, the titles of Zola's twenty novels, 'to be read without further delay'.

In bed on the eve of his departure, his eyes shining with enthusiasm, he told me his latest idea: 'Music must be given to those who love it. I want to give free concerts; that's the answer.'

I gave him an amused nod of approval. 'Do you know who'll resist the idea?' he asked. 'The promoters. They don't like that sort of thing.' Innocence and clear-sightedness. It was entirely typical of Richter. 'But I have the key to the problem. We'll place a large black hat on the stage, and those who want to contribute can do so.'

I saw him again in September in Vienna, where I was shooting some sequences for a film. He was scarcely in a fit state to get up. Nina, normally so willing to put a brave face on things, was close to despair. Given Richter's age and the state he was in, he could not continue to be shunted from pillar to post in this way. But where could he go? Where could he find a little sun and the peace and quiet that might restore his desire to go on living? It was at this point that I suggested that they might stay at an apartment that my family owned in Antibes, a quiet set of rooms with an attractive terrace and a beautiful view.

I thought again about the film, to which he had given me his implicit agreement but which we had not discussed for a whole year. I knew the layout of the apartment and told myself that, as long as he remained there for a few months, we might perhaps succeed in filming some of the sequences that were starting to become clear in my mind. On passing through Singapore in January 1997 I had unearthed and bought a tiny digital camera that might be suitable for filming Richter.

I left for Antibes with my cameraman, Raphaël O'Byrne, in order to inspect the location. Raphaël O'Byrne is a true gentleman, whom I introduced to Richter as my assistant. It was a question not of concealing the camera but of working out a system sufficiently discreet for Richter to be unaware of it. He should have the impression that we were merely picking up the thread of our conversations from the previous spring. I wanted to make a major film about Richter that would be worthy of its subject and so he had to appear on screen. Otherwise, we would make a third-rate documentary, with some nonentity providing the voice-over, the whole thing laboriously illustrated with conventional archival images that would all too soon start to pall. The moment was crucial: it was our last chance to succeed.

We would be very specific about the place where we put him – in a totally bare setting that we would take care never to identify – and we would set up the camera in such a way that it gave the impression of being part of the furniture. We would also have to work out the exact times of the day when we could film and when the sun provided a more or less acceptable degree of light (there was clearly no question of installing any artificial lighting) and we would connect the camera to a control room set up in the kitchen, with all the cables passing over the terrace.

The complexity of this set-up – which was actually extraordinarily rudimentary – stemmed from the fact that Raphaël could not be present in the room to frame the shots. It would have destroyed the illusion, and Richter would not have tolerated it.

As a working method, it was hazardous in the extreme. We would have to line up the shots without Richter, in an abstract way, and once the camera was running, there would be no one to adjust it to take account of our subject's movements. This might be made to work with a wide-angle shot that allowed him a certain freedom of movement; but with a much tighter angle concentrating on his face – indispensable to the expressivity of the image – there was no such margin for error. A slight movement to the right or to the left, a sudden bending forwards, and Richter would disappear from the field of vision.

A trial run proved fairly successful, but Richter was very tired. The previous year, when we were still working without a camera, he had replied to my questions in a laconic fashion – that was his nature – but he had spoken with wit and whimsy. But now that we had worked out a more or less fixed schedule, his replies were limited to 'yes' and 'no'. He must have come to hate me for my constant presence and relentless determination.

I had to find some other approach. It was then that I remembered the notebooks that he had written. Why not have him read from them? In itself, it would not be exciting viewing, but it might encourage him to want to express himself in other ways. Otherwise, it was hardly worth all the effort involved simply to get him to say 'yes' and 'no'. Above all, then, I had to have enough time, like those entomologists who, by dint of infinite patience, are finally able to observe the miracle of mating that they have so much wanted to see.

For months, the whole team from Idéale Audience and I had been ransacking archives all over the world, and I had been to Moscow on several occasions to visit Richter's flat. Nina had entrusted me with a set of keys, and Richter himself had explained where his private papers could be found. All were meticulously ordered. It was an apartment very much in his own image, vast, but completely bare, the apartment of a musical monk that housed two grand pianos and some furniture of positively ascetic frugality: some odd chairs, a table, an old divan and, in his bedroom, where I too slept, a metal camp bed and an unpretentious wardrobe containing a veritable treasure trove – the manuscripts of his own works, written while he was a child or adolescent, the autograph of Prokofiev's Ninth Sonata that Prokofiev himself had inscribed to him, and hundreds of photographs. All the walls were bare, and I had a very strong feeling that I was in the home of someone with no sense of ownership or at least of someone who had long since renounced the idea of ownership. Even the collection of marvellous paintings that he had built up over the years and that contained a number of canvases by banned artists for whom he had organized exhibitions at his own home had gone. He had donated them to the Pushkin Museum, where they could be seen in the Sviatoslav Richter Room.

Now that we had access to his notebooks, we had decided to film Richter for a whole week during a further visit to Antibes. I had prepared things in great detail and chosen extracts from his notebooks that he would read aloud and that corresponded with archival material already located. As I had hoped, this prompted a reaction from him. In the middle of lots of 'yes, buts' and 'well, there you ares', I managed to coax a few precious phrases from him in the course of the week, together with the odd look of burning intensity. When he came out of his room in order to work with us – and we never knew when that would be – I would sit him in a chair, the position of which had been fixed down to the last centimetre. Beside it was a table over which he could lean if he wanted to. Raphaël O'Byrne started the camera rolling and immediately headed off for the kitchen. Sometimes Richter grew animated and leaned slightly to one side; I was worried that in doing so he would disappear from the camera's restricted field of vision and that there was nothing I could do to prevent it. At risk of coming into the shot myself by leaning towards him, I made all sorts of gestures in my attempts to bring him back into line with the camera. In this way we developed a sort of silent *mise-en-scène*. Whenever I failed to draw him far enough back into the field of vision, the situation became frankly comical. Raphaël would sneak in from the kitchen and I would get up and pretend to lose my place in the notebooks through which I had been leafing just long enough for Raphaël to reframe the shot as best he could. Meanwhile my body served as a screen that prevented Richter from seeing all the paraphernalia behind me.

He needed encouragement. But he was worried about the result and at the end of each session asked me if I was satisfied, if he had understood what I was wanting to know and if he had been clear enough. He then went to lie down on the divan at the far end of the room, which took him past the two cameras that were then no more than a few centimetres away from him. It was impossible for him not to see them, I told myself, and not to notice that we were filming. But he seemed not to be aware of them, nothing, not a word. He slumped on to the divan, we then sometimes listened to some music and the next day we began all over again.

Two days after we had started filming, Milena rang me at my hotel. She was laughing so much that she could hardly speak.

'I went into Maestro's room this morning; I wanted to take his kaftan' – a beautiful Scandinavian cardigan – 'to be cleaned. But he refused point-blank: "No, I want to keep it, it's nicer for Bruno."'

The phrase was clearly intended to reach my ears, but what did he mean by it? Was it a reproach or a sign of approval? I really did not know how best to interpret the remark and felt particularly ill at ease throughout the whole of the subsequent session. That evening he could not conceal his pride at taking us out to dine at a sumptuous restaurant that he had discovered on the Côte d'Azur. I was at the wheel of his car, and we had just installed him beside me when, out of the blue but with his usual air of sadness, albeit seemingly illuminated by an affectionate smile, he asked: 'Were you able to do any filming today?'

I was stunned. It was the first time he had pronounced the forbidden word. I answered as though nothing was amiss: 'Yes, Maestro.'

'With this?' he asked, pointing at his cardigan.

'Yes, Maestro, it's very nice.'

And we left it at that. It was a delightful way of letting me know that he knew, that it was exactly what he wanted and that he himself was party to this semi-secret filming. The ambiguity had finally been resolved, and by Richter himself in his own inimitable manner.

A few days later, I left Antibes to make an immediate start on editing the film. I had several hours of sound interviews, a few precious minutes of Richter on film, a large number of photographs and a mountain of documents unearthed by the combined efforts of the researchers lined up by Idéale Audience: Jacques Spohr, Marie-Nicole Féret and Sophie Germain in Paris, and Victor Bocharov in Moscow and St Petersburg. There was no order to this raw material. I would have to give it a sense of structure, if possible both solid and expressive, and it would have to be of an impressive length. Above all, it would have to be based on a script drawn up only after the event. I would have to edit the material word by word and phrase by phrase, hoping and praying that in this way there would gradually emerge the increasingly clear outlines of the extraordinarily complex and multifaceted individual whose portrait I was tracing. I still had to find the guiding principle into which would fit a multitude of successive or simultaneous themes, deciding on the moments when the tension would be increased and decreased, creating a harmonious and polyphonic texture of facts and ideas, finding a contrasting and fluent rhythm and providing a channel for the floodtide of impressions that would carry the film along from start to finish. In a word, I had assembled the thematic material for my symphony. Now all I had to do was sit down and compose it.

Richter returned to Paris towards the end of May after spending a few weeks at the monastery at Jouques near Aix-en-Provence, where he had given some concerts a few years earlier. He moved into rooms at 44 rue Hamelin in the very building in which Proust had spent the last years of his life and where he had died. From here he paid a final visit to the Fêtes Musicales de Touraine, where he attended two concerts. On his return to Paris at the end of June, he demanded his piano, and I can still see him calmly and interminably practising the same page of a Schubert sonata – Richter's famous 'three hours a day'.

A rebirth?

By early July my film was starting to take shape. We now had a sort of outline, a rough cut in which the structure of the narrative was more or less organized, even if the structure of the film itself was still lacking. This allowed me, above all, to pinpoint what was missing and work out what we would need to film in Russia when we joined Richter there, as we had already arranged to do.

He had decided to spend the summer at his attractive little dacha near Moscow, where he had invited me to visit him in order to complete our work on the project. And so I suggested showing him the film as it was, a veritable monster of a documentary lasting almost three and a half hours, still very incomplete and largely lacking any images – one of the problems, of course, was to find illustrative material for the words that I had recorded on tape and to create a perfect continuity between the voiceover and whatever appeared on screen.

On the eve of his departure we organized a showing, through which he sat motionless, a picture of intense concentration. By the end, he was visibly moved and all he could say was: '*Eto ya*' – 'It's me'.

Nothing could have touched me more than this laconic response of his. He raised no objections and radiated a sort of inner satisfaction. We returned to his hotel and I remained with him until well into the night. His active and conscious involvement was finally and joyously established.

'When will you come to Moscow?' he wanted to know. 'There are so many things I'd like to show you there. And we've still a lot to do.'

I told him that on this occasion I'd come with a proper film crew and that we would film specific sequences that I would write in advance and that would fill the gaps in our film. If he liked, I could come to Moscow as soon as next week.

'No, not next week. I'm flying, and so I'll need time to recover.'

He hated flying. Only a few years earlier he had driven all the way from Moscow to Japan and back, giving nearly one hundred concerts within the space of only a few months while crossing the Urals and Siberia. He was altogether exceptional as a person.

'What about the end of August?' I suggested.

'*Budyet posdno!*' – 'That would be late.' I was dismayed by this idea of the ineluctible that he had now raised for the first time. He had said these words in such a plaintive voice, but with a sense of mischief in his eyes. It could not be a premonition, as he immediately went on, as though still making up his mind: '*Po tomu shto, mozhet byt' konzerty*' – 'Because, who knows, there may be concerts.' Only a few days earlier he had started to play the piano again for real and was thinking of returning to the concert hall.

I suggested arriving four weeks later, on 2 August.

'That will be perfect; we'll work together for a whole week,' he replied.

He died on 1 August.

Sviatoslav Richter's career and his impact not only on his audiences but also on his colleagues – he is the only pianist whom they all agree to have been one of the greatest in the whole history of music – cannot be reduced to a classical model. After a childhood and adolescence in Odessa, where he was allowed to run wild and where he received no academic training but taught himself the piano and music, he became a *répétiteur* at the local opera at the age of fifteen and it was not until 1937 that he left for Moscow. At an age when most great pianists are already starting their careers, Richter became a student.

Heinrich Neuhaus, one of the most famous Soviet pianists of his generation, was captivated by the 'genius' of this unknown musician and immediately admitted him to his class at the Moscow Conservatory. Here Richter led a wholly marginalized existence. However incredible it must seem, at the height of the Stalinist era he refused to submit to the discipline imposed on the rest of the students, who were required to attend classes in 'politics', and was twice expelled but on each occasion readmitted at Neuhaus's insistence. He came to the attention of Prokofiev, who asked him to perform his Fifth Piano Concerto under his own direction, a work which had remained stubbornly unsuccessful whenever he had played it himself. The result was a resounding success. This was in 1941, and it was now not so much a career that was launched as a legend that was born.

From this date onwards, Richter toured the length and breadth of the Soviet Union, gradually expanding his repertory to the point where it reached arguably unequalled proportions. Without counting chamber music and a large number of operas, including the words and music of all Wagner's music dramas, he had some eighty different recital programmes in his head and fingers by the end of his life. For reasons that remained unclear at the time but which, as we shall see, were bound up with his family background, he was not allowed to travel abroad, except within countries belonging to the Socialist bloc. But Richter made no demands and had no ambitions in terms of either international acclaim or personal comfort,* unlike most of his colleagues, for whom only concert tours in the West could offer any prospect of material improvement. He was also

---

*In the archives of the Gnesin Institute in Moscow, where Richter often practised in 1947, I discovered a document that affords striking evidence of the conditions under which the most eminent Soviet artists lived and worked at this time. The following is the text of a letter to A. G. Kalashnikov, a member of the soviet parliament:

> We are writing to ask you to intervene with the relevant authorities with a view to obtaining accommodation for the pianist Sviatoslav Richter.
> Sviatoslav Richter is one of the greatest musicians and pianists of our country, and even, if the truth be told, the leading pianist of our time.
> This man, known and loved throughout the entire Soviet Union, has nowhere to live or to work in peace and quiet.
> Is it normal that so talented an individual, who gives concerts eagerly listened to by the whole country, should be forced to scour the capital, begging the hospitality of people he knows, simply to be in a position to prepare his concert programmes?
> The piano that Richter has been able to acquire thanks to the prize he received by winning the USSR Music Competition is currently with friends outside Moscow, in the absence of anywhere to house it in the city. Thank you for the help that you may be able to offer.
> Professors Gnesin, Gedike and Lebedeva

he only great soloist of his generation and of his country to eschew membership of the Communist Party, an eschewal due less to a deliberate decision than to radical indifference: Richter was no rebel, merely refractory. He had nothing to fear from an exclusively Soviet career. He had nothing to fear from anything. Nobody had a hold over him. That would be his great strength.

By the time he finally travelled to the West – initially to Finland in May 1960, then to the United States in the October of that same year – Richter was already forty-five years old. His American début comprised eight recitals and orchestral concerts at Carnegie Hall that sent shock waves all round the world of music. He subsequently visited England, France, Germany, Italy and Scandinavia, returning to each of these countries on frequent occasions throughout the 1960s. Japan came later.

But it was not long before he tired of the conventions of the international concert circuit; positively allergic to long-term planning, he played only where and when he wanted, often imposing unusual programmes on audiences mesmerized by the earth-shattering power and infinite delicacy of his playing.

After four tours of the United States, he turned down all further invitations to appear in a country he loathed, with the exception, he said, of its 'museums, orchestras and cocktails'.

In 1964, he founded a festival in France (the Fêtes Musicales de Touraine at La Grange de Meslay near Tours), then another in Moscow (the December Nights at the Pushkin Museum), but he would sometimes disappear for months on end.

He clearly enjoyed playing chamber music in the company of regular partners of the stature of Rostropovich, David Oistrakh and the Borodin Quartet. He accompanied Nina Dorliac, Dietrich Fischer-Dieskau and Peter Schreier in *Lieder* recitals. And he also performed with many young musicians, including the violinist Oleg Kagan and his wife, the cellist Natasha Gutman, the viola player Yuri Bashmet and the pianists Zoltán Kocsis, Andrei Gavrilov, Vassili Lobanov, Elisabeth Leonskaja and Andreas Lucewicz, in each case helping to establish their reputation. In concertos, he was accompanied by countless conductors: Kurt Sanderling, Evgeny Mravinsky, Kyrill Kondrashin, Lorin Maazel, Leonard Bernstein, Rudolf Barshai, Herbert von Karajan, Sergiu Celibidache, János Ferencsik, Christoph Eschenbach, Riccardo Muti, Charles Munch, Eugene Ormandy and, above all, the two conductors whom he liked most, Václav Talich and Carlos Kleiber.

From the early eighties, he performed only with a score in more or less darkened halls where it was difficult even to make out his massive silhouette, but where he created a gripping atmosphere, convinced that he was preventing the spectator from succumbing to the demonic temptations of voyeurism.

Yamaha placed two grand pianos at his permanent disposal, together with the staff necessary to maintain them, and they accompanied him wherever his imagination took him. Well, not quite everywhere. They remained behind when, over seventy, he left Moscow by car and did not return until six months later, covering the distance from Vladivostok and back, not counting a brief sortie to Japan, in conditions one can barely imagine, giving a hundred concerts in the remotest towns and villages in Siberia. A missionary at heart, he thereby signalled his preference for the simple enthusiasm felt by listeners in Novokuznetsk, Kurgan, Krasnoyarsk and Irkutsk, rather than the artificial acclamations of Carnegie Hall.

If I have spent so long recounting the last two years of Richter's life, including an account of my film's eventful genesis, it is partly because these were the only two years in his life of which I was a first-hand witness and, as such, the only ones I feel competent to describe. But it is also, in part, because my daily contact with this genius, whose obvious strangeness was in no way calculated but merely the outward sign of a wild and intractable purity, resulted in some of the most intensely moving moments in my entire life. Does it all hold together? These countless meetings, the film and, at the start of it all, this book?

'Maestro wants Bruno to "do" his biography.'

This book is in no way a biography. I do not have it in me to be a biographer – someone who examines events from day to day, questioning witnesses and giving them their chance to speak. Having had the chance to persuade Richter to speak, it seemed to me preferable to offer the reader the remarks I recorded in a form which, however carefully reorganized, is – I believe – entirely faithful.

Of course, there could be no question of offering a simple transcript of our conversations, as the subjects we broached were discussed in a totally random manner, and Richter's replies were sometimes no more than simple interjections, brief phrases that made no sense when divorced from the context of my questions. Starting from a barely coherent mass of more than one thousand pages, I had to try to compile an account that had some semblance of continuity, adopting a sort of montage technique, while taking advantage of the latitude offered by the non-material nature of the written word, an advantage not shared by film-editing techniques: I did not, for example, have to take into account the often considerable differences in acoustic ambience that prevented me from splicing together phrases recorded several months apart, nor did I have to worry about the poor articulation of certain words or the absence of numerous names where Richter simply referred to 'them' and which made no sense unless replaced by the names of the people about whom he was speaking. Nor, finally, did I have to deal with microphone noises caused by his sometimes violent hand movements.

Richter's way of speaking could not, in any case, be transcribed without further ado. He kept hesitating and his thoughts came in fits and starts, depending to a large extent on promptings from me, so that I clearly needed to make considerable changes in order to adapt what he said to the written form. And this need became all the greater when I decided in writing this book that I would cast it not in the form of a dialogue but in that of a continuous narrative, a first-person narration. This seemed to me to correspond better to what the reader would be hoping for and to result in greater clarity, without abandoning the occasionally Celinian aspect of the syntactical oddities and unexpected incongruities in Richter's spoken style. But I was particularly keen to recapture on paper his highly idiosyncratic speech rhythms or at least, by dint of the necessary stylistic changes, to create the illusion that the words on the printed page reflect the way he spoke – *tel sur le papier qu'à la bouche*, as Montaigne would have said.

To flesh out the narrative, I have occasionally had recourse to sources other than my own. Here I am particularly thinking of the only section that I have transplanted wholesale into the present narrative in the form of Richter's wonderful essay on Prokofiev, the only text he ever published. Here the joins are bound to be noticed by the reader on account of the essay's different style. I could have adopted an alternative solution and reproduced it as an appendix, but it seemed to me to be far more effective in the place I have chosen to insert it.

In the course of our conversations, I would have felt that I was inhibiting the narrator's imagination by imposing any chronological structures on him. It was only after the event that I attempted to impose some sense of order on the events that he had wanted to describe so that I could correct the most glaring errors that have circulated about him – more from lack of information than from malice. Richter's life was exclusively devoted to music, the cause of which he served with consuming intensity, while rejecting all trace of conformism. But as a result of his loathing for all forms of self-promotion and the obstinate silence that he maintained throughout the whole of his turbulent life (and throughout a period in history that was itself no less turbulent), it was inevitable that so internationally celebrated an artist should be the object of incessant rumours. Although far from frightened of scandal, he was concerned, above all, with order and truth – the desire to be true to the score, to be true to art, to be true to himself in his behaviour, in short, the truth of a child.

Anecdotes about his musical activities struck him as wholly devoid of interest, and I noticed afterwards that, through lack of time, but also through lack of anything that he himself regarded as interesting, our conversations rarely went beyond the late 1960s. 'You'll find all that in my notebooks,' he would say.

These notebooks pick up where the conversations leave off and provide the material for the second part of this volume. Richter began writing them at Christmas 1970 and continued, sometimes sporadically, until the autumn of 1995 – the time of our meeting and his departure for his final visit to Japan.

As we shall see, he says very little about himself here, while at the same time proving utterly revealing. Here, there is no theorizing, only personal impressions, undeveloped, concise, noted down as they happened, with no desire for empty effect. The manuscript is astonishing. It is headed 'On Music', a title that sums it up to perfection. As a result, Richter does not describe the people he meets, the countries he passes through, the scenery he enjoys, the museums he visits, the events that take place, the thoughts that assail him on reading a book, nor – above all – does he discuss the tours that he undertakes. He is content, rather, with sober and candid descriptions – often acerbic or bitter, but also impassioned and fervent – of his reactions to concerts, operas and gramophone recordings.

The diaries he entrusted to me run to seven large school exercise books, each double-sided page of which was completely filled. The left-hand page gives the date (with only a few omissions), place, programme (including the opus numbers, keys and, in the case of *Lieder* recitals, the complete title of each song) and a detailed list of performers, whether instrumentalists, singers or conductors (but rarely naming the orchestras). Finally, this page also includes the names of all the people in Richter's party, assuming that he attended the performance in the company of others, as was often the case. Except for a single instance – a musical soirée at his flat – I have not reproduced these names.

The right-hand page is reserved for Richter's comments. Since everything had to fit into a single page and as the comments are often – though by no means always – more substantial than the description on the left-hand page, Richter would also write in the spaces between the already narrow lines, sometimes making it difficult to decipher his writing, which was otherwise exceptionally clear.

Needless to say, I have been selective in reproducing passages from these notebooks, and in this followed his express wishes. I have removed entries that merely repeat others, while taking care to retain those repetitions that reveal a fundamental aspect of their writer's character. (Such passages include those that concern his repeated listening to works he did not understand but to which he was seeking to gain access, or his habit of listening tirelessly to his favourite works, which included, first and foremost, Debussy's *La mer*, the operas of Wagner and the cantatas of Bach.)

I also felt obliged to omit certain entries that contain *ad hominem* attacks on living people, attacks so violent that they might almost appear defamatory. Richter's attitude to the world of music and its practitioners was sometimes acidic in its virulence, appearing all the more cutting for being expressed so concisely and without the usual rhetorical niceties. Those who may be the butt of such comments should remember that Richter's devastating sense of humour and the violence of his critical views were no less extreme than his enthusiasms and were often directed, in the first instance, against himself.

Following on from the notebooks, I thought that the reader might be interested in a complete list of the works in Richter's repertoire. This appears as an appendix and may serve to complement the discography that is available elsewhere. This list does not include every detail of the vocal works that Richter performed, and it also takes account only of those works that he performed at least once in public. Excluded are those that he may have studied, played and even learned but which in the end he did not keep on.

I cannot deny the part of me – my part in Richter's life – that figures in the pages that follow. The whole thrust of the questions with which I bombarded him over such a long period, the way in which I have organized the account, turning it from a dialogue into a monologue, replacing the spoken with the written word and transforming a sort of chaotic jumble into what, I hope, is a more or less coherent structure and, finally, my passionate involvement in this whole adventure made it inevitable

that some of my own preoccupations would become part of this monologue. No doubt, in my final version of the text, I have insisted on
episodes that would have seemed secondary to Richter. (How many times
I heard him end this or that anecdote with a laugh: 'But it's not important, it has nothing to do with music!') And there is no doubt that, in
turn, he provided, at best, elliptical answers to questions that seemed to
me to be of the utmost interest. But is not this cross-fertilization of
thoughts, after all, one of the most satisfying aspects of the interaction
between two individuals? Yet I can say categorically that I have not made
anything up and, as for the finished product, I have the odd but intense
conviction that I have in fact been faithful to Richter.

The reader will appreciate that the whole conception of the present
book was inextricably bound up with the film whose difficult birth I have
recounted. The editing process took a whole year and in the course of it,
the film underwent countless changes. When I started on it, I was certain
of only one thing, that it would begin and end with the first and last bars
of the slow movement of Schubert's final B flat major Sonata, one of the
most sublime and heart-breaking works by the composer in a performance to match.

I had thought of introducing the final scene with a brief episode
designed to give it the right emotional setting and of assuming the role of
the public's spokesman, entering the shot, taking Richter's hands and
asking: 'Was it a great effort for you to make this film?'

'Terrible . . .'

'Thank you, Maestro . . .'

To the visual accompaniment of Richter's infinitely sad smile, we
would then hear the sombre semiquavers in the bass that Schubert added
in the coda of his second movement, in order to underpin the main subject's harrowing melancholy. And we would then see a close-up of Richter
playing this sonata in the concert hall some twenty years earlier.

The episode was moving but superfluous, and I cut it at the final edit.
My gratitude, like that of the general public, for all that he had given us,
went without saying.

Bruno Monsaingeon
1 August 1998

Richter in his own words

Prolegomenon

People have written and said such false and improbable things about me that I wonder who could have invented such stories. In some cases they are people I know – people like the film-maker Andrei Konchalovsky who, without being a close friend, is someone I've met on several occasions. Where did he get hold of the idea – as he claims I told him in the course of 'numerous conversations' – that I was for ever complaining 'about having fingers as big as sausages and not having enough room between the black notes and the white ones'? I've big hands, it's true, but my fingers are actually quite slender. Well, it's not a serious point and not important either, but even so . . .

People have also written that I owe the start of my career to Ribbentrop because, following his visit to Moscow and the Non-Aggression Pact between Germany and Russia, the Germans insisted that I be allowed to start giving concerts. What Germans? What insistence? What concerts? No Germans knew me at that time, no one did. I don't know why I met with success, but it came of its own accord, and much later! Still, if it had only been a question of anecdotal stories about concerts . . . but there was the war, which was something far more terrible.

Sometimes the absurd things that have been written about me go too far and are no more than a fanciful embellishment of the true facts. To read some French hacks, you'd think I'd spent my whole time protesting against Stalin. Where have people dredged up these stupid ideas, when I was never interested in politics and never had any connection with a world that I detest? These journalists have put it about that I played at Stalin's funeral – it's true, I did play on that occasion – and that I 'specially chose a long fugue by Bach to protest against the dictator'. But how could I have chosen what I wanted to play, when a special commission set up by the Ministry of Culture had drawn up a programme to which each of the artists involved clearly had to conform? 'The audience', we're told, 'began to boo.' But what sort of audience would have booed at Stalin's funeral? It took place in the Hall of Columns, which was full to bursting with official guests. In the face of my refusal to interrupt Bach – 'One doesn't interrupt Bach,' I'm said to have exclaimed – the police apparently dragged me away from the piano and threatened to shoot me. In fact, I was in a confined space, surrounded by the orchestra, and not even playing a proper piano, but a frightful upright. And it was the second movement of Beethoven's *Pathétique*. We were so cramped that no one could have got to me.

I remember all this very well; it's not important, but it's indelibly printed on my mind.

I was on tour in Tbilisi when I received a telegram informing me that the dictator was dead and demanding my immediate return to Moscow. It wasn't easy: the weather was appalling and there were no more available flights. In the end I was bundled on board a plane full of funeral wreaths. I was the only passenger. Yes, I travelled alone, buried in funeral wreaths.

Because of the bad weather, we had to land at Sukhumi on the Black Sea, where I was told that Prokofiev had died. Then, after a night at the airport, we flew on to Moscow. From there I went straight to the Hall of Columns, where I found Oistrakh, Nikolayeva, the Beethoven Quartet, the conductor Alexander Melik-Pashayev, a full symphony orchestra, everybody, already waiting. We were confined there for two days, which was how long the ceremony lasted, with no possibility of leaving.

The coffin had been placed directly above us. We couldn't really see it, and in any case I wasn't looking. But I remember – what was his name? – Malenkov. He looked scared to death. No doubt he had good reason to. I immediately thought: 'Ha ha! There's someone who's afraid he'll be killed.' He was the favourite to succeed.

He wasn't killed, but he didn't get Stalin's job either.

The only thing that bore any resemblance to an incident was when I was about to start playing and I realized that the pedals on the wretched upright didn't work. Nikolayeva, who had played before me, hadn't noticed. I said to myself: 'I'm not going to play like that.' I found some scores and asked someone in the orchestra to help me wedge them under the pedal, so that it would more or less work. At that moment I was supposed to be playing the slow movement from Bach's D minor Concerto. While I was busy repairing the piano, I noticed people running around in the gallery. No doubt they thought I was planting a bomb under the piano. As for a scandal, that was all there was to it. Stuff and nonsense!

In any event, there was no escaping it: we had to play and I found the whole experience deeply repugnant. Also, it was horribly uncomfortable as we were in a terrible draught. One of the officials even died from it, unless he was killed . . . A Czech, Gottwald.* No doubt he caught a chill.

People were still pouring into the building. It was just like being in the street. They were all very worked up, still in thrall to a man they had worshipped. In fact, I think the real reason they came was to be sure that 'he' was really dead. Everyone wanted to see it with their own eyes. And I don't know how many people were trampled to death at that time!

Afterwards I made a drawing of what I had seen through the hall window. You could see Dimitrova Ulitsa, the flags all at half-mast, and the people filing past, forced on to the pavement and channelled towards the building by the police. It's quite successful as a drawing, it has a sense of atmosphere, a simple pastel. I was doing lots of pastels at that time.

I still recall a particularly unpleasant episode – from the artistic point of view, you understand. It was nearly midnight, and they were preparing to remove Stalin's body. But there were still a few minutes to go, and so we had to continue playing. The conductor, Melik-Pashayev, started Tchaikovsky's Sixth Symphony again, but just as he reached the development section – musically, the most inconvenient moment imaginable – he had to stop, as he was interrupted by the military band playing Chopin's Funeral March. Disgusting! I was furious, but, at the same time, I felt little sympathy for 'Sir' and so I thought: 'He's got what he deserves.' After the ceremony, as I was finally leaving the Hall of Columns, I heard the words 'Our new leaders' bellowed forth on the loudspeakers. Already, all you could hear in the whole of Moscow was: 'Beria! Bulganin!' And the other one, too: 'Malenkov!' In short: 'The king is dead, long live the king!'

* Leader of the Czech Communist Party. (B.M.)

I detested Stalin, but this really made me sick.

I returned home. All I wanted to do was to take a shower. This whole episode was of no real concern to me, and it certainly wasn't the start of my life.

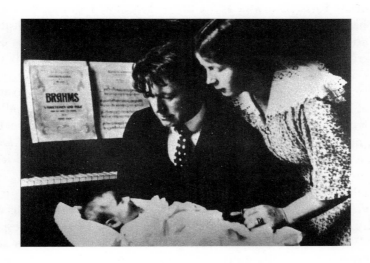

1 Childhood

I suffer from a terrifying, non-selective memory that quite literally torments me. Wherever I've been in Russia and elsewhere – and as I'm nomadic by nature, I've been to lots of different places – I've met countless people. The names of all these people are filed away inside my head, together with their first names, and I'm for ever rattling them off in my mind.

Sometimes some of them slip from my memory, and that's the worst, because I then try to remember them, as if it mattered. It happens at night, when I can't sleep. It's a real nightmare.

All these memories of a life that has lasted eighty years – some of them may be of a certain interest, I suppose, but it's all I can do not to detest them.

Zhitomir, the town where I was born, is now part of the Ukraine, but when I was born in 1915, the Ukraine didn't exist, it was Russia, 'Little Russia'.

I was born a dual national in a country that didn't admit to such things – I'll come back to this later. My paternal grandfather was a German from what is now the Western Ukraine but was then in Poland. Like many Russians who came to Russia in an attempt to make their fortune, he arrived towards the middle of the last century and set himself up as a piano-maker in Zhitomir; it was there that my father was born.

In many Russian towns and cities – Moscow, Odessa, even a small town like Zhitomir – there was always a German quarter with its own population, its own schools and *Kirche*. Although my father was born in the Ukraine, he was still a German, not just because of his family origins but as a result of his education. As soon as he was old enough to do military service, he left Zhitomir to study the piano and composition in Vienna. Here, on the benches of the Hochschule, he became friendly with the composer Franz Schreker, who was a fellow student. A great composer, now well and truly forgotten, but his opera *Der ferne Klang* left such an impression on me as a musician that, having sight-read it at the piano as an adolescent, I still know every note of it even now, seventy years later.

In Vienna, my father also got to know Grieg, but Schreker was a close friend. Later he told me lots of stories about the Vienna Opera, especially about Wagner. Indeed, I was so fascinated by these stories that as soon as I got my hands on a piano, it was Wagner's operas that I first attempted to sight-read. But he also told me a lot about the city itself, with the result that when I went there for the first time in 1961, I had no need to ask the way when I went out for a walk. The city was completely familiar to me, I already knew it like the back of my hand.

My father remained in Vienna after completing his course. He worked there as a *Hausmusiker* and gave concerts. This lasted nearly twenty-two years, although he always came back to Zhitomir for the summer. And it was there, in the summer of 1912, that he met my mother, who became his pupil.

My mother, whose maiden name was Anna Pavlovna Moskalyova, was Russian. Her father, whose distant ancestors were Polish, German, Swedish and Tartar, was a landowner and for a long time he refused to allow his daughter to marry a commoner. But in the end my father married my mother, in spite of everything. He was forty-two. As was usual at that time, they went off on their honeymoon – to Vienna. It didn't last long. One day they returned from a visit to the surrounding countryside to find the city swathed in black. It was 1914, and the assassination in Sarajevo had just ignited the powder keg that was Europe. They left at once for Russia.

Shortly after I was born, my father was offered a teaching post at the Conservatory in Odessa, where my family settled. For the first two years we divided our time between Odessa and Zhitomir, where we spent the summer. Then came a period of chaos, with all the changes of government.

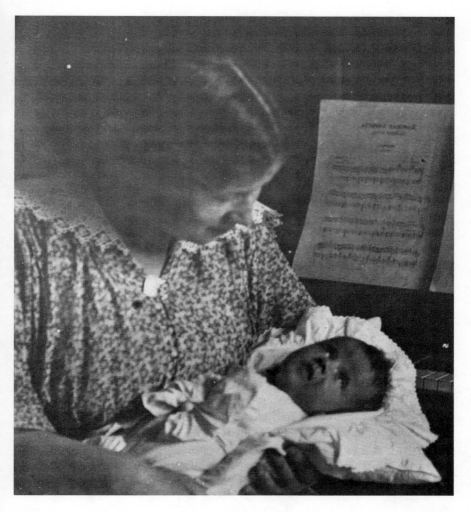

Richter outside his parents' dacha at Zhitomir with his maternal uncle's family

Seated from *l.* to *r.*: Tyotya Mary, Slava, Richter's grandfather and his mother and father

It was difficult to travel. At the end of the summer of 1918 I caught typhus. My mother had already rejoined my father in Odessa: once there, she found herself caught between the White Russians and the Red Army. It wasn't until four years later that she was able to return for me. I spent these four years with Tyotya Mary, Aunt Mary, my mother's sister, Tamara Pavlovna Moskalyova, whom I loved very dearly.

Mother took me back to Odessa by goods train, a distance of around four hundred kilometres. The journey lasted a week. It was during the troubles, a difficult period. I found it exciting.

In Odessa, we lived in the German quarter. My father carried out his duties as choirmaster at the church, as he was also an organist by training, and at the same time he taught the piano at the Conservatory.

At home, we spoke more Russian than German, but we had lodgers, one of whom, Fräulein Stabuch, was virtually a member of the family. She was a remarkable woman, originally from Lithuania, and it was she who taught me German.

I've always read a great deal. Around the time I was ten, I almost literally devoured books. My mother told me off for not liking Tolstoy, and it's true, I didn't read him; but I adored Gogol, whom I read while I was still very young, as well as Dickens. I was completely spellbound by Maeterlinck – *Pelléas et Mélisande*, of course, and also *La princesse Maleine*.

I came to poetry only much later. I still love Racine, Rimbaud, Shakespeare, Pushkin and Pasternak, but it's a form of expression that doesn't stick in my head; I can never manage to remember the lines, whereas I can remember all the prose I've ever read.

But the fact remains that I used to read so much that one day – much later, in Moscow, during the war – the organist and composer Alexander Gedike confided in a friend: 'RRRichter' – he pronounced the 'r' in the German way – 'really must be told that it's dangerous to read while walking in the street.' He had passed me in the street somewhere in Moscow, but I was so engrossed in reading Goethe's *Dichtung und Wahrheit* that I hadn't acknowledged him.

When I was nine, I penned a sort of drama, *Dora*, a short play in eight acts and fifteen scenes, with thirteen characters, which we performed at one of the soirées that my parents sometimes organized in their little flat. On other occasions there might be masked balls, a tradition I continued when I got my own place in Moscow.

It was wonderful. Until I was eleven, I had a happy childhood. But then came the most terrible period in my life: school! I hated school; even today, the mere thought of it makes me shudder. I loathed every aspect of it, but above all the fact that it was obligatory. The children were real scoundrels, even though the school was German and had a good reputation. Our main teacher was a terribly strict woman by the name of Frau Peters. We went in absolute fear of her, all the more so because she was generally so calm. She remained the picture of sweetness and composure, then suddenly she'd scream 'Get out!' in a voice that would have brought down the walls of Jericho.

She was actually quite pretty, with something of the Mona Lisa about her, and seemed relatively well disposed towards me, even though on one occasion she exclaimed – in German, which made it sound even worse – 'Alle sind so faul, faul, alle! Aber der Richter, der stinkt von Faulheit!' (You're all lazy, the whole lot of you! But Richter, he's bone-idle!) It's true that I never did any work. I've always been lazy. It's one of my failings; I'm passive by nature.

One day I set off as if to go to school, but didn't, and spent the day wandering round Odessa. My escapade lasted ten days. I wanted to get to know the world, but in my own way, not because they were trying to drum it into me. I learned far more by playing truant than I ever did at the German School.

At all events, it ended when I was fifteen or sixteen. I just managed to scrape through my exams; I understood nothing about arithmetic, but was completely absorbed by music, which I'd discovered when I was around eight, when I started to play the piano.

My father was in fact a remarkable pianist, and when he was free, he would practise for two or three hours in the evening; needless to say, I always listened. The impressions left by his playing undoubtedly had a great influence on me. But whenever I sat down at the piano myself, he was horrified by what I did. I can still hear him exclaiming: 'It's terrible what the lad's doing!'

To begin with, I practised with him, but he would immediately lower his arms as I wasn't showing him any respect. He was a very gentle, taciturn man. He had a delightful pupil, a Czech harpist, who subsequently went to San Francisco and became principal harpist at the Opera. She gave me some lessons, and I soon learned all you're supposed to know, the things that children are taught at the very beginning, and at all events what I needed to know in order to devote myself to the only thing that interested me: sight-reading. At that point I decided her lessons were no longer necessary.

Richter with his grandfather (*above*) and parents (*below*)

As a good German, my father was clearly not in agreement with this method or, rather, this absence of any method. My mother, on the other hand, kept telling him: 'Leave him alone, let him do as he likes, it's best not to put any pressure on him.' There's no doubt that she was right. On some level she realized that I should be allowed to run free. She would say: 'If he doesn't want to practise scales, all right, he doesn't need to.' As a result, I've never practised scales. Never. Nor any other exercises. Never, not at all. Czerny neither. The first piece I played was Chopin's First Nocturne, followed by his Study in E minor, op. 25 no. 5. Then I tried sight-reading Beethoven's sonatas, especially the one in D minor. Then, because I often heard my father playing Wagner – he was a fanatical Wagnerite, he spent all his time in Vienna listening to Wagner at the Opera, and he'd told me all the stories – I began to take an interest in Wagner and to study the vocal scores of *Tannhäuser* and *Lohengrin*. You can imagine what my performance must have sounded like! But I played everything I wanted, Wagner and Verdi, Mascagni and Puccini.

We had a three-room flat. The main room was divided in two by a large cupboard. On one side was my mother's bedroom, and on the other side was the dining room. But we always ate in the kitchen. The piano was in the smaller room, and it was there that I slept. Sometimes I would get carried away. I'd say: 'This evening I'm going to play this opera from start to finish.' My mother would get annoyed: 'No, it's too late, it's time you were in bed.'

I also composed. To begin with, my father wrote down my compositions, but afterwards I started to do so myself. They were short works, extremely inept, obviously, all for the piano. My first serious 'work' was an opera, of course. It was based on Lermontov's *Bela*. But it had no words, only music. Later there was a sonata–fantasy and a foxtrot on Jewish themes (both for piano) and a fairy-tale opera, *Ariane and Bluebeard*. But it remains a fact that nothing became of me as a composer. Perhaps I could have been a composer, as my first little pieces – the ones I wrote when I was eleven or twelve – were in fact quite original; but as I grew older, I started to imitate others. I began to write in the style of Franz Schreker, as I'd discovered his opera and fallen under its spell. Never mind. The most important thing was this insane attraction that the theatre had for me. My father had a remarkable quality, a very special gift: he could improvise wonderfully well on the organ, and he had been offered a post as organist at the Odessa Opera. As he worked there, I too had access to the place. I still remember the second act of *The Tsar's*

Bride, the third act of *La bohème*. I was won over and gradually I got to know them all, *Aida*, *Rigoletto* . . .

It was this that interested me, not the piano. And it was opera that provided me with the essentials of my education.

2 Odessa in the Thirties

During the summer of 1931 we returned as usual to spend two months at Zhitomir. I was sixteen, and my father introduced me to his old friends and admirers, the eight Semyonov sisters. They lived together in a charming house with colonnades. You'd think you were in a short story by Turgenev. They were delightful women, but slightly comical, because they behaved like girls although they were in fact around seventy. They were already old women and always wore very old-fashioned clothes. Everyone made fun of them, but they were really quite extraordinary, each in her own way. Real eccentrics!

They organized a kind of family concert at their home, in the course of which I played the Schumann Concerto – on a single piano, taking both the piano part and the orchestral part. The next day they sent my parents a bunch of flowers from their garden, which was laid out beside a monastery, with a deep gully running alongside it. It was very beautiful.

And so these eight sisters were my first audience. It was with them that I enjoyed my first success. In fact, this concert decided my future, as it was then that I conceived the desire to become a pianist. Imagine! Eight admirers at once!

The idea of becoming a pianist, in the professional sense, had never

The family home at Zhitomir

Richter at the piano in Zhitomir

struck me before. Even so, I had already worked as an accompanist at the Sailors' Club at Odessa when I was only fourteen. There was a group of amateur singers there who staged operatic excerpts with piano accompaniment. I spent a lot of time there, it interested me. And because they were amateurs, they too enjoyed it. Of course, they were incredibly bad singers, with dreadful voices, but even so it gave me a certain experience. In this way I accompanied a whole act of Tchaikovsky's *Cherevichki* and *The Queen of Spades*.

At fifteen, I was invited to perform as an accompanist in clubs, at little concerts. I toured all the clubs in the region; I'd be sent off somewhere, outside the city, in the evening, it was all new. Everything had to be sight-read on stage, you never knew in advance what to expect. Anything was possible. I had to accompany singers, violinists, a ballet, a circus, and always at a moment's notice. Sometimes the performances were outside, so that one day the piano got soaked in a shower. On another occasion I was accompanying a violinist in Bazzini's *La ronde des lutins*. Within a few bars we were producing the most frightful din. What he was playing bore absolutely no relation to what I could see in the score in front of me. The page-turner had turned over two pages at once. We started again and had just survived the perils of the earlier passage unscathed, when disaster struck again. Another page had been missed out. I felt him tapping me on my shoulder: 'All right, sonny boy, I've just about had enough of you.'

I felt I'd brought dishonour on myself. But it was the score. It was falling apart. Whole pages were missing. We never rehearsed for these concerts. You came on stage and had to play.

(A few years later I spent the summer at a rest home near Odessa: there were distribution difficulties at the time, and I'd been found a place at a rest home belonging to the Ministry of Justice. I was working as a cinema pianist, improvising the music while the films were showing. I also stood in as librarian.)

It was thanks to these concerts and clubs that I started to earn a bit of money. I was fifteen at the time. Sometimes I was paid in kind, which was even better. One evening, in a club, after a concert, I was given a sack of potatoes, which was more than welcome. It was just after collectivization, a very difficult time, it was a struggle to survive. But ultimately that was of no concern to me . . .

My mother had started to make dresses to bring in some extra money. She did it on the black market, of course, not officially. She was always the centre of attention and dressed very well for the time. She was an exceptionally brilliant woman, very fashionable – almost too much so. She was also very much abreast of the times. She took a passionate interest in current events, in all that was going on, both in Russia and abroad, but this produced a reaction in me. There's no doubt that this is at the root of my total aversion to this kind of thing. And she was always telling me off: 'Why aren't you interested in politics?' I really wasn't interested in it in the slightest and have never paid the least attention to it before or since.

I wanted to work, and, of course, my mother thought this was an excellent idea, not because of the money but so that I could appear on stage. That was something I really wanted to do.

And so, when I was eighteen and because we knew lots of people at the Opera – I used to go with my father whenever he was playing the organ there and was always buried away in the orchestra pit – I was finally taken on as a ballet *répétiteur*.

The chief conductor was Samuel Alexandrovich Stolerman, an extremely professional and decent conductor, not very likeable as a person, but someone I could respect. He had killed his wife. She was jealous and had destroyed all his compositions. He was completely drunk when he shot her in her sleep. What a lovely wife! From jealousy! Burned all her husband's work!

He was acquitted.

I learned a lot under his direction and, after having accompanied the ballet for a while, I became *répétiteur* for the opera chorus.

At this point in its history, the Odessa Opera was at the forefront of the avant-garde. It was here, for example, that the Russian premières of Puccini's *Turandot* and *Il trittico* were given. They also staged Krenek's *Jonny spielt auf*, which was hugely successful at the time but was later forgotten. It remained in the repertory for two years before it was banned.

Be that as it may, it was an excellent theatre, with a fine ensemble. Stolerman, who was well disposed towards me, even promised to let me conduct, which tempted me enormously. The work in question was Glazunov's *Raymonda*, not particularly easy as a piece. But in the end someone else conducted it, someone who toed the line and who was a Party member. *Raymonda* includes a two-page variation in which the piano has a solo. I had to settle for playing the piano part.

It was round about this time – in other words, during the early 1930s – that something happened that was to have important repercussions. My father was officially invited to teach at the German Consulate. The consul needed someone to teach his children the piano and a Soviet official in charge of relations with the foreign consular staff sent along my father, who taught there for a number of years.

The consul had a box at the Opera and, having heard me play the solo variation in *Raymonda*, invited me to perform at the soirées at the consulate. To mark Hindenburg's death, I played the funeral marches from Beethoven's op. 26 Piano Sonata and *Götterdämmerung*.

We were on good terms with the consul and his family; we were virtually friends and on several occasions we spent the New Year with them. But the consul was summoned back to Germany soon after Hitler came to power.

I remember that on one occasion my father was questioned on what he'd seen at the consulate – you can imagine where the interrogation took place. He told us that they'd said: 'No doubt you have to shout "Geil Hitler" all the time.' That's how *'Heil Hitler'* is pronounced in Russian. To my ears it sounds so funny that it only underlines the ridiculousness of the expression.

In short, my father's lessons and all these soirées rapidly came to an end, but it had all had German associations. There's no doubt that it all added weight to the files that were kept on me and my father.

I was nineteen when I had the mad idea of giving a solo recital. I was an accompanist, a *répétiteur* at the Opera, I had no proper training as a pianist and I virtually never practised the piano repertory *per se*, to which I was in any case not particularly drawn at this time. But during the summer of 1933 I attended a recital given in Zhitomir by David Oistrakh. His accompanist was Vsevolod Topilin, whom I got to know much later and who was arrested after the war, for no reason, or rather simply because he hadn't been killed in battle. During the first half of the concert he gave a magnificent performance of Chopin's Fourth Ballade.

'If an accompanist like Topilin can do it,' I asked myself, 'why can't I?'

Without prevaricating any longer, I prepared a Chopin programme and the concert was held at the Odessa Engineers' Club on 19 March 1934. It was a small room, and the audience was largely made up of family friends and acquaintances. It was a rather foolhardy venture. I'd prepared the programme on my own and, not to put too fine a point on it, in a very amateurish way. The programme wasn't all that easy. To play the *Polonaise–fantaisie* and Fourth Ballade for the first time in your life – well! It was terrifying to find myself all alone on stage, and I almost died of stage fright. Bizarrely, I started with the posthumously published Prelude in C sharp minor and then, after a few nocturnes and preludes, the first half ended with the *Polonaise–fantaisie*. After that came the Fourth Scherzo, another nocturne, a mazurka and two of the op. 10 Studies. It was very bad! Lots of wrong notes; all the runs in the Fourth Scherzo no more than approximate . . . In spite of what people told me afterwards, there were lots of frightful things about this concert – after all, I was there myself, so I know. However much I may suffer from a natural severity, a sort of German pedantry, I still tend to draw a line in my own case between what's more or less good and what's downright bad.

But to go back to the recital, it ended with the Fourth Ballade, which was in fact fairly successful. And as an encore I played the Fourth Study from the op. 10 set. Not too badly either.

The experience wasn't to be repeated for a number of years. The concert had taken place; one can't say that it created much of a stir. The press, it appeared, had been present, but remained hidden. I knew a certain Apfelzweig who wrote under the name of 'Largo' and whose articles covered the musical life of Odessa. I was told that he'd written a piece praising the concert, but when I asked if I could see it, I was forced to realize that he'd not written anything at all.

That was Odessa!

An attractive city, admittedly, but it lost all its charm in 1933, when they set about destroying all its churches. In their place, they built schools, shoddier than anything you could ever imagine. Rabbit hutches in the latest fashion! It was the same all over Russia. It was the time of the 'general demolition programme'. Buildings were being blown up everywhere, all that was left were a few blackened shells.

My father wasn't popular in Odessa. He was for ever being humiliated, probably because he was an excellent pianist and sometimes gave recitals. The other teachers at the Conservatory couldn't bear that; they were jealous of him. He felt he was suffocating and in the end was hounded from the Conservatory. It was in Odessa that he died, shot by the Soviets. I'll come back to this later.

I sometimes passed through Odessa in later life. But I swore never again to perform there in public, and I never gave any more concerts there. Never!

In 1935–6 people were frightened when they heard the doorbell ring, especially at night.

I still remember an odd dream that I had in this connection. A dream of astonishing stupidity. There's a ring at the door. I go to answer it. 'Who is it?'

And from the other side of the door comes a terrifying voice: 'Don't open up, I'm a burglar!'

And I would wake up, bathed in sweat. My dream was clearly bound up with this fear of the doorbell ringing, as, needless to say, there were arrests. The situation at the Opera was terrible. It was the time of the 'purges'. People were fired, everyone was accused of one thing or another, dereliction of duty, corruption, debauchery. There were countless meetings where everyone was expected to denounce everyone else and unmask the 'enemies of the people'.

The principal director at the Opera – the one who had staged Krenek's *Jonny spielt auf* – was a man of the first rank. A meeting was organized in the main auditorium and everyone had to produce a diatribe against him. The prima ballerina, who was really a very respectable person, was forced to declare that 'this man was really vicious'. And one of the men in charge of props had to denounce him; he found the whole idea so repugnant that as soon as he opened his mouth, he fainted. But this merely made things worse for the director, on whom further insults were heaped: 'That's what his work leads to.'

His photograph was plastered all over the walls of the theatre, with the caption 'Enemy of the people'. He was driven from his post and replaced by an absolute bastard.

The nightmare lasted a long time, there was no end to it, and after a while I thought that I could take no more. On top of everything – my friends don't like me saying this, but it's true – I was threatened with military service. That's why I suddenly decided to abandon everything – theatre, parents and friends – and go to Moscow. It was 1937, the most terrible year you could imagine, and I was twenty-two. I'd made up my mind to find out whether I could become a pianist, and so I went to see Heinrich Neuhaus with the aim of enrolling at the Conservatory and joining his class.

Richter in Neuhaus's class

3 Heinrich Neuhaus

I'd already heard Heinrich Gustavovich Neuhaus during one of his visits to Odessa and had been bowled over by his playing – he played Beethoven's Hammerklavier Sonata – and, indeed, by his whole manner. There was something about his appearance that strongly reminded me of my father, but he was really much more light-hearted. In fact, you could say that I had three teachers: Neuhaus, my father and Wagner.

We had friends in Moscow who had agreed to put me up, an act of extraordinary generosity when you think that, like most people, they lived in a wretched communal flat. As soon as I arrived in Moscow, the Lobchinskys – Mrs Lobchinsky was herself one of his pupils – took me to see Neuhaus so that I could play for him. Among the pieces I chose was my warhorse at that time, Chopin's Fourth Ballade.* At the end of

* Neuhaus himself left the following account of Richter's arrival in his class: 'I'd been asked to audition a young musician from Odessa who wanted to enrol in my class at the Conservatory. "Has he finished preparatory school?" I asked. "No, he hasn't studied anywhere." I must say that the reply left me a little perplexed. A boy who had had no musical training and who was preparing to enter the Conservatory was certainly not lacking in audacity! I was curious to get to know him. A young man arrived, tall, thin, fair-haired and blue-eyed. His face was alert and incredibly intense. He sat down at the piano, placed his long, supple and powerful hands

the audition, we talked about this and that, including Wagner. I must have made a good impression on him as I was admitted to the Conservatory without any examination or competition, on the one condition, however, that I promised to attend all the mandatory courses. These courses had nothing to do with music, but were a half-baked political and philosophical shambles that were totally alien to my nature but the object of extremely testing exams. I couldn't bring myself to attend them and I was twice expelled from the Conservatory during my first year. I returned to Odessa, fully resolved never again to set foot in an institution that didn't suit me. I didn't dare breathe a word to my parents about what had happened, but, to my horror, they received a letter from Neuhaus along the lines of: 'You're my best pupil. Come back!' It was so cordial a letter that it proved the instrument of my salvation. Neuhaus was then rector of the Conservatory, and it was no doubt he who had arranged for me to be admitted without any formalities. And it was he who now smoothed out the difficulties caused by my behaviour.

Neuhaus was like a second father to me. He was so generous by nature, we were all mad about him. I've never met anyone else with so much charm; such a delightful man, so utterly lacking in gravitas! Almost easy-going, and yet . . .

Like my father, he was of German and Polish extraction, a cousin of the composer Karol Szymanowski. In his youth he had been friendly with Vladimir Horowitz, and throughout his life he was close to Artur Rubinstein. At the beginning of the century, he had studied not only in Russia, but also in Berlin, in Italy, where he spent several years and which he loved, and in Vienna, where he was a pupil of the great pianist Leopold Godowsky. He was immensely cultured and widely read in literature, philosophy and the arts. He spoke fluent Russian, Polish, German, French and Italian. This sort of knowledge of languages was relatively common in Russia in the past, but was rarely found after the country was shut off from the outside world in the wake of the Bolshevik Revolution. Although he had only small hands, he was a tremendous pianist, but as he was never allowed to travel abroad, it was only his reputation as a

---

over the keys and began to play. His style of playing was reserved, simple and austere. The extraordinary musical perception that he showed won me over from the outset. I whispered to a female pupil who was sitting beside me: "I think he's a musician of genius." Following Beethoven's Sonata no. 28, he threw himself into Chopin's Fourth Ballade, then played some works of his own and sight-read. Everyone present wanted him to go on and for it to last for ever. That day Sviatoslav Richter became my pupil.'

Richter with Neuhaus

teacher that reached the outside world. His German origins cost him dearly. At the start of the war, during the Germans' lightning advance on Moscow, he stayed in the capital and refused to be evacuated with the rest of the staff from the Conservatory because his son was in hospital, suffering from a terrible type of tuberculosis that attacks the bones. A boy of fifteen. He said that as long as his son wasn't evacuated, he wouldn't leave either. They then checked his internal Soviet passport, which described him as 'Russian' under the heading 'Nationality'. He was accused of having deliberately concealed his German origins. It meant that he was thrown into prison.

But he was so utterly charming that he even succeeded in winning over the authorities. He was freed after ten months and evacuated to Sverdlovsk, where he taught for two years, leading a pitiful existence in a tiny room in which he also gave his lessons. All this left its mark on him, and he began to drink more than was good for him.

You might have thought that his small hands would have had an adverse effect on his playing. But nothing could be further from the truth. He produced a magnificent tone. It's to him that I owe this habit of sitting upright at the piano. He was right, everything depends on this.

He played Schumann and Scriabin splendidly. His performances of Chopin's E minor Concerto and Beethoven's 'Emperor' were so astounding that I always refused to include them in my own repertory. But his playing was sometimes uneven, as he spent so much time teaching that he had no time left for practising. Teaching is a terrible thing. It kills you as a pianist. And how can you teach when you need all your time to learn new things, to keep on learning new things?

I remember a Schumann recital that he gave. He'd begun with the sonatas and played them like a cobbler, with masses of wrong notes in every bar. Next on the programme came the *Kreisleriana* – marvellous. As for the *Fantasie*, you'd have thought it was Schumann himself at the piano. Never before, I'm sure of it, nor afterwards has it been possible to hear a performance like it.

I remember attending another of his concerts that was *really* bad. He had probably come to the concert hall straight from the classroom. But as an encore he played Rachmaninov's G major Prelude so well that I'd happily have sat through three other recitals as bad as this one just for the privilege of hearing that piece.

I learned a lot from him, even though he kept saying that there was nothing he could teach me. Music is written to be played and listened to

and has always seemed to me to be able to manage without words –
commentaries on it are utterly pointless – and I've never really been any
good with words. But there was a time when I was almost incapable of
speaking, especially in society, even with people for whom I felt no
antipathy – quite the opposite. This was exactly the case with Heinrich
Neuhaus. In his presence I was almost always reduced to total silence.
This was an extremely good thing, as it meant that we concentrated
exclusively on the music. Above all, he taught me the meaning of silence
and the meaning of singing. He said I was incredibly obstinate and did
only what I wanted to. It's true that I've only ever played what I wanted.
And so he left me to do as I liked.

The only work I've ever played without really wanting to was
Beethoven's Sonata in A flat major op. 110, which Neuhaus gave me to
practise during my first year at the Conservatory. He told me I couldn't
ignore it and that I'd find a lot of instructive things in it. I didn't want to
learn it: it seemed to me almost too genuine, almost indecent, almost in
bad taste, with its Arioso framing the final fugue. Also, I was never able
to bring myself to play all Beethoven's sonatas. I play twenty-two of
them, that's enough. If I've played the op. 110 Sonata fairly often since
then, it's because it's relatively easy to play. No comparison with the
op. 101 Sonata, which I played on arriving in Neuhaus's class and which
is horribly difficult, more so than the op. 111, and even riskier than the
Hammerklavier, though such a claim will seem heretical to many people.

But it remains a fact that with the op. 110 Sonata Neuhaus taught me
to obtain a singing tone, the tone that I'd always dreamed of. It was probably already in me, but he freed it by loosening my hands and teaching
me to open up my shoulders. He helped me get rid of the harsh sound
that was a legacy of the time I'd spent as a *répétiteur* at the Opera.

The other work he gave me to practise during my first year was Liszt's
Sonata. The essential point about this piece, he taught me, was the
silences, the sound of the silences. Thanks to him, I devised a little
stratagem, a dangerous stratagem that would almost certainly not work
for others but that has rendered me sterling service. It's at the beginning
of the sonata. What does this beginning consist of, in fact? A single note,
that's all: a G. What can you do to ensure that this miserable G sounds
somehow special? Here's what I do: I come out on to the stage. I sit
down, and I don't move a muscle. I create the sense of emptiness within
myself, and in my head I count up to thirty, very slowly. This causes panic
in the audience: 'What's happening? Is he ill?' Then, and only then, I play

the G. In this way, the note sounds totally unexpected, but in an intentional way. Clearly, there's a sort of theatricality about all this, but the theatrical element seems to me very important in music. It's essential if you want to create a feeling of unexpectedness.

I know lots of pianists who play splendidly, but who serve everything up on a plate. You know in advance what's on the menu. It's good, no doubt about it, but it's familiar.

The unexpected, the unforeseen – it's this that creates an impression. That's what I'd come to discover from Neuhaus and what he showed me. He put the finishing touches to what I was looking for.

The three pillars of the Russian piano school (apart from Rachmaninov, who left the country and who, as far as I know, never taught) were Goldenweiser, Igumnov and Neuhaus. Goldenweiser represented the older tradition, a pianist of the pedantic kind. For him, the important thing was knowing whether to play ta-ri-ra, ti-ra-ri or ti-ra-ra. An academic pianist, with no imagination. Igumnov, for his part, was an excellent musician and an original pianist. There was no panache to his playing, but it was lyrical; his tone was radiant and refined, but fairly limited in range. He belonged to another generation, he was much older than Neuhaus, and it was to Neuhaus that all the pianists in Moscow beat a path. Among those of more or less my own generation in Neuhaus's class was Emil Gilels. He was an honest musician and a marvellous pianist. It was he who gave the first performance of Prokofiev's Eighth Sonata: I was in the audience, and his performance was quite simply phenomenal. As for Prokofiev's Third Sonata, what he did with it was so magnificent that I decided not to play it. It's a sonata that I like enormously, but, having heard Gilels play it, I felt there was nothing I could add.

Gilels and I played together only once, on the radio during the war. It was the Variations on a Theme of Beethoven by Saint-Saëns, a composer I like a lot. (Gilels used to play his Second Concerto superbly, though a bit too seriously, so that I preferred Oborin's more engaging way with this work.) We'd have done better not to have bothered. It was pretty awful, no doubt because the piece itself is hardly a great success.

Our relations – friendly at the outset – were rather odd. Gilels was in fact a very great pianist, but a complex individual. He had a frightful temperament, was extremely touchy and was always sulking. He was pathologically jealous, which was terrible for him, as it reinforced the feeling that he was unhappy. He would sometimes put himself in the most ridiculous situations. One day he was at the Conservatory when a

With Emil Gilels (*centre*)

woman spotted him in the corridor and, amazed to see the great Gilels
there, went up to him and said to the little girl who was with her: 'Do
you know who this is? The greatest pianist in our country!' Whereupon
the kid exclaimed: 'Sviatoslav Richter!' Just a child. Gilels stormed away,
slamming the door behind him.

With Neuhaus, he behaved appallingly badly. Towards the end of
Neuhaus's life, he did something quite dreadful. He wrote to the papers
and also to Neuhaus in person, saying that he'd never been his pupil. He
disowned him. Neuhaus, for his part, worshipped him, but he was always
very frank with him and sometimes, of course, he would criticize him –
in a positive way, just as he criticized me. But Gilels was so touchy that he
couldn't bear the slightest criticism. It was enough to make him commit
this unforgivable act. Everyone in Moscow knew that he had been
Neuhaus's pupil and they were all indignant. When I heard what he'd
done, I refused to acknowledge Gilels in the street. Neuhaus was terribly
affected by it and died soon afterwards.

If it hadn't been for this permanent and consuming jealousy – a feeling
totally alien to me, it doesn't matter what area you apply it to – Emil
Gilels had it in him to be happy as an artist, given his exceptional talent.
But the circumstances surrounding his death are appalling. Before setting
off on a tour, he went into hospital for a check-up. He was given an injection, and three minutes later he was dead. It was the Kremlin Hospital.
Everyone knows that the doctors there are chosen because of their
political background. The result is that, through sheer incompetence,
they gave him the wrong injection and killed him.

But my great friend in Heinrich Gustavovich's class was a strange chap
by the name of Anatoly Vedernikov. He was five years younger than I and
had been a child prodigy. At the time of my arrival in Moscow in 1937,
he was seventeen and was already studying with Neuhaus. He played
divinely. His parents were very famous singers who had left Russia for
Japan, where he'd performed with great success as a child prodigy.
They'd then gone on to China where, as the result of a bizarre set of
circumstances like something out of a novel, they'd abandoned him. His
adoptive parents weren't musical. In 1937 – the year I arrived in Moscow –
they decided to return to the Soviet Union, where they were, of course,
arrested. It was an unsavoury tale of a kind all too common at this time.
Vedernikov and I became friends at once. I'd nowhere to stay, and so he
put me up for the night. He was a remarkable pianist with whom I
really enjoyed playing, and I often did. Even before war broke out in

1941,* if I remember aright, we'd already performed Bach's Concerto for four pianos on the radio, with Kurt Sanderling – he was still very young, it was my first meeting with this great conductor. The other pianists were Neuhaus's assistant, Emmanuel Grossman, and Theodor Gutman, one of Neuhaus's star pupils, who had won first prize in the Chopin Competition in Warsaw and who was already teaching at the Conservatory. Together with Vedernikov, we'd attended one of his recitals; he was a phenomenal interpreter of Chopin, one of the best I've ever heard. The way he played the studies was quite incredible, and I've never been able to understand why he remained unknown.

At the beginning of the war, Vedernikov and I gave a two-piano recital, with Chopin's *Rondo*, Liszt's *Concerto pathétique* and, in the second half, Debussy's suite *En blanc et noir* and Rachmaninov's Second Suite. It was an attractive programme and was well received.

Much later, we also played Bartók's Sonata for two pianos and percussion; one of the percussionists was Andrey Volkonsky, a harpsichordist and a fine avant-garde composer who now lives in Paris.

There's also a recording that we made, Vedernikov and I, of Bach's Double Concerto in C major – a fairly successful recording in which it's impossible to tell who is playing the first piano and who is playing the second: there's perfect unity between us.

Above all, however, there was the Students' Circle that Vedernikov and I ran from 1939 onwards. We met every Thursday in one of the Conservatory classrooms and played music for four hands, with my classmates Tolya Vedernikov, Vadim Guzakov, Volodya Tchaikovsky, Oleg Agarkov and Victor Merzhanov. The works we played were barely known or completely forgotten. We kept a little handwritten diary, and people would come and listen – students, teachers and their friends – in increasingly large numbers. I played complete operas here – *Die Meistersinger*, *Tristan*, Richard Strauss's *Salome* – and, in versions for four hands or two pianos, the symphonies of Bruckner, which people were unable to hear elsewhere. And also lots of contemporary works by living composers: Myaskovsky's Symphony no. 21, Hindemith's *Mathis der Maler* and *Nobilissima visione*, and works by Szymanowski. Neuhaus used to say that this Students' Circle was far more useful than all the subjects we were taught. But we were also serious competition for the Conservatory's official concerts, whose halls emptied as our own

---

* It was not until June 1941 that the Soviet Union was drawn into the Second World War. (B.M.)

Bust of Richter in polished granite, by I. E. A. Matyiszovna 'class' filled. In 1941 we planned to give the whole of Wagner's *Ring*. On the evening I was due to play the last act of *Götterdämmerung* with Vadim Guzakov, the Conservatory rector, Alexander Goldenweiser, refused to allow the performance to go ahead as no one had turned up for the recital scheduled to take place in the Conservatory's main auditorium. It was the Circle's one-hundredth meeting. *Götterdämmerung* proved its death blow. I should add that this was 21 June 1941 and that German troops invaded the country that very evening.

Vadim Guzakov, my partner for *Götterdämmerung*, was a delightful layabout but not without talent, and he sometimes joined in the Circle's activities. He showed an insane admiration for me simply because he was mad about Wagner. One evening, I'd gone round to his place and played the whole of *Tristan* for some of our friends. There were four or five of us in all. At the end he exclaimed in a rather puerile way, 'I propose that we all kneel before Slava!'

I protested, of course, and so he went on: 'All right, then! If you don't want me to kneel, spit on me! Please, spit in my face as much as you like.' He was a fanatical Wagnerian, who knew all Wagner's works, of course, but so extreme that there was something almost ridiculous about him. He spent his time trying to demonstrate to whoever was prepared to listen that Wagner was the greatest composer of all. It may be true, but even so!

Vedernikov was more interesting as a musician, more avant-garde. He could play anything and had stockpiled a number of new works that nobody at that time dared include in their repertory: Stravinsky's Sonata, Hindemith's *Ludus tonalis*, Debussy's twelve *Études* (one of his most successful achievements, in my view) and Schoenberg's Concerto. But there was a question mark over his playing, and Neuhaus had struggled hard to deal with it – his tone lacked beauty. He was terribly pig-headed and played using only his hands instead of his whole body. Neuhaus was always arguing with him on this point. But he refused to accept the weight of Neuhaus's arguments, although Neuhaus knew more than anyone about tone. Unfortunately, Vedernikov was also rather difficult as a person or, to be more exact, he had a lot of complexes. He always did the opposite of what he was told, out of a spirit of contradiction, and rubbed people up the wrong way. He had a theory that 'artistism', as he called it, by which he meant artistic individuality, was an obstacle to music. It was absurd! Not that the artist should push himself forward, but nor should he disappear. Rather, he should act as a mirror for the composer, embodying the latter within himself. In any case, these ludicrous

ideas were immediately refuted by his playing, but he spent his time spouting things like this, more out of obstinacy than to provoke people, and always managed to turn them against him.

He had another theory that consisted in claiming that the piano was merely a percussion instrument and couldn't be made to sing: the sound of the piano decayed as soon as the note was struck. All this is clearly debatable. One day we were listening to my recording of *Pictures at an Exhibition*, in which the last note of 'Catacombs' has to resound for a long time. And on the recording, the sound does indeed continue to resonate for a very long time. Having heard this, and in the face of all the evidence, he exclaimed: 'You see, you can't hear a thing!' On principle. Stubborn as a mule. As soon as you said anything good about something, he'd invariably say something bad. On another occasion, we'd taken a look at the score of Dvořák's Piano Concerto and discovered that it contained lots of interesting things. I took the work into my repertory and a year later played it in the Grand Hall of the Conservatory. After the concert, he came to see me in my dressing-room and said: 'Slava, why do you play such worthless music?' A third example proved the final straw. We'd both been deeply moved by a recording of Britten's *Peter Grimes*, but when I got to know Britten himself a few years later it was enough to make Vedernikov announce that Britten had 'only ever written worthless music'. You'd take him a present – Strauss's Alpine Symphony, for example, which we'd played in a version for four hands – and as soon as he put the record on, he'd exclaim: 'What frightful music!' The same thing happened with Pfitzner's opera *Palestrina*, a remarkable work from every point of view, with an excellent libretto. 'Impossible to imagine a stupider subject!' No doubt because it was I who had given him a copy of the score.

But the fact remains that I'd had enough. We'd been good friends at the beginning, but we stopped performing together. I didn't feel like it any longer.

At the height of our friendship, I was living in Moscow or, rather, dividing my time between Moscow and the surrounding area. I often went to the dacha owned by the five Hekker sisters, five young ladies who assiduously attended our Students' Circle. One of them was a pianist, another was a violinist, the third a painter and the fourth and fifth nothing at all. They were German and suffered more or less the same sort of problems as Neuhaus did in 1941. Three of them were arrested and later deported. Why only three of them? Because the other two weren't at home when the police came looking for them. Afterwards the authorities forgot about them and they remained at home without being troubled

Richter in Kiev

Richter outside the family dacha in Zhitomir

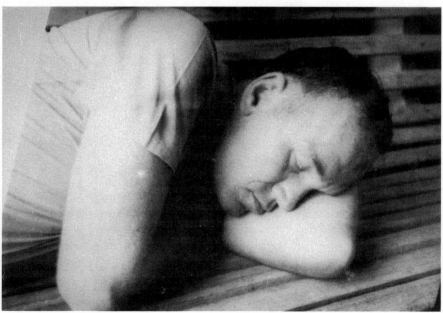

any further. An example of what's called *khaltura* in Soviet slang: a shoddy or botched piece of work.

But Vedernikov – and this is why I've mentioned them – had married one of the sisters. And so he found himself in a German environment where he felt completely out of place. He had a little boy who caught meningitis. Stubborn as he was, he announced: 'I've no faith in doctors,' and so no doctor was called to the child's bedside. There were complications, and his son was left a deaf mute. (He became quite a good painter.)

During my studies, I regularly performed at concerts given by Neuhaus's pupils in the Small Hall at the Conservatory. It was there, in 1939, that I played the Bach Double Concerto with Vedernikov and there that I first performed Brahms's Second Piano Concerto, Schubert's 'Wanderer' Fantasy, Schumann's *Fantasie*, Debussy's *Préludes* and Ravel's *Valses nobles et sentimentales*. I practised wherever people would let me, in the classrooms at the Conservatory, at the Gnesin Institute or at the homes of friends such as the painter Anna Ivanovna Troyanovskaya, where I could turn up whenever I liked, day or night. An extremely interesting woman who later encouraged me to paint pastels. The piano on which I practised there had belonged to Nikolay Medtner, to whom she had been very close.

There's a Russian saying: 'You lack ten roubles, you've one hundred friends.' There's some truth in it. Wherever I went, even at the height of the war, I always found a potato to eat. I didn't mind not having a home. I slept wherever people would have me: at Anatoly Vedernikov's, at Volodya Tchaikovsky's, at the home of the mathematician Igor Shafarevich. I felt comfortable everywhere. Above all, however, I was put up by Neuhaus for several years. He was so generous that his pupils could call on him without warning, even at four in the morning. His wife was equally amazing and welcoming. She never slept; if you turned up in the middle of the night, she'd be drinking tea or wine and was delighted for people to come. And she'd say to you: 'You've nowhere to sleep? Well, you can spend the night here.' They had a tiny flat.

At Neuhaus's, I slept under the piano.

4 The War Years

I heard Prokofiev play his Sixth Sonata in private in 1940, at the home of some fellow musicians. He'd just completed it. The work fascinated me from the outset and I decided to learn it.

Some time later, Neuhaus told me that he had to give a recital of works by Soviet composers in Moscow. Pretending that he hadn't practised enough (but really because, generous as ever, he wanted to introduce me to a wider audience), he suggested that I should share the programme with him. In the first half, he'd play pieces by Myaskovsky, Kreyn and Alexandrov, while I'd feature in the second half.

That's how I came to play the Sixth Sonata and got to know Prokofiev. I'd already started to practise it during the summer in Odessa; but in fact I didn't really begin to learn it until ten days before the concert, as I only worked regularly when faced with a deadline. It's a highly effective piece and, of course, it was a great success with the audience. Prokofiev came to congratulate me after the performance and asked me to play his Fifth Concerto under his own direction.* A couple of years previously I'd played his Second Sonata at a student concert, a piece he'd dedicated –

* See Chapter 5.

like his Fourth Sonata and Second Concerto – to his great friend, the pianist Maximilian Schmidthoff. Before the First World War, Prokofiev was due to perform his Second Concerto at Pavlovsk. He was very young, but already famous, and he'd been the butt of a great deal of hostility on account of the innovative nature of his music. The critics took him to the cleaners. But it so happened that the concert hadn't taken place, because the weather was so bad! To that degree, one must admit that critical dishonesty is fairly rare. Much later I had a similar experience, but in the other direction. One morning, *Pravda* ran the headline: 'Great success yesterday evening for concert with Nina Dorliac, Anatoly Vedernikov and Sviatoslav Richter.' It was supposed to be a concert in memory of Rachmaninov, but I'd fallen ill and had cancelled.

There are few tragic works by Prokofiev, who was actually rather genial and positive by nature, but these three pieces – the Second and Fourth Sonatas and the Second Concerto – are certainly tragic. The last two were in fact dedicated posthumously. Prokofiev and Schmidthoff often corresponded, until one day Prokofiev received a letter from Schmidthoff announcing: 'Seryozha, another bit of news. I've shot myself through the head. Maximilian.' His body was found two months later in a forest.

Sergey Prokofiev was an extremely interesting person, but . . . dangerous. He was capable of hurling you against a wall. One day a pupil was playing him his Third Concerto, accompanied by his teacher at a second piano, when the composer suddenly got up and grabbed the teacher by the neck, shouting: 'Idiot! You don't even know how to play, get out of the room!' To a teacher!

He was violent. Completely different from Shostakovich, who was for ever mumbling 'Sorry'. No, he was solidly built, bursting with health, qualities that I'd rather tend to admire. Also, he had little time for principles, although in 1948, at a meeting of the Central Committee that condemned new music and where he was savagely attacked by Zhdanov for formalism, he had the courage to go up to Zhdanov and, looking him straight in the eye, to ask: 'What right have you to speak to me like that?'

But principles weren't exactly his strong point. If necessary, he was perfectly capable of writing to order, as was the case with *Zdravitsa*, which was commissioned to mark some birthday or other of Stalin's, an ode in his honour. It's a work you couldn't perform now: 'Hail to Stalin, the father of us all.' Unless you changed the words. But the piece is absolutely brilliant. A monument, it's true, but a monument to himself, to Prokofiev! He wrote it with a kind of insolence, a noble amorality: 'Stalin? Who's that? But yes, why not? I can do anything, including this sort of thing.' For him, it was a question of writing music, and that was something he knew how to do.

I was due to give my first public recital – my first solo recital – in the Small Hall of the Conservatory in October 1941. In the heat of my preparations – and this was to be the case throughout my life – I paid little attention to what was going on around me. The recital was cancelled, of course, as the Germans were already at the gates of Moscow. Even so, I appeared in the Grand Hall in December, performing the Tchaikovsky Concerto for the first time, and later played the Prokofiev Concerto that he'd asked me to perform under his own direction. All this helped, of course, to establish my reputation. I finally gave my first recital, which had been postponed from the autumn, in July 1942. My proposed programme was Beethoven's *Pathétique*, Schubert's 'Wanderer' Fantasy and, in the second half, some Chopin. They wouldn't let me and I was told to play Prokofiev. I did as I was told and played his Second Sonata in the second half of the programme, together with six Preludes by Rachmaninov, a composer whom Prokofiev loathed, no doubt because he had been influenced by him. (It's enough to look at the cutting-edge *Études-tableaux* to see that Prokofiev's piano style stemmed, to a large extent, from Rachmaninov's. It was these works that he hated most of all. Of course, it was his right to like neither Rachmaninov nor Chopin, just as another great composer, Benjamin Britten, detested Brahms and Beethoven, although this really *is* going a bit far!)

At all events, it was a bad programme, a frightful hotchpotch. You really can't follow up the *Pathétique* and the 'Wanderer' Fantasy with Prokofiev's Second Sonata. That's why, shortly afterwards, I gave another recital of my own choice, this time in the Grand Hall, with a programme of Russian music: Tchaikovsky's G major Sonata, some Rachmaninov, Glazunov's Suite on the Name 'Sacha', and a group of Scriabin Preludes and the *Fantaisie* in B minor.

So my career began with the war. I remained in Moscow throughout its duration, unlike most other musicians, who were evacuated. I often had to keep watch on the roof-tops and stand guard during air raids. Sometimes I organized excursions on foot within a hundred-kilometre radius of the city. I've always loved walking and I've several times managed to cover fifty kilometres on foot in a single day. In the first place, I can't stand having to wait, it's part of my character, and whenever I had to wait for a tram or if it was full, I preferred to set off and walk. Before the war, I did quite a lot of climbing in the Caucasus. Of course, there was no question of that any longer; but now I explored Moscow and its surroundings. I remember walking on my own through a forest and suddenly finding myself bellowing like a wild animal in a sort of atavistic reflex. All on my own and without warning: grrr! Ow-ow-ow! Like a tiger, a lion or a wolf. It started up all at once, but I soon realized that I was doing something odd. It was as though I'd been turned into an animal wandering through a primeval forest. As an episode, it had no particular significance, except that it took place at all and that it occasionally resurfaces in my recollections.

On another occasion, I'd set off on an expedition with my friend Igor Shafarevich, the future mathematician. It was five days after war had been declared, and we'd said to ourselves: 'Has war broken out? Now's the moment to go, while there's still time.' We'd wanted to do this walk for some time. It wasn't without danger, but we weren't aware of the fact. We'd walked for around forty kilometres through woodland when we came across a woman, who immediately started squawking. Alerted by the noise, the local peasants took us to be saboteurs or spies sent by Hitler and bundled us off to the nearest police station. They discovered the word 'German' on my ID card. And when he saw Shafarevich's, the chief of police couldn't conceal his surprise: 'What's all this, then? Nineteen and already in your second year at university? That's rum.' I tried to explain: 'It's because he's very gifted . . .' Shafarevich found this irresistible and burst out laughing. The police chief, who had been extremely threatening until now, suddenly relaxed: 'You know what you're going to do? Get on the first train home without delay.' We were escorted to the station. Having been disciplined, we followed them to the station, gossiping with them as we went. It seemed these peasants had taken a liking to us. Everything was sorted out, though it was two in the morning when we finally got back to the Shafareviches', where I was staying at the time.

I was then invited to play not only in Moscow, where the musical life of the capital continued as usual, without interruption, but also in Kiev and in the Caucasus. I was sent partly because they knew that I would at least be properly fed there, and so I was able to spend three months giving concerts and dividing my time between Tbilisi, Baku, Yerevan and Sukhumi. Life was relatively easy in Georgia – it always has been. The intelligentsia had been eradicated here as elsewhere, but in a certain way

Fancy-dress ball at home

Richter on tour in the Caucasus

despotism didn't weigh as heavily on people here, while the war seemed a very long way off. Mobilization appeared not to affect the young people of Tbilisi, whom you could see strolling along Rustaveli Prospekt in the evening, and there was plenty of food. It was in Tbilisi that I first played Mozart's D minor Concerto – on the radio. The conductor was a dubious individual, you could tell a mile off that he was a member of the People's Commissariat of Internal Affairs – the NKVD – and as a conductor he was quite simply abysmal. I'd been given a room on the sixth floor of the hotel that I had to share with an accompanist whose name, strangely enough, I've forgotten. I had friends in the town and I sometimes spent the night at their place, and each time I returned to the hotel, I had to account for my absence. One day I told my room-mate that I'd return to the hotel in two days' time and collect the music for the concerto that I was to record the next morning. When I returned, it was fairly late at night and the door to the room was locked. I knocked . . . knock knock knock! 'I have to collect the score.' Knock knock knock! There was no answer, but I could hear stifled laughter coming from inside the room. What should I do? A few doors away lived a circus artist, extremely likeable, and I'd noticed from the outside that his room gave on to a ledge that ran all round the building. So I thought he might let me in and I could then get out on to the ledge. He agreed to help. It was raining. It was also about one o'clock in the morning, and here I was, scrambling from one ledge to another, six storeys up, in an attempt to get back to my room. As it was wartime, it suddenly struck me that if anyone saw me, they'd shoot me like a rabbit, but nothing of the sort happened. A few minutes later I entered my room through the window, greeted by shrieks of terror. I realized that my room-mate wasn't alone. 'Don't be afraid,' I said, 'I shan't even put the light on.' And I stretched out on my bed. I didn't sleep a wink all night, but the next morning I was at the radio station at nine, playing the Mozart Concerto with my NKVD official.

Oddly enough, this D minor Concerto is bound up with other strange memories. On another occasion I played it in Leningrad with Karl Eliasberg, the conductor of the local Radio Orchestra, a frightful man. He was very intelligent and cultured, but you can't imagine a more unpleasant person. Orchestras hated him. During the rehearsal, at the trill at the end of the cadenza, I said to him: 'Sorry, I'm going to play that passage again.' To which he retorted, disdainfully: 'Perhaps you could do that at home.'

He was a true conductor, highly professional, but an absolute horror!

But I really don't think there are many good conductors who aren't hated by orchestras.

It was also in Tbilisi that I set about studying the second book of Bach's *Well-Tempered Clavier*. I learned it by heart in a month and immediately played eight of the preludes and fugues, first for students, then in public, before performing the whole work in Moscow the following year.

Because the traditional Romantic repertory was so well established, Bach was rarely played by pianists in the Soviet Union. *The Well-Tempered Clavier* never appeared on concert programmes. Only transcriptions by Liszt or Busoni of one or other of the organ works seemed to have gained acceptance, while the 'Forty-Eight' were considered good enough only for examination pieces at the Conservatory. Before me (and, later, Maria Yudina), I see that only Samuel Feinberg included them in his recitals. Feinberg was a fanatical admirer of Scriabin and Nikolay Medtner (an extremely fine composer, I may add, but such a professional that in the throes of writing down his works he could never bring himself to settle on one variant rather than all the others that were jostling for his attention, in which respect he was the very opposite of a composer like Schubert, for whom only one solution ever seemed possible). He played Bach after his own fashion, not like Bach but like late Scriabin, terribly quickly and cleanly. This didn't stop him from having lots of admirers, which is entirely justified, as he was a great musician.

Maria Veniaminovna Yudina was a *monstre sacré*. I knew her, but only from afar – it has to be said that she was so odd that everyone avoided her. For her own part, she showed herself somewhat suspicious and critical of me. She said of me: 'Richter? Hmm! As a pianist, he's good for Rachmaninov.'

On her lips, that wasn't a compliment, even though she herself occasionally played Rachmaninov. She had graduated from the Petrograd Conservatory in the early twenties, at the same time as Vladimir Sofronitsky – a giant of a man who played Schumann and Debussy magnificently and Scriabin like nobody else. By the end of her life Yudina was an outrageous figure, a sort of Clytemnestra, always dressed in black and wearing sports shoes for her concerts. She was immensely talented and a keen advocate of the music of her own time: she played Stravinsky, whom she adored, Hindemith, Krenek and Bartók at a time when these composers were not only unknown in the Soviet Union but effectively banned. And when she played Romantic music, it was impressive – except that she didn't play what was written. Liszt's *Weinen und Klagen*

Maria Yudina

Maria Yudina

was phenomenal, but Schubert's B flat major Sonata, while arresting as an interpretation, was the exact opposite of what it should have been, and I remember a performance of the Second Chopin Nocturne that was so heroic that it no longer sounded like a piano but a trumpet. It was no longer Schubert or Chopin, but Yudina.

During the war she had given *The Well-Tempered Clavier* at a splendid concert, even if she polished off the contemplative Prelude in B flat minor from Book Two at a constant *fortissimo*. At the end of the concert, Neuhaus, whom I was accompanying, went to congratulate her in her dressing-room.

'But, Maria Veniaminovna,' he asked her, 'why did you play the B flat minor Prelude in such a dramatic way?'

'Because we're at war!!!'

It was typical of Yudina. 'We're at war!' She absolutely had to bring the war into Bach.

She also used to wander around with a revolver, which she would show to all and sundry. It really was a bit much. She used to say: 'Hold this thing for me, but be careful, it's loaded.'

One day she developed a crush on someone who didn't return her advances. One can understand the poor man; he must have been terrified of her. And so she challenged him to a duel.

By the end of her concerts I always used to have a headache. She subjected her audiences to such a degree of intensity, an incredible intensity! And then there was her way of coming onstage; you had the impression she was walking through the rain. And she carried a crucifix and crossed herself before launching into the first note. I've nothing against this, but in Soviet Russia, at that time!!!

She had a vast crowd of admirers. Audiences worshipped her, no doubt because of her powerful artistic personality, but probably also because she made no secret of her religious convictions. For my own part, I found her behaviour exaggeratedly theatrical and her religious beliefs somewhat false and ostentatious. At the time of her final public appearances, she couldn't resist reading some lines of Pasternak, even though lots of her concerts had been cancelled by the authorities, who had made her promise that if she wanted to continue to appear in public, she would have to abandon this kind of provocation. But she couldn't resist her own impulse to read Pasternak's poetry. The spectacle was all the more appalling in that she no longer had any teeth.

Of course, she cared for the poor, took them in and lived like a tramp herself. An eccentric woman and an extraordinary artist, but someone who always felt the need to invent things. To tell the truth, I really didn't like her. No doubt she was sincere, but her relations with composers seemed to me to be dishonest. Even so, I played at her funeral. Rachmaninov.

And so I learned Part Two of *The Well-Tempered Clavier* in the autumn of 1943 while giving concerts in the Caucasus, mainly in Tbilisi, but also wherever I happened to be staying, taking advantage of the breaks between concerts. At the hotel in Sukhumi there was a frightful little upright piano on which I practised relentlessly. Unfortunately, I kept being interrupted by people coming in and asking: 'Wouldn't you play us a little waltz?' I found that the best way of getting rid of them was to continue practising my fugues.

I'm no great fan of complete cycles. I don't play all Chopin's studies, for example, for the very good reason that I don't like some of them, such as the ones in octaves. Nor do I play all the Beethoven sonatas, but only twenty-two of them. The only exception is *The Well-Tempered Clavier*, which, it seems to me, all pianists should play. I made myself learn them out of defiance, out of a desire to excel. I forced myself to learn them as a kind of challenge, out of a desire to surpass myself. Originally, I was not all that fond of them, and if I made up my mind I was going to learn them, it was no doubt because of this kind of reverence towards *all* music that my father had instilled in me. But once I was immersed in the work, I came to understand and love it passionately. By 1945 I'd also learned the whole of Book One. I played the whole lot virtually everywhere and so often that I received letters from female admirers: 'When will you stop inflicting Bach's music on us?' But I took care to spread each book over six different recitals: eight preludes and fugues in the first half, followed in the second half of the programme by works by Mozart, Beethoven or Brahms. It was in this way that I first performed the *Appassionata* in Tbilisi. It has the reputation of being a difficult, virtuosic work, but next to *The Well-Tempered Clavier* it seemed to me almost easy. To tell the truth, my concert in Tbilisi was extremely bad, whereas two days later, at Baku, it went much better.

In Baku, I made a rather unpleasant discovery. I was under surveillance and was being followed. I was returning to my hotel one evening and, as I was late, I started to run. Out of habit, I looked round and noticed a man running behind me. Wanting to find out the truth, I arrived in front of the hotel but, instead of going in, I continued on my way as far as the

next corner, where I waited. The other man was still running as fast as his legs could carry him. I turned round and threw myself at him with all my might. We fell. He, of course, pretended that nothing was wrong, but now I understood. Later, I looked down into the street from my balcony window and saw that he was still there with another man. This surveillance lasted several months – it left an extremely unpleasant impression. I was followed everywhere, in Moscow as well as elsewhere. But I played a few tricks on my pursuers. One day, one of them was standing in front of me in the bus. I asked him: 'Are you getting out at the next stop?' 'Yes,' he replied after a momentary hesitation. 'Well, I'm not!' He had to get off, but I must say he looked terribly offended.

Even some of my own friends were summoned to the NKVD and asked for information about me. But they replied that I'd long since rumbled their little game. Even so, the surveillance continued all winter, then suddenly stopped.

After several months in Moscow, I was sent to Arkhangelsk and Murmansk, an adventurous journey in trains with no lighting or heating that took us to the front line and the trenches. Here I played for soldiers and the wounded. One of them asked me my name and, when I told him, exclaimed: 'Are you the namesake of the Richter in Moscow?' I looked very young, younger than I was, and for him, Richter could only be a professor, whereas in front of him stood a mere strip of a youth.

At Murmansk, I recall playing Rachmaninov's G minor Prelude, which I love, even though it's performed far too often. But it needs to be played at a *tempo di marcia*, mysteriously. I learned afterwards that it was on the very day that I played this wonderful prelude that Rachmaninov died, in March 1943.

I didn't stay long in Murmansk. Shortly after I arrived, the authorities woke up: 'What's this? A German here? Blah-blah-blah! Oh no!' I was sent back to Moscow on the first available train. In this way, I escaped the bombardment that had stopped just before I arrived and that started up again the night I left. The place was almost entirely destroyed, everywhere was in ruins. I particularly remember one occasion when I was walking among the rubble in search of the public baths. It was raining and the sky was overcast. There was sadness everywhere. Suddenly, in the street, the loudspeakers started to broadcast the slow movement of Tchaikovsky's Violin Concerto, played by Oistrakh. I remember it as it caught to perfection the startling melancholy of the mood and of the place.

The shelling had been terrible, though nothing in comparison to what

Leningrad suffered. In Moscow, there was danger everywhere, but it was at least possible to survive after a fashion, whereas Leningrad was absolute hell.

I first played in Leningrad on 5 January 1944. The trains were often shelled, but I arrived safe and sound on 31 December. I knew no one in the city and spent the evening alone in my hotel room staring out of the window, from where I could see St Isaac's Cathedral and hear the exploding bombs. That's how I spent New Year's Eve.

The following morning I went to the Philarmoniya and spent the whole day practising there. In Leningrad, the air raids were announced on the radio only after they had begun. That evening, as I was leaving the hall to return to my hotel, bombs started to rain down on the city. The streets were strewn with frozen corpses. In spite of everything, I continued on my way back to the Astoria Hotel, which wasn't very far away. I found the whole episode exciting. The next day I returned to the Philarmoniya. The glass in the windows was all broken, and only gaping holes remained. A shell had fallen on the Russian Museum next door. Even so, the concert went ahead. The audience was wrapped up in coats and was extraordinarily moved. My memory of the concert is that it went well; as soon as you start playing, you stop feeling cold.

Even so, I had to decamp yet again. My ID card had been examined: 'You can't stay here, you're German!' It was always like that. The Russians told me: 'You're German.' And the Germans told me: 'You're Russian.'

I returned to Leningrad in 1945, also in January. I was terribly disappointed. It wasn't at all the same city. The siege had been lifted, of course. The streets were full of people, and there was this mood of exhilaration that couldn't have been more nauseating if it had tried. This second visit left a nasty aftertaste. The first time, everything was dark, on account of the curfew and the bombings, the city was beautiful, mysterious, there were shells . . . And now, everything was utterly banal.

A particularly important event took place in my life in 1943. Prokofiev had just written his Seventh Sonata and had decided to entrust me with its first performance. I received the manuscript score only shortly before the première and had only four days in which to memorize it. I was almost responsible for the death of Neuhaus's second wife, Sylvia Fyodorovna, who was ill with a temperature of 40° and whose apartment was the only place I could find to rehearse. The piano was in her bedroom. The poor woman had to submit to the onslaughts of the final movement for three or more hours at an end, over a period of four whole days.

The sonata was a huge success with the audience. It's a fantastic work, but I still prefer the Fourth and, above all, the Eighth, the one dedicated to Gilels, which he played with such sovereign skill. I soon had occasion to perform this work, too, in public, when I was finally talked into taking part in the All-Union Piano Competition in 1945. It was an idea that I'd long resisted.

My attitude towards these competitions has always been entirely negative. I loathe them, as neither the people who take part in them nor the jury emerge unscathed. How can one listen to the same work played twenty or more times, each time by a different performer? How can you do that without going mad?

On the subject of competitions, let me digress for a moment. In 1958, I was forced to be a member of the jury at the first Tchaikovsky Competition, in which everyone who thought he was anyone on Moscow's musical scene owed it to himself to take part. I resigned myself to serving on the jury, but it was the first and last time. The composer Dmitry Kabalevsky was also there. Neuhaus summed him up rather well when he called him the poor man's Prokofiev or Shostakovich. I knew him, but it would never have occurred to me to play his threadbare music. Another composer of the same sort was Aram Khachaturian. He was much more talented, but he was also much more simple-minded, and incredibly lazy. Kabalevsky was a true intellectual, someone who was genuinely cultured, but as a person he was compromised, and deeply unpleasant. During the war, I'd been accused of 'pessimism' – the worst crime of the period – for playing Schubert's 'Wanderer' Fantasy. 'When you play this work,' I'd been told, 'there's nothing left but to throw yourself in the Moskva.' At the time of the Tchaikovsky Competition, Kabalevsky added his own accusation, but on this occasion, I thought, it was for something positive: he accused me of 'individualism', simply because I held views of my own. It was the first international competition to be held in Moscow, and it was vital that it should be won by a Soviet pianist. But during the preliminary rounds it was Van Cliburn who played best. He was miles better than any of the others. He was talented, he played with sincerity, even if he swamped Prokofiev's Sixth Sonata with too much pedal and adopted wrong tempi in the Tchaikovsky Concerto. By giving a zero mark to all but three of the other candidates (one of these three, Lev Vlassenko, had played the Liszt Sonata superbly, rather in the manner of Gilels), I'd decided to eliminate the others and leave only him. The public had in any case fallen madly in love with Van Cliburn and they were ecstatic when he won.

In 1945 the unwilling candidate had been me. The competition was a complete waste of my time, as I was already giving lots of concerts and couldn't see what I would achieve by getting mixed up in all this. But Neuhaus had finally persuaded me to let him put my name forward. I'd chosen one of the Liszt Transcendental Studies, *Wilde Jagd*, for the first round. For one reason or other, it left a deep impression, not least because there was no electricity in the hall and they'd had to place a candle on the piano. While I was playing, it fell inside the instrument.

It was at this competition that I first played Prokofiev's Eighth Sonata. On the day in question, I was still learning it – I always left everything to the last minute – and arrived ninety minutes late. Everyone was waiting, including Prokofiev himself: no doubt he wanted to hear his own work.

One of the other competitors was Victor Merzhanov, an excellent pianist, and it was he who won first prize. The war had just ended, and it was necessary for a true Russian, not a German, to win. In the end, however, he had to share it with me. Shostakovich was president of the jury and he later told me that Molotov had telephoned him: 'You're afraid of awarding the first prize to Richter? It's been decided to authorize you to do so, don't worry.' This prize allowed them to say on my concert posters that I'd won some prize or other, so they could later add 'Lenin Prize', 'Hero of Socialist Labour' and 'People's Artist of the USSR'. The Soviet mentality was very fond of these totally meaningless titles.

Work on Prokofiev's Eighth Sonata, which I'd spent whole nights practising before arriving late for the competition, had left me exhausted. Two days later, I had to play the Tchaikovsky Concerto; in the meantime, I'd spent a whole day in bed, trying to force myself to practise, but falling asleep and not managing to do any work. I couldn't rehearse the concerto until the day of the concert and I played abominably. It was a work I'd often played, starting in 1940 at a student concert, when I was accompanied by Goldenweiser playing the orchestral part on a second piano, then, later that same year, in the Grand Hall of the Conservatory. Technically speaking, this is perhaps the most difficult work in the repertory, together with Dvořák's, a piece that virtually no one plays but which occupies a special place in my affections. In Dvořák's concerto there are some terrifying passages from a technical point of view, with these double thirds in both hands. It was in Philadelphia that I played it for the first time, before making a recording – much later – with Carlos Kleiber. It's not a good recording, I'm afraid, because the atmosphere wasn't good. One of the players, idle as always – the oboist or horn player, if my memory serves – had said to him: 'If you continue to make remarks like that, I'm leaving.' To speak like that to Kleiber, the greatest living conductor! I was furious. Besides, I wasn't on form and neither was Kleiber. Be that as it may, it's a very attractive concerto, perhaps not as successful as the cello concerto, although that's a matter for debate.

Other composers of Dvořák's generation deserve a better press in musical circles – someone like Grieg, for example, of whom I'm very fond and who's a remarkable composer, almost a genius. Alfred Brendel says that it's music for a chambermaid. May God have mercy upon him! I know what it is that makes Grieg sound cheap but, when all's said and done, it's a positive feature: he's easy to play. He wrote marvellously well, not only for the piano, but also for the orchestra and the strings. It's enough to listen to *Peer Gynt*, the violin sonatas or the quartet, which is so well written that you'd think you were listening to an orchestra. And as for the songs! I've accompanied quite a lot of them for Galina Pisarenko and, in the past, for Nina Dorliac.

It was towards the end of the war that I first started to appear with any frequency with Nina Dorliac. When I enrolled at the Conservatory in 1937, a clarinettist had just died and there was a civilian funeral, a sort of memorial concert that I attended and that many musicians took part in. Igumnov played a movement from Tchaikovsky's *The Seasons*, Neuhaus a Brahms intermezzo, Gedike accompanied the cellist Shirinsky at the organ in Rachmaninov's *Vocalise* – not at all together. And, finally, a singer performed Solveig's Song and Lullaby. It took my breath away, the singer seemed to me so wonderful. Also, she was extraordinarily pretty, a real princess. I started to ask everyone around me: 'But who is she? Who is she?' I was told it was Nina Dorliac. She was often asked to perform on such occasions. As she herself used to say, good-humouredly, 'I fulfilled the function of a professional mourner.'

Nina Lvovna Dorliac's father was born in Russia, but he was French in origin, his own father having come from Toulouse and settled in Russia. I don't know the circumstances, as Nina didn't like talking about it. They were the sort of things that one concealed; it was dangerous to mention them. In any case, he died before the Revolution – 'Thank God,' Nina used to say, as he would certainly have been made to account for himself.

On stage with Nina Dorliac

Rehearsal with Nina

Her mother, Xenia Nikolayevna, had been a great Wagnerian singer in her day. At the time that I got to know her, she had a famous class at the Moscow Conservatory. She, too, was of mixed descent – French and German. These French roots can also be found in Nina, although she never stops repeating that she's Russian, as she's both obstinate and nationalist. And, of course, she adores St Petersburg – whereas I hate it. She was born there and was noticed by Glazunov, who commented on the purity of her voice. Certainly, she sang very well: hers wasn't a large voice, but it was very beautiful. And she really *knew* how to sing; she had had a good teacher in her mother.

It was the conductor Nikolay Anosov – the father of Gennady Rozhdestvensky – who encouraged me to accompany her, which I did from 1945 onwards. Between then and 1961, when she gave up singing, we gave countless recitals together. Russian music, of course, but also Debussy and Ravel, which she sang in perfect French, and a number of German *Lieder*, which she wasn't allowed to sing in the original language at that time and which were barely known in the Soviet Union. Hugo Wolf was completely unknown, so much so that when Nina Lvovna first included Wolf in one of her recital programmes in Moscow, hardly anyone turned up. Some days later, she met a female pianist of her acquaintance and asked whether she'd attended the concert. The answer came as something of a surprise: 'No, I never go to concerts of Soviet music.' The sound of the name had confused her.

Even Schubert was rarely sung or played, although he managed to maintain a modest place in the repertory of pianists, who were happy to play the Impromptus and, if necessary, the 'Wanderer' Fantasy, whereas nobody seemed to have even heard of the sonatas. But this was also the case in the West before Artur Schnabel. I was the first to play them in the USSR, and when I started, people thought I was mad. The professors of the older generation said to me: 'Why are you playing Schubert? What an idea! He's so boring. Play Schumann instead.'

Anyway, I don't play for the audience, I play for myself, and if I derive any satisfaction from it, then the audience, too, is content. My whole attitude while I'm playing relates to the work, not to the audience or the notion of success, and if I have any contact with the audience, it's through the work that that contact is forged. To be frank and to put it crudely, I don't care about the audience. Not that they should take offence at this. People shouldn't take my remarks in the wrong way: it's just that the audience doesn't concern me, I don't need them, there's a sort of wall between them and me. And the less I need them, the better I play.

In fact, my first Schubert concert met with a considerable response. Not only in Moscow, but also, much later, in Paris, where I devoted my second recital to two of Schubert's great sonatas, the unfinished one, which I was playing for the first time, and the very last one. The concert was held at the Palais de Chaillot, which the organizers despaired of filling with a programme like that. They were wrong, it couldn't have gone better. I only wanted to play good music.

With Nina, with whom I went to stay in 1946, as I still had no apartment of my own whereas she had two tiny rooms in a communal flat that also housed another couple and a family of three,* I often performed Schubert, Schumann and Brahms. But this was also an opportunity for me to discover the world of Russian song.

The year 1948 saw the absurd decree against new music, against Shostakovich and Prokofiev. I never read the papers. In my view, they serve only to dirty the fingers of those who leaf through them. Instead, I always find out about things by talking to other people. And so I didn't read Zhdanov's famous decree and took no interest in it, though I knew they wanted to muzzle these two composers. Of course, there was no formal ban on public performances of their music, but it was just as if

---

* I came across two more letters that complement the earlier ones. These, too, were written with the aim of persuading the authorities to provide Richter with accommodation. The first dates from 18 March 1950, by which time Richter had already been awarded the Stalin Prize and had been triumphing in concerts halls all over Russia for several years. It is addressed to Marshal Voroshilov, vice-president of the Council of Ministers of the USSR and points out that

> Richter has been living in a student hall of residence since 1937. During the war he was registered as living at the home of Heinrich Neuhaus, where he lived in makeshift accommodation. [. . .] As a soloist with the Moscow Philharmonic, he receives a salary of 25,000 roubles, which prevents him from even thinking of applying for a cooperative flat.

This letter received no reply, and so Richter was no doubt advised to write in person to the marshal, which he did on 18 November of the same year. In excerpted form, his letter reads as follows:

> I have decided to trouble you as a last resort. [. . .] Mos-Soviet offered me a room in a communal apartment block in Peschanaya Ulitsa, after I'd waited patiently for a number of years in the hope of receiving a reply from the committee in charge of cultural affairs. [. . .] I had to decline the offer of the room made by Mos-Soviet, as it would not have improved my situation. I need a two-room flat where I can practise for between twelve and fourteen hours a day, including the hours of darkness, without disturbing anyone. It is vital that two grand pianos can be installed in one of these rooms. [. . .] I can assure you that no other musician with such a busy concert schedule is in a situation like mine.

Richter had to wait almost two more years before his request was granted. (B.M.)

there was, and certainly that's what was intended. Oistrakh was due to give the first performance of the concerto that Shostakovich had dedicated to him, but, as a result, he had to abandon his plans until 1955. It was disgusting. It merely served to persuade me to go on playing the works of those whom the authorities wanted to sideline. We paid no attention to the decree, Nina Dorliac and I, and put on a programme made up of Rimsky-Korsakov in the first half and Prokofiev in the second, a delight-ful combination. It went ahead. No doubt they hadn't seen the poster.

The hostility to Prokofiev lasted a long time. In 1952 there arose the question of the first performance of his Symphony–Concerto for cello and orchestra that Rostropovich was due to play. It was known that the Ministry of Culture was opposed to it, and people were too frightened to conduct it. No conductor would touch it. Now, it so happened that I'd broken a finger – in a brawl, if you must know. I'd gone on an expedition with some female friends, planning to be away for eleven days and to cover between twenty and twenty-five kilometres a day on foot. We'd completed our expedition and had just arrived at a small station with the intention of catching the train back to Moscow. While waiting for it, we were having something to eat in the buffet when a young sailor, com-pletely drunk, began to argue with the cashier. He'd lost control and was smashing everything up. I tried to grab him and make him leave, but he was as strong as an ox and kicking out in every direction. Even so, I managed to get him outside. He wanted to throw himself under the train, but I spoke with him at length and in the end he calmed down. But the next morning I felt a violent pain in one of the fingers of my right hand, which was bleeding. I went for an X-ray and they told me I'd broken it. My immediate thought was to take advantage of the situation and learn Ravel's Concerto for the Left Hand – which I played, in fact, soon after-wards. And because of the enforced reduction in my activities, I also thought of this Symphony–Concerto that nobody else wanted to conduct. I very much wanted to conduct. Perhaps I could risk it, I told myself, because it had been rejected. I spun a tale to the authorities, arguing that I might never play the piano again. It was pure blackmail. The injury to my finger really wasn't all that serious; a miserable little fracture, that's all. But they fell for it. The concert took place on 18 February 1952.

I had ten days in which to learn how to conduct, and during that time Kondrashin gave me lessons. I had to acquire a certain technique, as I didn't have any. It was the first time in my life that I'd tried conducting. The work isn't particularly easy, quite apart from the fact that we had

Richter conducting

only three rehearsals, during which Kondrashin remained seated at the back of the orchestra, ready to offer me his advice. It was a real experience! I was afraid that I'd be no good at giving the cues and, on top of everything, the cellists in the orchestra all behaved like boors, chuckling away as they listened to Rostropovich's part, which – it's true – bristled with passages of a literally unheard-of novelty. But I came out of it not too badly, as Prokofiev told me afterwards that he had 'finally found a conductor for his works'.

This Symphony–Concerto is in any case one of his best works. Rostropovich gave a fantastic performance and it was warmly received by the audience, while the powers-that-be pulled a distinctly long face. There was a passage in the finale that Prokofiev unfortunately later cut, at Rostropovich's request, a very interesting passage in which the soloist plays triplets against semiquavers in the first cello in the orchestra. It was a marvellous passage, but Rostropovich, wanting to create more of an impression, insisted that Prokofiev change it. I could never forgive him for this. He got his way and the new version is undeniably effective, but the music lost something by being rewritten, and the very end of the concerto became somehow rather ordinary. Will it ever be possible to reconstruct the original? I very much doubt it.

I never conducted again. There are two things that I hate: analysis and power. A conductor can avoid neither the one nor the other. Conducting's not for me.

Following Prokofiev's death, I wrote a piece about him in which I recounted some of these episodes and others besides. Everyone, including my own friends and his, was afraid to read what I'd written. They dreaded the trouble that my frankness might cause. This was the fifties, after all, and many passages were criticized, including, for example, one in which I described his first wife. She took offence. I'd said, in all innocence, that she was 'an attractive woman, interesting, with an expression of impatience about her'. She read this and reacted badly to it: 'What's he trying to insinuate? That I'm a manhunter or something?' She wasn't very likeable, but it's true that she'd been arrested and spent eight years in a camp, which doesn't necessarily make you very likeable. Meanwhile, Prokofiev had remarried. His new wife was Mira Mendelson, a pleasant enough woman, but boring and with an insufferable voice, for all that she wrote the libretto for *War and Peace*.

And so I resigned myself to removing a number of passages. Moreover, it was enough for me to open my mouth for people to think that I was criticizing the government, and so, although my article was published, the censor had stuck his oar in. Many of the things that gave the article some interest failed to get past him. The text lost part of its *raison d'être*.

5 On Prokofiev

I had more contact with Prokofiev's music than with the composer himself. I was never particularly close to him as a person: he intimidated me. For me, he was always summed up by his music: encounters with his works are encounters with Prokofiev himself, and of them I feel competent to speak. In playing these works, I say more or less everything that I could say about him in words (herein lies the whole difficulty of my position). None the less, I shall always retain an exceptionally vivid memory of a number of meetings with Sergey Sergeyevich.

My First Encounter

The first thing I think of when I hear Prokofiev's name is the March from *The Love for Three Oranges*, a piece which, when it was new, everyone played and liked. And when Prokofiev came to Odessa to play his own works, people said that the only piece of his that was any good was the March. At his recital, he played a whole series of pieces, but it was the March that people were waiting for. Musicians nodded in agreement: 'Yes, that's all very well, all very well . . .' But in reality only the March counted. It was published with a cover illustrated with little circles and squares. (New! Futurism!)

This was in 1927. I was twelve. All of us – Papa, Mother and I – lived in Odessa. My father taught at the Conservatory. I liked to stay at home and play the piano, sight-reading all the operas that fell into my hands – from the very first note to the last. One day Papa took me with him: Prokofiev was to give a recital in the Grand Hall of the Conservatory.

It was winter and so it was dark in the hall. A tall young man with long arms came out on to the platform. He wore a fashionable suit that was clearly of a foreign cut, short in the arm and leg – it looked almost as if he had outgrown it. And all in checks, like the cover of *The Love for Three Oranges*!

He had a funny way of bowing to the audience: he sort of bent in two – crack! His eyes did not change their expression, but continued to look straight ahead, so that, when he straightened up again, they were fixed at some point on the ceiling. And his face seemed devoid of expression.

But then he sat down at the piano. I remember being struck by his way of playing virtually without any pedal. And his manner was so polished. He played his own little pieces, and each was like an elegant delicacy in a carefully planned menu. It seemed to be altogether exceptional and different from anything I had heard before. As a result of my childish stupidity, I also had the impression that everything he played sounded exactly the same. (Bach's works had the same effect on me at this time.)

To finish, there was the March.

The audience was pleased. And so was Prokofiev. He bowed with an air of evident satisfaction: part conjuror, part character out of one of the tales of Hoffmann.

Thereafter, I heard no more about him. No, that is not quite true. I heard some musicians mention a Classical Symphony, which was said to be good, even excellent: it was a sort of model for new composers.

And I was also told that the opera *The Break-Up* and the ballet *The Carmagnole* by the Odessa composer Vova Femelidi were influenced by Prokofiev. Later, I, too, became convinced of this, though at the time they struck me as original.

And that is all. About Prokofiev himself, I knew nothing. One might have thought he had gone out of fashion and been forgotten. I knew of the existence of composers such as Rachmaninov, Puccini and Krenek (it was at this time that the Odessa Opera put on *Turandot* and *Jonny spielt auf*) and even Pfitzner (I had at home a vocal score of *Palestrina*). I knew about Stravinsky – I had heard his *Petrushka* twice – and I knew about

Shostakovich – I had looked through the vocal score of *Lady Macbeth* –
but about Prokofiev, I knew nothing.

And so ten years passed with no further mention of him.

Moscow

I arrived in Moscow in 1937 and became a pupil of Heinrich Neuhaus. I
now found myself living in the real world of music. Completely new
horizons opened up. I learned who Myaskovsky was. Then there was the
first performance of Shostakovich's Fifth Symphony. A major event! And
at the Conservatory, people were talking about Prokofiev.

One sunny day, I was walking along the Arbat when I noticed a
strange individual. He had a defiant air about him and passed by me like
an apparition: bright yellow shoes, a check jacket and an orange-red tie.
I could not help turning round to look at him. It was Prokofiev.

Now I could see him all the time. There were almost daily opportuni-
ties: I was staying with the Neuhauses, and Neuhaus and Prokofiev were
living in the same building. And so he became a part of my everyday
surroundings.

In the courtyard you would often hear people say: 'Those kids playing
there are a delight . . . They're Prokofiev's little boys: the older one, and
the other one, look, pretty as a picture!' I kept meeting Prokofiev's wife,
an elegant woman with a dark-blue beret and an impatient expression. I
saw them together at concerts. On one occasion we were returning home
from a concert in the Grand Hall of the Conservatory, Neuhaus, Tolya
Vedernikov and I, and were just emerging from the Kurskaya Metro
station in Chkalova Ulitsa, when Neuhaus exclaimed delightedly: 'Why,
Sergey Sergeyevich, hello!'

They were walking ahead of us, talking. Prokofiev was saying something about Richard Strauss and apparently making ironical remarks
about his ballet *Josephs-Legende*. Neuhaus disagreed. Tolya and I walked
along behind, watching and joking at their expense, while wondering
who Neuhaus most looked like and who Prokofiev most resembled. Our
remarks were not very respectful, but were pardonable in view of our age.

As for Prokofiev's music, I still had reservations or, to be more precise,
I still had to come to grips with it. I always listened to it with interest, but
I remained passive. The problem was that I had been brought up on
Romantic music: for me, the last word in new music was Richard Strauss.

Then, when Prokofiev's Cello Concerto appeared in 1938, I was unex-
pectedly asked to rehearse it with the cellist Berezovsky. I approached it

as I would any other task that I had accepted to earn some money. Virtually every day for the next two months, I went to Berezovsky's sixth-floor flat on Krivokolenny Pereulok. For me, it was just another job, and I was in the mood for work. For his part, Berezovsky was pleased to have received this commission but at the same time the music was foreign to his nature. He shrugged his shoulders and sighed, groaning at the difficulties and becoming terribly upset, but finally memorizing the work. I cannot say that I liked the concerto, but I felt that my work with Berezovsky was beginning to engage my attention.

We performed the concerto for the first time in a smoke-filled room at the Composers' Union, which was then in a little Gothic building not far from the Arbat. It was enthusiastically received: 'A real event! Every bit as fine as the Second Violin Concerto!' There was a lively and positive discussion, and everyone present wished Berezovsky well. No one doubted that the work would be a tremendous success. 'This is a new page in our history.' But a setback lay just around the corner.

We went to play the concerto for Prokofiev. He opened the door himself and led us into a little canary-yellow room. On the walls were sketches in pencil or Indian ink of what I assumed were the sets for *Three Oranges*. He began by sending away his children. 'Be off with you!' he shouted at them. 'Leave us in peace!' Then he sat down. Berezovsky looked terribly confused, and it was no doubt because of this that Prokofiev, clearly in no mood for compromise, immediately sat down at the piano himself and began to say things like: 'Here it should be like this, there it should be like that.' I stood in a corner, out of harm's way. Prokofiev was businesslike, but not pleasant. Berezovsky's questions clearly annoyed him. I was pleased that his demands coincided with my own view of the work. He wanted to hear what was in the score – nothing more. Berezovsky had a tendency towards sentimentality, but could find no way of exploiting this propensity. He was determined, however, to find a passage in which to show off his tone quality. But, as if on purpose, such passages were not in the least bit sentimental. Not once was I asked to sit down at the piano. We then left.

Berezovsky then passed into the hands of Melik-Pashayev, who was conducting the concert. How they worked together was no longer my concern and I have no idea how it went. I attended the first performance and sat in the amphitheatre. My heart was beating wildly and I was suffering from stage fright, simply on account of the work, but also for Berezovsky, of course. The ground seemed literally to be pulled from under his chair while he was playing, as Melik-Pashayev's tempi were as impossible as they were wrong. It seemed to me that he utterly failed to grasp the work's inner essence.

It was a total fiasco. The performers bowed as best they could. And with that it was all over.

A Change of Heart

Shortly afterwards, Prokofiev conducted a concert of his own works. On the programme were the Suite from *Egyptian Nights*, the Second Violin Concerto played by Boris Goldstein, the *Scythian Suite* and the Suite from *The Tale of the Buffoon*. Again I found it 'interesting'.

But the work that first compelled me to like it and, with it, the composer himself was the First Violin Concerto. Later I met many people whose love for Prokofiev's music was fired by this work. No one who loves music could fail to submit to its spell. You can compare its effect with the sensation you get when you first open your window in spring and are assailed by the sounds rising up from the street. I fell in love with the concerto even before I knew the violin part, simply by listening to Anatoly Vedernikov practising the accompaniment. From now on, each time that I got to know a new piece by Prokofiev, it was with an extraordinary feeling of excitement and even of envy.

Won over by the Violin Concerto, I decided that I really must play one of Prokofiev's works myself. I even dreamed of playing the Second Sonata, and so I made up my mind to learn it. But it turned out to be completely different from how I had imagined it. I learned it during my second year at the Conservatory, in 1938, but with no particular pleasure. And it now ceased to be one of my favourite works.

It was at about this time that I met Sergey Sergeyevich at the Composers' Union. Anatoly Vedernikov and I were playing through Stravinsky's *Oedipus rex* on two pianos. Vedernikov played the orchestral part, I the choral part. It was organized as a proper performance, including a narrator. Before it, something had taken place in the hall, a meeting, I think, attended by a large number of composers.

Someone asked Prokofiev: 'Are you staying to listen?'

'What for? Without orchestra and chorus? No, I'm off.'

But he was talked into staying.

We played with the requisite spirit and energy. A few young composers walked out ostentatiously. When we had finished, Prokofiev went over to Vedernikov, who was at the first piano. I could see that he was pleased.

He said that he had not expected it to sound so good on two pianos.

The performance of his Third Symphony in 1939 left a tremendous impression on me. The composer himself conducted. Never before had I felt anything like it when listening to music. The impression was staggering; it was like the end of the world. Prokofiev uses extraordinarily intense expressive devices in this work. In the third movement – a Scherzo – the strings play a flickeringly jerky motif from which plumes of asphyxiating smoke seem to issue, as though the air itself were on fire. The final movement opens with a sort of sombre march – a grandiose orchestral tumult, a veritable apocalypse followed by a brief lull before starting up again with redoubled force in a swirl of tocsin-like bells. I sat there as though turned to stone. I wanted to hide. I glanced at my neighbour, who was crimson and sweating profusely. Even during the interval, shivers still ran up and down my spine.

Neuhaus suddenly appeared from nowhere: 'That's Sergey Sergeyevich for you! Always something new up his sleeve! First there was *Romeo*. Now he's written a new opera, and what an opera! I was at one of the rehearsals – tremendous!'

The work was *Semyon Kotko*.

The first performance of this opera was a momentous event in my life, one with which Prokofiev won me over in the fullest sense of the word.

Together with a whole crowd of students, I went back to see the opera three or four more times after that, though the production and the performances left a lot to be desired.

It was also around this time that I saw the film *Alexander Nevsky*, of which the music, more than anything, left a lasting impression. Never before had film music impressed me to such an extent. I have still not forgotten it to this day.

It seems to me that it was only after his Fifth Concerto that Prokofiev forged a style for himself that was both new and accessible to all. In my own view, *Semyon Kotko* is one of these works. It is also one of the richest and most perfect of all his creations and, without a doubt, the finest Soviet opera.

With *Semyon Kotko*, Prokofiev followed the path traced out by Mussorgsky. Other composers had already done so, each in his own way – Debussy and Janáček, for example – but I think that Mussorgsky's direct descendant in the field of popular national music drama is our own Prokofiev. His music is based on the intonational patterns of the spoken language, and to it he brings the most perfect contours. Listening to the opera you become one with it, become one with a work that breathes not only youth but also the time and period of history that it depicts.

This work is so perfect and so accessible that an appreciation of it depends only on the listener's willingness to listen. And there is always such a listener. That is my profound conviction. It is sufficient for him or her to have the chance to hear this pearl of the operatic repertory.

The evening that I heard *Semyon Kotko* for the first time, I knew that Prokofiev was a great composer.

The Sixth Sonata

A whole company of musicians and serious music lovers used to meet at the Lamms',* in their old dark Moscow flat, which was filled almost entirely with scores. The nub of this group was made up of Muscovite composers and prominent musicians of the older generation. Myaskovsky always turned up, taciturn and extraordinarily tactful. If you asked him his opinion, he spoke as an expert, but very quietly and as though it were no concern of his. Pianists and conductors were often invited. The meetings were held on a regular basis, as if carrying on the tradition of the Russian musical circles that had existed in Balakirev's day.

It was all very informal. Essentially, we played music for eight hands. And tea and biscuits were served. The piano arrangements were made by Pavel Alexandrovich himself, with every Wednesday spent busily preparing something new for the following day's meeting.

One day Neuhaus invited me to join them. It was to be a special occasion: Prokofiev had been invited.

It was rather dark. A mark on the wall – mould. The next moment I found myself sitting at the piano, playing Myaskovsky's Thirteenth Symphony arranged for eight hands and sight-reading the manuscript transcription with Shebalin, Nechayev and Lamm.

Prokofiev entered the room. He came not as a regular, but as a guest – you could sense it. He had the slightly arrogant air of someone who was celebrated.

He had brought his Sixth Sonata. 'To work,' he announced at once. 'I'll play it for you.' What speed and impetuosity! He was younger than most of those present, but we sensed from his manner that he was implying

---

* The musician and music historian Pavel Alexandrovich Lamm taught at the Moscow Conservatory. It is to him, not least, that we owe the reconstruction of the original score of Mussorgsky's *Boris Godunov*. (B.M.)

something with which we were all in any case in agreement: 'I may be younger than the rest of you, but I'm as good as anyone here!' But his disdain did not extend to Myaskovsky, to whom he was particularly attentive.

Prokofiev behaved in a businesslike, ultra-professional way. I remember that he took Neuhaus's advice, agreeing that the A in the bass could not be sustained for five bars, and so he immediately corrected it.

As far as I remember, he played the sonata twice before leaving. He played from the manuscript and I turned the pages.

Later, during the war, I heard him play his Eighth Sonata, but by then his playing was no longer as good.

But on that particular day, even before he had finished playing, I had already decided that I would play this sonata.

The remarkable stylistic clarity and the structural perfection of the music amazed me. I had never heard anything like it. With wild audacity the composer broke with the ideals of Romanticism and introduced into his music the terrifying pulse of twentieth-century music. Classically well-balanced in spite of all its asperities, the Sixth Sonata is an utterly magnificent work.

The sonata also interested me as a performer. I had never played anything like it before, and so I thought I should try my hand at it. Neuhaus agreed. And so, when I returned home to Odessa for the holidays, I took the music with me.

Papa acknowledged the merits of Prokofiev's music, but even so the sonata was too extreme for his ears. 'Terrible,' he said. 'It's like being slapped in the face again and again. Wham! Bam! Wham!' And he pretended to take aim . . .

For my own part, I recall studying it with immense pleasure. I mastered it in a single summer and played it at a concert on 14 October. This was my first public appearance outside the student concerts. And what a responsibility! Neuhaus had included me – a fourth-year student – in the programme of one of his own recitals. During the first half he played works by Myaskovsky, Alexandrov and Kreyn, and during the second half I played works by Prokofiev. Three short pieces – the Rondo from *The Prodigal Son*, the Pastoral Sonatina and *Landscape* – were by way of an introduction to the Sixth Sonata. I was terribly nervous. I spent the three days before the concert locked away in a classroom, practising for ten hours at a time. I remember not being satisfied with my performance, although the sonata itself was a great success. The audience was a specialized one and made up almost entirely of musicians. Everyone

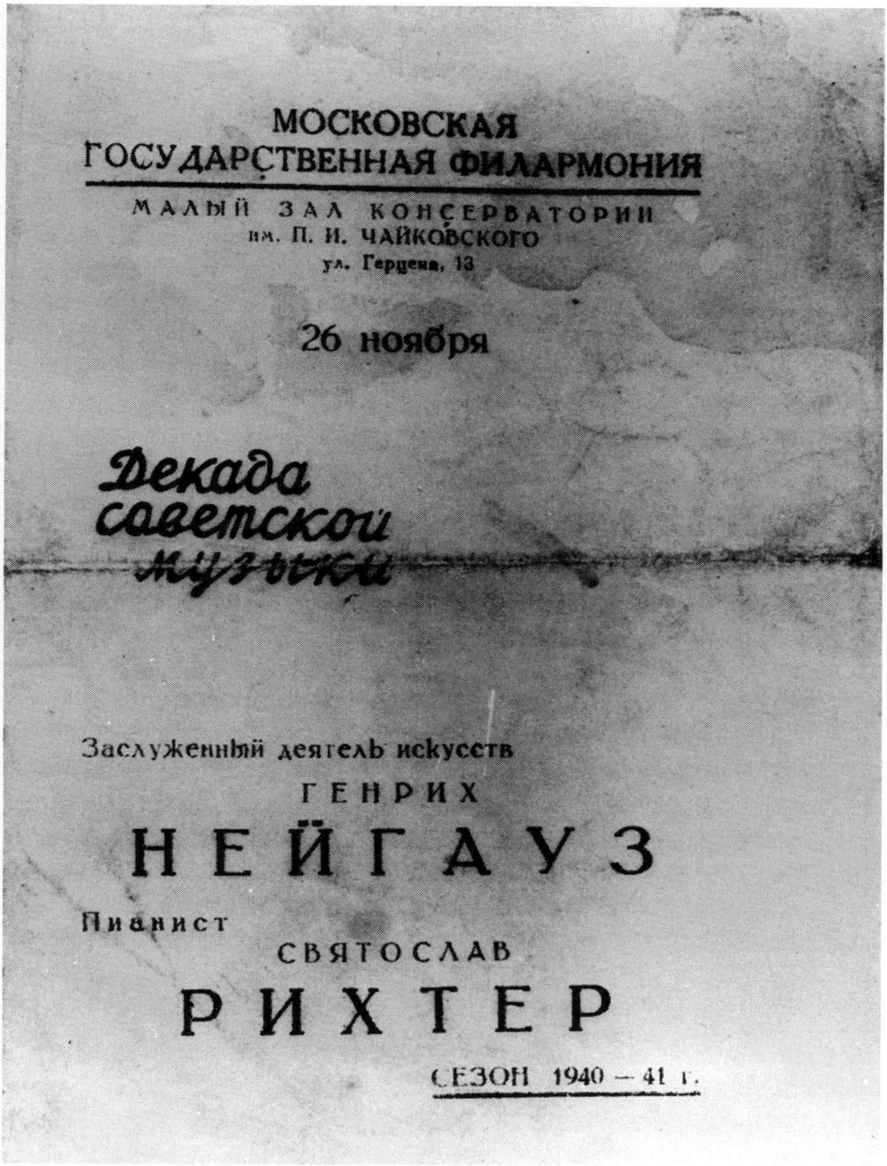

Poster for the joint recital with Neuhaus

2-е отделение

С. ПРОКОФЬЕВ —

Рондо, op. 52

Пейзаж, op. 59

Пасторальная сонатина, op. 59

Шестая соната A-dur, op. 82

1. Allegro moderato

2. Allegretto

3. Tempo di valzer lentissimo

4. Vivace

(в первый раз)

исп. С. РИХТЕР

Начало в 9 часов вечера

Цена 20 коп.

Л67122   Зак. 6262   Тир. 250

Тип. „Москопромпечать", Рождеств бульвар, 22

Poster for the joint recital with Neuhaus

was 'for', no one 'against'. People liked both the sonata and the way I played it.

The Fifth Concerto

Smiling, Prokofiev walked the whole length of the hall in order to shake my hand. Then, backstage, he asked: 'Perhaps this young man would agree to play my Fifth Concerto, which has always been a fiasco and never proved a success? Perhaps he'll play it and audiences will like it?'

I did not know the Fifth Concerto, but I was immediately taken by the suggestion. When I finally got hold of the music, I did not care for it very much. And Neuhaus, too, had his doubts, recommending that I take a look at the Third instead. Certainly, the Fifth had a poor reputation at that time. And so I looked at the score of the Third Concerto, which I had already heard on a number of occasions. There was even a recording with Prokofiev himself as the soloist. It was considered the best, but for one reason or another, it did not appeal to me. I looked at it again, and again I thought: no, I shall play the Fifth. And once Prokofiev himself had asked me, my fate was sealed.

I returned to Odessa in February 1941, taking the score of the Fifth Concerto with me. A month later, I was back in Moscow with the concerto under my belt. Prokofiev wanted to hear me. We met at Neuhaus's, where I played through the concerto twice accompanied by Anatoly Vedernikov.

Prokofiev had brought his wife with him, and the room was filled with the powerful smell of French perfume. He suddenly started to tell us some tall stories about gangsters in America, everything told in his inimitable way, extraordinarily businesslike and yet not without humour. We sat at a small table with barely enough room for our legs, drinking tea and munching the slices of ham that Neuhaus invariably provided.

Then we played.

Prokofiev was clearly pleased. He had been standing in front of us, facing the two pianos and conducting, and at the end he produced two bars of chocolate simultaneously from both his pockets and presented them to us with a grand gesture. There and then we agreed on dates for the rehearsals.

At the very first rehearsal, he sat me down at the piano so that the orchestra could get used to the piano part. Prokofiev's conducting manner suited his works like nobody else's, so that the players performed quite well, even if they understood little of the music. Prokofiev did not beat about the bush: 'Kindly do this . . . And you, be so kind as to play it like this.' He was naturally demanding. In all, we had three extremely productive rehearsals.

The day of the concert drew closer. Prokofiev was to conduct the whole programme, which comprised the *Lieutenant Kijé* Suite, the *Scythian Suite*, the Fifth Concerto and the Classical Symphony.

The order of the programme seemed strange to me and I did not particularly care for it. I would have preferred it to end with the *Scythian Suite*.

I arrived early at the Tchaikovsky Hall and listened from the wings. Nervousness, lack of confidence and the impressions produced by the *Scythian Suite* were all mixed up in my head. I thought: I shall walk out on stage and it will be a disaster. I shan't be able to play anything.

I gave an accurate enough performance but, because of my nervousness, it gave me no pleasure.

There was none of the usual applause at the end of the first movement. I glanced out into the hall and saw the aggrieved expressions in the front row. I had the impression that no one understood anything. There was a a chill in the air – and in any case the hall was half-empty. Only recently I had played the Tchaikovsky Concerto to a packed house.

And yet the concerto was a great success. We were called back on stage countless times and Prokofiev exclaimed: 'It's amazing! Look, a success! I'd never have thought it . . . Hm . . . Hm!' Then, all of a sudden: 'Ah, I know why they're clapping like that – it's so that you'll play them a Chopin nocturne.'

I was happy. At twenty-two I had decided to become a pianist and now, at twenty-five, I was playing a work that no one except the composer himself had performed. At the same time, I had a feeling of dissatisfaction caused, in part, by my nervousness (try playing the Fifth Concerto and you will understand) and, in part, by a vague premonition that I would not play it again for a long time – it was to be almost eighteen years.

The Seventh Sonata

Soon after that, war broke out, forcing us all apart, and I did not see Prokofiev again for a very long time.

I was preparing for a concert – my first recital in Moscow – which had been announced for 19 October 1941. There were posters throughout the city. But I was so nervous that I was oblivious to what was going on all around me.

Round about the same time I had played a Bach concerto, the Schumann Concerto, the Brahms Quintet and, together with Anatoly Vedernikov, Bach's Double Concerto in C major, but the prospect of my début recital made me literally quake with fear.

In view of the circumstances, the concert was cancelled and rescheduled for July 1942. The programme was now Beethoven, Schubert, Prokofiev and Rachmaninov. And so I played a piece by Prokofiev at my début recital – the Second Sonata – but did not play it particularly well.

It was at around this time that the opera *War and Peace* was unveiled. An extraordinary event! An opera based on Tolstoy's novel! It seemed impossible. But since it was Prokofiev who had undertaken it, you had to believe it.

Vedernikov and I played through the work to a group of musicians, including Shostakovich. It was during the dark winter days, when night came early.

Early in 1943, I received the score of the Seventh Sonata, which I found fascinating and which I learned in just four days.

A concert of Soviet music was being prepared and Prokofiev wanted me to perform his new sonata. He had just returned to Moscow and was staying at the National Hotel. I went to play the sonata for him. He was on his own. There was a piano in his room, but it turned out that the pedal was not working, so Prokofiev said: 'All right, let's fix it.' We crawled under the piano and were straightening a piece of metal when we banged our heads together so hard that we both saw stars. 'At least we managed to fix that blasted pedal!' Sergey Sergeyevich later recalled.

It was a businesslike meeting. We were both concentrating so hard on the sonata that we spoke little. I have to say that I never had any serious conversations with Prokofiev. Our remarks were precise and to the point. Admittedly, I was never alone with him except just this once. And if there happened to be a third person present, it was always this person who did all the talking.

The sonata received its first performance in Moscow's Hall of the House of Trade Unions. I was its first performer. The work was a huge success. (This was invariably the case wherever it was subsequently performed, except in a single city – Kiev. It was the same with the Second Sonata.)

Prokofiev attended the concert and was called out on stage at the end. Once most of the audience had left and only musicians remained (and there were many, including Oistrakh and Shebalin), they all wanted to

hear the sonata again. There was an extraordinary atmosphere in the hall, a mixture of elation and seriousness. And this time I played well.

The audience clearly grasped the spirit of the work, which reflected their innermost feelings and concerns. (This was also felt to be the case with Shostakovich's Seventh Symphony, which dates from more or less the same period.)

With this work, we are brutally plunged into the anxiously threatening atmosphere of a world that has lost its balance. Chaos and uncertainty reign. We see murderous forces unleashed. But this does not mean that what we lived by before thereby ceases to exist. We continue to feel and to love. Now the full range of human emotions bursts forth. Together with our fellow men and women, we raise a voice in protest and share the common grief. We sweep everything before us, borne along by the will for victory. In the tremendous struggle that this involves, we find the strength to affirm the irrepressible life-force.

I now had to play the Seventh Sonata at the Sovinformbureau, where all manner of new works were premièred during the war. The whole of political and official Moscow assembled in the old palace in Kalashny Pereulok. On this particular evening, writers read from their works. Conditions were hardly auspicious. The piano was carved and gilded, but the keys barely worked. I played extremely badly and almost lost my way completely at the entry of the second subject.

Afterwards, Sergey Sergeyevich said: 'Something odd happened there, but it doesn't matter. You got out of it extremely well. But I wondered how you'd go on.'

I remember Sergey Sergeyevich in quite different circumstances, when he seemed almost like a young boy. I had always noticed his interest in strange or unusual phenomena. There was something about him that recalled a young boy or an explorer. When I played his First Concerto for the first time in 1943, he sat in on the rehearsal. Immediately afterwards, he suddenly said: 'Do you know what an amazing thing I saw? When you began the final octaves, the chairs around me started to move in time with the music! Just imagine, the chairs, too . . . Now, isn't that incredible!'

That year, I undertook my first concert tours of the country. Among the works I played were the Fourth and Seventh Sonatas.

The Eighth Sonata

My next important meeting with Prokofiev was bound up with the first performance of his Eighth Sonata in 1944. Prokofiev himself played it at the Composers' Union, but it was Gilels who gave the first public performance.

Prokofiev played it twice. Even after a single hearing, it was clear that this was a remarkable work, but when I was asked whether I planned to play it myself, I was at a loss for an answer.

Sergey Sergeyevich now had difficulty playing. He no longer had his former confidence, and his hands fluttered helplessly over the keys.

After the second hearing, I was firmly resolved to learn the piece. Someone began to snigger: 'It's completely outdated! You don't really want to play it?!'

Of all Prokofiev's sonatas, this is the richest. It has a complex inner life, profound and full of contrasts. At times it seems to grow numb, as if abandoning itself to the relentless march of time. If it is sometimes inaccessible, this is because of its richness, like a tree that is heavy with fruit.

It remains one of my three favourite works, alongside the Fourth and Ninth Sonatas. Gilels played it magnificently at his recital in the Grand Hall.

The All-Union Piano Competition was about to take place and my closest friends urged me to enter, in spite of my own reservations. I included the Eighth Sonata in my programme.

I had no accommodation of my own at this time and was staying with Vedernikov in the suburbs.

I was to play last but, having mixed up the time, I arrived very late. They had already finished. Prokofiev had waited for a long time. Many people had already left the hall, but they returned when they heard that there was more to come. Sergey Sergeyevich, too, returned. He was very strict about punctuality, and always reacted badly in such cases, but on this occasion he simply said: 'Ye–e–s . . . an hour late . . . Well, we'll have to hear the sonata anyway.' Clearly, he wanted to hear his own work.

I remember that the Eighth Sonata left a deep impression on Gedike: 'You know, Slava, this music really is good. What a magnificent sonata!'

There was one more curious episode involving Sergey Sergeyevich – that most punctual of men – and me. It was in 1946: I was to play the Sixth, Seventh and Eighth Sonatas at a subscription concert of his works in the October Hall of the House of Trade Unions. Nina Dorliac and I had just returned from Tbilisi, where concerts begin at nine in the evening. They called us at eight to ask what was wrong and why we were not there. It was Victory Day – 9 May – and there was no public transport, and the streets were teeming with people. We were staying in the Arbat and it was not until a quarter past nine that I arrived at the hall.

Sergey Sergeyevich was waiting with the rest of the audience. A man came on stage and announced that the concert would start with the Sixth Sonata, whereupon an elderly, quite intelligent-looking man stood up in the middle of the hall and exclaimed: 'This is scandalous. It's intolerable!' And with that he walked out. He had expected the concert to be cancelled.

Sergey Sergeyevich was pleased that the concert took place. He commented on my late arrival, but in an entirely good-natured way.

He had changed greatly since I had last seen him. He had become gentler and more forgiving. Of course, I was never once late for a working session with him. He would have been furious. Whenever we arranged a meeting, he was always careful to say: 'And the time, you're sure that's all right?' He stressed the need to be punctual.

The Flute Sonata and the Akhmatova Cycle

On completing his Seventh Sonata, Prokofiev wrote a Flute Sonata, which he later transcribed for violin as flautists seemed in no great hurry to perform it. Now all violinists have it in their repertory and it has become known as his Second Violin Sonata, even though the original version for flute is incomparably better.

It was first performed not at a public concert but at an audition organized by the State Prize Committee in the Beethoven Hall at the Bolshoy Theatre. I played it with Kharkovsky, but it failed to win an award. We later played it at concerts together, and it was always a great success.

It was also performed at a concert of Prokofiev's works in 1945. This was also the first time that I accompanied Nina Dorliac at a public concert. She sang the Five Songs to Poems by Anna Akhmatova. It was a particularly dense programme: Melnikova sang the Twelve Russian Folksongs – magnificently. Tsomyk played the *Ballade* for cello. And I ended the concert with the Sixth Sonata.

Prokofiev's works were constantly in the repertory and it was impossible to imagine the musical life of Moscow without them. He worked indefatigably, tirelessly adding to the treasure-house of modern classics.

Nikolina Gora

It was Prokofiev's birthday, and he invited me to visit him for the first time at his dacha at Nikolina Gora. 'I've something interesting to show you,' he announced as soon as I arrived, whereupon he produced the sketches of his Ninth Sonata. 'This will be your sonata. But don't think it's intended to create an effect. It's not the sort of work to raise the roof of the Grand Hall.'

And at first glance it did indeed look a little simplistic. I was even a tiny bit disappointed.

Oddly enough, I cannot really describe the rest of this day, however important and interesting it may have been. It was the first time I had really been close to Prokofiev, in his own home, amongst his friends, and I could not conceal my shyness and confusion. Everything seemed to pass me by.

I remember that there was talk of *War and Peace* and *The Stone Flower*, both of which he hoped would one day be staged. I also remember that it was early spring, and I recall the turn-off to Nikolina Gora, crossing the Moskva River by ferry (there was no bridge at that time), Sergey Sergeyevich coming to meet me in the garden, the elegant luncheon, which we took for the first time on the cool veranda, and the scent of spring . . .

Another Meeting

It was now 1948. I do not understand people's attitudes to Prokofiev's work at this time.* My concert with Nina Dorliac was announced for 28 January. On the programme were Rimsky-Korsakov and Prokofiev. Everything about it proved successful: the programme, the performance . . .

It was a great success for Sergey Sergeyevich. He was called out on to the platform. He thanked Nina Dorliac, smiling and saying: 'Thank you for reviving my dead works.'

Illness

Then I remember Sergey Sergeyevich as a sick man. The Kremlin Hospital. Mira Alexandrovna† and I visited him in his room. He seemed very run down, but there was a note of indignation in his voice when he said: 'They won't let me write . . . The doctors won't allow me to write.'

Mira Alexandrovna tried to placate him. 'Seryozhenka . . . Seryozhenka!' She spoke as one would talk to a sick child, soothingly and droningly. He complained that they had taken away his writing paper, but instead he

---

* Richter later told me that he was expressing himself euphemistically here: in 1948 Zhdanov denounced 'formalism' in music. The music of both Prokofiev and Shostakovich was included in his denunciation, and it required great courage to perform it in public. (B.M.)
† Prokofiev's second wife. (B.M.)

Sergey Sergeyevich Prokofiev and his wife Mira Mendelson-Prokofieva at Nikolina Gora

Autograph score of Prokofiev's Ninth Sonata with dedication 'To Sviatoslav Richter'

wrote on small paper napkins, which he then proceeded to hide beneath his pillow.

It was difficult to square all this with the image one had of one of the giants of Russian music. One refused to face up to reality. Here was a man who, creative energy itself, was now so utterly helpless. It was hard to come to terms with it.

We visited him a second time, a month later. He was getting better. He was able to write. He joked and talked, lovable, likeable and radiant.

He accompanied us to the stairs and when we reached the bottom, he waved goodbye to us – with his foot. There was something of the naughty schoolboy about him.

Sixtieth Birthday

In 1951 he turned sixty. On his birthday Prokofiev was once again ill. On the eve of his birthday a concert was held at the Composers' Union and he listened to it over the phone. It was on this occasion that I played the Ninth Sonata for the first time, a radiant, simple and even intimate work. In some ways it is a *Sonata domestica*. The more one hears it, the more one comes to love it and feels its magnetism. And the more perfect it seems. I love it very much.

The Second Cello Concerto

It was enough for Rostropovich and me to play Prokofiev's Cello Sonata for Rostropovich to fall madly in love with Prokofiev's music in general. When you saw them together, you would think Sergey Sergeyevich was his father, so much did they resemble each other. At one of his recitals, Rostropovich played the Cello Concerto – the piece that Berezovsky had played – but with piano accompaniment. Sergey Sergeyevich and Rostropovich then sat down and revised the work, which became the Second Cello Concerto. But they did not know who would conduct it. As it happened, I had recently injured one of the fingers of my right hand and had just played Ravel's Concerto for the Left Hand. My injury helped to persuade me to make my début as a conductor. Kyrill Kondrashin gave me some lessons. Sergey Sergeyevich seemed pleased, and we pressed ahead with the rehearsals.

This whole episode was wildly exciting. Throughout the rehearsals, no matter how hard the orchestral players tried to be tactful and accommodating – they were students from the Moscow Conservatory – there were bound to be differences of opinion. Some of them screwed up their faces in comic amazement or had difficulty stifling their laughter. They were reacting to the augmented sevenths and the harsh orchestral sonorities. The solo writing was of unprecedented difficulty and novelty, unleashing violent hilarity on the part of the rank-and-file cellists.

Kondrashin sat with the orchestra, following each of my gestures with his characteristically immobile expression.

In all, we had three rehearsals, which were just enough to put things right. We had agreed with Rostropovich that during the passages when he was not playing, no matter what happened, he would smile at me benignly in order to give me moral support. Joking apart, it was an immensely risky undertaking. Sergey Sergeyevich did not come to the rehearsals, as Rostropovich thought, with good reason, that his presence would have paralysed us. He attended only the concert itself.

As I came out on to the platform, I started to tremble all over: not a piano in sight. Where should I go and stand? I stumbled against the podium. The whole of the audience gasped. But by losing my footing I managed to get rid of my stage fright. I started to laugh at myself (what a thing to laugh at!) and calmed down. We were greeted by frenetic applause, which infuriated me: I cannot stand anticipatory applause. For his part, Rostropovich responded to the ovation by bowing and scraping to the audience, who refused to let us begin.

What I feared most did not happen, and the orchestra started together. The concerto passed off like a dream. But the tremendous tension left us completely exhausted. We could not believe that we had played the piece and that it was over, and we so forgot ourselves that we omitted to invite Prokofiev to join us on stage. It was from the hall that he shook hands with us. We were absolutely dumbfounded and as soon as we were off the platform we literally jumped for joy. But the work had not been a success. Everyone criticized it and tore it to shreds. As always, Prokofiev adopted a pragmatic approach and said simply: 'I can stop worrying now that I know there's a conductor capable of conducting my works.'

The last occasion on which Sergey Sergeyevich attended one of my recitals was on 4 April 1952 in the Grand Hall of the Conservatory. The first half of the recital was devoted to his works. He sat in the director's box in the company of Nina Dorliac and Boris Alexeyevich Kuftin.* He died the following year.

* A friend of Richter and Nina Dorliac, Boris Alexeyevich Kuftin was an eminent Soviet archaeologist. (B.M.)

A Great Musician

As long as Prokofiev was alive, you could always expect a miracle, as if in the presence of a conjuror who, with a wave of his magic wand, could produce the most fabulous riches. Swish! And there are your *Stone Flower* and *Cinderella*!

I am thinking of one of his very finest compositions – the brief *Zdravitsa*, a work of genuine inspiration. And I am also thinking of *The Year 1941*, a work like a dry-point engraving, concise yet acerbically vivid.

Nor shall I ever forget the first performance of his Fifth Symphony in 1945, on the eve of victory. This was the last time that Prokofiev appeared in public as a conductor. I was sitting in the third or fourth row. The hall was probably lit as usual, but when Prokofiev stood up, it seemed as though the light poured down on him from on high. He stood there, like a monument on a pedestal. A moment later he mounted the podium and a hush fell over the hall, when artillery salvoes suddenly started to rumble in the distance. His baton was already raised. He waited for the cannon-fire to stop before he began. There was something deeply significant, deeply symbolic in this, as if this moment marked a dividing line in the lives of everyone present, including Prokofiev himself.

The Fifth Symphony reveals his full inner maturity, while at the same time looking back on his life and all that had happened as though from a very great height. There is something Olympian in this.

In his Fifth Symphony, Prokofiev rises to the full stature of his genius. The work bears within it both time and history, war and patriotism and victory. Victory in general and Prokofiev's own private victory. And here he triumphed completely. He had always triumphed before, but this time he triumphed as an artist, and for all time.

Prokofiev himself considered it to be his best work.

After this, the final stage in Prokofiev's life began. It was noticeable in his music. He rose to new heights, perhaps the greatest heights of all. But it remained the final stage . . .

I learned that Prokofiev had died one morning as I was leaving Tbilisi by plane for Moscow. We had had to put down in Sukhumi. Snow heavier than anything seen before was falling ceaselessly on the Black Sea and its sombre palm trees. A dismal sight.

I thought of Prokofiev, but without sadness.

How could it be otherwise? After all, I had not been saddened by the deaths of Haydn or Andrey Rublev.

Richter and his mother, Anna Pavlovna

6 A Dark Chapter

In our country, everything was hushed up. It isn't hard to guess why. As far as my father is concerned, no one has ever dared to describe events exactly as they happened. People said nothing about his execution – he was shot by the Soviets in 1941, before the Germans arrived in Odessa. I didn't discover the truth until twenty years later, as it all happened at the beginning of the war. My last visit to Odessa had taken place a few weeks earlier; I myself was living in Moscow, cut off from all communication with my parents. It's the darkest chapter in my existence.

During the early thirties, while still a young man, I'd had some private lessons in theory and composition with a teacher in Odessa who was so boring that he robbed me of any desire to write music. He was extremely well read and had gone to three universities, studying law, geology and music. He'd even been a pupil of Taneyev in St Petersburg. He was certainly not ungifted, but I couldn't abide him, and as soon as he started to talk, all I wanted to do was to fall asleep. Sergey Kondratiev, for that was his name at this time, played a fateful role in my life. We'll see how and why in a moment.

In a sense, I myself was the cause of it all. It was through a certain Boris Dmitriyevich Tyuneev that I'd got to know Kondratiev. Tyuneev was quite well known as a musicologist in Odessa. He was a delightful old man, cultivated, inquisitive and slightly mad. His beard made him look like Ivan the Terrible, and he had a permanent tic that was a legacy of his misfortunes during the Revolution, when he had been racked by fear as a result of the charges of spying that were brought against him.

Anyway, it was Tyuneev who one day took me to see Kondratiev. He advised me to have lessons with him. Kondratiev taught composition and even numbered a very gifted composer among his pupils, Vova Femelidi, a composer of Greek extraction whose ballet, *The Carmagnole*, was really quite decent, certainly superior to anything written by other composers at that time. It contained moments that even Prokofiev would not have disowned. I can still remember the complete score of this ballet, which was written under Kondratiev's supervision and which had been a real event when staged in Odessa.

On another occasion Tyuneev and I turned up without warning at Kondratiev's – he never went out – and found the door closed and the flat plunged into darkness. We went in and discovered Kondratiev stretched out on the ground, gasping for breath. He'd choked on something. Tyuneev wanted to clear off at once, but, all of fifteen years old, I stopped him and alerted the neighbours so that they could help. They brought him round.

Afterwards, I often associated this episode with *Hamlet*: if I'd not been present on that occasion, I'd not have been guilty of saving him. Kondratiev, who was the source of so much misery for me and my father, would have gone to meet his maker without causing us any harm.

He was the son of a senior official of the Tsar. He was of German extraction and his real name was German. After the Revolution, he had to go into hiding and change his name – not for the last time. He'd then fled from Moscow to Odessa, hoping to save his skin in that way. His friend, the conductor Nikolay Golovanov (who was married to the most famous singer in Russia, Antonina Nezhdanova), helped him to assume a new identity, arranging his departure from Moscow and going to some lengths to get him a job at the Conservatory in Odessa.

In spite of his new name, Kondratiev clearly didn't feel safe here. He went in constant fear of arrest and soon gave up his classes at the Conservatory, preferring to teach at home, where he could maintain a more discreet presence. There was a sort of aura about him and young people queued up to attend his courses, so he can't have been such a bad teacher, though he was a complete maniac. He never stopped talking, and it's no doubt because of him that I'm not much of a chatterbox myself.

He claimed to suffer from a particular type of tuberculosis that affects the bones and took to his bed for twenty years, getting up only when the Germans arrived. It was a pretence, a pretence that lasted twenty years or more!

Mother waited on him hand and foot, and my father, of course, knew what was going on. Then, when war broke out, Kondratiev moved in with us. In the face of the German advance, it was suggested that my parents should be evacuated, but when everything was ready for their departure, my mother suddenly refused on the grounds that they couldn't take 'the other one'. My father was arrested and shot. It was in June 1941.

Rumour had it that it was because Kondratiev, hoping to get rid of my father, had written an anonymous letter. Of course, it was easy to denounce other people at this time on the flimsiest of pretexts; and Kondratiev was a dubious individual, in spite of his origins and education. But I still find it hard to believe that he'd stoop so low.

It was in Tbilisi in 1943, during my first visit to the city, that I learned that my father was dead. I wasn't told how. I simply learned that he was dead. A woman whom I'd known as a child told me. She came up to me in the street and started to speak. I didn't find her very sympathetic and, out of a sudden feeling of hostility, I said 'Yes, I know', whereas in fact I knew nothing. I didn't want to have to listen to her. And so it was only much later that I understood what had really happened.

My mother and Kondratiev left the country in 1941, with the Germans. Thanks to my father's old contacts with the consulate, they were somehow able to settle in Germany. They got married. Kondratiev changed his name yet again and became known as Richter. I never understood how my mother could have let him do this. He told everyone he was my uncle, then, once I'd acquired a certain reputation in the USSR but without having set foot outside the country, he even had the nerve to claim to be my father. Of course, I wasn't there to deny it, and people believed him. You can imagine my anger when, some years later, I was touring Germany and I heard people say: 'We know your father.' '*Ihr Vater, Ihr Vater!*'

I saw my mother again in 1960, the first time in nineteen years, in America, where she and her husband had gone for my début there. It wasn't a happy reunion. I later visited them in Germany, as I wanted to take Mother to Bayreuth – a long-standing dream of mine. When I arrived at their house, I saw their name-plate on the door: 'S. Richter.'

Richter with Kondratiev, Nina Dorliac and Anna Pavlovna

'What am I doing here?' I asked myself, then I remembered he was called Sergey.

My mother had completely changed – he'd cast a spell on her with his inane chatter, never leaving her alone for a moment, never letting her get a word in edgeways, even when she was with me, but prattling on all the time. It was impossible to talk to him on account of his logorrhoea. At a farewell party in New York, at the end of my first American tour, all my relatives from the Moskalyov side of the family – people unconnected with the world of music – were there. He spent the whole evening over supper explaining Rimsky-Korsakov's treatise on harmony. It was of absolutely no interest to anyone, but it was impossible to stop him. And when I visited them again in Germany, shortly before Mother's death, she was in hospital. After having been to see her, I needed somewhere to sleep and had to go back to their place, at Schwäbisch Gmünd, near Stuttgart. I'd come from Paris and had to return there early the next morning for some more concerts. Mother had said to him: 'Please, Sergey, don't talk too much. Promise me that you'll let him go to bed no later than one thirty.' But he wittered on until six in the morning. I was flat out and had long since stopped listening, but he still went on and on. Always the same rubbish that I'd heard a thousand times before. Music, current events. On and on. A complete maniac.

The worst thing of all was my first recital in Vienna. I'd arrived from Italy on the eve of the concert, having just appeared at the Maggio Fiorentino, and I really wasn't on form. And there he was, on the day of the concert: 'My wife's dying.' To break the news to me in this way! To come straight out with it like that!

I'd never played in Vienna. My recital was a disaster, and the critics didn't let me off lightly: '*Abschied von der Legende*' – 'Goodbye to a Legend'. It's true, I played very badly.

7 Foreign Tours

I've never felt any difference between concerts in Russia and concerts abroad. Tours of the Soviet Union satisfied my passion for travel. I sometimes played in villages there, especially when I toured Siberia not all that long ago; I'm interested in everything new and, to tell the truth, I'd much rather have got to know the whole world than have to visit the same place twice.

On an artistic level, life in Moscow at that time was really quite exceptional, especially in terms of the theatre. When I arrived there, the Moscow Art Theatre was at the very peak of its form, and unforgettable productions were staged there, directed by Stanislavsky and Nemirovich-Danchenko. I saw virtually all Shakespeare's plays there, as well as those of Gorky, though I'm not a great admirer of his and find him quite weak as a writer. But when staged by Stanislavsky and Nemirovich-Danchenko, his plays were really quite gripping. A number of inferior Soviet plays were also so well staged that they ended up seeming good.

At Neuhaus's place, I met writers, including Boris Pasternak, who had just married his first wife and sometimes read from his translation of *Hamlet*, as well as from works of his own.

We spent the summer of 1949 at Koktebel in the Crimea, on the shores of the Black Sea, at the dacha of Olga Leonardovna Knipper-Chekhova, Chekhov's widow, a phenomenal actress, whatever people might say about her, and someone to whom I was very close. Chekhov had bought her this house, which was built on rocks in a magnificent setting. It is said that Pushkin used to spend his holidays here at the beginning of the last century.

I remember that on 27 June – shortly before leaving for the Crimea – I'd for once in my life given a really good performance of the Tchaikovsky Concerto, at Dzintari, near Riga, on the Baltic. I hadn't admitted anyone to my dressing-room – I never let anyone in – and had fled the building through a side door. I ran about a kilometre, tore off my tailcoat on the beach and threw myself into the sea. It was almost dark, and the waves were an absolute treat. A really successful concert.

Anyway, to cut a long story short, apart from my curiosity about new experiences, I felt no particular wish to travel outside Russia. At all events, the idea was thoroughly incongruous.

Prague was the first foreign city I visited, in 1950. It remains one of my favourite cities, along with Venice, Paris and Vienna. Prague was very attractive in the spring, with its chestnut trees in flower, and there was a sense of happiness that later disappeared, replaced by a feeling of sullen moroseness. It was there that I first heard Václav Talich, one of the greatest conductors I've ever worked with, even if our recording of Bach's D minor Concerto is unfortunately not very good.

I wasn't on my own, but was part of a delegation that included the cellist Daniil Shafran, the great mezzo Zara Dolukhanova and the conductor Kyrill Kondrashin. A frightful person by the name of Kaloshin 'accompanied' us. He was in charge of our group and was also our guide, and of course he was instructed to keep an eye on us. One day I wandered off with an interpreter in a separate car to visit a castle. On our return, Kaloshin created a scene and threatened me with heaven knows what reprisals. To hear him, you'd think I'd just defected. It was all very embarrassing. In spite of what people may think, I'm not completely insensitive and used to resent this constant pressure. But in general I pay no attention to life's little excitements and I told myself that these inanities would soon pass, thank God, and that it wasn't worth allowing them to upset me. By withdrawing into myself, I thought I could overcome my aversion. This man annoyed me, but I reckoned that he had been recruited to the job because he was an imbecile. He even accused me of having found a wife for myself in the person of our interpreter. A boorish individual . . . bah!

Richter with Karel Ančerl in Prague

Richter with Picasso at Mougins in 1964

I gave my first recital at Plzen. It wasn't a success, no doubt because I was from Russia. Also, I had to play in factories. Red banners had been unfurled in the hall, bearing slogans celebrating Soviet–Czech friendship and similar idiocies. I noticed this nonsense when I arrived for the concert and, unable to bring myself to play in such a setting, I asked: 'What's all this then? Are you holding a Party meeting or something?' Those responsible reacted like startled rabbits. I insisted: 'Why have you strung up these tatty bits of cloth?' 'But they're in your honour!' 'I'm not holding a meeting!' They took them all down.

A few days later, in Prague, I played Mozart's D minor Concerto, Schumann's *Konzertstück* and Brahms's Second Concerto under the direction of Kyrill Kondrashin. They held a great celebration in our honour. Our imbecile of a minder woke up just in time for the speeches.

It was on my return to Moscow, at the end of this tour, that I started doing pastels. Some visual impressions had remained with me. One day, when I was tired of practising at the piano, Anna Ivanovna Troyanovskaya, a former pupil of Serov, Pasternak and Matisse, at whose home I was practising, gave me a paintbox, saying: 'You must be fed up with so much practising, do something with this.' And so it was that she tempted me away from my work that evening. I painted for three days in a row. I did landscapes, from memory, based on impressions and recollections. It was a distraction that lasted more than ten years. As long as I wasn't travelling abroad, I was often able to return to Moscow and set aside some time in which to paint and try to acquire a technique. I'd always been very interested in painting, so that later, when I got a large enough flat, I organized a number of exhibitions there, in addition to balls and musical evenings. One of them was called *Encounters with a Musician*. Not all the canvases belonged to me, but they were all connected with me, either because I knew the artist or because I knew the sitters. I'd assembled works by Robert Falk, Krasnopevstev, Shukhayev and Troyanovskaya; also Magalashvili's portrait of Neuhaus, in which the image is so powerfully evocative of the sound that you really think you can hear him playing an intermezzo by Brahms; Ulyanov's portrait of Olga Knipper-Chekhova; the portrait of Pierre Joliot-Curie that Picasso gave me when I visited him at Mougins; my own portrait, in crayon, that Kokoschka drew while drinking a flask of whisky as I was practising the Fugue from Beethoven's op. 106 in Lucerne and that captures the sense of effort so powerfully; and Kustodyev's splendid portrait of Shostakovich as a boy. In 1957, another exhibition, this time devoted to Robert Falk, lasted six weeks. I organized it in my own flat for the very good reason that Falk was banned from exhibiting his work in public. Robert Falk was very famous in Russia, but virtually unknown abroad, even though he had lived in Paris for many years. Quite apart from the fact that I admired his canvases, including a portrait of me as a young man, I had other reasons to be grateful to him. From time to time I used to go and practise painting at his studio, and it was on one of these occasions that he made the following comment, which I immediately applied to the piano: 'Do you know what's the most difficult thing in painting? It's to draw a perfect circle. But it's less difficult if you use both hands and draw two circles simultaneously.' It's exactly the same with the piano. Symmetry! Everything has to be symmetrical. And then he told me that when you practise a lot, you reach the point where 'the water begins to boil' and that it's this moment that is essential.

But let's return to my travels. My tour of Czechoslovakia had remained an isolated event and I didn't go abroad again until 1953. But in 1953, Stalin – *auf Wiedersehen*!

During the years that followed, I often performed in Poland, Romania, Bulgaria and Hungary, and it was in Hungary that I started to familiarize myself with the music of Bartók, a composer I admire intensely but who, even today, remains something of a closed book to me. I really don't understand him any more than I understand Hungarian. But when I heard his Second Concerto, I liked it so much that I decided to learn it. It didn't take me all that long: whereas I needed more than two years to get the Dvořák Concerto into my head, I needed only two months to assimilate Bartók's. True, the circumstances in which I did so were idyllic. It was during the summer, in the little wooden house that we'd had built near Tarusa on the banks of the River Oka. The house was accessible only on foot, and to get to it you had to walk several kilometres through the woods or along the river bank, and it had the advantage of having no running water or electricity. But I'd managed to have a piano transported by water and delivered to me in that way. The surrounding countryside was among the most beautiful of any that I know in Russia; I worked there better than anywhere else.

And so I played Bartók's Second Concerto in Budapest under the direction of that excellent conductor János Ferencsik. There's a recording of these concerts, but unfortunately it can't be released as there's a spectacular split note on the trumpet after the *presto* passage in the second movement that ends on a top C. I was sent a copy of the recording after it had been

Richter in his flat

Portrait of Richter by Kokoschka

patched up using takes from the concert and rehearsals, but I noticed straight away that the unfortunate note on the trumpet hadn't been edited out, so I refused to authorize its release.

Recordings have always been a problem for me. I don't like them, especially my own. I'm always disappointed when I listen to them as I hear exactly what I'm expecting to hear, a lack of freshness, no sense of the unexpected. Even so, there are exceptions, such as Liszt's Fantasy on Hungarian Folk Themes, which I also recorded with Ferencsik. There was an imbecile of a critic – it must have been in France or in England, where they also hated the Dvořák Concerto – who no doubt thought he was paying me a compliment but who wrote the most unspeakable nonsense, saying that 'the end was no longer Liszt but made one think of Khachaturian's Sabre Dance'. Merciful heavens! There's no piece I hate more than this Dance. Liszt's Fantasy on Hungarian Folk Themes is no doubt a relatively lightweight piece, but whatever does it have in common with a work like the Sabre Dance, a work that stinks to high heaven?

The country gradually opened up to the outside world and Moscow started to receive visits from foreign musicians. Glenn Gould came in 1957. I attended one of his concerts. He gave a stunning performance of the Goldberg Variations, but without the repeats, which took away some of my pleasure. I've always thought one should boo musicians – and there are lots of them – who ignore the composer's instructions and omit the repeats.

Next came the Philadelphia Orchestra under Eugene Ormandy. In 1958 I played Prokofiev's Fifth Concerto with them, and the return match followed soon afterwards: after a handful of concerts in Finland, I was packed off to America in the autumn of 1960.

I'd been told that the impresario Sol Hurok came to Moscow each year to organize tours of Soviet artists to the United States. David Oistrakh had started the ball rolling in 1955, after which Emil Gilels and Mstislav Rostropovich had both given recitals on the other side of the Atlantic, but each time Hurok asked about me, he was told I was ill. In the end, he reached an agreement with Khrushchev and signed a cultural accord that included me as part of the deal. I'd have been only too pleased to perform in western Europe, but I'd no desire to go to America. I almost didn't go at all. On the day I was due to leave, a delegation of friends came to the station to say goodbye; for my own part, I'd insisted on walking, but had gone to the wrong station, and it was only on my arrival that I realized my mistake. I had to jump into a taxi, which whisked me across Moscow

Richter in his dacha on the River Oka

at high speed – the train was due to leave in only a few minutes' time – and deposited me at Belorussky Station just as the train was preparing to pull out. How many times afterwards I thought of how happy I'd have been if only I'd missed the train. I'd never have got to know America, and would have been all the better for it. True, American orchestras are of the very first rank, as are its art galleries and cocktails. But the noise, the cheap culture, the advertising and the language! I've never really felt comfortable in London either, but the language that they speak there and that I don't particularly like either still sounds more agreeable to my ears than the slang that they speak in America.

And so I caught the train to Paris and Le Havre, from where we set sail for New York. I'd been given what they called a 'bodyguard', a young man by the name of Anatoly who had just graduated from the NKVD and who was perfectly decent, but who was himself supervised by another 'bodyguard' called Byelotserkovsky, who kept pestering him with instructions: 'Follow him, keep an eye on him, listen to what he says, see who he meets.' One day I'd gone to the Art Institute in Chicago and, as I was leaving, I discovered Anatoly hiding behind the door. He was horribly embarrassed and whispered to me: 'It's him! It's him who sent me! Him!' For his part, Byelotserkovsky never stopped drumming it into me: 'Your job is to play!' It was as though I had no right to take any interest in my surroundings. They virtually expected me to wear blinkers and ignore the magnificent American countryside.

Basically, these minders were decent types who were simply doing their job, but their mere presence was annoying. One day, for example, at the end of a rehearsal of Beethoven's First Concerto with the Boston Orchestra, I was so moved by the wonderful accompaniment that I kissed Charles Munch on the hand. Byelotserkovsky was appalled by what I'd done and complained to me about it afterwards: 'How can a Soviet artist sink so low as to kiss the hand of a foreign conductor?' He was such a boor that on the evening we were invited to the home of the violinist Efrem Zimbalist, who was of Russian origin, he encouraged Zimbalist to return to Russia, where he'd be 'offered a flat and see what a real funeral was like'. How tactful! Zimbalist must have been over eighty at the time.

Sometimes the employees of the said institution really did go too far. On another visit to America, I'd been lumbered with the former director of the Leningrad Philharmonic, Ponomarev, who in his original job had been excellent. But when I discovered that he was demanding presents from impresarios that he claimed were for me and that could range from

Meeting with Glenn Gould in Moscow in 1957

TV sets to carriage clocks – none of which I ever saw, of course – and that he did exactly the same when he 'minded' Mravinsky, I decided I'd had enough. From that day forth I had no further trouble from guardian angels.

I was terribly nervous during this first American tour and in a state of almost permanent panic. At my first concert in Carnegie Hall, I discovered that my mother was present, with her second husband. She'd come over from Germany to see me. I was too upset to see her before the concert – I'd simply have been in no fit state to play. And I didn't see her either at the end of the concert as I was unhappy with my performance. Bunches of wrong notes! It wasn't until the next morning that I called a taxi and, unbeknownst to my minder, went to see her. She had her own 'minder' with her in the person of her second husband. We'd not seen each other for nineteen years, but he didn't leave us alone for a moment.

There was also the recording of Brahms's Second Concerto with Erich Leinsdorf, one of my worst records, even though people still praise it to the skies. I can't bear it. I've lost count of the number of times I've listened to it in an attempt to find anything good in it. Each time I'm appalled. Tam, param, taram, param. A Tempo di allegretto, you bet! Leinsdorf took it at an *allegro*, constantly pressing ahead.

And then all the praise that was showered on me and that even today serves only to ruin my relations with the public. A concert should be a surprise. It loses all its freshness if you tell the audience in advance that they should expect something special: it prevents them from listening. That's why I now play in the dark, to empty my head of all non-essential thoughts and allow the listener to concentrate on the music rather than on the performer. What's the point of watching a pianist's hands or face, when they really only express the effort being expended on the piece?

Another reason why I played badly in America was because I was allowed to choose my own piano. I was presented with dozens and I spent all the time thinking that I'd chosen the wrong one. Nothing is worse for a pianist than to choose the instrument on which he's going to have to perform. You should play on whichever piano happens to be in the hall, as though fate intended it so. Everything then becomes much easier from a psychological point of view.

I remember Igumnov saying to me one day: 'You don't like pianos!' 'Possibly so,' I replied, 'I prefer the music.' I never choose a piano and don't try them out before a concert. It's useless and demoralizing. I place myself in the hands of the piano tuner. If I'm on form, I can adapt to no

With Byelotserkovsky and Nina Dorliac on board the *Queen Mary* en route for New York

Richter with the Boston Symphony Orchestra and Charles Munch

matter what instrument, whereas if I'm in doubt, I never succeed in doing so. You have to believe, more than St Peter, that you'll walk on water. If you don't believe it, you'll go under, and straight away. But I have to say that since Yamaha placed their pianos at my disposal, I've found what I was looking for: the possibility of individualizing the sound and the ability to produce a true *pianissimo*, an extreme *pianissimo*. There can be no more ravishing effect than this.

In deepest Russia, I didn't always have these fine instruments – far from it; but I paid no attention. In any case, there have been times when I've played on terrible pianos, and played extremely well. Some years ago, for example, I had to give a recital at the Soviet Embassy in Paris. The piano tuner took one look at their Steinway and told me that in his opinion it was unplayable. I immediately cancelled the concert. The ambassador – it's always the same with these people – ignored my cancellation. At five o'clock in the afternoon of the day of the concert, he rang me: 'The audience is coming. What shall I do? Shoot myself?' His words moved me to pity and so I decided to go there in spite of everything, convinced that the concert would be a disaster. I went out on to the platform, thinking 'To hell with the piano and the rest of them', and launched into Brahms's Sonata in F sharp minor. It was probably my best concert of the season.

People say I'm capricious and that I cancel concerts for no good reason. Someone even went so far as to write that I was better known for my cancellations than my concerts. Another journalist! It's true that I've occasionally fallen ill and cancelled concerts; in fact, it's happened several times. But people have been led to believe that I've done so out of whimsy, which is completely untrue. Also, whenever I've cancelled, I've always rescheduled the concert at some later date.

I hate all the planning that there is in the world of music. If I've a work ready and want to perform it, I'm happy to do so anywhere, in a school or anywhere else, just like that, free of charge. I do so with pleasure, and it's a matter of complete indifference to me whether it's in a large hall or a small one. People always say that I like small halls, but it's not so much that I like them as that the large halls are booked up well in advance and I can't stand long-term planning. I've nothing against performing in large halls, but on the evening I'd really like to play there, the hall in question is in use – a concert by, well, Philippe Entremont or Moura Lympany. What can I do?

I now know from experience that things planned too far in advance

Richter in Paris and Venice

always end up being aborted. Always! Either you fall ill, or you're prevented from appearing for some other reason, whereas if you improvise –
'The day after tomorrow?', 'Of course, why not?' or, if the worst comes
to the worst, 'Next week?' – everything passes off smoothly. I may be on
form today, but who can tell what I'll feel like on such-and-such a date in
the more or less distant future?

People wonder why I play so few concertos nowadays. Here the problem
is even more acute. In Europe, orchestras demand that I accept engage-
ments four or five years ahead. They're always booked up when I'm free.
In Russia, yes. Everything was different. Maybe it wasn't very ethical, but
if I wanted to play such-and-such a programme and felt ready to give it
the very next day, they'd cancel a concert that was already planned and
put me on in its place. Or if the hall was booked in the evening, I'd play
at two in the afternoon or at ten in the evening. No need to advertise. The
programme was scrawled on a scrap of paper on the day of the concert
and posted up, and through word of mouth the hall would be full. That's
not done in the West.

And so, when I arrive in a country, I prefer to open a map and show
my impresarios the places that have certain associations for me or that
excite my curiosity and, if possible, that I've not yet had a chance to visit.
We then set off by car, followed by the pianos, avoiding motorways like
the plague. And then I may play in a theatre or chapel or in a school play-
ground, at Roanne, Montluçon or in some remote corner of Provence. All
that matters is that people come not out of snobbery but to listen to the
music.

Richter with Karajan

8 Silhouettes

I disapprove of transcriptions, unless they are by the composer; the original always strikes me as better. Much as I love Ravel's music, I find his orchestral transcription of Mussorgsky's *Pictures at an Exhibition* an abomination, a terrible, decorative travesty of the most profound masterpiece of Russian piano music. There was a time, unfortunately not entirely past, when pianists – and audiences – were fond of this sort of attack on art. I've never allowed myself to inflict anything like this on my audiences, with three exceptions: Rachmaninov's transcription of Kreisler's *Liebesfreud*; and Liszt's transcriptions of Wagner's *Liebestod* and Schubert's *Erlkönig*. In *Erlkönig*, Schubert's original accompaniment is already testing enough, but in Liszt's version the difficulties are practically insurmountable. I've always been afraid of it, even if I sometimes emerged from performances unscathed, so I didn't risk it for long. Technical difficulties of this order are harmful to your health, I decided.

Conversely, I often used to play duets as a young man, which enabled me to get to know countless symphonies and the string quartet repertory, to which I would otherwise never have had access. During my years at the Conservatory, we produced transcriptions for two pianos of everything that fell into our hands and that seemed to us worthy of our interest.

It was during the war that I started to play actual chamber music – the Brahms and Schumann Quintets with the Beethoven Quartet and, later, lots of similar works with the Borodin Quartet. A brief association with the cellist Daniil Shafran gave me little pleasure. He was a great cellist, with a distinctive tone, but whenever he played, you always had the impression that he was thinking only of the moment when he would have an ingratiating high note that he could hold on to and produce an attractive sound. He also suffered from nerves. I stopped performing with him in 1951 and he then joined up with Grigory Ginzburg. Ginzburg was an excellent student of Neuhaus's and I often played Liszt's *Concerto pathétique* with him. A very fine musician, a very fine pianist and extremely likeable as a man, but passive and lacking in any vestige of artistic ambition. It was no doubt this that persuaded him to accompany Shafran, who spent all his time splitting hairs with him, probably because he had no self-confidence. When I started to play with Rostropovich, who was then emerging into the limelight, Shafran kicked up an enormous fuss: 'Why are you playing with Rostropovich?' On and on he went. As a musician, if not as a cellist, Rostropovich was incomparably more interesting, an artist of far greater stature. He dwarfed him completely. My relations with him lasted longer. They began in 1949, when we gave the first performance of Prokofiev's Cello Sonata. Before playing it in concert, we had to perform it at the Composers' Union, where these gentlemen decided the fate of all new works. During this period more than any other, they needed time to work out whether Prokofiev had produced a new masterpiece or, conversely, a piece that was 'hostile to the spirit of the people'. Three months later, we had to play it again at a plenary session of all the composers who sat on the Radio Committee, and it wasn't until the following year that we were able to perform it in public, in the Small Hall of the Conservatory on 1 March 1950. We took advantage of this delay to work on two Beethoven sonatas and the Brahms E minor and to discover that we were in fact happy playing together. Over the years we performed a large part of the cello repertory together, and even though there are lots of things for which I have to forgive Rostropovich, I remain grateful to him for introducing me to Benjamin Britten. With Rostropovich, I found a common language; at the time, we were on good terms, not only as far as music was concerned, but in all manner of idiotic ways. I remember an evening when we were invited to a masked ball at the tiny apartment of a dear friend, Bulgakov's widow, Elena Sergeyevna. (She's the Margarita of Bulgakov's novel, it's her to the life.) Rostropovich and I decided to go as crocodiles. It was a lot of work, and we had the costumes, masks and claws made by someone who normally made theatre props. It took us so long to get ready that we didn't arrive till two in the morning, instead of ten in the evening. We went by taxi and, in those austere times, I'm sure the driver thought we were up to no good. We entered Elena Sergeyevna's flat on all fours, each by a different door, to shrieks of laughter and terror. At another masked ball – this time at my own place – we all dressed up in traditional Russian costume. Anna Ivanovna Troyanovskaya, who had already turned seventy at the time, sang songs accompanied on the balalaika by Slava Rostropovich decked out in a long false beard and gold pince-nez. He'd written the words himself. I myself featured in one of them:

'I heard Sviatoslav and lost my heart / And since then I can't tell A major from C minor. / Our audience, under the terror, / Has learned to listen to Bach. / He's restored a sense of discipline, / The spirit of the air reigns in the room.'

And Slava tailored the accompaniment to the words, playing quotations from Bach on his balalaika. He was incredibly talented in this respect, a real joker.

But later we drifted apart, for all kinds of reasons. He always took the credit for everything and harboured ambitions that had nothing to do with music – and this from a man who was a musician to the very core of his being. That's something I've never been able to tolerate. I don't like it, there's nothing I can do about it. One of our last attempts to perform together was Beethoven's Triple Concerto, which we recorded in Berlin, Rostropovich, Oistrakh and me, under Herbert van Karajan.

I'd known David Oistrakh for a long time – my father had introduced me to him in Odessa when I was still quite young. I was around twelve, Oistrakh must have been seventeen. He was an utterly delightful young man, an incredibly handsome youth and extremely likeable. I later attended a lot of his concerts, and of all the violinists I've heard, for me he's the greatest. A tone of almost unimaginable beauty, and a strength without any sense of strain. He barely moved when playing, the violin was an extension of his body, everything was supported on his legs and diaphragm. Later, when I played with Oleg Kagan – by far his best pupil, a violinist of the very first order, a true musician and a delightful man, who had to contend with so many problems unrelated to music – I always had to remind him that the most important thing is the stomach and the legs. However comical it sounds, it's the stomach and legs that produce a good tone.

I played with Oistrakh only quite late in my career, following the death of Lev Oborin, with whom he had formed a superb partnership. He was so modest that he kept asking me: 'Slava, tell me the truth, do you get very bored playing with me?' How could it possibly have bored me! In all the three or four programmes that we put on together, we had only one slight disagreement, over the Franck Sonata. He played it well, of course, but didn't take it very seriously, considering it little better than salon music, whereas I was passionate about Franck and this wonderful sonata. After all, isn't it Vinteuil's Sonata in Proust?

David Oistrakh and Rostropovich, Rostropovich and me, Oistrakh and me – we'd all played together on frequent occasions, but never all three of us at once. The first time we found ourselves sharing the same platform was in Moscow, for Beethoven's Triple Concerto. It was a good concert. And it was clearly an attractive billing, as we were then invited to record the work with Karajan, with whom each of us had already worked on his own. It's a dreadful recording and I disown it utterly. As for the actual recording sessions, I remember them only as a total nightmare. Battle lines were drawn up with Karajan and Rostropovich on the one side and Oistrakh and me on the other. Rostropovich was falling over himself in his attempts to do everything Karajan wanted, whereas Karajan had a superficial and clearly wrong-headed view of a work that has never had a good press but of which I'm personally very fond. Among other things, the second movement was taken far too slowly. He held back the natural flow of the music. He was faking it, and neither Oistrakh nor I had any time for this. But Rostropovich had gone over to the enemy, trying to push himself forward, whereas what he has to play here is no more than figurations. Karajan could see I wasn't happy and that Oistrakh was sulking. He asked why. I was intentionally remaining in the background, not so much to annoy him, but because I found Rostropovich so exasperating.

Suddenly Karajan decided that everything was fine and that the recording was finished. I demanded an extra take. 'No, no,' he replied, 'we haven't got time, we've still got to do the photographs.' To him, this was more important than the recording. And what a nauseating photograph it is, with him posing artfully and the rest of us grinning like idiots.

On the whole, Karajan's behaviour was not particularly attractive. One day, while we were talking, I happened to say *'Ich bin ein Deutscher'* (I'm a German), to which he replied: *'Also, ich bin ein Chineser'* (In that case, I'm a Chinaman).

Richter shifting copies of Karajan's recordings

But there are other things for which I can't forgive him. In our recording of the Tchaikovsky Concerto, there's a disgraceful mistake that's due entirely to his own pig-headedness. It's in the second movement, when the main theme returns after the cadenza. He stopped conducting, although I'd specifically asked him to give me the upbeat. He obstinately refused to do what I wanted, which was no more than rhythmic precision. The result was this mistake, an absolute abomination.

Of course, Karajan was a phenomenal conductor. I heard him do some fantastic things – Mahler's *Das Lied von der Erde*, *Parsifal*, the *Missa solemnis*. I also remember an excellent Beethoven Fifth, though I can honestly say that I prefer Boulez; Boulez's Fifth in London was simply amazing. Karajan was also quite good in Shostakovich's Tenth Symphony, though he took it a bit too fast. Mravinsky was more restrained and was in any case the finest interpreter of Shostakovich. Mravinsky and Kurt Sanderling were both scrupulous musicians, true conductors, and I always enjoyed working with them. Whenever I had the choice – which was only rarely the case, of course – it was with them that I chose to work in the Soviet Union, just as at a later date in Europe, it was Carlos Kleiber, the greatest conductor I've ever been privileged to meet. Unfortunately I never heard either Wilhelm Furtwängler or Roger Desormière in the flesh. For me, Desormière's recording of Debussy's *La mer* – a piece that I rank alongside the *St Matthew Passion* and the *Ring* as one of my favourite works – is the most beautiful in the whole history of the gramophone. From time to time, I invite twenty or so friends round to my home to listen to music. If it's an opera, I ask them to read the libretto in advance and, for my own part, I prepare large sheets of paper on which I write out in capital letters the subject matter and plot of each act, and I turn the pages while we listen to the opera. This helps the listener to follow what's going on and allows his or her imagination free rein, without any interference from directors more interested in parading their own pygmy-like personalities than in respecting the nature of the music and what's written into the score. I haven't forgotten a performance of *Götterdämmerung* in Bayreuth, magnificently conducted by Pierre Boulez – not very intensely, yet extremely precisely – but ruined by a pretentious staging by Patrice Chéreau. How many times I've had to endure such acts of vandalism at the opera! Obviously this wasn't the case at home, with the musical evenings I organized there. One year we devoted four evenings like the ones I've just described to the *Ring*, conducted by Furtwängler. What can I say, except that there's an unbridgeable gulf between him and all the others!

With Evgeny Mravinsky

With Kurt Sanderling

With Carlos Kleiber in June 1976

I remember on one occasion being outside the Odessa Opera. It was dusk, and the street lights hadn't come on. There was a man staring at me. He had white eyes, with no pupils. Suddenly I realized that it was Shostakovich. I went weak at the knees.

Although this was the first time I'd seen Shostakovich, I recognized him from a photograph in the score of his opera *Katerina Izmaylova*, an opera for which I felt no sympathy on account of the naturalism of its libretto. On a practical level, the score itself gave off a nauseating smell of glue, which I can still smell even when merely recalling it. I already knew Shostakovich's symphonies and string quartets, as well as *The Nose*, an extraordinarily satirical opera that I saw many years later conducted by Gennady Rozhdestvensky, an extremely professional conductor, but one who has never inspired me, whereas his wife, the pianist Victoria Postnikova, has always struck me as a major talent on the few occasions I've heard her.

My real encounter with Shostakovich came much later, when he visited me at my flat to rehearse his cycle *From Jewish Folk Poetry*, of which Nina Dorliac and Zara Dolukhanova were preparing to give the first performance, with Shostakovich himself at the piano. It was as though Tchaikovsky had come to call on us. At about the same time – in other words, in the late forties – I sight-read a piano-duet version of his Ninth Symphony with him, at his own place. It was a real torment to play with him: he'd start at a certain tempo, but then he'd start to get faster or slower. He played the bass part, and so it was he who had responsibility for operating the pedal, but he ignored it completely. And he played *fortissimo* all the time, including passages of pure accompaniment, so I had to play even louder to bring out the main themes; without the use of the pedal to give it some sort of outline, I was fighting a losing battle, not least because I could hear him muttering to himself all the time: 'Toon . . . toorooroo . . . toorooroo . . . tooroorooroom!'

So that's how we got to know each other . . . it was all a bit too close for comfort. After the read-through, at which only a few close friends were present, we moved on to the cognac and toasts. It was terrible, as all the others said they didn't want anything to drink, and Shostakovich kept refilling my glass. I emptied more than a bottle out of sheer politeness, a dreadful failing of which I'm guilty all too often. The evening dragged on until nearly midnight, when his first wife, Nina Vassilyevna, suddenly appeared from nowhere. A real beauty! He seemed terrified of her, and brusquely gestured the rest of us to leave: 'Clear off, clear off!'

I staggered out and fell into the gutter at the side of the road, where I spent half the night, oblivious to my surroundings. When I finally came round, I set off in search of shelter at the Neuhauses', where Neuhaus's wife welcomed me with her usual five-o'clock pick-me-up. I spent the whole day sleeping.

As I say, Shostakovich's first wife was beautiful, but authoritarian. She understood nothing about music. I can still see the expression on her face at the first performance of the Piano Quintet, a dazzling and fantastically successful work. She was sitting in the third row and, as the applause broke out at the end, she looked all round the hall, as if to say: 'Are these people mad, or what?' She was very ostentatious, but of all Shostakovich's 'wives', she was undoubtedly one of the most interesting.

As for Shostakovich himself, he was really quite touchy. He was hurt when Mravinsky refused to conduct his Twelfth Symphony, a work that is actually pretty second-rate. Same attitude with regard to me. I've played lots of his works, the Quintet, the Trio and sixteen of his Twenty-Four Preludes and Fugues, all major works that I regard as some of the most important to have been written during the twentieth century – when all's said and done, Shostakovich is descended from Beethoven, via Mahler and Tchaikovsky. But he wanted me to play all twenty-four. There was no reason for him to feel offended: I played the ones I liked, why should I play ones that I didn't? He took offence. He was consumed by irritability, but at the same time extremely well-mannered. One evening, Neuhaus was sitting next to him at a performance of some symphony or other that was being badly conducted by Alexander Gauk. Neuhaus leaned over to whisper in Shostakovich's ear: 'Dmitry Dmitriyevich, this is awful.' Wherepon Shostakovich turned to Neuhaus: 'You're right, Heinrich Gustavovich! It's splendid! Quite remarkable!' Realizing that he'd been misunderstood, Neuhaus repeated his earlier remark: 'Yes,' muttered Shostakovich, 'it's awful, quite awful.'

That was Shostakovich to the life. Unlike Benjamin Britten, whom I regarded as a true friend, there was never any real friendship between Shostakovich and me, except perhaps when I gave the first performance of his Violin Sonata with David Oistrakh. I had difficulty getting used to his presence, I always went weak at the knees. He was too jumpy and clinically depressed. A genius, but completely mad, like the rest of us. Why did I say 'like the rest of us'? I'm not mad, I'm the most normal person you could imagine. I just mention that in passing. Perhaps I might have wanted to be mad. It's always like that . . .

With Shostakovich and Oistrakh in Moscow in 1968

With Jessye Norman

With Elisabeth Schwarzkopf in Tours

With the conductor Christoph Eschenbach

With Arturo Benedetti Michelangeli in Tours

With Pierre Boulez in Tours

In Alexander Calder's studio

With Dietrich Fischer-Dieskau

With Sergiu Celibidache in 1962

With Lisa Leonskaja

With Oleg Kagan

In Tours with Natasha Gutman

Yuri Bashmet at the Grange de Meslay

With Natasha Gutman

9 The Mirror

I've got the reputation of being a workaholic. It's been said that I'd spend ten or twelve hours a day at the piano and that after each of my concerts I'd lock myself away for nights on end in order to continue working on the pieces I'd just played. Nothing could be further from the truth. If I worked after a concert, it was to rehearse or to put the finishing touches to new works for the following day's concert. Also, with my German pedantry, I decided ages ago that three hours a day at the piano would be my normal ration and that I'd stick to it as far as I could.* Let's work it out. 365 times 3 is 1,095. That makes 1,095 hours a year that I need. Days spent travelling by car without touching a piano, concerts demanding several hours of rehearsals (which I don't count as instrumental practice), bouts of illness or indisposition and periods of interruption which, on occasion, have lasted up to five months at a time – they all have to be

---

* See p. 62n. As soon as we broached this question of practising, I was immediately struck by the vehemence and, at the same time, the evident sincerity of Richter's remarks on the subject. Yet all the evidence, including the accounts of the people who were closest to him, to say nothing of my own observations, contradicts his claim about these 'three hours' a day. Richter admits to so many exceptions, many of them of a frankly bizarre character, that in the end I am convinced that he finished up believing what he said. (B.M.)

made up for. I keep a stopwatch on the piano and try to keep an honest record of the time I actually spend working, but I admit that there have been times when I've had to work a lot more, especially on the final day – for example, when I had to learn Prokofiev's Seventh Sonata in four days or Rachmaninov's Second Piano Concerto (not such an easy work!) in a week. But, in general, no. These stories about me practising for twelve hours are absurd. On the other hand, I feel the need to remain in touch with the piano, and I can't imagine working without producing some sort of sound; and so I use every minute of my three hours a day at the piano and set out from the very straightforward principle that what's easy is quick to learn and what's difficult takes time. But there are various kinds of difficulty: those of a strictly virtuosic nature that you find in works like Scriabin's Fifth Sonata or Liszt's First Mephisto Waltz, devilishly difficult pieces, the most difficult – I believe – in the repertory, all of which I played a lot before finally giving them a miss. You have to practise them endlessly. There are other difficulties that aren't so easy to define. The Handel Suites, of which I'm extremely fond, are harder for me to learn than most of Bach's works, perhaps because I find less music in them than in *The Well-Tempered Clavier* or the English Suites. Mozart is a similar problem for me. I can't keep him in my head. I prefer Haydn, whose works have a greater freshness, a greater element of surprise, at least where the piano sonatas are concerned. As a rule, as long as the music has the upper hand, I allow myself to be carried along by it, and everything becomes infinitely easier.

Be that as it may, I adopt a purely repetitive method whenever I've got to learn a new piece; I identify all the really fiddly bits and study them first, practising them mechanically. I take a page at a time, go over it as often as I need to and don't move on to the next until the first one is under my belt. And only when I've finished the second one do I move on to the third. However difficult it may be, there isn't a passage that doesn't become easy if practised a hundred times. Sometimes I play the passage slowly, but I do this very rarely, as I prefer to work at the actual speed from the outset. Purely repetitive work of this kind may appear stupid, and I admit that it comes close to being so; and so there's no better antidote than to keep on studying new works. If I'm asked to give a recital in such-and-such a place in five days' time, I take advantage of the occasion to include a new piece that I've not played before, a new sonata by Haydn, for example, which always goes down well. And all at once I feel reinvigorated, as there's nothing I detest more than constantly repeating the same old works. I always need something new.

I never play a piece in its entirety until I've learned each page separately. But I often leave things to the very last minute – which isn't a good thing, but that's how it is: if I didn't have the pressure of a forthcoming concert, I'd never force myself to do any work. As a result, it's not unknown for me to play through a whole piece for the first time on stage. That was the case with Schumann's *Humoreske*. I'd included it in the programme of one of my recitals, but ran out of time. I'd started to practise it only a week before the concert. On a purely technical level, it bristles with all manner of difficulties – all, that is, except for the finale, and so I set this to one side. Having spent the week studying the rest of the score, I couldn't make a start on the final movement until the night before the concert. I knew it would be less difficult to manage. I must say the concert wasn't too bad.

In the past, I always played from memory, but I stopped doing so in the late seventies. In spite of what people call my temperament, I'm actually someone who always remains level-headed and can view things objectively. I used to have perfect pitch and could reproduce everything by ear, but I noticed that my hearing was getting worse. Today I mix up keys and hear things a tone or sometimes two whole tones higher than they actually are, except the bass notes, which I hear as being lower than they are, as the result of a kind of softening of the brain and weakening of the auditory system, as though my hearing were out of tune. Before me, Neuhaus and Prokofiev were both afflicted by a similar phenomenon – in Prokofiev's case, he heard everything up to three whole tones too high towards the end of his life. It's sheer torture, and of course it also affects the coordination of your fingers. What it costs to have devoted one's life to music!

I've known periods of chronic depression, the most serious of which was in 1974. It was impossible for me to live without a plastic lobster that I took with me everywhere, leaving it behind only at the very moment I went out on stage. This was accompanied by a type of auditory hallucination that tormented me for months on end, day and night, even while I was asleep. I started to hear a recurrent musical phrase a few bars long, violently rhythmical and rising in pitch. It was based on a chord of a diminished seventh. In the cold light of day I tried to work out what it meant, even though the torment was permanent, even telling myself that such a phenomenon might be of interest to medical science. But try telling doctors about chords of a diminished seventh! Sometimes I would lie

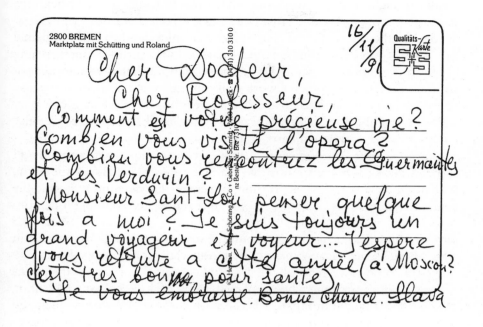

Cher Docteur,
    Cher Professeur,
Comment est votre précieuse vie?
Combien vous visité l'opera?
Combien vous rencontrez les Guermantes
et les Verdurin?
Monsieur Saint-Lou penser quelque
fois a moi? Je suis toujours un
grand voyageur et voyeur... J'espere
vous retrute a cette année (a Moscou?
c'est tres bonne pour santé)
    Je vous embrasse. Bonne chance. Slava

GROSSETO
Palazzo della Provincia
Provincia Palais
Palace de la Provincia
Provincia Palast
Trees cher Docteur, voeux
Mersi pour votre bonnes / voeux
et pour Seurat (qui je tres aimer)
J'espere vous sete tres bien a Chicago,
le seule citta, qui je aime en Ame-
rique porqeque je déteste (?) les
autres (et beaucoup!). . Voila
Nina arrivee per moi a Pamplona
et reste aussi en Italie
    Avec mes meilleurs voeux pour
votre fortune et chance.
    Je reste votre Fidele Klient
P.S. Excuse mon grand Mère. Slava.

Postcards to René Marteau

awake all night trying to work out what I was hearing – I wasn't hearing it, but just *thought* I was – or to work out its pitch. I was for ever trying to identify the notes and these primitive harmonies and to correct them, as it was the most frightful nonsense – ta raaa ra riii ri rii – going through my head in every conceivable key. I finally realized that it was a kind of variant of a relatively modest work built on rudimentary harmonic steps and one, oddly enough, that had had a great effect on me as a child: it was Rachmaninov's *Vocalise*. It was this that had been the unconscious model of some of my own early compositions.

Curiously, the phenomenon disappeared overnight, as soon as I stopped taking the medication that I'd been prescribed. But it returned with each new bout of depression, whereas the deterioration in my hearing is permanent. If I start to play in A minor, for example, I hear it in B minor and so, in an attempt to correct it, I transpose what I'm playing, with the result that, without intending to, I land up in G minor, which is clearly extremely inconvenient, especially if I'm playing with an orchestra. Following an absolutely frightful concert that I gave at the Fêtes Musicales de Touraine, when I played eight of Liszt's Transcendental Studies, and a recital in Japan, where I took fright even before launching into Beethoven's op. 106 Sonata, I made up my mind never again to play without a score.

In any case, what's the point of cluttering up your brain when there are far better things to do? It's bad for your health, and it also smacks of vanity. True, it's not as easy to retain the same degree of freedom with a score open in front of you – it doesn't work straight away and requires a lot of practice – but now that I've got used to it, I find that it has lots of advantages. In the first place, I've never made any distinction between chamber music and music written for a solo performer. But one always plays chamber music with a score; why should one have to perform without one as a soloist? In the second place, it's easy enough to memorize a Haydn sonata, but I prefer to play twenty while reading the music, rather than limiting myself to two performed from memory. As for contemporary music, there are only a few exceptional artists who are able to memorize a piece by Webern, or Hindemith's *Ludus tonalis*, but it's a waste of time and effort. It's not *practical*. Moreover, even if the element of danger and risk aren't totally foreign to music, you feel more secure and can concentrate better if you've got the score in front of you. Finally, and above all, it's more honest to play like this: you've got how it has to be in front of you and you play exactly what's written. The interpreter is a mirror, and performing music doesn't mean contaminating the piece with your own personality, it consists in performing *all* the music, nothing more and nothing less. Who could ever remember *all* the performance markings indicated by the composer? Failing that, performers start to 'interpret', and it's that that I'm against.

By freeing the brain of the useless task of memorizing the music, you can also stop inflicting the same endlessly repeated programmes on audiences – and on yourself. I have no time for works that are hackneyed. It's enough for anyone to mention Chopin's B flat minor Sonata in my presence, and I feel physically sick. Yet, it's a work of genius. Same thing with the four Ballades – his finest works. Much as I love them, I simply can't face the idea of having to play them again and again. And then there are Beethoven's Fourth and Fifth Concertos. What, not again!? Magnificent works, I've nothing against them, and I enjoy listening to them, but they're not for me. There are still so many things that I've never played – Schoenberg, Scarlatti and Janáček, a composer of whom I'm immensely fond, though I've only ever played his *Capriccio*. With the exception of Janáček, I have to admit that these are composers whom I don't always find very persuasive. Scarlatti seems to me to cut a pitiful figure next to Bach, even though he wrote some real jewels. Schoenberg strikes me as a composer who set out to destroy, even though he conceived the incredible Five Orchestral Pieces and other masterpieces besides. But, having attended a remarkable performance of *Moses and Aaron* in Düsseldorf, I couldn't help wondering how they managed to learn it and whether it was worth all the effort. You can't do everything, you can't read everything, see everything. There are too many masterpieces, and I'm laziness and passivity personified. I simply try to bring a little freshness to the music I play by performing what people don't expect, rather than what everyone else plays. I've worked it out. My repertory runs to around eighty different programmes, not counting chamber works. I'm an omnivorous animal with a large appetite. I've tried to eat all I can, and up until the sixties I continued to take on new works in order to provide myself with a basis on which to keep on changing my programmes. I don't reject a score because I'm not satisfied with what I've done with it in the concert hall. A performing artist doesn't develop in a straight line, it seems to me, but in a spiral. I can be patient and if a piece hasn't worked to my satisfaction, I continue to work on it and play it over and over again.

From the seventies onwards, my decision to stop playing from memory meant that I could continue to enlarge my repertory, but at a less frantic pace. Among the works that I'm virtually the only person to perform, there isn't a single one that I haven't genuinely liked. Take the Rimsky-Korsakov Concerto, one of the first things I ever recorded with an orchestra. It's a modest piece, but highly successful in its way. I played it out of a fanatical admiration for the composer. I don't rate it above the Tchaikovsky Concerto, which is clearly a more important work, but Rimsky is more to my taste and I'm mad about his music. The *Capriccio espagnol*! Heavens! What a work! What restraint, and what orchestration! If you compare it with painting, it's not in oils, but a pastel or a watercolour. Rimsky wrote nine operas, the first of which – *The Maid of Pskov* – is absolutely amazing. You'd really think it was music from that period. Mussorgsky and he lived together and wrote at the same table, *Boris* on the one hand, *The Maid of Pskov* on the other. And *The Snow Maiden*? And *Christmas Eve*? And *Kitezh*, this Russian *Parsifal*? And *The Golden Cockerel*? And *The Tale of Tsar Saltan*? They're all fantastic. I'm less fond of *The Tsar's Bride*, though it's his most widely performed opera. I find that it doesn't ring true because he was trying to imitate Tchaikovsky. He succeeded . . . but it's not him. And *Kashchey the Immortal*? It's a fairy-tale opera, already anticipating Stravinsky. They're all descended from him, Debussy, Ravel, Prokofiev and Stravinsky.

Two other Russian composers who have now more or less fallen into oblivion also used to figure in my repertory: Glazunov and Myaskovsky. Glazunov was an excellent composer, a musician who knew all there was to know and who had a great influence on the musical life of Russia, even though he died in exile in Paris. I met him in Odessa, where he sometimes came to conduct his own works, perfectly crafted and extremely elegant symphonies and ballets. I played his Concerto, a highly contrapuntal piece of great complexity. Here, too, I had to learn it in five days, as I was immersed in Bach just then and, as always, running short of time.

Myaskovsky was a member of the old school, serious and withdrawn. He wrote music in a style that combined Tchaikovsky with Scriabin, though he was a friend of Prokofiev. He wrote close to thirty symphonies, some of which – nos. 4, 5, 6 and 21 (the one we presented to the Students' Circle) – are really quite remarkable. I used to play his Third Sonata, an emotionally highly charged, not to say grandiloquent, piece, but of a healthy complexity. I'd place him on a par with a composer like Aaron Copland (whose Piano Quartet I've played), in spite of a musical language that is clearly far less contemporary.

As for contemporary non-Russian music, I've essentially tackled Britten,

With Benjamin Britten and Dietrich Fischer-Dieskau

With Lorin Maazel

Playing duets with Benjamin Britten

Hindemith, Stravinsky, Berg and Webern. The first work of Britten's that I played was the Cello Sonata, which I performed with Rostropovich, and later with that extraordinary musician Natasha Gutman, one of the people with whom I've derived the most pleasure from making music. Then there was the Piano Concerto, a work full of youthful energy, written under the influence of Ravel and Prokofiev, perhaps a little immature, but extremely likeable in its English way. I recorded it under Britten himself, but he was already ill, he hadn't long to live and had little energy. As I didn't really feel on form myself, the recording isn't very successful. We also played duets together, Mozart and Schubert and his own Rondo alla burlesca for two pianos. I staged two of his operas in Moscow as part of the December Nights Festival at the Pushkin Museum, *Albert Herring* and *The Turn of the Screw*. A long time ago the young Lorin Maazel suggested that I should stage the *Ring*; of course, I was tempted by the idea and could already imagine a revolving set, with a rock in the distance on which enormous trees rose up; a rock turning all the time, avenues, horses, and sopranos who remained seated, never moving, while everything around them revolved; clouds scudding past and trees swaying, the whole scene being visible only in flashes, as if in flashes of lightning. The effect of movement produced in this way would have reflected the waves of music. It never happened. But I can still picture those productions of Britten's operas. Moments of great excitement. I firmly believe that Britten is one of the century's leading composers, as is Paul Hindemith, perhaps the last great representative of 'Germanness' in music. I also like Max Reger, another composer who's rarely performed. I played his grandiose Variations and Fugue on a Theme of Beethoven for two pianos with the young Andreas Lucewicz – we needed months of rehearsals to master it – and Hindemith often reminds me of him. Each of them is a master of compositional technique, but in Hindemith's case there's also a sense of humour that people fail to recognize. I've played around ten of his works: his four violin sonatas with Oleg Kagan – the early ones are a bit like Richard Strauss, but the others are Hindemith at his best – and the Viola Sonata with Yuri Bashmet. But, for me, the real masterpieces are the *Suite '1922'*, a work of monumental power, and the *Ludus tonalis*, which Nadia Boulanger recommended to me in Paris. It's a phenomenal piece. He himself illustrated it – in extremely poor taste but absolutely brilliantly none the less – with animal figures for each voice. I don't like the drawings in themselves and I detest caricatures in general, but here his way of drawing a lion with its four legs in the air to illustrate invertible counterpoint is irresistible. And what can one say about his scandalous operas, *Neues vom Tage*, *Mörder, Hoffnung der Frauen*, which he wrote in collaboration with Kokoschka, and *Sancta Susanna*! He was a serious composer, but his works have this other aspect to them, totally unexpected, the reflection of a man who was insanely cheerful and with a clearly brilliant mind.

A sense of humour certainly wasn't the dominant feature of a composer like Webern, whose music is of such translucency that, in spite of its complexity, you immediately notice if even so much as a single note is missing. The same is true of Mozart. Berg is another composer who wasn't exactly a bundle of laughs. I spent almost a year working on his Chamber Concerto. One hundred rehearsals proved necessary to overcome the hair-raising difficulties of this exceptional piece, and it would have been impossible for me to have performed it without them. I played it with an orchestra made up of young students from the Conservatory under Yuri Nikolayevsky, an unknown conductor, but one who's very meticulous. I also played Stravinsky's *Movements* with him. I've never encountered such enthusiasm for sheer hard work as I did with these young musicians. Whenever the conductor said 'That's enough for today', they'd protest: 'No, more!' You never get that with orchestras. Later they became professional orchestral players, and I've no doubt that their desire for work lost some of its edge. In any case, the rehearsals were held at my own place, which must have contributed to their enthusiasm: they were fed.

I've listened to some famous recordings of the Chamber Concerto, including the one with Boulez and Barenboim, which was probably made after six rehearsals. I know this music inside out, yet I didn't understand a thing in their performance of it. Our own recording was made live at the Théâtre de l'Athénée in Paris. The sound engineer didn't know the work and turned up the volume in places where he should have turned it down. But, apart from that, it's one of the recordings of which I'm most proud.

I didn't explore contemporary music in any greater depth, even though I was fascinated by a number of pieces by Berio, Stockhausen, Boulez and Xenakis. In another context altogether, Ravel and Debussy always seemed to me to be more representative of Spanish music and to give it a more universal significance than composers from the country itself. And so I didn't venture any further into this field, except to accompany Nina Dorliac in Falla's Seven Popular Spanish Songs. There was one French composer I could never make up my mind to include in my programmes,

At the Grange de Meslay

Rehearsing with David Oistrakh in Tours

Olivier Messiaen. I find him interesting, especially when played by Yvonne Loriod. The works of his that I've heard often start magnificently, but their initial promise is never realized, and you get these sugar-water climaxes that I can't stand. Splendid ideas, then suddenly Gershwin, cloying sweetness! Having said that, I like Gershwin a lot. He's excellent in his own field, and less sentimental than Messiaen.

My festivals in France and Moscow were also a chance to play music that's out of the ordinary and to perform in places that are as inspiring for the performers as for the audience. For years, the Fêtes Musicales de Touraine were one of the greatest delights of my life. While touring France in the early sixties, I took time off to explore the Touraine and see for myself its famous châteaux. I was so attracted by them that I immediately thought of organizing concerts there. But their poor acoustics and the size of the rooms that were shown to me made this dream impossible, at least until the architect Pierre Boille told me about a thirteenth-century barn that seemed to meet my criteria, the Grange de Meslay. When I went there, it was full of hay and hens were running around everywhere, but I fell in love with it there and then. I asked for the necessary acoustic changes to be made, and we set to work. I'd imagined the Fêtes Musicales as a real celebration, in which music would be central to other delights and everyone would have time to meet everyone else, an idea that reflects the lightness of the place and of the air. I invited a number of young musicians who had already impressed me – people such as Zoltán Kocsis, one of the most talented pianists of his generation; Lisa Leonskaja, with whom it was always a pleasure to play; Eliso Virsaladze, an incomparable interpreter of Schumann; and a number of famous artists, including Dietrich Fischer-Dieskau – for me, the greatest singer of the century – and David Oistrakh. It was at the Grange de Meslay that we first performed together. I'm not always sure that the locals were aware of the quality of the programmes on offer, but the Fêtes Musicales were soon being talked about not just in France but elsewhere, too, and even as far afield as Russia.

One day Irina Alexandrovna Antonova, the director of the Pushkin Museum, came and challenged me to organize something similar in Russia. She allowed me to use the beautiful White Room at the museum, and it was in this way that the December Nights came into being. The month of December has symbolic resonance in Moscow, of course, and I thought that that would suit the festival we had in mind. It suited me less, as I hate spending the winter in Russia, where I'm always ill, but no matter. We organized evenings around particular themes. I was able to

specify the programmes and invite whoever I wanted. I remember a particularly successful evening devoted to Schubert, Schumann and Chopin. We'd laid out the room in a special way, with a large window at the back, through which you felt the presence of the snow. And on stage, around the piano, were 'guests' wearing evening dress and talking. The scene recalled the musical soirées of the Romantic period, a Schubertiad or an evening with George Sand at Nohant. We continued to rehearse even after the audience had started to arrive. They tried to make out what we were saying on stage. 'When's it going to start?' we heard them whispering. Then someone brought in some beautiful sprays of flowers and placed them at the front of the stage, at which point I sat down at the piano and played Chopin's Ballades and Schumann's *Blumenstück* and Toccata, but without announcing the programme, as though it were all improvised and we were performing among friends at home.

The essential thing, of course, is to play well, not to worry about the setting. But a certain element of theatricality, which seems to me to be sadly lacking in the formality of the concert hall, must exist for the music to be heard.

I don't like having a score in my hands when I'm listening to music. My aim isn't to judge the work, but to enjoy it. I find it almost off-putting to know in advance at what point the flute or oboe is to enter; I dislike it because things then lose their charm and mystery, a mystery I have no desire to fathom. They then assume an academic aspect. In any case, I'm not in favour of study and analysis. I never look at the orchestral scores of the concertos I'm playing. I don't look, I listen. In this way, everything is a surprise to me, I can have the whole of the score in my head and allow my imagination free rein.

The interpreter is really an executant, carrying out the composer's intentions to the letter. He doesn't add anything that isn't already in the work. If he's talented, he allows us to glimpse the truth of the work that is in itself a thing of genius and that is reflected in him. He shouldn't dominate the music, but should dissolve into it. I don't think that my way of playing has ever changed. Or if it has, I didn't notice. Perhaps I simply started to play with greater freedom as I threw off the shackles of existence and rejected the superfluous and all that distracts us from the essential. It is by shutting myself away that I've found freedom.

I might have had doubts about the extent to which I managed to play what I intended, but from the beginning I was always certain that, for each work, it was in this way, and no other, that it had to be played. Why? It's very simple: because I looked closely at the score. That's all that's required to reflect what it contains.

Kurt Sanderling once said of me: 'Not only can he play well, he can also read music.'

That wasn't such a bad way of putting it.

With Natasha Gutman in Tours

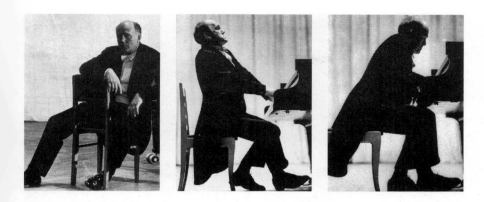

In the film *Glinka*, with Richter as Franz Liszt

At Carnegie Hall in October 1960

In Vienna in 1963

At Tours Station in 1973

With Irina Alexandrovna Antonova

During filming of *Richter: The Enigma*

Notebooks: On Music

24/XII,
Christmas Eve 1970
Moscow
Recording
Bach
*Two arias from
Cantata 51:
1) 'Jauchzet Gott in
allen Landen'
2) 'Sei Lob und Preis
mit Ehren . . . Alleluja'*

1) These two arias are like twins; both are in C major.
2) Trumpet and soprano soloist vie with each other in virtuosity.
3) The inspired lightness of this music seems so self-evident that you'd think it was written without premeditation (perhaps, by the same token, it was equally quickly forgotten by the composer). In at one ear and out of the other, but like air, the sky and warmth – things we don't even think about. There's absolutely no doubt that it's the very epitome of perfection.
Bach's cantatas: you can listen to them at any time and ought really to hear them all. They introduce us to a world of plenitude and harmony, a world of inner discipline. How sad that, given the number of them, it's virtually impossible to know them all!

24/XII
Recording
Schumann
*Humoreske op. 20
Sviatoslav Richter*

Whenever I listen to my recordings, I'm always disappointed, as what I hear bears absolutely no relation to what I was expecting.
Disappointment at finding no freshness, no sense of surprise.

25/XII
Recording
Bach
*Christmas Oratorio,
Part I*
26/XII
*Christmas Oratorio,
Part II*
27/XII
*Christmas Oratorio,
Part III*

How many times we've already met to listen to this wonderful oratorio at Christmas! It's become a tradition that we've all got used to.
I know this work virtually by heart, but I still marvel at its richness and beauty.
It's enough to hear the first timpani strokes at the beginning for my heart to leap with joy.

Recording
Brahms
*2nd Concerto in B flat
S.R. Orchestre de Paris
conducted by Lorin
Maazel*

What hard work this recording was for the marvellous musician that Maazel is and for the third-rate orchestra that the Orchestre de Paris is! They all fancy themselves as soloists and constantly press ahead without paying the least attention to the conductor. That's why the quality of this recording is rather debatable, though it's still better than the one with Leinsdorf.

3 1/XII, New Year's Eve **Ravel** *Boléro* *Conductor:* *Charles Munch*	Charles Munch's *Boléro*. A New Year present. This tremendous ascent, this triumph of rhythm; although I've heard it so often, it always feels as though it's the first time. And then for weeks you can't get it out of your head, thereby prolonging the pleasure. Bravo, Monsieur Ravel!
1/I **Bach** *Christmas Oratorio,* *Part IV* 3/I *Christmas Oratorio,* *Part V* 6/I *Christmas Oratorio,* *Part VI*	The last three parts are appreciably shorter than the first three. Everything is now fixed and perfectly clear. And the world is reborn. There's real integrity to this performance, so that everything sounds as it should, with no attempt at over-interpretation, which would be inappropriate here. The two men's voices (Traxel and Fischer-Dieskau) are remarkable, as are the two women. Kurt Thomas conducts the chorus and orchestra with perfect evenness and simplicity; he is convincing in carrying out his high calling.
Ljuba Welitsch 1) Richard Strauss: *Salome* 2) Puccini: *Tosca* 3) Johann Strauß: *Die Fledermaus* *The Gypsy Baron*	A famous singer in her day. Felicitous combination of a natural gift and a dazzling technique. What a shame her career was so brief!
Lehár *The Merry Widow*	This performance is utter perfection! The work is a delight by virtue of its sheer inanity. Everything about it is mere playfulness, charm, lightness, Viennese elegance. There's something about it that reminds me of alchemy: out of nothing and emptiness a gem is created.

Performance at the Moscow Operetta Theatre **Kálmán** *Paris in Spring*	Odd that I should go to a performance at the Moscow Operetta Theatre, but . . . It turned out that there wasn't too much coarseness in this production, except in the finale, where the director seems to have gone out of his way to ruin his production by presenting a sort of B-movie revue in execrable taste.
Recording **Debussy** *La mer*	One day, after listening to this work, Anna Ivanovna exclaimed: 'For me it's exactly the same miracle as the sea itself!'
Concert at Tchaikovsky Hall *Galina Pisarenko* **Beethoven**	There's no question about it, from now on neither we ourselves nor any of our friends will miss any of Galya's concerts. The Moscow public loves her for her attractive voice, the charm of her interpretations and her sheer physical beauty. I think audiences in the provinces also love and appreciate her. She very much likes to sing, even more than the works she sings.
Bach *Organ music* *1) 'Dorian' Toccata and Fugue* *2) Toccata, Adagio and Fugue in C major* *Helmut Walcha*	It's the first time I've heard this. I'm not a great connoisseur of the organ repertory (and perhaps I'm no connoisseur at all). The 'Dorian' Toccata is splendid, severe to the point of glaciality. The Toccata, Adagio and Fugue in C major: here the composer gives free rein to a staggering imagination! Walcha is inimitable!
February **Schumann** *String Quartet in A major op. 41 no. 3* *Parrenin Quartet*	After having lived apart for forty years, here we are together again, me and the world of the quartet. I feel the same enthusiasm at this reunion as I did when I was young and first attempted to sight-read the quartet repertory using pocket scores. I'm happy to be so constant in my affections.

Schumann
Piano Quartet in E flat
op. 47
Parrenin Quartet
Pierre Barbizet

This is a bit like the Quintet's little brother. It, too, is in E flat and it, too, is magnificent (and easy to live with).
Good recording.
Pierre Barbizet is unquestionably a true musician, his head teeming with ideas, his fingers precise.

Barber
1st Concerto
John Browning
Erich Leinsdorf

An eclectic concerto written in a thoroughly professional manner and brilliantly played by John Browning (a serious and thoughtful pianist whom I heard and got to know at Spoleto).
A good recording.
But I could never play this music. I always give a very wide berth to this type of piece. Copland has so much more talent and is so much more interesting than Barber.

Henri Sauguet
1st Piano Concerto
Vasso Devetzi
Conductor: Gennady
Rozhdestvensky
Les forains (ballet)

Sauguet's Concerto is very superficial; I'd even say it is rubbish, God forgive me.
I think that if Vasso Devetzi plays it, it's in order to advance her career, but she makes a gallant stab at it. As for the ballet, it, too, is worthless, but not ineffectual. No doubt it's easy to dance to.

Recording
Bruno Rigutto
Schumann:
Kinderszenen
Toccata
Liszt:
Mephisto Waltz
Transcendental Studies
in D flat and F minor
Petrarch Sonnet in
A flat (no. 123)

Début recital by this young musician. Fine temperament, youthful freshness and – if you can trust the recording technique – rather lovely sound. In sum, an attractive proposition. But . . .
There's also a certain ungainliness in the way he separates the phrases and individual episodes.
Is this really an incurable ill with all pianists?!

Recording
Pavel Stepán
Brahms
opp. 117, 118, 119

A true musician, cultured, experienced, intelligent and, moreover, a good pianist.
So why is it I don't feel like listening to this recording again?

Boulez *Le marteau sans maître*	This isn't unlike Goethe's *The Sorcerer's Apprentice*. An enigmatic and speculative work that's difficult to understand. It could just possibly be a masterpiece.

Badings *Evolutionen* **Varèse** *1) Hyperprism* *2) Octandre* **Stockhausen** *Zeitmasze* **Dallapiccola** *Goethe Lieder* *Elisabeth Söderström* **Schoenberg** *Five Orchestral Pieces* *nos. 1–3*	This whole collection of contemporary works brings with it a certain feeling of nostalgia. On the one hand, there are some interesting and diverting sounds (Badings) and, on the other, the sort of ponderous, elephantine music (Varèse) that lots of people like. The Stockhausen is also quite entertaining but I don't find it at all persuasive (unlike Berio, for example). Dallapiccola is more serious, but even here there is a certain strangeness. Schoenberg is the only one who's original (but, frighteningly, isn't he already considered old hat?). In sum, it's like a bouquet made up, for the most part, of thistles.

Bach *1) Fifth French Suite in* *G major* *Tatyana Nikolayeva* *2) Fifth English Suite* *Margarita Fyodorova*	Two pianists play Bach suites. 1) Fifth French Suite. A pupil of Goldenweiser. A famous artist; even so, her performance is so unconvincing that I keep realizing that I'm not listening. 2) Fifth English Suite. A pupil of Neuhaus. I'm not expecting much, but I listen to the whole Suite with interest and say to myself: 'What a phenomenal piece!' (In other words, the interpretation didn't disappoint me.) Might this be the result of a lesson with Heinrich Gustavovich just before the recording?

Bach
Sixth English Suite in
D minor
Anatoly Vedernikov
	You can't get better than this:
	  a sense of form
	  pianistic brio
	  irreproachable musicality
	  impeccable taste
	  concentration on the execution of the work
	Odd impression: the pianist is playing in an airless environment.

March **Brahms** *Heine settings* Fischer-Dieskau, Demus **Wagner** *Wesendonck Lieder* Hannelore Kuhse **Wagner** *Brünnhilde's War Cry* (*Die Walküre*) Frida Leider	We listened to these in response to a request from Ninoshka, and they are all magnificently performed. Impossible to pick and choose among so many fine singers. And the music is in a class of its own. Miracles really do exist in this humdrum world of ours!
Recording **Haydn** *Sonata in F major* (London) *Sonata in C major* (Moscow) S.R.	Sonata in F major. The one and only time I played this sonata was in London. Dear Haydn, how I love you! But other pianists? They're rather luke-warm towards you. Which is a great shame.
Salle Pleyel in Paris **Hindemith** *1st Sonata in A major* S.R.	This was far from being one of my most brilliant concerts, in spite of my love of this sonata.
Massenet *Manon*	An extraordinary recording under the direction of Pierre Monteux, with Victoria de los Angeles in the title role. And what an adorable work, with its sentimental lyricism that's so light and so purely French! And Massenet, what talent all the same!
Haydn *Sonata in E major* *no. 37** **Schumann** *Novelletten op. 21* *No. 1 in F major* *No. 2 in D major*	I really love Haydn's E major Sonata. It's the first time I'd played it. And obviously I love the Schumann. And Chopin even more. As for Debussy! My principle is to play only works that I really love (and not just those that are currently accepted).

* Here and elsewhere the numbering of Haydn's keyboard sonatas follows that of Christa Landon's Vienna edition of 1963–6.

Chopin *Ballade in G minor* *op. 23 no. 1* **Debussy** *Twelve Préludes* *(Book Two)* *La sérénade interrompue* *(Book One)* *Danseuses de Delphes* *(Book One)* S.R. *(recording of* *Spoleto concert)*	I've <u>almost</u> always stuck to this principle.

Osaka **Bartók** *Fifteen Hungarian* *Peasant Songs* **Szymanowski** *Masques op. 34* **Prokofiev** *7th Sonata op. 83* *Waltz in E flat op. 96* *no. 1 (War and Peace)* **Debussy** *Cloches à travers les* *feuilles* S.R.	In the first half I think I played Schubert's C minor Sonata, then everything listed above. The recital ended with Prokofiev's 7th Sonata, the rest being encores. The concert was fairly successful: it was my first in Japan. Everything there was so new and unusual, I felt a certain apprehension, though it soon wore off. Our stay was really quite interesting; we went to Nara, to the World Fair and so on. Since then, I've often returned to Japan and got used to the pace of life there, to its customs, its cooking . . . There you are!

Akademgorodok **Britten** *Concerto in D major* *op. 13* *Conductor:* *Rudolf Barshai* S.R.	We played the Britten Concerto very well and derived great pleasure from it. Barshai accompanied magnificently. But I sensed that the academicians didn't understand the work. Virtually no one expressed an opinion. The weight of tradition, and what a weight!

Kate Klausner Beethoven *Concerto in C major* *op. 15*	It was either at the opera or at a concert that we met this middle-aged and very cultured woman. She was sitting beside us in the stalls and struck up a conversation. Quite repulsive in appearance (like a witch) and eccentrically coiffed in the Spanish style. But our conversation wasn't uninteresting

and more than once she said how friendly she was with Karajan, even giving us the impression she was to appear with him on the concert platform.

As a result we met her from time to time at the Salzburg Festival.

Anyway, one day she presented me with a tape of herself playing Beethoven's 1st Concerto (accompanied by a second piano) so that I could hear her. (I'm not certain, but I think it was before a concert by Karajan.) Horror of horrors! Her playing is unspeakably awful, heavily accentuating the left hand, without the least *piano* nuance, but with the most incredible self-assurance and arrogance, and totally lacking in talent.

When she reaches the cadenza, she starts to reel off the notes like a woman possessed. In the second movement, a complete lack of sensitivity, but the most overbearing self-confidence. The main subject in the final movement is a total fiasco.

Moreover, the piano is recorded very close, almost directly over the strings, whereas the second is barely audible.

That's the lady for you: a shameless strumpet.

Since then, we've avoided all meetings with her.

12/IV, in honour of Heinrich Neuhaus's birthday
Recordings
Chopin
Nocturne in B major op. 32 no. 1
Fantasie in F minor
Heinrich Neuhaus
Szymanowski
'Tantris the Clown'
(Masques op. 34 no. 2)
S.R.
Debussy
La mer
Conductor:
Roger Desormière

We had lots of visitors this evening in Nezhdanova Ulitsa. With the obvious exception of Gilels, we'd invited all Heinrich Gustavovich's former pupils (I remember Yakov Zak bringing a bunch of roses). A well-appointed table, wine and an enthusiastic ambience.

I'd arranged things so that everything went well. We listened to Neuhaus's recordings: his inspired Nocturne in B major and the *Fantasie* in F minor that Heinrich Gustavovich played so often and that I myself heard him interpret on numerous occasions, both in Moscow and in Odessa, a city I always found so unwelcoming. On each occasion it was so inspired that you'd have thought it had been written with him in mind.

In Neuhaus's honour, I also put on my own recording (lack of modesty on my part?) of the very short piece from Szymanowski's *Masques*, 'Tantris the Clown', which is dedicated to our master, and, finally, the work by Debussy that he loved above all others ('Slava, put on *La mer*,' he almost always used to say whenever he came round here).

Our guests stayed till very late. It seems the evening was a success.

He sometimes had such flights of inspiration in the concert hall! Unforgettable!

But it was uneven – simply because he practised so little. He worked mainly with his pupils – a sheer waste of time, in my view.

Recording **Mozart** *Variations in D minor* *(Serenade no. 17)* [K 334]	I'd completely forgotten these variations; for me, this is virtually the rule with Mozart's music. I don't know why (perhaps some deficiency in my brain?), but I can never remember it. Sometimes I remember the first subjects, but the second subjects and the rest are always a disaster! Nothing stays in my head. *We're still living in Nezhdanova Ulitsa, but the flat in Bolshaya Bronnaya Ulitsa is already awaiting us. From there, we'll have a view over the whole of Moscow.*
Recording **Tchaikovsky** *Waltz in A major* *Sergey Rachmaninov*	I went to see Yakov Zak. He has masses of books in his tiny room, all piled up on top of each other, albeit in some kind of order. This is entirely typical of a person I once said resembles Goethe. Just for me, he put on this waltz, played by Rachmaninov. It was magnificent, with an innate nobility and a warmth wholly characteristic of Tchaikovsky.
April Bolshoy Theatre **Prokofiev** *War and Peace* *Conductor:* *Mstislav Rostropovich*	Worthless! New ways of solving the problems of staging this remarkable opera really must be found. P.S. It's a chamber opera! Slava Rostropovich had sent me two stalls seats and so I took Galya Pisarenko. Oh! the Bolshoy's gilded auditorium!

The performance proved tiresome in the extreme. First, Slava: he's obviously delighted to be conducting and is visibly in love with this music, but what he did with it had nothing to do with Prokofiev. From a musical point of view, then, it was really bad.

As for Pokrovsky's production, it's cumbersome, misguided and outdated. As Natasha, Galina Vishnevskaya is like a wicked old witch. Mazurok (as Prince Andrey) sings as though he's at a Party meeting. I can't even remember who sang Pierre. Arkhipova no longer has the *physique du rôle* for the part of Hélène. The battle scenes are totally unconvincing. Napoleon (Kipkalo) is like a character out of an operetta. Vedernikov as Kutuzov is more or less correct, though his voice is not particularly attractive; as Kuragin, Maslennikov is just about adequate, and only the gypsy Masha (I don't know her name) shows real vitality and is by far the best thing in the cast.

I don't think this magnificent epic opera has yet found a place for itself in the repertory. At the same time, it is already beginning to bore its listeners: it's become just another routine production for the Bolshoy, whose art is moribund and uninteresting. As a result, I didn't even go to thank Rostropovich for his invitation – my conscience wouldn't let me.

Recording
Stravinsky
Capriccio
Monique Haas
and the composer

I really wanted to listen to this wonderful Capriccio, which I've spent my whole life preparing to learn and to play. When shall I ever get round to it?

18/IV
Britten
Cello Symphony
Mstislav Rostropovich

Very interesting work, written specially for Rostropovich.

With Britten, speculative powers are always combined with human feelings – he's a representative of what's called 'human music' – and you notice this both in his choice of subjects for his operas and in his other works.

Rostropovich plays it magnificently (I was present

at the première in Aldeburgh, and it left a powerful impression on me then).*

22/VI
Bach
Triple Fugue in D minor
Orchestrated by
Rudolf Barshai

Rudolf Barshai is a magnificent musician; formerly a viola player, he went on to form the Moscow Chamber Orchestra.

He's always on the look-out for relatively forgotten works in order to perform them in public in the most perfect manner. He's very keen to conduct large symphony orchestras, but things aren't working out for him in this respect, and I don't think this will ever change. I'm not sure why; perhaps he lacks something of the artistic calibre needed to conduct large orchestras; perhaps he's too obsessed with detail, which offends the omnipresent sensibilities of large symphony orchestras (I'm thinking here of my own disastrous experience with the Leningrad orchestra in Beethoven's 2nd Symphony): they positively loathe pedants, whereas you really have to struggle to fire their imaginations.

I like playing with him as he gives me confidence and support. In his appearance, Barshai (with his beret) inevitably reminds me of Wagner, and he's always flattered when I tell him this.

Unfortunately, the orchestra he founded has recently started to rebel and to throw tantrums: their conductor is no longer to these gentlemen's liking. It's clear that they no longer want to rehearse sufficiently and that they prefer to live it up, an attitude typical of virtually all orchestral players.

2/VII, Tours
Schoenberg
Pierrot lunaire
Marie-Thérèse
Escribario
Pierre Boulez

Boulez Festival at Meslay. This was the first time I'd heard Schoenberg's famous *Pierrot lunaire*. Arresting in its strangeness and bizarrerie, but it interests me! The singer–*diseuse* is extremely musical and I find her versatility quite astonishing. Hugely talented. As a conductor, Boulez, too, is compelling. But it is this that distinguishes him.

---

* The Aldeburgh performance on 18 June 1964 had been preceded by the world première in Moscow on 12 March 1964.

3/VII
Harrison Birtwistle
Verses for Ensembles
Pierre Boulez
Stockhausen
Messe du temps présent
[unidentified]

Even when a work is not one of the peaks of the repertory, he still manages to turn it into a mountain and make it a success (but not everyone has such a musical audience). There's a certain fanaticism here with regard to contemporary music: it's a point of honour.

3/VII
Pierre Boulez
Domaines
Clarinet: Alan Hacker

Domaines is a work that's both very unsophisticated (for me) and very likeable. It's almost entirely homophonic. The clarinettist (fabulous) is seated in an armchair on castors and moves around. He plays each solo in a different place (it's true that he's obliged to be in an armchair because it seems that he's paralysed in both legs). Visually, it's quite entertaining and, without it, Boulez's pastorale might appear a little monotonous. But . . . I can't make up my mind if this music has any real substance or whether it's totally hollow. (Great success! The work was encored.)

4/VII
Mozart
Adagio and Fugue in
C minor
Haydn
Symphony no. 99
in E flat
Pierre Boulez

Boulez presented Mozart and Haydn in a beautiful musical mirror, but in the Haydn he unfortunately ignored the repeats; I'd never have expected this of him.

10/VIII
Menton
Beaux Arts Trio
of New York
Schumann
Trio no. 1 in D minor
Beethoven
Trio in B flat
('Archduke')

A splendid trio, especially Menahem Pressler (the pianist). Initially, one was rather put off by his superfluous gestures (expressive of his enthusiasm), but after five minutes you no longer noticed (and in any case he does it with total sincerity). Schumann. This was the first time I'd heard this work, and it made me want to play it myself. The Beethoven, which I know of course, also whets my appetite (how I love the piano part, with all its ornaments rising to the top of the instrument's register).
A brilliant concert. Down below twinkled the

lights of Menton, while a refreshing breeze blew in off the sea.

8/VIII
Monte-Carlo
Richard Strauss
Metamorphosen
Tod und Verklärung
Dance of the Seven Veils
Conductor:
Lovro von Matačić

At this concert in the Palais Princier de Monaco I played Mozart's C minor Concerto, replacing Elisabeth Schwarzkopf, who was ill. I can't say that Matačić's accompaniment was to my liking – Mozart isn't his cup of tea. The second half of the concert, by contrast, was splendid: here's someone who's made for Richard Strauss. All three works are engraved on my memory, especially the Dance of the Seven Veils from *Salome*. Matačić performs all Strauss's rubatos in so natural and arresting a manner that I don't think I've ever heard anything as successful (even with very famous conductors).

Afterwards we dined with Elisabeth [Schwarz-kopf], Walter [Legge] and Christian.*

29/VIII, Salzburg
Donizetti
Don Pasquale
Conductor:
Riccardo Muti

This was Riccardo's Salzburg début (very impor-tant for him). It was the first time I'd heard this opera. Because of its comic character, it didn't really reflect the mood I was in that evening.

I recall Graziella Sciutti's great and well-deserved success in the main part.† And I also remember the scenery in the form of the ace, knave and seven of hearts and other playing cards. But to be quite frank it all left very little impression on me. I feel far greater affinity with other operas of Donizetti – *L'elisir d'amore*, for example (I recall an old film with the young Tito Gobbi), and *Lucia*, which I've never seen but which has always appealed to me. In fact, of all the Italian composers of this period, the one I prefer is Bellini and I know *Norma* very well, having enjoyed it as a child when I used to play through the vocal score.

We'll remain in Salzburg a little longer and hear some other concerts. I'm also doing some recordings at

---

* The Austrian actor Christian Ghera was a friend of Richter's.
† Graziella Sciutti sang the part of Norina in 1972. In 1971 the role was taken by Emilia Ravaglia.

Schloß Kleßheim – in a room that was once the office of a certain Mr Hitler.

28/VIII **Bruckner** *Symphony no. 8* *in C minor* *Conductor: Karajan*	My favourite symphony (I've known it since I was an adolescent and used to play an arrangement for four hands). I also think it's Bruckner's finest work. I'm particularly fond of the first movement, where it's all so intense and unexpected. But the rest, too, is tremendously beautiful. This time Karajan was magnificent – expressive and human: rarely does one achieve such fulfilment. He touched me.

30/VIII **Verdi** *Otello* *Conductor: Karajan* *Vickers* *Freni*	This luxurious wide-screen performance of *Otello* under Karajan's direction initially left me completely cold both musically and in terms of the staging (the production, too, is by Karajan) – indeed, not just initially, but for the whole of the first three acts. And not just me: you could also sense it from the applause. The conductor made no effort to raise himself up to the requisite level. Coldness and indifference. But, in order to ensure that the evening ended on a high note and to earn his laurels, his conducting of the fourth act was beyond reproach, and the applause almost literally raised the roof.

September Schloß Kleßheim *Recordings* **Schumann** *Bunte Blätter* *Symphonic Studies* **Beethoven** *Sonata in E minor* *op. 90* **Brahms** *Intermezzo in A minor* [op. 118 no. 1] *Ballade in G minor* [op. 118 no. 3]	This was a lot of work, but the result is three new records. These recordings seem to me entirely professional and won the approval of the musicians and technicians who were working with me. In spite of the fact that they are studio recordings, there's a real atmosphere and a genuine sense of life to them. Let's say they're a success. I'm grateful to the team with whom I worked: the elderly and sympathetic Herr Ganss (who once worked for the Fascist administration); the artistic director, Herr Waldeck, a rather forbidding individual of a somewhat sceptical frame of mind who reminds me a little (not without charm?) of Tolya Vedernikov; and Herr Lindler and Herr Karo,

*Intermezzo in E flat
minor op. 118 no. 6*
Rachmaninov
*13 Preludes
opp. 23 and 32*
S.R.

who both proved excellent and hard-working colleagues. Kostia and Inge Metaxas had to climb up on to the roof on several occasions in order to chase away the birds that were making such a noise there.

The weather was splendid, everywhere was green. Not long afterwards I had to say goodbye to Salzburg and return to the East.

8/x
Moscow
Mozart
*Variations in G minor
for violin and piano*
Stravinsky
*Duo concertante for
violin and piano*
*Oleg Kagan
and Lisa Leonskaja*

Today Lisa and Oleg came to regale us with their playing. It's interesting to hear works one doesn't know, in good, honest interpretations. Theirs are perfectly controlled, and they know how to read the score accurately.

Quotation about me by Kurt Sanderling: *'Er kann nicht nur gut spielen, er kann auch Noten lesen'* [Not only can he play well, he can also read music].

I've recently seen quite a lot of these young musicians and always enjoy their company. Perhaps one day I'll play with Oleg Kagan, but it'll involve a lot of hard work (my partnership with David Oistrakh places an obligation on us).

The Mozart Variations are authentically classical. As always, the piece by Stravinsky is perfectly structured and of crystalline purity.

24/x
Recording
Bach
*English Suite no. 3
in G minor*
S.R.

A very old recording, certainly outdated in terms of recording techniques. But I understand absolutely nothing about these things, which are a matter of total indifference to me.

As long as a piece is correctly played, the recording technique shouldn't bother you. But nowadays many listeners seem to attach great importance to the technical quality of a recording. I think this is because it's something they understand and that they care more for it than they do for the music. They're simply incapable of appreciating the true value of an interpretation. It's a reflection of this century, with its concern for machines and technology. People are further away than ever from nature and from genuine human feelings and are gradually turning into machines themselves. (How brilliantly and how wittily Prokofiev made this point in his 6th Sonata!)

In my own view, this recording of the English Suite isn't too bad. I still remember the extreme effort I put into learning it. At the same period I was also playing the Italian Concerto, the *Capriccio sopra la lontananza del fratello dilettissimo* and the 4th and 5th Sonatas.

I was then taking a very serious interest in the *galant* Bach, whom I've always found much more problematical than the 'strict' Bach of *The Well-Tempered Clavier*.

Perhaps it would be no bad thing to do some more work on Bach. After all, he's the 'beginning and end' of all music. (Between ourselves, I'm not entirely sure that he's 'the end'.)

The English Suite in G minor is unsurpassably harmonious and beautiful.

24/XII
Paris
Notre-Dame
Bach
Prelude and Fugue in E flat major
Marcel Dupré
?
Pierre Cochereau at the organ

Christmas Eve with Ninoshka at Notre-Dame in Paris. We were so looking forward to it, but it was a terrible disappointment. The Parisians treat their cathedral as a place for an evening stroll. On this special night, they chatted at the tops of their voices, clattering around the building as though in hob-nail boots and behaving in a thoroughly inappropriate manner, without paying the least attention to those of us who were seated and who had come to hear a concert of sacred music. We were deeply angered and disappointed by the behaviour of the French, who, after all, have the reputation for being a well-bred and intelligent nation.

There was no question of listening to the music while it was being played: it was simply imposs-ible to hear it.

And this in this fabulous city and fabulous cathe-dral, in this land of art!

How shameful!!!

We left, not feeling in the least bit like enjoying Paris by night.

1/I, New Year's Day Moscow **Bach** *Toccata, Adagio and* *Fugue in C major* *Helmut Walcha* *at the organ*	This is the second time I've heard this utterly inspired work. This time it was to mark the arrival of 1972. It's already been around for quite some time. May it never be forgotten (I say this to everyone, not just to organists).
8/I and 9/I **Bach** *Christmas Oratorio,* *Parts I–VI*	None of the people whom we invited for these two evenings has forgotten them completely, I hope, nor – above all – the music, which we've often listened to at Christmas celebrations in the past. Isn't this D major tonality magnificent?
7/I Grand Hall of the Conservatory **Mahler** *4th Symphony* *Conductor:* *Kyrill Kondrashin* *Galina Pisarenko,* *soprano*	With what exquisite taste this work was composed, and with what originality Mahler invested this music! The pantheism of the 3rd [*recte* 4th] movement, its humanism without arrogance, its humour, and this naïve and religious text! And everything is exactly in place.
13/I *Recording* **Brahms** *Die schöne Magelone* *(15 songs)* *Dietrich Fischer-Dieskau* *and S.R.*	I still remember all the work that went into this cycle: it wasn't easy. Dieter's insistence on every vowel and every consonant often got in the way of the free flow of the music and I wasn't able to adapt to it. This recording has been very successful, but I don't particularly care for it – any more than I do for the work itself. Benjamin Britten had no time for Brahms, or for Beethoven. But that really *is* going a bit far!
27/I Grand Hall of the Conservatory *Leningrad Philharmonic* *Orchestra* **Shostakovich** *6th Symphony*	We've been waiting a long time for Evgeny Alexandrovich and his orchestra to visit us in Moscow. There's absolutely no doubt that Evgeny Mravinsky is our finest conductor – this was immediately obvious after the conducting competition held in Moscow in the late thirties. I remember his

Stravinsky
Apollon musagète
Tchaikovsky
Francesca da Rimini
Conductor:
Evgeny Mravinsky

performance of Liszt's *Préludes*, at the end of which all the other competitors turned pale (they included Rakhlin, who had given his all, and Ivanov, whose only real success was the overture to *Romeo and Juliet*).

Mravinsky and Shostakovich are made for each other (as were Strauss and Hofmannsthal). What a pleasure to hear this wild and incomparable 6th Symphony again in this particular reading!

Then Stravinsky's *Apollon*, performed with rare elegance and an entirely classical rigour. The Tchaikovsky (which I'd already heard on record) wasn't at all good. The orchestra rumbled along without ever getting under the skin of the music; a disappointing impression. Yet the work is astonishingly beautiful (I don't think it has ever suited Evgeny Alexandrovich). He looked drawn and has aged visibly. He, too, hasn't had an easy life.

6/II
Recording
Bartók
Music for Strings,
Percussion and Celesta
The Miraculous
Mandarin

In both these works, Bartók reveals his true stature as a giant among composers. There are no two ways about it: he's a phenomenon unique unto himself.

Whereas Bartók is generally something of a closed book to me (just like the Hungarian language), here I lay down my arms and manage to understand him thanks to a kind of seventh sense: he literally forces you to submit to his music.

10/II
Recording
Mozart
Piano Quintet in E flat
major K 452
Philadelphia Wind
Ensemble
and Rudolf Serkin

This Quintet is sheer beauty as performed by these American musicians: an impeccable performance, full of life and authentically Mozartian.

20/II
Belgrade
Britten
The Rape of Lucretia

I didn't know this opera at all, and this was the first time I'd heard it. It seems to me that the present performance was excellent both musically and in terms of the production. A star of the

Yugoslav Opera (whose name I unfortunately forgot to note down) was the Lucretia and gave a performance of consummate intelligence. Not only does she have a very good voice, but she acts well and is pretty. But what impressed me most was the Prologue and Epilogue of the opera, taken by two singers (a man and a woman). This is the best part of the work, it seems to me.

The actual subject matter I find very unappealing and even see a certain banality in it, a quality I'd rather not associate with Britten.

The opera clearly contains a goodly measure of *verismo* that finds its most obvious expression in Lucretia's final solo before her suicide. The 'rape' scene is accompanied by somewhat agitated music that left little impression on me.

Let's say that I far prefer Ben's other operas, but perhaps it was due to a not entirely authentic performance by the Yugoslav company?

That's by no means out of the question.

In that case my verdict carries no weight whatsoever.

7/IV
Moscow
Recording
Debussy
La mer
Conductor:
Roger Desormière

La mer again; shall I ever tire of listening to it, of contemplating it and breathing its atmosphere?

And each time is like the first time! An enigma, a miracle of natural reproduction; no, even more than that, sheer magic!

Recording
Richard Strauss
Alpine Symphony
Conductor:
Rudolf Kempe

I've known mountains in the past (the mountains of the Caucasus) and have personally savoured the epic feeling of climbing to the very top.

Whenever I listen to this work, I sense – without really knowing if it's true – that Strauss, too, stayed at these altitudes and reproduced his impressions in this symphony. And how faithfully!

15/IV
Recording
Stravinsky
Petrushka
Conductor: Seiji Ozawa

I'm not really taken by Ozawa in this work, which is so clearly Russian. Of course, he's very gifted, but his gift is rather that of the mimic, and he lacks some of the depth for this kind of music. He certainly knows how to create an effect. From that point of view, his success is assured.

19/IV
Recording
Mozart
*3rd and 5th Violin
Concertos in G major
and A major*
Oleg Kagan
*Conductor:
David Oistrakh*

Recordings that attest to the supremacy of the Russian violin school.
The mere fact that David Oistrakh is accompanying his talented pupil says much for the extraordinary scrupulousness and democratic character of this great artist.
Oleg Kagan reveals a true understanding of Mozart, and I think that in the near future I'll try to join him in this miracle of music-making. (Could my intentions have made David Fyodorovich a tiny bit jealous? After all, he's announced that he's going to give a cycle of Mozart sonatas with the pianist Badura-Skoda.)
It's worth listening several times to this recording of these two concertos. You appreciate them all the more and derive a real pleasure from doing so.

20/IV
Recording
Beethoven
*1) Quartet in F major
op. 18 no. 1*
Gewandhaus Quartet
*2) Quintet in E flat
major op. 16*
*Rudolf Serkin and the
Philadelphia Ensemble*

Even in his magnificent first quartet, Beethoven's genius is already fully revealed. From the outset he demonstrates the most total mastery. The same is true of Schubert (*Erlkönig*) and Brahms (1st Piano Sonata).
The E flat Quintet, too, is phenomenal, except that I disagree with the tempo adopted by the Philadelphia players in the slow movement – disagree totally.

21/IV
Recording
Schumann
*Phantasie in C major
op. 17*
Scriabin
12 Études

An old recording from London, made up of bits and pieces; you can't help feeling that it's been patched together and it's not really a success. I recall having wrestled all night with the Schumann *Phantasie* for the sake of the recording, before returning to the sauna at the Imperial Hotel (which has long since disappeared).

from opp. 2, 8, 42, 65 *6th Sonata op. 62* S.R.	The Scriabin is a live recording; there are quite a few wrong notes in the 6th Sonata, but it's still not without interest and has a certain life and integrity to it. As for the op. 65 Études, they're not without merit. At all events, they're not a disaster.
26/IV *Recording* **Bartók** *1st Violin Sonata* *Oleg Kagan* *and Alexei Lyubimov*	I played this sonata with Oistrakh, and there's even a live recording of us. It's a difficult piece and I've never really got to the bottom of it (the main problem is the last page, where I did not make the F sharp tonic sufficiently clear). Oleg and Lyubimov play it with clarity and precision.
1/V and 2/V *Recording* **Bach** *The Well-Tempered Clavier* *24 Preludes and Fugues* *(Part One)* S.R.	My recording of Part One is undoubtedly more successful than that of Part Two. In the second volume, it's the most significant preludes and fugues that have turned out the worst – those in E flat minor, F sharp minor and the splendid Prelude and Fugue in B flat minor, and this weighs heavily on my conscience.
7/V *Recording* **Hindemith** *3rd Piano Sonata* *Maria Yudina*	Maria Veniaminovna Yudina was always keen to play Hindemith's works, which suited her very well, unlike Chopin, Rachmaninov, Scriabin and other 'composers of sentiment'. Here she doesn't get up to her usual mischief but remains true to the text.
Recording **Shostakovich** *Violin Sonata* *David Oistrakh* *and S.R.*	This recording is of documentary interest: the first performance of a work which, however remarkable it may be, is not – I have to admit it – particularly close to my heart and which, as a result, didn't come easily to me during the rehearsals. It was enormously successful, and Shostakovich came up on stage to congratulate us, muttering to us – he was afraid of falling while walking – 'I don't want to cause a scene. You understand, I don't want to cause a scene . . .'

10/v
Recording
Boulez
Le marteau sans maître
Conductor:
Robert Craft

The present recording is clearly '*sans maître*': the conductor is a certain Mr Craft (a permanent member of the entourage of great composers) and, if one had any choice in the matter, it would be better if '*Le marteau*' were '*sans Mr Craft*', an individual wholly without talent who specializes in 'new' music.

18/v
Recording
Mussorgsky
Pictures at an
Exhibition
S.R.

There are two recordings of *Pictures* by me, one from a concert in Sofia, the other a studio recording made in Moscow. Both have enjoyed some success, though I'm not satisfied with either of them; there's something missing that's difficult to pin down: perhaps a certain sense of reality. I'd like something more here, something more universal in scope, the suggestion of a whole world in its myriad contradictions.

I loathe and abhor the orchestral version of this piece, which is the best Russian work *for piano*. Amen.

Recordings
Haydn
Piano Concerto
in D major
23/v
Jean-Bernard Pommier
25/v
Vasso Devetzi
Conductor:
Rudolf Barshai

I enjoyed listening to these two recordings of Haydn's Concerto.

I really must make an effort to learn it and show people the right tempo for the first movement.

All its interpreters play it as if they had a train to catch, and as a result the music sounds dull. It's curious – but I've noticed this before – tempos that are exaggeratedly quick or simply wrong-headed make the music sound boring. It's a fact.

Musicians should give serious thought to this.

25/v
Strauss
Salome
Conductor:
Clemens Krauss

Salome again, with its strange and, as it were, lubricious orchestration, its tremendous flights of fancy and returns to earth, its almost Viennese charm, its bizarre moon and pools of blood in which Herod stumbles. '*Das ist ein schlechtes Zeichen*' [It is an ill omen].

What imagination there is on the part of these creative artists; nightmares and gardens of delight, beauty and death: it all exists side by side and has more real presence than our actual lives.

29/v
Recording
Beethoven
Sonata [no. 27
in E minor] *op. 90*
Schumann
Symphonic Studies
S.R.

My recording of the Symphonic Studies is fairly successful.

The Beethoven is less good; there's something not quite right about it.

I've played my new recordings to friends, who naturally sang their praises. It's always like that . . . unfortunately.

Recording
Schumann
Bunte Blätter op. 99
Brahms
Intermezzo in A minor
op. 118 [no. 1]
Ballade in G minor
op. 118 [no. 3]
Intermezzo in E flat
minor op. 118 [no. 6]
S.R.

Same thing with this recording. Everything seems more or less correct, but somewhere in the depths of my soul there lurks a certain dissatisfaction.

It's no doubt the fault of the recording techniques that always break the sense of continuity. What remains is beautiful, but it's never more than a residue.

24/vi, Tours
Song recital
Mady Mesplé
Vivaldi
Schubert
Richard Strauss
Fauré
Roussel
Poulenc
Debussy

This singer is very popular in France. Her programme was well chosen and easy on the ear. There's absolutely nothing you can say against her. She doesn't arouse wild enthusiasm on the part of the audience, who are no doubt used to her, but I think that if she appeared in Moscow, she'd bring the house down and be hugely successful.

After the concert, Nicolette Le Chevallier said proudly: 'Elle est méridionale comme moi.' To be 'from the South of France' isn't universally appreciated by the French. I remember Angèle Van de Velde speaking to me about this same Nicolette with the merest trace of disdain in her voice: 'Seulement, elle est un peu méridionale.' Ultimately, it's not very important and, after all, Mistral, too, was 'méridional'.

We left the concert well satisfied.

25/VI
Tours
Juilliard Quartet
Haydn
*Quartet in G major
op. 77 no. 1*
Bartók
3rd Quartet
Beethoven
*Quartet in E flat major
op. 127*

A fabulous concert! Impossible to play better!
I've never heard a quartet scale such peaks. It's
hard to describe . . . A miracle remains a miracle!
And so I shall say nothing more.

1/VII
Tours
*Orchestre de Paris
Conductor: Georg Solti*
Bartók
*Music for Strings,
Percussion and Celesta*
Beethoven
7th Symphony

The Grange was specially laid out for this evening's
concert, so that the orchestra was positioned not
in the middle of the hall, as is usually the case
here, but at one end (for acoustic reasons).
Solti is in his element in this piece by Bartók.
There's no doubt that it's Bartók's masterpiece, a
masterpiece of sonority, rhythm and atmosphere.
In the Beethoven, Solti proved to be terribly
unsophisticated and I really wasn't impressed by
his interpretation.
I didn't sense any affinity with the great Spanish
classic (perhaps this is something I've merely
imagined). I didn't sense the great sword thrust of
the opening bar. I didn't sense the 'pilgrims' pro-
cession' in the second movement and, finally, I
didn't sense the vision of the cross on the horizon
in the D major Trio.

July–August
Innsbruck
Recording
**Three arias from
Macbeth**
Maria Callas

Three perfect miracles by the great diva and trage-
dienne of the operatic stage. What tremendous
force to her delivery!
Signor Verdi, too, is at the very peak of his powers.
Impossible to match such prodigies.

Rachmaninov
*Rhapsody on a Theme
of Paganini*
Gary Graffman

I really enjoyed listening to the Rhapsody (I didn't
know it had been conceived as a ballet, but why
not???).
Gary Graffman, whom I met some time ago in
America and who struck me as very sympathetic,

played the piano part brilliantly.

But I've no desire to play this piece, in spite of its marvellous qualities: if you restrict yourself to the theme, Brahms is better in a different way; and as for the final bars, I think they're a veritable insult to the work.

August, Salzburg
Mozart
Così fan tutte
Conductor: Karl Böhm

Reri Grist dazzled us as only she can. Janowitz brought refinement and humour to her part. It was all very interesting and, of course, hugely successful. *Großer Aufwand* [Great extravagance] . . .

But what a poisonous plot! For example, when the boat returns, you're overcome with terror, and yet everything's so lively and cheerful and comical and . . . vicious. This was the second time I'd heard *Così fan tutte* in Salzburg.

The first time was certainly better: Elisabeth Schwarzkopf, Christa Ludwig, Fritz Wunderlich* and Hermann Prey, and a better production in an old-fashioned, realistic style.

This time (Janowitz, Fassbaender, Reri Grist, Fischer-Dieskau), the production was no less good, but the scenery was sometimes conventional and really rather boring – a piece of scenery representing Vesuvius in the background naturally takes up all your attention, so that I inevitably felt a (rather childish) desire to see it erupt in all its splendour.

But it was nothing special, with no more than a little puff of smoke that you'd have thought had come from a cigarette.

Böhm conducts magnificently, but there's nothing new in that. The artists in Salzburg owe it to themselves to be of the very best; that's something we know and appreciate and accept as our due. But the tickets are exorbitantly overpriced.

The presence of Fischer-Dieskau lends the ensemble an exceptional lustre. What he does with the role of the scheming Don Alfonso is extraordinarily imaginative and entertaining.

* Wunderlich never sang Ferrando in Salzburg. It was Waldemar Kmentt whom Richter would have seen in Günther Rennert's production, presumably in 1964.

August
Salzburg
Alban Berg
Wozzeck
Conductor: Karl Böhm
(again he revealed his
power and tremendous
talent)
Anja Silja: Marie
Walter Berry: Wozzeck
(1st performance)
Theo Adam: Wozzeck
(2nd performance)

Let me say straight away that Anja Silja is the ideal Marie; and the same is true of the two Wozzecks, even though Theo Adam is probably better on a purely theatrical level.

I think that with *Wozzeck* Berg reached an impasse, albeit one that was brilliant in its way. There had been nothing like it before him, and it's unlikely that it will be repeated in the future; perhaps it's a typically Austrian phenomenon.

But I know that Britten was much influenced by Berg (as he also was by Dargomizhsky's *Stone Guest*!!!). Yet Britten found a completely different and original approach as an opera composer. For his part, Büchner is utterly amazing: how up-to-date his play seems and how negative his view of the world.

Büchner and Berg are clearly made for each other, and this combination exerts a powerful hold on the listener and spectator.

This was the first time I'd encountered this work and I decided to see it twice. It left a tremendous impression on me. The music plays a slightly different role here, a role that is almost imperceptible and yet wholly indispensable – in the sense of its inevitability. The theme of the rolling head transports you into a state close to that of a trance. The finales of the first and last acts, with their earthquakes in the orchestra, have something literally unheard-of about them. As for the subject matter, of course, the denouement has a slight sense of *verismo* about it, but Berg gives everything a colour that belongs to it and it alone, and the ending, again, is entirely novel.

The performance was splendid: wasn't this work born in Salzburg and universally consecrated here? If so, the cards were placed in good hands.*

---

* The opera was written in Vienna and premièred in Berlin in 1925.

Salzburg **Emilio de' Cavalieri** *Rappresentatione di Anima e di Corpo*	A very interesting work (I don't even know in which century it was written),* archaic and like nothing else I know. Unfortunately, I can no longer remember the first thing about it; there's something rather abstract about it, and it's difficult to find words to describe its qualities. It was very odd to hear and see it. Salzburg sometimes has surprises of this kind to offer, even if the festival overall is the height of conservatism.
Salzburg **Mozart** *Le nozze di Figaro* *Conductor:* *Herbert von Karajan*	A total triumph for Salzburg and one which, frankly, I wasn't expecting. It's now clear who Karajan is! And of what he's capable. Of all the *Figaros* I've seen, this was one of the best, in every respect. First, musically. No point going into detail. From the first bar to the last, Karajan revealed total mastery in his approach to Mozart. You couldn't conceive of a better cast (Janowitz as the Countess,† Stratas as Susanna). Everyone sang superbly and, theatrically, proved ideal. The production by Ponnelle (including his sets) is splendid and exemplary in style: it's a veritable feast for the eyes and goes perfectly with Mozart's music. Of all the operas I've ever been privileged to see, this was one of those rare examples of how it should all be done.
Innsbruck *Recording* **Schubert** *Sonata in C minor* *Sonata in B flat major* S.R.	These recordings of mine of two of Schubert's posthumous sonatas have more good points than bad ones, especially the first movement of the B flat major which, in my own view, adopts and maintains just the right tempo from start to finish.

* First performed in Rome in February 1600.
† Elizabeth Harwood sang the Countess in 1972.

September
Vienna
Alban Berg
Lulu
Conductor:
Christoph von Dohnányi
Anja Silja
Dietrich Fischer-Dieskau

In every respect, a magnificent performance of a work which, musically and theatrically, is as disturbing as it is repellent.

Anja Silja is made for the part of Lulu: I think it's her best role. Dohnányi conducts the orchestra with rigour and clarity, so that the music – which the ear sometimes has the greatest difficulty in assimilating – appears in its very best light. Everything on stage is exactly as it should be, and Lulu's appearance in Act III,* when she throws her shoe at the ceiling, is spectacular.

6/x
Moscow
Recording
Bartók
2nd Piano Concerto
Orchestre de Paris
Conductor:
Lorin Maazel
S.R.
Prokofiev
5th Piano Concerto
London Symphony
Orchestra
Conductor:
Lorin Maazel
S.R.

Needless to say, the Bartók, which caused us such problems when we were recording it, isn't a success. The orchestra proved so dreadful that I feel sick just thinking about it. It was the result of an article that appeared in the French press declaring them 'the best' in the world. There was nothing poor Lorin could do. On two occasions he even broke his baton. There wasn't even a trace of real temperament on the part of the percussionist (and this in Bartók!), and the whole recording took place against a background of indolence and carelessness; no one showed any interest.

That's what you get when a stupid piece appears in the papers. A disgraceful recording.

<u>Prokofiev</u> with the Londoners.

Here everything was different. Honest toil, and an attempt to achieve the highest possible standards. And so the results are more than respectable.

It's interesting to note that Maazel and I play perfectly (and even ideally) together, whereas listening to it at home, you have the impression that he'd like to have taken it a bit slower. Curious phenomenon.

25/xi
Tbilisi
Bach
The Well-Tempered
Clavier

It does no harm to listen to Bach from time to time, even if only from a hygienic standpoint.

---

* Presumably an error for Act II: the three-act version was not seen in Vienna until 1983.

Part One: Preludes and
Fugues in C major,
C minor, C sharp major
and C sharp minor
S.R.

27/xii
Recording
Bach
Christmas Oratorio,
Parts I and II
28/xii
Christmas Oratorio,
Parts III, IV, V and VI

Our annual tradition continues. Assembled once again are all our old friends and Bach, people who are used to spending their Christmas evenings together with us here.

The D major – the prevailing tonality of this work – colours these days of happiness with its light-heartedness and shades of greenish blue.

29/xii
Recording
Bach
Partitas nos. 1 and 2
Glenn Gould
30/xii
Bach
Partitas nos. 3 and 4
Glenn Gould

Glenn Gould, 'the greatest interpreter of Bach'. Glenn Gould has found his own approach to Bach and, from this point of view, he deserves his reputation.

It seems to me that his principal merit lies on the level of sonority, a sonority that is exactly what suits Bach best.

But, in my own view, Bach's music demands more depth and austerity, whereas with Gould everything is just a little too brilliant and superficial. Above all, however, he doesn't play all the repeats, and that's something for which I really can't forgive him. It suggests that he doesn't actually love Bach sufficiently.

31/xii
Recording
Beethoven
Missa solemnis
Schwarzkopf, Ludwig,
Gedda, Zaccaria
Conductor: Karajan

To start the New Year, here, once again, is the *Missa solemnis*, a work that few people really know (even among musicians).

That's why I put on this recording and made all our visitors listen to it. Only then did we wish each other a Happy New Year, only then did we chink glasses and drink rivers of champagne.

7/i
Recording
For children
and grown-ups

Today is a holiday. In the middle of our huge room is a large and magnificent Christmas tree in the finest tradition. Festive decorations (perhaps a little outdated) throughout the flat.

Humperdinck
Hänsel und Gretel

Between each scene of the opera, Natalia Zhurav-liova explains what happens so that all the children present can understand.

In the second scene, following the Evening Prayer and at the very moment that the angels appear and watch over the children as they dream, I light the candles on the tree, which is now a blaze of light. By the end of this delightful opera (which isn't as straightforward as all that, as is clear from the childlike Overture in the manner of *Die Meistersinger*), the table has been laid and is covered with Christmas gingerbread and other delicacies.

A true Christmas Eve.*

9/II
Recording
Mahler
***6th Symphony
in A minor***
Conductor:
Eduard Flipse

I'm passionately fond of this symphony and each time I hear it I'm amazed. Unfortunately, Flipse comes nowhere near a true understanding of the work, but that doesn't really matter, such a musical monolith can't leave one indifferent.

But I beg you, I entreat you: the first movement should be followed by the Andante, not the Scherzo!! <u>It's better like this!</u>

10/II
Recording
Britten
Violin Concerto op. 15
Mark Lubotsky
Conducted
by the composer

It was this work that made me fall in love with Britten. You find here the incomparable charm of a whole number of musical phrases that are entirely new and original. But you need to listen to it several times to grasp all its qualities. And to think that it's the work of such a young man.

17/II
Recording
Ovchinnikov
***1) Overture to
A Russian Festival***
Conductor: Provatorov
2) 1st Suite
Conductor: Zhuraitis

This foray into Soviet music didn't leave much of an impression on me. All these works by Ovchinnikov left a sugary aftertaste.

---

* In the Russian Orthodox tradition, Christmas is celebrated on 6 January.

Vienna
Recording
Bach
The Well-Tempered
Clavier
Part Two
S.R.

It was at Tbilisi in 1943 that I first learned and played the Second Book of Bach's *Well-Tempered Clavier* – it was a risky undertaking, but I had a sporting chance and so I pulled through: unless I'm much mistaken, I learned it in a month (by heart, I mean). It wasn't until later that I learned the First Book, this time in Moscow.

In Tbilisi I had a lot of help in this 'marathon' from Valentina Konstantinovna Kuftina. She was a very special woman, a pianist who taught at the Tbilisi Conservatory. I first gave *The Well-Tempered Clavier* for a student audience, before playing it in the concert hall (at the same time as the 'Appassionata', which I was also performing for the first time). This was the real beginning of my 'career', not the concerts in New York, as people all over the world believe.

19/III
Budapest
Marionette Theatre
Bartók
The Wooden Prince
The Miraculous
Mandarin
Stravinsky
Petrushka
(recording by
the composer)

The Marionette Theatre in Budapest is a strange set-up – not at all the right place to stage these ballets by Bartók and Stravinsky.

When you see such a worthless staging (I'm thinking here of the production and the choreography), you no longer feel like listening to these magnificent scores (although the recordings are excellent). This evening left me feeling completely depressed, and not even Pavel* was up to reviving my spirits, which isn't like him at all.

As a result, Budapest struck me as deeply unattractive, with its neon signs and frightful hoardings in every colour of the rainbow.

As for the dinner afterwards, everything tasted of paprika.

4/IV
Moscow
Recording
Bach
1st Partita
Dinu Lipatti

In this performance, this partita is really prodigious.

Bach's beauty and charm; a magnificent piano tone and a magnificent pianist!

---

* A Hungarian friend of Richter's, Pál Fejér, was then director of the Hungarian State Opera.

7/IV
Recording
Shostakovich
9th Symphony
Sergey Koussevitzky

What a brilliant performance! I think this is just what is needed in this symphony. Bravo, Koussevitzky!

12/IV
Tchaikovsky Hall
Annie Fischer
Mozart
Sonata in C minor
Schumann
1st Sonata
Beethoven
Sonatas nos. 19 and 23 ('Appassionata')
Chopin
Nocturne in F major op. 15 [no. 1] and Waltz in A flat
Debussy
Mouvements and La cathédrale engloutie

A wonderful musician and pianist, '*die große Dame des Pianoforte[s]*' [the *grande dame* of the piano], with an interesting, if somewhat eclectic, programme. I had quite a lot of reservations about some of her interpretations, which weren't always completely coherent in their freedom, but clearly one can forgive her everything, except the lack of a repeat in the final movement of the 'Appassionata', which sounds skimpy as a result. Then the encores – Chopin, Debussy: I'm not sure if they were really appropriate.

16/IV
Recording
Chopin
Concerto in E minor
Heinrich Neuhaus
Conductor:
Alexander Gauk

Each time I listen to this recording (and I've lost count of the number of times I've heard it), I feel I'm in the presence of an exemplary, living interpretation of Chopin.
An aristocratic reading, in other words, simple and natural.

18/IV
Recording
Bartók
1st Piano Concerto
Zoltán Kocsis
Conductor:
György Lehel

Kocsis is at the very peak of his powers, but the conductor is a very long way behind him, which is a great shame, as everything ought to be a unified whole, with a perfect balance between pianist and orchestra.
The work is original and authentically Bartókian. Should one play it like this, with this semi-rubato? Probably, yes.

22/IV, visit from Annie Fischer *Recordings* **Prokofiev** *5th Concerto* S.R. **Chopin** *1st Ballade* S.R. **Chopin** *E minor Concerto* *Heinrich Neuhaus* **Liszt** *Es muß ein* *Wunderbares sein* *Dietrich Fischer-Dieskau* *Jörg Demus*	It was lovely to have Annie Fischer round here on this beautiful sunny spring day. She immediately expressed a desire to hear some of my recordings (I wasn't expecting her to ask), which she listened to with great curiosity. She was absolutely amazed at Prokofiev's 5th and full of enthusiasm about it (but she clearly hadn't heard it before). She genuinely liked the Chopin Ballade and was equally amazed at it. We then listened to Chopin's 1st Concerto and a song by Liszt with Fischer-Dieskau. She's very direct and, I think, completely lacking in diplomacy, so you can believe her, she tells you everything, looking you straight in the eye. I remember the way in which she – quite rightly – criticized my interpretation of Bach's French Suite in C minor and Mozart's F major Sonata. A pity we meet so rarely (almost never).
29/IV, Easter Day Musical soirée for Easter *Recordings* *1) Bells of Rostov* *2) Rachmaninov* *Vespers op. 37* *Choir conducted* *by Sveshnikov* *3) Rachmaninov* *13 Preludes* *opp. 23 and 32* S.R. *4) Stravinsky* *The Rite of Spring* *Conductor:* *Ernest Ansermet*	This evening our guests are musicians, and the programme starts off as 'Orthodox', then becomes 'profane' and finally 'pagan'. But everything is springlike and authentically Russian, which is entirely appropriate to today's date. 1) <u>The Bells</u> would be better without the commentary, which is extremely off-putting. 2) <u>Vespers</u>. I don't find this sort of thing in the least bit overwhelming. I'm sorry, but I soon start to get bored; it's far too monotonous in style. 3) <u>Rachmaninov</u> is Rachmaninov. 4) As for the pagan <u>Stravinsky</u>, as conducted by Ansermet, you couldn't ask for anything better.
30/IV, Easter Monday *Recording* **Schumann** *Songs from Spanisches* *Liederspiel and Myrthen*	Nina was very insistent that we should listen to these songs in performances by this incomparable artist. Schumann always suits him fantastically well, but this is true of everything he sings. However, it would be better if he didn't sing roles

Dietrich Fischer-Dieskau
and Jörg Demus

such as Macbeth, Rigoletto and Hans Sachs that aren't written for his voice, which is incredibly soft and caressing. It's very dangerous for him.

30/v
Kiev
Palace of Culture
Haydn
'London' Symphony
[no. 104] in D major
Moscow Chamber
Orchestra conducted by
Rudolf Barshai

What pleasure it gave me to renew acquaintance with a work that I played as a youth with Natasha Verbitskaya in an arrangement for four hands. I understand Sergey Prokofiev when he said that his favourite composer was Haydn. I'd happily follow suit, but there are so many other composers that I like as much (more than I can count on the fingers of one hand).

29/vi, Tours
Grange de Meslay
Francis Poulenc
1) Banalités: 5 songs on
poems by Apollinaire
Bernard Kruysen
and Noël Lee
2) Trio for piano, oboe
and bassoon
Bruno Rigutto, Pierre
Pierlot and Paul Hongne
3) Tel jour, telle nuit:
9 songs on poems
by Paul Éluard
Bernard Kruysen
and Noël Lee
*4) Sonata for two piano*s
Gabriel Tacchino
and Bruno Rigutto

This Poulenc recital was extremely interesting, in terms of both the choice of works and the high standard of the performers, all of whom are excellent musicians.
With the exception of the sonata (or concerto) for two pianos, all the works were new to me, and so I got to know lots of new things, most of them charming and elegant, if occasionally not without a touch of sentimentality.
I don't consider Poulenc a particularly great composer, but I understand the love that the French feel for him and am not far from sharing it with them.
Noël Lee and Bruno Rigutto played magnificently. The locals adored them.

30/vi
Grange de Meslay
Jessye Norman, soprano
Irwin Gage, piano
Schubert
4 Lieder
Brahms
4 Lieder

A star! A black woman with a splendid, opulent voice and a deeply imposing appearance.
You'd think she was a giant from legend. You can't help but be struck by her singing, which has an almost infinite dimension to it, and by her total authenticity of emotion. She is generous in expressing this emotion, which she offers, like a present, to the listener. She's phenomenal.

Satie
3 *mélodies from 1916*
Wagner
Wesendonck Lieder
Mahler
Solo from
2nd Symphony

Unfortunately, she suffers (temporarily, no doubt) from a single failing, in that she sometimes has a tendency to sing a little flat, and it's the sort of thing one always notices. Let's hope that she soon resolves this problem.
She has a most enviable understanding of music. Bravo, Jessye Norman.

1/VII
Grange de Meslay
Concert of prizewinners
from the Concours
Marguerite Long–
Jacques Thibaud
Gabriel Fauré
Nocturne no. 6
(as an encore the final movement of Chopin's B flat minor Sonata)
Jacques Taddei
Prokofiev
7th Sonata
(as encores two sonatas by Scarlatti)
Olivier Gardon
Franck
Violin Sonata
Rossudana Gvassalia
Inna Kolegorskaya

As always, this type of concert doesn't remain lodged in your memory for long. The programme is always too varied and the performers too diverse, so there's no thread running through the concert and you forget who the people are. It was the same this evening with these prizewinners from the Concours Long–Thibaud. I don't know if it's tiredness or forgetfulness on my part, but I remember nothing. I hope other listeners were more attentive and that they took away from the concert more than just their own private opinions. In time, they'll no doubt forget those, too. Oblivion is our future, unless it be our past.

7/VII, Grange de Meslay
Handel
Concerti grossi op. 6 nos. 7 and 10
Bach
1) Double Violin Concerto
2) Harpsichord Concerto in D minor
Munich Bach Orchestra
Conductor and harpsichord: Karl Richter

Karl Richter has such a modest air about him and always seems so unsure of himself; he delighted us today with his programme and performance. I like these well-structured, stylistically coherent programmes. There's discipline and real harmony here.
It was an absolute delight.
And at Meslay, beneath these thirteenth-century wooden beams, the music sounds to be in harmony with this wonderful architecture. And those who aren't particularly musical can admire and enjoy this magnificent hall.

15/VIII, Salzburg
Kleines Festspielhaus
Vivaldi
Concerto grosso in
A major [RV 158]
Mozart
Symphony in C major
Conductor:
Riccardo Muti

Riccardo Muti is now a 'star' and conducts almost every year at Salzburg. He has all the qualities a conductor needs: precision, an excellent memory, genuine self-confidence, the ability to communicate with orchestral musicians and splendid gestures; and, of course, he likes power, something which unfortunately can't be avoided by those in a position of authority over a group (even if it's a group of musicians). He's an excellent conductor.

August (at the home
of Gerhard A.)
Innsbruck
Recording of a recital
from Tours
Myaskovsky
Sonata no. 3 in C minor
Shostakovich
Preludes and Fugues
in G minor, B flat and
E flat major
S.R.

Extremely unpleasant visit to some friends of Christian. But I listened to a recording of one of my recitals at Tours with which I'm more or less satisfied. I listened to it on my own, while my friend preferred *zu tratschen* [to gossip] with his hosts; for reasons that escape me, they were falling about laughing at a concert on television given by the old Zarah Leander, who was helped on stage by two young people. It didn't strike me as at all funny.

August
Mitterdorf
Televised broadcast
Marlene Dietrich sings

Marlene is always a pleasant surprise, always one of life's little extras, even here in this village. She's superb, irresistible, and sings with phenomenal taste and talent. What more can one say?

27/IX
Moscow
Recording
Richard Strauss
Sinfonia domestica
Conductor:
Richard Strauss

I love this symphony perhaps more than any other work by Strauss. It's also the one I know best – from my childhood, in fact. It seems to me that most of the conductors who tackle it do so with such a mania for giganticism that its 'domestic' character is lost. It should be conducted in a more unobtrusive, more appealing way. It's difficult to form any idea after only one hearing; the composer is clearly in total control and does everything right; yet I'm still uncertain. A complicated situation.

30/IX
Warsaw
Warsaw Philharmonic

I've always been impressed by Lutosławski as a composer, quite apart from the fact that he's utterly charming as a person. The works included in the

Witold Lutosławski
1) Preludes and Fugue
for 13 Strings
2) Cello Concerto
Conducted by the
composer

present programme merely served to confirm my feelings towards him. But . . . it's really not enough to hear such new music only once!

14/x
Moscow
Incomplete recording of
a recital in Budapest
Wolf
Mörike Lieder
Dietrich Fischer-Dieskau
and S.R. (6/X)

With Wolf, things went much better than with Brahms's *Schöne Magelone*. We managed to establish an excellent rapport and both of us enjoyed performing these works. Of course, these Mörike settings themselves helped; it's not even worth discussing them. Everything is so clear.

19/x
Recording
Schubert
Sonata in C minor
Impromptu in A flat
major op. 142 no. 2
S.R.

Here, finally, is a recording with which I'm fully satisfied (from start to finish). Perhaps only the tempo of the final movement of the Sonata is slightly on the fast side. But what's really good is the Impromptu.

19/x
Recording
Beethoven
Fidelio
Conductor:
Lorin Maazel
22/x
Fidelio
Conductor:
Herbert von Karajan
24/x
Fidelio
Conductor:
Wilhelm Furtwängler

Fidelio, in an ascending curve. All three recordings are good and are of great interest to the listener. There's absolutely nothing that one can criticize. But, like it or not, listening to the same work three times in this way clearly provides enough material for criticism. In the first place, it really allows you to appreciate the merits of this opera and to understand it – this 'difficult' masterpiece – and each exposure to it draws us more deeply into Beethoven's soul, as do these three extremely different interpretations by these very different artists. In this way, one can examine the work from every angle, as if through a prism (Chekhov's *The Proposal*). But it is the third interpretation that wins the day, this is actually always the case with this great conductor. Indeed, it's difficult at present to see to whom he may have handed on the torch. Perhaps he never did so.

We spent three extraordinary evenings in the company of Beethoven's inspired work.

Recording of a sonata recital with David Oistrakh in the Grand Hall of the Conservatory
Brahms
2nd Sonata in A major
Bartók
1st Sonata
Prokofiev
1st Sonata in F minor

Here I am again in Stankevicha Ulitsa in the company of Buneyeva and Veprintsev. A real pleasure. I think there are some successful things in the Prokofiev Sonata.
And the Brahms isn't irremediably bad, either.
The Bartók is less good, but we'll try to get something out of it.

13/XI
Recording
Bellini
Norma
Maria Callas
Conductor:
Tullio Serafin

What's the point in commenting on Maria Callas? She's a unique phenomenon in art that can never be reproduced. She's movement itself, imperious and peremptory. She's perfection.
'Opinions differ,' said a woman from Warsaw.

22/XI
Benjamin Britten's
60th birthday
Recording
Britten
Peter Grimes
Conductor: Britten

This was the first opera – and the first piece in general – that I heard by Britten. It was in Budapest. I was immediately ensnared by it. Right away I felt that, if I'd been a composer myself, this is how I'd have written. I became a fervent admirer of Britten's music and have remained so ever since.

2/XI
Recording
Beethoven
'Eroica' Symphony
Conductor:
Rudolf Barshai

A fine and powerful performance of this work by Barshai, and one that gives the lie to the usual view that he's incapable of conducting anything other than chamber music. I was delighted to discover this, as I've always thought very highly of a musician whom I've known since my days at the Conservatory.

3 1/XII, New Year's Eve
Recording
Mozart
Don Giovanni
Conductor:
Carlo Maria Giulini

To mark the New Year, it was Mozart this time (rather than our usual Bach), in the form of what is undoubtedly his most important and coruscating work (though one shouldn't forget *Die Zauberflöte* and *Idomeneo*). Here Mozart shows us the punishment visited on the insane libertine and the way everyone delights in his downfall. The work is devoid of all human sentiment; you could almost say that it's a cold work and that ultimately we are fairly indifferent to the 'sufferings' of the monster's victims, whereas he himself . . . oh no! <u>he's</u> not a matter of indifference to us! We even like him! (How amoral!)

It's very hard to define ourselves by reference to the opera's plot. But with the music, everything falls into place; it's enough for us to hear even the first few bars to fall under Mozart's spell and to succumb to the dissolute Don Giovanni and, indeed, to all the characters. Life and blood runs through all his veins, here the wine really sparkles, here are all the vices of the world, and everywhere there's an astonishing beauty!

Giulini's recording is splendid, but here you really need the flesh-and-blood theatre, with its scenery and performers in Spanish costumes. This is an integral part of the piece. That's how it was conceived by Wolfgang Amadeus, the precursor of our own Alexander Sergeyevich.*

1/I
New Year visit from
the Snezhnitskys
Recording
Beethoven
1st Symphony
in C major
Conductor:
Wilhelm Furtwängler

F major?!
No! C major . . .
From the very outset there's a sense of surprise – luminous, welcoming, self-confident . . .
And Beethoven? What sort of a mood was he in when he conceived this symphony, this gift to humanity?

* Pushkin.

2/1
Recording
Beethoven
Sonata op. 106
(Hammerklavier)
Artur Schnabel

No, you should never trust metronome markings. As proof, here is Schnabel's recording of the Hammerklavier: it's totally unacceptable, absolutely impossible to listen to.

3/1
In memory of
Shereshevsky
Recordings
Schubert
Sonata in B flat major
op. post.
S.R.
Wagner
Dutchman's monologue
from Der fliegende
Holländer
Dietrich Fischer-Dieskau
Conductor:
Franz Konwitschny
Brahms
3rd Symphony
(live recording)
Conductor:
Wilhelm Furtwängler

I'd invited round the well-known critic, David Rabinovich, who's very knowledgeable about music and who was very close to Rusya Shereshevsky. I think this was our last meeting; so fate decreed. He spoke a lot this particular evening (no doubt a little too much), as most music critics do, and in the process gave a rather prosaic touch to the evening. But I think he must have been pleased with it and with the fact that he'd been invited.

Schubert. I think this recording is a success, even if the 2nd movement could have been better.

Fischer-Dieskau. Phenomenal in the monologue from *Der fliegende Holländer*.

Brahms and Furtwängler. Could one wish for anything better?

Over the years Brahms's symphonies have become increasingly popular and well-loved. Perhaps they'll even become as popular as Tchaikovsky's. Things ripen little by little without your expecting it.

4/1
Recording
Penderecki
St Luke Passion

A highly theatrical but effective work. I don't hear any great depth in it. It has been immensely successful with its audiences, but will it remain so? An accessible and slightly unsophisticated piece.

6/1, Russian Christmas
Recording
Bach
Brandenburg Concertos
nos. 1 and 2
Conductor:
Helmut Koch

Two absolute masterpieces (above all the 1st). Enchantment and exultation.
All one can do is kneel before the art of music and before Johann Sebastian Bach.

11/I
Grand Hall of the
Conservatory
Mozart
Violin Sonata no. 33
*in F major**
Schumann
Violin Sonata no. 1
in A minor
Oleg Kagan
Elisabeth Leonskaja

These two artists delighted us with two rarely
performed works that are so very different from
one another.
The interesting thing is that one is struck by the
essentially feminine character of the violin and the
masculine character of the piano, which corre-
sponds perfectly to the very essence of these
instruments. It also reflected the character of the
two musicians and gave their partnership a natural
and harmonious unity.
Thank you, Oleg! Thank you, Lisa!

21/I
Recordings
Wagner
Der fliegende Holländer
Conductor:
Ferenc Fricsay
22/I
Der fliegende Holländer
Conductor:
Franz Konwitschny

Two days devoted to Wagner's oceanic *Flying
Dutchman*.
The wonderful Hungarian conductor Ferenc Fricsay,
who died prematurely, was already familiar to me
from his splendid recording of *Die Zauberflöte*.
He's not quite as successful in the Wagner, especially
if you compare his recording with Konwitschny's,
which deserves nothing but praise and produces
in the listener the effect of a veritable maritime
tempest.
As the Dutchman, Fischer-Dieskau scales dizzying
heights (in his first monologue). In the third act,
the altercation between the two crews creates such
an atmosphere of terror (mercifully they don't sing
right into the microphone – an absolutely hideous
effect – as they do with Fricsay) that it's impossible
to remain indifferent. Everything about this
recording is entirely worthy of Wagner. The conductor is temperamentally on the same wave-
length as the composer.

1/II
Playthrough of our
recording with David
Oistrakh in the studios
in Stankevicha Ulitsa
Brahms
Sonata in A major

I'm pleased that this recording has finally seen the
light of day (we had to make quite a lot of correc-
tions to the 2nd and 4th movements of the
Prokofiev to achieve a good balance, but it seems
we've got the desired effect).
Bartók. This could, of course, have been better.
We haven't lived with this sonata for a long enough

---

* No. 33 is in E flat; nos. 8, 15, 24, 25 and 36 are in F.

Prokofiev	period of time.
Sonata in F minor	<u>Brahms</u>. I think listeners may like this.
Bartók	
1st Sonata	
David Oistrakh and S.R.	

February	(Listened to it four times in succession)
Recording	I followed the enthusiastic advice of the performers
Butsko	and of Ninoshka and listened to this work with an
White Nights	open mind. Certainly, everything is in place, there's
Galina Pisarenko	a Dostoyevskian sense of humour, it's magnificently
Anatol Mishchevsky	sung and I even liked the bells . . . But then came
Conductor: Gennady	the fatal question: is this opera really necessary?*
Rozhdestvensky	

February	Extremely enjoyable and convivial evening at the
Dinner at the Oistrakhs'	Oistrakhs', in the course of which we listened to
Recording	this work, which Beethoven twice revised.
Beethoven	I think it's infinitely better suited to the violin, and
Piano Concerto in	so I turned down their suggestion that I should
D major (Beethoven's	play it myself.
own transcription of	The performance by Vederzinke and Masur is cor-
his Violin Concerto)	rect and precise, but there's no sense of freshness.
Amadeus Vederzinke	Nothing to get carried away by.
Conductor: Kurt Masur	

25/II	I got to know the composer in the south, at
Recording	Dubrovnik, if I recall correctly. We dined together
Penderecki	in the shade of some vine leaves, and the man proved
St Luke Passion	to be extraordinarily sympathetic and full of inter-
	esting plans concerning orthodox religious music.
	How sad that his music doesn't speak to my soul . . .

1/III	This concerto is almost as profoundly original as
Recording	the 2nd, and Kocsis's reading of it is a model of
Bartók	textual fidelity. It seems to me that this pianist is
1st Piano Concerto	by no means as well known as he ought to be and
Zoltán Kocsis	that he doesn't yet have the impact he deserves
Conductor:	among international audiences. The conductor,
György Lehel	for his part, is mediocre.

* Based on Dostoyevsky's novel, Yury Markovich Butsko's *White Nights* was broadcast on Russian radio before receiving its stage première in Dresden on 15 September 1973.

3/III
Peredelkino (blinis at
Stanislas Neuhaus's)
Recording
Bartók
2nd Piano Concerto
Zoltán Kocsis
Conductor:
György Lehel

Zoltán Kocsis plays superbly in every respect, exactly as he should and as I feel it should be. But the conductor comes nowhere near scaling these heights, which detracts terribly from the merits of this recording.

6/III
Recording
Chopin
12 Studies op. 10
Dezsö Ránki

Extraordinary skill and virtuosity, a real thorough-bred. How easy these young pianists make it all sound! It's only later, once they are in thrall to their profession, that things start to get more complicated for them.

10/III
(following a walk to the Donskoy Monastery)
Recording
Chopin
Two Studies op. 10
nos. 11 and 12
Nocturne op. 9 no. 3
First and Second
Ballades
Dezsö Ránki

There's absolutely no doubt that Ránki possesses a real talent and genuine musicality. He's less spectacular than Kocsis, but this is simply a matter of time. As a person, he's adorable, in complete contrast to Kocsis, who is as wild and temperamental as a child.

12/III
Recording
Penderecki
St Luke Passion

I've now listened to this work three times, and I like it less each time. These obsessive cries are terribly theatrical. I see in them only affectation and empty rhetoric. We're a thousand leagues from the sincerity of the Glagolitic Mass. A disappointment.

7/IV
Vienna State Opera
Richard Strauss
Salome
Leonie Rysanek
Conductor: Horst Stein

A beautiful and traditional production in Klimt's original sets, which, in my view, are really quite successful.* Everything is there, except the feeling of horror that's so characteristic of this work and that one barely notices in this performance. Stein's conducting is assured and fairly convincing and tempestuous, but where's the depravity?

*The designs were by Jürgen Rose, albeit inspired by Klimt.

Rysanek is brilliant from start to finish (even the 'dance' is a complete success). In short, a first-rate show. The audience went wild (because of Rysanek). But there's a certain old-fashioned routine lurking behind these sets.

22/v
Tokyo
Recital
Galina Pisarenko
**Handel, Purcell,
Beethoven, Schubert,
Tchaikovsky,
Mussorgsky**

Great success for Galina's recital in Tokyo. Programme a bit too varied but a pleasure to listen to. Everything's well balanced and correctly weighted. Moreover, Galina is always easy on the eye, which is clearly important. The appearance of a soprano is decisive, on condition – of course – that she sings well.
The Japanese appreciated all these qualities. And there's another one: her magnificent diction.

9/VI
La Scala on tour
at the Bolshoy
Verdi
Simon Boccanegra
*Conductor:
Claudio Abbado*

A magnificent performance in every respect. Abbado's conducting was assured and spirited. Of the singers, Freni and Cappuccilli were absolutely splendid. The amazing cohesiveness of chorus and orchestra resulted in a real sense of ensemble. The production* doesn't give itself airs and graces and derives from a fine tradition that isn't yet dead. The opera itself is musically superb, and even though it's long, you never feel tired.
I've rarely attended an opera performance as good as this; it gave me tremendous pleasure.

17/VI
Live recording
Shostakovich
***Six Romances on Verses
by Marina Tsvetayeva***
*Irina Bogachova
Conductor:
Rudolf Barshai*

I really detest the Tsvetayeva cycle. I loathe this kind of tension, this tendentious grandiloquence and, finally, this music which, even if it clearly bears the hallmarks of a composer of genius, irritates me beyond measure.

19/VI
Stockhausen
Hymnen

'*Viel Lärm um nichts*' [Much ado about nothing]. A long, noisy, eccentric piece (I think it even includes a saw among other things).

---

*By Giorgio Strehler.

As a person, Stockhausen creates a sympathetic impression.

August Munich *Recording coming from* *next door's apartment* **Puccini** *Turandot*	Each evening someone next door puts on this opera – every note of which I already know – at full volume. It's a sort of leitmotif accompanying our return home. It's almost always the final scene, in which Turandot attempts to solve the riddle to the sound of off-stage trumpets.
Paris **Wagner** *Piece in A flat* *('Schmachtend')* * *(in Visconti's film* *Ludwig)*	The first time I heard this little piece I was completely thrown by it, of course. Later I've often played it as an encore. Audiences, who, as it happens, can be fairly stupid, have invariably thought that it was by Scriabin, or at least something Russian.
Nino Rota *Soundtrack to* *Fellini's Amarcord*	What talent! So much lightness and charm in the writing! What a shame this composer felt he had to restrict himself to trifles.
November (at Dorothy's) Milan *Recording* **Glazunov** **Piano Concerto** **in F minor** *S.R. and* *Kyrill Kondrashin*	I played my recording for the Baroness;[†] she was clearly impressed above all by the second movement, which is not unlike a ballet score. Having been a ballet dancer in the past, she even started to wave her arms around in time to the music. I find this recording quite successful, and I like this concerto, the musical material of which is so cleverly developed. I also like it for a sort of noble Russian sentimentality.
Kurt Weill *Die Dreigroschenoper* *Directed by Strehler*	An excellent performance in terms of both music and production. An accomplished, entertaining piece, somewhere between an opera and an operetta and not unlike Krenek's *Jonny spielt auf*, but less interesting. That magnificent artist Milva was first-rate. What

* WWV 93, a thirteen-bar fragment begun in Venice in 1858 and completed in Palermo in 1881.
† Baroness Dorothy Lanni della Quara, the former German ballerina who founded Gioventù Musicale in Italy.

talent! The direction bears many of Strehler's hall-marks.

14/XII *Warsaw Philharmonic* **Mahler** *1st Symphony* **Stravinsky** *Octet* *Conductor:* *Witold Rowicki*	This was in fact my last meeting with Rowicki, with whom I played a concerto in the first half of the programme. In spite of its qualities, the 'Titan' Symphony has never been among my favourites. Rowicki conducted it superbly, and after the concert, once the audience had left, he repeated the Octet specially for me – I'd not been able to hear it earlier as it had been performed before the concerto. This time he didn't conduct but just sat to one side on the steps leading up to the stage. It was a wonderful present for me. The musicians played it impeccably. Things then took a terribly dissolute turn, as we went off to celebrate with the performers of the Octet, and the vodka had its usual effect, so that I no longer remember how I got back to my room in the Europa Hotel.
22/XII and 23/XII Moscow *Recording* **Hans Pfitzner** *Palestrina* *Nicolai Gedda* *Dietrich Fischer-Dieskau* *Conductor:* *Rafael Kubelik*	Long ago in Odessa, I was given the vocal score of this remarkable opera for my birthday (Papa went to some lengths to get hold of a copy of the score through the German Consulate, where he gave music lessons to the children of the consul, Paul Roth) and I then studied it in depth and fell in love with it. Pfitzner picks up and continues the tradition laid down by Wagner. The – splendid – libretto is by the composer himself, and the music is both austere, original and extremely profound.
24/XII Christmas Eve with candles lit on Christmas tree *Recording* **Bach** *5th Brandenburg* *Concerto* *Conductor:* *Helmut Koch*	For me, the 5th Brandenburg Concerto is obviously the most seductive of the lot (for the simple reason that I can join in), even if I consider the 3rd to be more perfect. But I prefer the 5th. It's impossible not to like it.

1/1
New Year celebrations
Recording
Mozart
Exsultate, jubilate
Elisabeth Schwarzkopf
Conductor:
Walter Susskind
Nino Rota
Amarcord
Johann Strauß
Auf der Jagd (Polka)
Conductor:
Willi Boskovsky

Traditional New Year party. How many have we had so far . . .

The musical programme is intended to impose a certain discipline on our guests: after all, it's not enough to gossip, drink wine and celebrate after wishing each other a Happy New Year and listening to the bells in Red Square.

And so here is Elisabeth, as magnificent as ever, at the very peak of her powers. She's followed by *Amarcord* and Johann Strauß, so that things don't get too serious. Let's hope that this year will be happier than the last one. Who knows . . .

February
Cologne
Recording made
in Monte Carlo
Schumann
Concerto in A minor
Grieg
Concerto in A minor
S.R.
Conductor:
Lovro von Matačić

I've been waiting for this recording for a long time. It's the second time I've recorded the Schumann (the first time was with Rowicki). Unfortunately, I'm not completely satisfied with this one either, even though it's my favourite concerto. I can't quite put my finger on exactly what's missing, but, whatever it is, it's something essential, something poetical . . .

The Grieg, by contrast, has my full approval.

March
Innsbruck
Recording
(Salzburg Easter Festival)
Ravel
Boléro
Conductor:
Herbert von Karajan

Once again, this magical work, with its endless and bewitching repetitions of the theme and the totally unexpected modulation at the end. A miracle remains a miracle!

June
Glyndebourne
Stravinsky
The Rake's Progress
Conductor:
Bernard Haitink

Even in itself, the journey to Glyndebourne was worth the effort. Somewhere out in the country, Nina and I took our seats on board a coach, a special luxury coach, and set about studying our travelling companions.

Here's snobbery for you! The women in decadent

dresses accompanied by their little dogs, a handsome young man in a dazzling white suit, whose anxious winks already revealed that he was in search of some amorous adventure, some delightful young ladies who offered us champagne and, finally, a famous 'stopping for pissing' [in English in the original], in the course of which several of our company, including our fair-haired fop, elegantly relieved themselves along the side of the coach, alternating with the little doggies and the ladies, before we could continue on our way.

When we reached Glyndebourne, with its wonderful gardens, everyone got out their picnic baskets. The lilac was in flower, and the lawns freshly mown. The watchword is pleasure. Finally, it was time for the opera. It was conducted by Haitink, who is completely unsuited to Stravinsky, so the whole spirit of the work was lost. Conversely, the sets and costumes by David Hockney were brilliant. Impossible to wish for anything better.

The singers, especially the heroine (whose principal aria was cut as a favour to her), were not really convincing; they were too cold and externalized. But I have the impression that this is the general style here. The important thing is that it should be a pleasant way of passing the time. I really didn't like that.

June
(on the radio while driving to Dover in Lilian Hochhauser's car)
Mendelssohn
Scherzo and Finale from Octet in E flat
Performers include Heifetz and Piatigorsky

Heading towards Dover with the music of Mendelssohn. As always with Mendelssohn, there's a sort of Mozartian perfection that puts you in a positive, whimsical frame of mind.

But it's dangerous to allow yourself to be too carried away by this kind of relaxation, as if that went without saying. To tell the truth, I think one should try to resist it as we're not dealing here with a pleasure that's the simple result of a gift, but with an intense intellectual effort on the part of a musician of genius. This is something that needs to be taken into account and fully understood.

3/VI Prague USSR Embassy Club Concert by artists from the Bolshoy *Yury Mazurok* **Songs by Dolukhanian** **('I'm a citizen of the** **Soviet Union'),** **Rubinstein,** **Rachmaninov, etc.** *Tamara Milashkina* **Songs by Rubinstein,** **Rachmaninov, etc.** *Vladimir Atlantov* **Songs by Tchaikovsky**	Strewth! This concert proved how painful singing can be – not through lack of a voice, but because of the frightful execution. <u>Mazurok</u>. He has a voice and can sing quite decently, but he is so physically off-putting (he is quite unbelievably smug – I'm tempted to see it as a symptom of 'bureaucratism'). Was this a concert or a Party meeting? A total absence of feeling . . . <u>Milashkina</u>. She simply sings out of tune – to such an extent that it's difficult to know what notes she's actually singing. <u>Atlantov</u>. This is better. A fine voice, and a traditional, if ordinary, delivery (as with all tenors).
June Snape **Britten** *Death in Venice*	I attended two performances. Poor Britten, terribly ill, hunched up in his box, but apparently pleased with the performance. Peter Pears, in the role of the professor, is dignified and stern; his singing and acting are both admirable, and it's on him that the whole performance rests. Mercifully, Tadzio (a young lad from the *corps de ballet*) isn't annoying. The opera is long and difficult and, it seems to me, not easy to stage. In my own view, the production is a total disaster. Everything seems unreal, and there isn't the least sense that we're in Venice. The children's ballet reminds us of a physical education class in a kindergarten, with no feeling of aesthetics or poetry. It should have been possible to take greater advantage of the music and create a more evocative staging, but it's easy to say this . . . Unfortunately, the result doesn't match up to my own vision of the work (as judged by Britten's music). What I saw was pseudo-realistic, unwieldy and hard to grasp. But, when all's said and done, Ben liked it.
June London Covent Garden	My first *Frau*. Highly impressive! Some people say it's a 20th-century imitation of *Die Zauberflöte*.

Richard Strauss
Die Frau ohne Schatten
Heather Harper
Helga Dernesch
Conductor: Georg Solti

Strauss wallows in an ocean of music – his own – and you have to admit that there's an awful lot of water. But there are also some islands (the scene with the Emperor, the Voice of the Falcon). I can't say I'm wild about the opera, which is fairly wordy and a bit strained in its gigantism. No, it's not Strauss at his best; here he seems overblown and indulges himself in a way that's a little too garish and hollow. In my view, Hofmannsthal's libretto suffers from the same shortcomings.

Even so, it's a piece that can stand on its own and that on this occasion received a magisterial performance.

26/VI, Tours
Grange de Meslay
Recital by Arturo
Benedetti Michelangeli
Beethoven
Sonata in A flat major
op. 26
Schubert
Sonata in A minor D 537
Debussy
Images
1) Cloches à travers les
feuilles
2) Hommage à Rameau
3) Reflets dans l'eau
Chopin
Sonata in B flat minor
Ravel
Le gibet

As always, beyond reproach. The notes exactly as written. Technically perfect. But it all remains glacial.

Beethoven. The Trio in the Funeral March is so formal and dry that you'd think it were a comic turn (rather than an artillery salvo).

Schubert. I liked this. The score was reproduced exactly.

Debussy. No objection. No impression.

Chopin. The Funeral March and above all the Trio were played with a degree of insight that was nothing short of inspired. Of the concert as a whole, this was by far the best.

Ravel. Same as Debussy.

A superb concert. But one doesn't sense any love of the music.

27/VI
Beaux Arts Trio
Isidore Cohen
Bernard Greenhouse
Menahem Pressler
Beethoven
Trio op. 1 no. 1

A magnificent programme! Whenever these artists perform, it's a real artistic event.

Pressler is particularly close to me as a musician. He captivates with his sincerity and, it seems to me, the music gives him immoderate pleasure. For him, giving a concert is a source of genuine happiness, and for this I envy him enormously.

For me, it was a sheer delight to hear the Ravel

Ravel
Trio in A minor
Schumann
Trio no. 1 in D minor
Dvořák
'Dumky' Trio

(how I'd like to play this work!). The Beethoven and Schumann also left a deep impression on me. When I asked young Kocsis whether he'd enjoyed it, he started to laugh without the least attempt at pretence; he'd clearly not liked it (he's not averse to this – it's a question of character). Pavel Fejér had already warned me about Zoltán's independent views.

28/VI
Grange de la Besnardière
Janáček
1) In the Mists for piano (1912)
2) Capriccio for piano left hand and eight wind instruments (1926)
Josef Páleníček and soloists from the Czech Philharmonic

I've known Páleníček for many years; hearing him play *In the Mists*, I was struck by the originality of this cycle. I'd very much like to play it myself.
This was the first time I'd heard the *Capriccio*. The work is scored for most unusual forces. Whatever he tackles, Janáček remains Janáček, unique in his way.
A highly successful concert.

29/VI
Bach
Goldberg Variations
Zuzana Růžičková, harpsichord

This is the first time I've heard Bach's monumental work on a harpsichord. I heard Gould play it in the concert hall, and have also listened to his recording. Some day I'd like to play it myself – if ever I manage to master it.
The harpsichordist, who is from Prague, played it with integrity and, thank God, with all the repeats (without them, you may as well not play it at all). For me, it's unusual to listen to a whole recital on a harpsichord; it takes some getting used to, but it sounds magnificent.

29/VI
Meslay
Irina Arkhipova
Igor Guselnikov
Mussorgsky
Marfa's Aria from Khovanshchina
Gopak

Irina Arkhipova is now the greatest Russian singer of our day. She has everything it takes to assume this mantle: voice, force of personality, musicality, artistry, refinement, polish and authenticity of execution. Her recital was a great success and a real lesson.
The French audience clearly had no idea of this singer's existence and gave her a resounding ovation.

Songs and Dances of Death
Glinka
5 Songs
Tchaikovsky
5 Songs

Personally, I didn't much care for her interpretation of the 'Lullaby' from the *Dances of Death*, in which she used an excessive amount of *secco* in Death's replies (but, after all, this is an unimportant detail).

Igor Guselnikov was an excellent and sensitive accompanist. I'd never heard him on stage before, and so it was a pleasant surprise for me.

Outwardly, Arkhipova is unsympathetic: you feel the whole weight of her forceful personality. Julia Ganeva said to me afterwards, with a note of sadness in her voice: 'What a great and wicked heart she must have.'

3/VII
Meslay
Recital by Zoltán Kocsis
Brahms
Intermezzo in A minor op. 76 [no. 7]
Bach
3 Preludes and Fugues from Part One of The Well-Tempered Clavier
Mozart
Fantasia in C minor and Sonata in A major
Beethoven
Sonatas op. 2 no. 1 and op. 110
Bartók
Excerpts from the Suite 'For Children'
Chopin
Waltz in C sharp minor
Bach
Prelude and Fugue in B flat minor from Part One
Brahms
Intermezzo in E flat major op. 117 [no. 1]

A fine recital. A serious musician, one of the most talented young pianists of our age. Not in the least narcissistic or affected and with no fanatical desire to prove himself wildly successful (all these things would have been possible in view of the fact that he's so foul-tempered and moody in real life).

There was nothing about his performance that I would criticize, except that in the op. 110 he took my own interpretation as his model, an interpretation in which I have difficulty recognizing myself. He was clearly a little put out when I told him this.

What was absolutely fantastic was Chopin's terribly hackneyed Waltz. He played it as an encore, while announcing that he was dedicating his encore to me. The other encores were likewise dedicated to musicians – Boulez and someone else. I really like this rather unusual habit of treating encores as personal presents.

4/VII
Meslay
*Ensemble Musique
Vivante under the direction of Pierre Boulez*
Brahms
*Serenade no. 2
in A major*
Wagner
Siegfried Idyll
Berg
*Chamber Concerto
for piano, violin and
13 wind instruments*
*Christoph Eschenbach
(piano)*
*Saschko Gawriloff
(violin)*

Boulez's translucent, concentrated and scrupulous reading of the Brahms Serenade was a real musical treat.

The Wagner was a little lacking in imagination.

As for the Berg, it left a very deep impression on me. I was bowled over by the breadth of this extraordinarily complex work, by its unusual colours, its construction and all these things put together, even if I didn't understand or accept everything (at the time, the work struck me as fairly strange).

Boulez conducted it masterfully, although I'll never forgive him for performing the final section without its da capo.

Eschenbach played magnificently, bringing considerable weight to the work merely by dint of his impressive artistic presence.

5/VII
Meslay
*Ensemble Musique
Vivante and Stuttgart
Schola Cantorum under
the direction of
Pierre Boulez*
Schubert
*1) Nachtgesang im
Walde*
2) Hymne
*3) Gesang der Geister
über den Wassern*
Stravinsky
*Symphonies of Wind
Instruments (in memory
of Debussy)*
Berio
*Laborintus II
for narrator, 3 voices,
tape and instrumental
and vocal ensemble*
Narrator: Luciano Berio

Boulez introduces audiences to interesting programmes made up of little-known works. This is one of his great qualities.

This was the first time I'd heard these pieces by Schubert – and in such fine performances! How many of these forgotten works are there?

I've always liked Stravinsky's Symphonies, with their 'strange chord' constantly repeated.

Again, Berio's work left an excellent impression. He's one of the most interesting of contemporary composers. The work in question is <u>naturally</u> extremely complex.

I went to congratulate him after the concert, as I wanted to get to know him; we'd scarcely met before he exclaimed: 'My hearty congratulations, you're a remarkable painter. I've admired one of your pastels at Lorin Maazel's.'

6/VII
Grange de la Besnardière
Janáček
*The Diary of One Who
Disappeared (1917)*
Robert Tear
Philip Ledger
Hanna Aurbacher
*Women's Voices of the
Stuttgart Schola
Cantorum*
Mozart
*Serenade for 13 wind
instruments K 361*
Ensemble Musique
Vivante
Conductor
Pierre Boulez

A most unusual and interesting work. As so often with Janáček, the opening bars sound naïve and unsophisticated. But it's precisely these qualities that are later refracted in all that's most valuable and interesting in this music. It's as though you'd bathed in the spring where the water is purest and which then allows you to understand everything. A compelling and penetrating performance. I'd very much like to be able to hear this remarkably original vocal cycle again.

Under Boulez, the Mozart was played to perfection and provided a delightful conclusion to this musical matinée at the Grange de la Besnardière. The cars parked in the green field then set off in their various directions, with everyone heading off for lunch.

The atmosphere was excellent, as was the weather.

6/VII
Meslay
Schoenberg
*Chamber Symphony
no. 1 op. 9*
Webern
*1) 5 Pieces op. 10
2) Entflieht auf leichten
Kähnen op. 2
3) Das Augenlicht op. 26*
Boulez
*cummings ist der
Dichter (1970)*
Stravinsky
Les noces
Ensemble Musique
Vivante
Stuttgart Schola
Cantorum
Conductor
Pierre Boulez

Schoenberg's Symphony isn't one of my favourite works, although I wouldn't deny that it has tremendous qualities from a musical point of view. It is stuffed full of typically Viennese elements – but is that really so surprising?

Webern attracts me, though there's a lot that I don't understand. His music is a combination of purity, complexity and abstraction in the very best sense of the term.

I was enormously taken by Boulez's piece, with its strange and innovative character.

To tell the truth, the Stravinsky, which I already knew, struck me as curiously monotonous and left me feeling bored and impatient. I think the problem is that *Les noces* should be staged as a ballet. When performed in the concert hall, the music isn't in the least convincing.

July Monte Carlo Opéra de Monte-Carlo *Recital by* *Artur Rubinstein* **Chopin** *Sonata in B flat minor,* *Nocturne, Scherzo,* *Barcarolle, Polonaise* **Debussy** *1st movement from* *Suite: Pour le piano*	Artur Rubinstein continues to play at an age when most pianists have long since stopped playing. It's quite an event! A whole host of pianists, musicians and conductors (including Maazel) having taken their seats in the auditorium of the Opéra de Monte-Carlo, Artur comes out on stage and, with incredible assurance, gets through all the works in the gala programme. Of course, there's no longer much freshness to it, but the technique remains flawless. Success and gratitude. I went backstage to congratulate him.
July *Listening to recordings* **Bartók** *15 Hungarian Peasant* *Songs* *S.R.* *Violin Sonata no. 1* *David Oistrakh and S.R.* *Eurodisc jubilee* *recording* **Tchaikovsky** *Excerpt from* *1st movement of* *1st Piano Concerto* *S.R. and Mravinsky* **Tchaikovsky** *Excerpts from* *The Nutcracker* *Gennady* *Rozhdestvensky* **Richard Strauss** *Till Eulenspiegel* *Franz Konwitschny*	The Bartók recording has its good points, but it's not beyond reproach. Whatever one might say, it remains a fact that we didn't get far enough inside the work. The most disappointing aspect is the final section, where the listener doesn't really manage to grasp the fundamental key (F sharp), because I didn't properly underline the modulation in the bass. As a result, the piece has no real ending. The jubilee recording: what a Russian salad; impossible to take this kind of thing seriously! Even so, the performance of *Till* is phenomenal (but it's true that it's <u>Konwitschny</u>).
7/ix *Recording* **Bach** *The Well-Tempered* *Clavier*	Unlike Part One, which is fairly successful, this recording of Part Two is riddled with mistakes, above all – unfortunately – in the most important preludes and fugues, such as those in F sharp minor and B flat minor (the latter I consider the

Part Two S.R.	most extraordinary of all, a piece that yields in nothing to the B minor from Part One). Unfortunately, it hasn't produced the results I'd been hoping for.
27/IX Nemirovich-Danchenko Theatre **Pergolesi** *La serva padrona* *Galina Pisarenko* *Leonid Boldin* **Offenbach** *Le mari à la porte* *(operetta)*	Not for me! I've never understood the 'charm' of Pergolesi's piece, neither when it was given at the Conservatory with the lisping Revliakina, nor today with Galya. I see nothing funny in this imbecilic opera, either in the subject matter or in the music, the only effect of which is to put me in a foul temper. Offenbach. A work of staggering banality. I'd scarcely stepped outside the theatre than all trace of this performance had been wiped from my memory.
8/X Musical gathering at home *Recording* **Pierre Boulez** *Le marteau sans maître* *1) Conductor:* *Robert Craft* *2) Conductor:* *Pierre Boulez*	We listened to this work twice in two different interpretations in a final attempt to understand it, something which – as I knew from previous experience – is difficult in the extreme. The first interpretation clearly isn't that . . . The second is by the composer, so here caution is in order. I think the evening was instructive. Some of those present expressed an apparently complete understanding and even an appreciation of the work. None the less, the question – and it's by no means an insignificant one – remains unanswered.
11/X Kirov Theatre **Andrey Petrov** *Peter I* *Conductor:* *Yuri Temirkanov*	It's a long time since I've seen or heard such trash. A badly finished piece halfway between an operetta and a musical comedy. Stylistically, the music is so eclectic that it's impossible to speak of any style at all but only of bits and pieces stuck end to end. As for the staging, whatever is going on? Some sort of 'historical' ramblings utterly devoid of any talent. And, to cap it all, we had to go there because one of Ninoshka's pupils, Lessi N., was playing the part of a harpy.

12/X
Grand Hall of the
Conservatory
(concert in memory
of Shostakovich)
Shostakovich
Suite on Verses by
Michelangelo op. 145
(orchestral version)
Evgeny Nesterenko, bass
Conductor:
Maxim Shostakovich

This magnificent work was magnificently performed by Nesterenko under the direction of
Maxim Shostakovich. A major event in Moscow's
musical life.

Maxim Shostakovich has a true understanding of
the spirit of his father's music. Nesterenko is at the
height of his well-deserved reputation.

I was deeply impressed, as was the whole of
Moscow's musical intelligentsia.

14/X
In memory of
Sofya Peltsova
Dvořák
Stabat mater
Conductor
Václav Talich
Mendelssohn
Venezianisches
Gondellied
in F sharp minor
Schumann
Papillons op. 2
S.R.

The *Stabat mater* is a masterpiece. It was a real
treat to hear it under Talich's direction. With
Karel's help, we prepared a large number of
photographs, attractively assembled, and these we
passed round, commenting on them for the bene-
fit of our guests.

I then played Mendelssohn's *Venezianisches Gondellied* in F sharp minor, then my Schumann recording,
of which Sofya was so fond. The score is covered
in signatures of Sofya's friends (for her it was a
relic). It, too, was passed round. A melancholy
evening.

15/X
German Consulate
Stuttgart Chamber
Orchestra
Vivaldi
Concerto grosso
op. 3 no. 11
Handel
Musette from Concerto
grosso op. 6 no. 6
Grieg
Holberg Suite
Gluck
Chaconne from

I loathe these concerts organized by politicians.
All these empty phrases about 'culture bringing
nations together' and 'music contributing to international understanding' and so on are coquetries
that don't ring true. That's why I avoid these official gatherings like the plague.

This time the conductor was Münchinger, with
whom I once – and very badly – played Mozart's
Concerto no. 22 at Aix-en-Provence. We were
both pleased to see each other again.

I listened to the concert patiently, but with no
great pleasure. The reason, of course, was the
place, the setting and the politics, all of which
have a negative effect on me. Amen.

Paride ed Elena
Bach
Fugue in G minor
Boccherini
Minuet
Britten
Aria italiana [*from
Variations on a Theme
of Frank Bridge*]
Conductor:
Karl Münchinger

17/x
Chamber Opera Theatre
Shostakovich
The Nose
Conductor:
Gennady
Rozhdestvensky

This opera has finally been revived after long being banned. Its revival is due to the obstinacy of Rozhdestvensky and the producer, Boris Pokrovsky. All credit to them! They've pulled it off. It's a real artistic event. I even went to congratulate Gennady Rozhdestvensky (somewhat under pressure, it's true, from Nina and his mother, Natalya Rozhdestvenskaya). He's someone with whom I have absolutely no rapport.

19/x, at the home of
Galina Pisarenko
Televised broadcast
Beethoven
Sonata op. 111
S.R.

I don't even know if I play this sonata well or only half well (it's considered Beethoven's finest work). It's hard for me to judge and I find myself in a state of the utmost uncertainty.
It's true that I detest televised broadcasts, especially those in which I myself am involved.

29/x
Musical soirée at the
home of Irina
Shostakovich
*Recital by
Galina Pisarenko and
Elisabeth Leonskaja
Songs and concert arias
by Mozart*

A musical evening at the home of Irina Shostakovich, with a programme made up of songs by Mozart. The guests are musicians and composers. An attractive programme, attractively sung by Galina Pisarenko, with Lisa Leonskaja at the piano.
But something funny happened: at the end of the concert, the composer Yuri Levitin protested violently, criticizing Leonskaja for using too much pedal (which hadn't been the case at all). When I objected, he replied to me: 'But I was watching and saw that she was pressing down on it all the time.' What a clot!

5/XI
Recording
Anatoly Vedernikov
Debussy
7 Études
Prokofiev
4th Concerto
Conductor:
Lev Ginzburg

Debussy's *Études* are among Anatoly Vedernikov's finest achievements. I'm enormously fond of this recording and it always gives me pleasure to listen to it. I'm also prepared to listen frequently to Prokofiev's 4th Concerto, which I like a lot. Unfortunately, the recording isn't perfect from a technical point of view, and the sound could be better.

November
Recording
Grieg
Concerto in A minor
S.R.
Conductor:
Lovro von Matačić

Today Andrei [Gavrilov] struck a B minor chord as hard as he could. I asked him what it was. It turns out it was the opening chord of the Grieg Concerto. Which means that my hearing is now a whole tone out. This is most annoying.

10/XI (anniversary of Mother's birth)
Recording (following my own works)
Schumann
Concerto in A minor
S.R.
Conductor:
Lovro von Matačić

An evening of memories. I remember that on this day in Odessa our flat was always filled with splendid and magnificent chrysanthemums; evenings with guests were always a celebration.

25/XI
Brno
Radio broadcast
Dvořák
1) Aria from
The Jacobin
2) Symphonic Scherzo
in D minor

These works, which I heard by chance, gave me a good deal of pleasure. So much authenticity and mastery to them.
How is it that Dvořák is the butt of so many doubts on the part of so many people, as though his music weren't really good? It's partly because, except in Czechoslovakia, it's so little known. It's not given the place it deserves – the same is true of Grieg. And what did Brahms say about it? He, at least, wasn't wrong.

23/XII
In memory of Antonin and Sofya Peltsova

During the last few days of the exhibition of paintings by Antonin Peltsov that I organized at my flat, we set aside an evening for friends and again

Recording **Josef Suk** *Asrael* *Conductor:* *Václav Talich*	listened to this funeral symphony in Talich's incomparable performance. And here again this impression that you're hearing it for the first time. And what a miracle this conductor is!
24/XII, Christmas Eve *Recording* **Bach** *Christmas Oratorio,* *Parts I and II* 25/XII, Christmas Day *Christmas Oratorio,* *Parts III, IV, V and VI*	The tradition continues. Bach once again for Christmas. Again the timpani. The D major aria with Fischer-Dieskau. The Pastoral Symphony that opens Part Two: a lullaby for eternity. The arresting fugal tenor aria. The children's chorus and, to end, the finale with the solo trumpet. The Christmas tree (a small one this year, but covered with glass balls). The table laid, the guests . . . I leave the rest to your fertile imagination.
31/XII (at five o'clock) In memory of Dmitry Shostakovich *Recordings* **Shostakovich** *1) 5 Preludes and* *Fugues* S.R. *2) 6 Songs op. 62* *Evgeny Nesterenko* *Moscow Chamber* *Orchestra conducted by* *Rudolf Barshai* *3) 9th Symphony* *Boston Symphony* *Orchestra conducted by* *Sergey Koussevitzky*	I find the five Preludes and Fugues recorded by Supraphon infinitely better than the French recording on the Chant du Monde label (which contains six). I'm told the composer thought the same. It was with interest and pleasure that I listened to the six songs to words by English poets performed by Nesterenko and Barshai. The 9th Symphony, as conducted by Koussevitzky, is brilliant. All the composer's sarcastic streak, his eccentricities, verve and liveliness are captured here with tremendous brio. An enthralling disc.
1/I *Recording* **Ravel** *Concerto in G major* *Benedetti Michelangeli*	To celebrate the New Year, the choice this time fell on Ravel's Concerto in G. It's clearly the best thing Michelangeli has ever done. I've never heard a better performance of this concerto. The coldness so typical of this pianist is entirely appropriate here and never for a moment at odds with the music.

It's an exceptionally fine recording, which we listened to with enormous pleasure.

14/I *Vladimir Visotsky* *sings his own songs* *accompanying himself* *on the guitar*	For the visit of Vladimir Visotsky and Marina Vlady, our large sitting room was transformed into a circus arena. All the walls were covered in posters, with comic phrases left over from a previous evening. Visotsky accompanied himself on the guitar, singing with obvious pleasure, while we lent a sympathetic ear.
17/I *Recording* **Grieg** **Concerto in A minor** *S.R.* *Conductor:* *Lovro von Matačić*	I consider this recording of the Grieg Concerto with Matačić one of my genuine successes. Even after listening to it several times, I haven't changed my mind. I only hope that I'm not wrong.
31/I *Recording* **Chopin** **Concerto no. 1** **in E minor** *Maurizio Pollini* *Conductor: Paul Kletzki* **Polonaise, Mazurka,** **Impromptu, Nocturne** *Maurizio Pollini*	All this is most likely played on one of those powerful and violently metallic Steinways. For this reason, it has nothing in common – in my own opinion – with a true Chopin sound. The style of playing, too, is powerful and no doubt even 'heroic'; it's all perfectly correct and virtuosic, but lacking in any kind of charm, dressed up in the latest fashion as though on purpose. 'Chopin cast in metal' – but is that what we want here? I'm afraid that I have only a negative impression of this recording: an icy performance that's proud and sure of itself.
1/II *Recording* **Haydn** **Quartet in B flat** **op. 76 no. 4** *Tátrai Quartet* **Schubert** **8 Lieder**	If I had any advice to give, it would be to listen more often to the Haydn quartets; they're such a source of pleasure that it wouldn't surprise me to learn that they're good for your health. You could also say more or less the same about Schubert, but the effect of listening to music that's accompanied by words is rather different, as it dispenses both music and poetry.

Dietrich Fischer-Dieskau
Gerald Moore

4/11 *Recording* **Beethoven** *Quartet in F major op. 18 no. 1* Gewandhaus Quartet	I made myself listen to some music for string quartet, which I always find rather difficult. But I've known this 1st Quartet from my childhood and it has remained more or less lodged in my memory ever since, which is why it's easier for me to listen to this one than to the others.
8/11 *Recording* **Glazunov** *Concerto no. 1 in F minor* **Rimsky-Korsakov** *Concerto in C sharp minor* **Prokofiev** *Concerto no. 1 in D flat* S.R. *Conductor: Kyrill Kondrashin*	Old friends. It was a pleasure to meet them again. Ever since I was an adolescent, I've felt a considerable affinity for Glazunov: didn't I see him with my own eyes during a rehearsal for his 7th Symphony at the Conservatory in Odessa? Then there was the ballet *Raymonda*, in which I often played the piano part at the Opera, and his 5th Symphony, which I performed in an arrangement for four hands. Yes, he's someone who's very close to my heart. Rimsky. Unless I'm much mistaken, this was my very first recording with an orchestra. Prokofiev's 1st Concerto. A total delight! Jubilation, unbridled passion, humour, technical brio and then . . . the epilogue in octaves.
10/11 *Recording* **Schubert** *9 Lieder* Dietrich Fischer-Dieskau Gerald Moore	An irreproachable performance of these Schubert songs by this phenomenal singer. They're a model of Schubertian interpretation. But you have to listen to them several times to appreciate so many splendid things. When you think that he has recorded all Schubert's Lieder and of the time this must have taken, you really can't help wondering how he managed it. Alas – aren't there almost too many masterpieces?
18/11 *Recording* **Vladimir Visotsky** *4 songs*	Nothing here to excite me, either in the music (which is total rubbish) or in the words (which are for people who read only newspapers). I feel no interest in or affinity with this. Visotsky himself certainly has lots of talent, in his way, and the crowd is behind him.

27/II Munich Opera **Verdi** *La traviata* *Violetta:* *Ileana Cotrubas* *Conductor:* *Carlos Kleiber*	Finally a *Traviata* that's true to the work (albeit with some scandalous cuts). Carlos Kleiber has rediscovered it. This is the first time that I've really enjoyed listening to a work for which I've had mixed feelings until now, unlike Niaz, for example, who considers it the best opera in the world. I was much taken with Cotrubas, as, indeed, with the whole of the cast. A decent production. The final act, situated in an empty hotel room with red armchairs, was memorable.
28/II Opera **Johann Strauß** *Die Fledermaus* *Conductor:* *Carlos Kleiber*	Resoundingly perfect. I can't imagine it ever being done better. Kleiber above all. And a production in the best tradition. We laughed till we cried. What more can one say? You can envy us having had the chance to attend such a marvellous performance.
29/II Opera **Wagner** *Siegfried* *Birgit Nilsson, etc.* *Conductor:* *Wolfgang Sawallisch*	To the Munich Opera in the company of Oleg Kagan. Musically and scenically, a pitiful performance. The whole thing had a rubbery feel to it. The single exception was Birgit Nilsson, who, vocally, is as magnificent as ever. Jess Thomas lacks power, verging on paralysis. After Act II, Oleg asked if it was worth staying for Siegfried's death. Completely uninteresting staging. Conductor unequal to the opera. No impression, except one of weariness. This is the kind of contrast you find at the opera.
5/IV Moscow *Recording* **Bach** *Partita no. 1 in B flat* *1) Anatoly Vedernikov* *2) Glenn Gould* *3) Dinu Lipatti*	A little competition at home on the subject of different interpretations of Bach's Partitas, the most beautiful of which may well be the present one in B flat major. <u>Anatoly Vedernikov.</u> An integrated scrupulous approach to Bach. The music is the main thing. <u>Glenn Gould.</u> Absolutely brilliant, very individual tone. Here it's the pianistic element that's the main

thing. (He doesn't do the repeats, which is bad.)
<u>Dinu Lipatti</u>. It's Lipatti who wins the day.

6/IV *Recording* **Bach** *Partita no. 2 in C minor* *1) Anatoly Vedernikov* *2) Glenn Gould*	<u>Anatoly Vedernikov</u>. A scrupulous approach to Bach, and this I find convincing. <u>Glenn Gould</u>. Not sufficiently scrupulous (here too he ignores the repeats), but it's so artistic, so interesting and so striking. Even so, it's not *my* Bach.
7/IV *Recording* **Bach** *Partita no. 3 in A minor* *1) Hugo Steuer* *2) Anatoly Vedernikov* *3) Glenn Gould*	<u>Hugo Steuer</u>. Boring, ordinary and painfully uninteresting. <u>Anatoly Vedernikov</u>. Very successful, no 'buts' about it. <u>Glenn Gould</u>. Same as with the other partitas.
8/IV *Recording* **Bach** *Partita no. 3 in A minor* *Anatoly Vedernikov* *Partita no. 4 in D major* *1) Anatoly Vedernikov* *2) Glenn Gould*	First, I wanted to check my impression of the Third Partita as played by Vedernikov. My opinion hasn't changed. The Fourth Partita, too, is a splendid work. <u>Vedernikov</u>. Excellent, with all the characteristics typical of this artist. <u>Gould</u>. Excellent, with all the characteristics typical of this artist.
9/IV *Recording* **Bach** *Partita no. 5 in G major* *1) Anatoly Vedernikov* *2) Glenn Gould*	This is a partita I'd like to play myself. <u>Vedernikov</u>. No doubt one would like a little more humour, but it's good. <u>Glenn Gould</u>. It's good (aber nicht wunderschön).
11/IV *Recording* **Bach** *1) Cello Suite* *in G major* *Daniil Shafran* *2) Partita no. 5* *in G major*	I've often listened to Shafran's recording of the First Suite, not without some difficulty . . . <u>Glenn Gould</u>. I listened with interest, but not without feeling remote from it. <u>S.R.</u> A very old recording. I hope it's not too bad, but I can't guarantee it.

Fugue in F sharp minor
Fugue in E major
(The Well-Tempered
Clavier, Part Two)
Glenn Gould
3) English Suite no. 3
in G minor
S.R.

12/IV
Recording
Bach
Partita no. 6 in E minor
1) Anatoly Vedernikov
2) Glenn Gould

Here I feel only unease. It is almost always the case with the key of E minor. I don't like it, and it doesn't like me. (Neither performer is to blame.)

15/IV
Recording
Bach
Concertos in D minor
and E major
Zuzana Růžičková,
harpsichord
Conductor:
Václav Neumann

I organized six days of celebrations with Bach and suddenly my mood has improved.
Each day's programme is very precious to me and a source of perpetual wonderment.
The main thing is that I start getting used to the harpsichord, and I owe that to Růžičková. That's good.

Bach
1) Concertos in E major
and D major
Zuzana Růžičková
Václav Neumann
2) Concertos
in D minor, A major
and F minor
Vasso Devetzi
Rudolf Barshai

Today in addition to Růžičková and Neumann we've got Vasso Devetzi and Barshai. Theirs is a typically mediocre performance, even though all the notes are in place. That's why it's so boring.

16/IV
Bach
Concertos in D major,
A major, F minor and
G minor

What can one say of these marvels? They're perfect, and we can only thank Bach in our thoughts (will they reach him?).

Zuzana Růžičková
Václav Neumann

17/IV **Bach** *1) Concerto in D minor* *S.R. and Václav Talich* *2) Concerto in D minor* *S.R. and* *Kurt Sanderling* *3) Concerto in F major* *Zuzana Růžičková* *and Václav Neumann*	Unfortunately, my recording with the great Talich isn't very successful. This is probably due to differences in our conception of Bach's style, also to the fact that I was very tense at the time of the recording. The one with Sanderling, by contrast, is extremely successful. The Concerto in F major with two flutes is magnificent, as is its twin in G major (none other than the 4th Brandenburg Concerto).

18/IV **Bach** *Concertos in F major* *and G minor* *Zuzana Růžičková* *and Václav Neumann*	One can listen to this music every day. But such days might then be too rich and luxurious . . . and possibly undeserved.

19/IV *Recording* **Bach** *St John Passion* *Conductor: Karl Richter*	Impossible to decide which is better, the *St John* or the *St Matthew Passion*. It seems to me that the less massive *St John Passion* is easier to listen to. Hence the question: which is better – that which is easier or that which is more difficult? The answers will vary depending on the listener, but all of them will be correct.

21/IV *Recording* **Bach** *St John Passion* *Conductor: Karl Richter*	Our Easter evenings have begun, during which it has become customary (here, with us, as in the rest of the world) to listen to Bach's Passions. People today feel real enthusiasm for this music and praise it to the skies. No doubt it is very necessary to them as an antidote to impoverished reality.

22/IV *Recording* **Bach** *St Matthew Passion,* *Part I*	We celebrated Holy Week by listening to Klemperer's extremely austere recording of the *St Matthew Passion*. I was keen that the ambience at home should be in harmony with the work – a frugal board and

23/IV *Part II* 24/IV *Part III* [sic] *Dietrich Fischer- Dieskau, Peter Pears, Elisabeth Schwarzkopf, Christa Ludwig, Nicolai Gedda, Walter Berry* *Conductor:* *Otto Klemperer*	limited conversation – and that these evenings should have a significance of a kind that we would not forget. As for the music, there's nothing one can say: it speaks for itself.
25–27/IV (Easter Sunday, Monday and Tuesday) *Recording* **Bach** *Magnificat* *Conductor:* *Kurt Thomas*	We celebrated Easter in beauty and splendour. To invite all our friends, we needed three evenings. The table groaned under the weight of so much food and was decorated not only with eggs tied with ribbons but also with bunches of violets and snowdrops. The mood was one of Eastertide rejoicing; we listened to Bach three times.
29/IV, in memory of Theofil Richter on the 104th anniversary of his birth *Recording* **Bruckner** *8th Symphony* *Conductor:* *Wilhelm Furtwängler*	We again listened to this splendid symphony by Bruckner – his best – which I've known and loved for so long. Furtwängler adopts some extraordinarily slow tempi, so slow, indeed, that you might think that he was flying in the face of the composer's intentions, but it's so magnificent and so convincing that it leaves no room for argument. It's something unique, a miracle.
26/V *Recording* **Brahms** *Cello Sonata in E minor* **Grieg** *Cello Sonata in A minor* *Mstislav Rostropovich and S.R.*	I don't like this recording, which was made at Aldeburgh, and find it really rather unsuccessful. Slava was so afraid that I'd drown him (!) that he managed to talk me into lowering the piano lid. The result is a frightful imbalance and, at the same time, there's a general impression of over-cautiousness and unharmoniousness and, ultimately, of total failure. An execrable recording.
2/VII Tours Grange de Meslay *Recital by Radu Lupu*	With this pianist, everything is so carefully calculated and weighed up in advance that there's nothing unexpected or surprising. The meal is

Bartók
Out of Doors
Brahms
4 Pieces op. 119 and
Rhapsody op. 79 no. 2
Schubert
Sonata in G major
op. 78

served up as though on a large tray, but you know in advance exactly what it's made up of.

And so it was with Schubert's G major Sonata – irreproachable and level-headed. Such an interpretation doesn't surprise you in any way, all the notes are perfectly in place. But is the result really interesting? No. It lacks any sort of thrill and leaves the listener (or me, at any rate) cold.

9/VII
Grange de Meslay
Recital by
Stanislav Neuhaus
Prokofiev
8th Sonata
Chopin
Ballade, Mazurkas,
Scherzo
Scriabin
5th Sonata

I was disgusted by this recital, which is hardly surprising: the pianist had sat up drinking all the previous night with his pupil, Radu Lupu, and didn't get to bed till six in the morning. In the circumstances, it would have been better to cancel than to play in this way.

In the Prokofiev, he skipped several pages, and what followed was much the same. He later apologized via Nina, but at the same time he wanted me to give my permission for his recital to be broadcast on French radio.

4/VII
Grange de la
Besnardière
Organ recital by Irzhi
Rheinberger
Bach

Bach on the organ!

What can I say? Yes, I listened; I've no doubt it was excellent or at least correct. But there's nothing I can do about it, I really don't have the ability to listen to the organ – or, for that matter, to string quartets.

6/VII
Grange de Meslay
Recital by
Andrei Gavrilov
Scarlatti, Ravel,
Scriabin, Tchaikovsky,
Balakirev, Chopin,
Paganini–Liszt

Today's morning concert passed unnoticed by the French – there were no more than thirty people in the hall. Someone had forgotten to shut the entrance and a dog capered around the barn.

Even so, it was the best concert of the whole festival. It was the first time I'd heard this young pianist, and I was genuinely impressed by his talent. Temperament (lots of people think he makes a bit too much of it, but for my own part I thought that what he did was just right), stature, brilliant technique, it all came together to make me think that we're dealing here with the most gifted pianist of his generation. The Scriabin was ideal, as was the Ravel. He triumphed. Gavrilov.

July
Vienna
Stadthalle
(Dress rehearsal)
Leonard Bernstein
Candide
(musical comedy)

This musical comedy is clearly the work of a talented musician, but there's no sense of novelty or freshness about the music. It's true that I have absolutely no time for musical comedy as an art form, so it was silly of me to go (it was Christian who took me).

2/VIII
Munich
State Opera
Verdi
Falstaff
*Falstaff: Dietrich
Fischer-Dieskau
Kirschberg
[recte Kirschstein]
Reri Grist
Fassbaender and others
Conductor:
Wolfgang Sawallisch*

Fantastic performance. Sawallisch showed himself in the best light, everything was exact, perfectly clear and in place. But the real sensation was Fischer-Dieskau. The production was minutely detailed, with the final fugue providing an impressive culmination to the opera. All the singers were excellent.
At the same time I realized that this Verdi isn't the real Verdi, even if his mastery is complete. It's a Verdi that comes more from the head than from the heart.

Bayreuth
Festspielhaus
Wagner
4/VIII
Das Rheingold
*Hans Sotin
Yvonne Minton
Heinz Zednik
Zoltán Kelemen*
5/VIII
Die Walküre
*Hans Sotin
Peter Hofmann
Hannelore Bode
Roberta Knie
Yvonne Minton*
7/VIII
Siegfried
*Hans Sotin
René Kollo*

Well, here finally was an exact, honest, clear and transparent (albeit unmagical) performance of the work I prefer to all others. No praise is too high for Pierre Boulez. For his part, Patrice Chéreau is clearly something of a paradox, and I don't like him for it, even if his staging did reveal one or two inspired ideas.
Das Rheingold was splendidly sung from start to finish, a feat all the more admirable in that the production – a veritable betrayal of the work and in permanent opposition to it – clearly gets in the way of the music and is extremely awkward for the singers.
In every respect, the best of the four evenings was Die Walküre.
Peter Hofmann is phenomenal. Singing and acting Wagner suit him very well, and we'll never forget his Siegmund (his jeans notwithstanding). Yvonne Minton is no less magnificent as Fricka.
There are lots of 'shocking' things in the production

Heinz Zednik
Roberta Knie
9/VIII
Götterdämmerung
Jess Thomas
Roberta Knie
Bengt Rundgren
Yvonne Minton
Conductor:
Pierre Boulez
Director:
Patrice Chéreau

(even if 'shocking' is overstating it: it's purely and simply bad scenography). For example, the Ride of the Valkyries takes place in an infirmary, where the wounded heroes are patched up. But an episode that worked particularly well was the Magic Fire, in which music and staging were in perfect accord: real sparks produced by gas ran round the stage and flew up into the air.

At the end, I went backstage to congratulate Boulez, who was in an excellent mood.

Siegfried. I can't say that I found the radiant hero (Kollo) particularly convincing, I'd have preferred Hofmann. Zednik as Mime was infinitely more convincing.

I can't make any sense of Chéreau's idea of having Wotan help Siegfried – either here or in *Die Walküre*. It changes the whole meaning of the work. The scenery is really quite appalling. But, musically speaking, it's superb.

Götterdämmerung. Even worse. How can Boulez like such a hotchpotch of ideas? The whole thing is simply arbitrary (previously it was Erda in a bag, now it's the Norns. The devil only knows why!). For reasons that escape me, Hagen has become a representative of the working class in a boiler suit, while Siegfried and Gunther are in dinner jackets (while out hunting!!). Hagen's final phrase 'Zurück vom Ring' isn't sung. Chéreau's 'mature' thoughts on the *Ring*: 'Evil will always exist on earth.' How original!

10/VIII
Festspielhaus
Wagner
Parsifal
Bernd Weikl
Karl Ridderbusch
Theo Adam
Peter Hofmann
Franz Mazura
Eva Randová
Conductor: Horst Stein

This was my first *Parsifal* in the theatre. Musically, Stein's conducting is honest and well within the Wagnerian tradition, but ultimately unilluminating. Much the same can be said of the production. Still, it wasn't unimpressive. Peter Hofmann is perfect as Parsifal: a handsome presence, young, a face worthy of the Middle Ages. Theo Adam was convincing as Gurnemanz, as was Eva Randová as Kundry. The chorus was impressive.

A good performance, nothing more. I expect more from *Parsifal*.

Director:
Wolfgang Wagner

11/VIII
Festspielhaus
Wagner
Tristan und Isolde
Spas Wenkoff
Kurt Moll
Catarina Ligendza
Donald McIntyre
Yvonne Minton
Conductor:
Carlos Kleiber
Director:
August Everding

I fear that as long as I live I shall never hear another *Tristan* like this one.

This was the real thing.

Carlos Kleiber brought the music to boiling point and kept it there throughout the whole evening (unleashing an interminable ovation at the end).

There's no doubt that he's the greatest conductor of our day. All the singers were on top Wagnerian form and we were carried away by them.

Eine Sternstunde in the fullest sense of the word.

The staging and scenery were a bit too austere for my liking and of the happy-medium variety, but at least they weren't distracting.

Following the performance, Kostia Metaxas persuaded me to seek out the conductor and share my impressions with him. He seemed rather depressed and displeased with himself.

I told him what I thought and he suddenly leapt into the air with joy, like a child: 'Also, wirklich gut?' [So it was really good?]. Such a titan, and so unsure of himself.

5/XII
Florence
Teatro Comunale
Shostakovich
5th Symphony
Conductor:
Riccardo Muti

In Shostakovich's 5th Symphony, Muti again showed himself in his best light. We heard the symphony as written, and it was a great success.

There's obviously a certain rivalry between these two Italian conductors. Which of them is better, Muti or Abbado?

I have the impression that they've got caught up in this competitive situation themselves. I don't find this sort of thing at all attractive or that it has anything to do with Art with a capital A, but perhaps it's just a way of getting on in the world of music, though in my own view this notion is devoid of all significance.

And what's the point of these comparisons?

17/XII
Warsaw
National Opera
Moniuszko
Halka
Halka: Hanna Lisowska
Conductor:
Antoni Wicherek

I played through the vocal score of this opera in my youth and once heard it at the Bolshoy (with Kruglikova). And so I've a certain affinity with the piece, the old-fashioned aspect of which doesn't bother me. Here in Warsaw the performance is traditional, ordinary and not very imaginative.
The changes made to the ending are an abomination and idiotic in their tendentiousness. The woman singing Halka (a Polish 'star') wasn't sufficiently tragic. She was merely cute, and why such short sleeves? So that we could admire her pretty arms?

19/XII
Brest-Litovsk
Televised broadcast
from the Grand Hall
of the Moscow
Conservatory
Beethoven
Sonata in F minor
op. 2 no. 1
S.R.

I'm fiercely opposed to these televised broadcasts (except when they're proper films); that's why listening to this sonata (and, unfortunately, seeing it as well) left me completely cold. The image prevents you from listening, and there's nothing interesting to see. It's natural to do something and to do it through to the end.

24/XII
Christmas Eve in front
of the candle-lit tree
Recording
Schubert
Impromptu in A flat
op. 142 no. 2
S.R.

This, I think, is my one and only recording that doesn't put me in a bad mood and with which I'm in total agreement. I simply feel that this is exactly how this impromptu should be played.

1/I, evening of New
Year's Day, after listen-
ing to a recording of
Boris Pasternak reading
excerpts from
Shakespeare's *Henry IV*
Beethoven
1st Symphony
Conductor: Wilhelm
Furtwängler

Beethoven's 1st Symphony is the ideal way of inaugurating the new year with music. It's a real treat.
It would be interesting to weigh up the reactions of each listener and draw up a balance sheet. But this is a matter, rather, for physics and medicine.

2/I
Recording
Liszt
*1) Hungarian Fantasia
(live recording from
Budapest)
Conductor:
János Ferencsik
2) Funérailles
(live recording from
Budapest)
3) Sonata in B minor*
(Carnegie Hall, New
York, 1965)
S.R.

Faults and technical imperfections (noises, crackling etc.) don't disturb me in the slightest, as long as I can feel that the music is well played and there's a palpable sense of atmosphere.
Such is the case with the present recording. In spite of everything, it's a success and (forgive me) I'm almost proud of it. Each time I listen to it, I do so with pleasure: but I mustn't listen to it too often, of course, as that would have an unfortunate effect on the record, which, like the rest of us, is subject to its little moods.

4/I For our friends
Recording
Liszt
*Funérailles
Sonata in B minor
Hungarian Fantasia
S.R.*

I couldn't resist the temptation and within a very short space of time have listened to this Liszt record on two further occasions.

5/I
For some other friends
Recording
Liszt
*Hungarian Fantasia
Funérailles
S.R.*

I simply had to play this record to some other friends and hear what they had to say. It's clearly a waste of time, but isn't *amour propre* a part of human nature? Yet it remains a fact that praise almost always provokes a negative reaction in me, and I then try to find out what didn't work.

7/I
Recording
Franck
*1) Les Djinns
S.R. and
Kyrill Kondrashin
2) Prélude, choral
et fugue
S.R.*

1) This is a fairly successful recording, and I like it, just as I like all Franck's music.
2) The first time I heard the *Prélude, choral et fugue* was an awfully long time ago in Odessa in the Hall of the Stock Exchange at a recital given by Egon Petri. I fell madly in love with the work and immediately decided to play it (even though I didn't have the least prospect at that time of embarking on a career as a soloist).
The first act of *Palestrina* is the strongest part of

Pfitzner
Palestrina (Act I)
Gedda
Fischer-Dieskau
Conductor:
Rafael Kubelik

this music drama. I can understand why Richard Strauss had so little time for such a serious rival.

15/I
Recording
Berg
Chamber Concerto
Ivan Strauss, violin
Zdeněk Kožina, piano
Conductor: Libor Pešek

Here is a relatively satisfying recording of Berg's Chamber Concerto. Probably only a few people will listen to this recording, in spite of all its merits and its (professional) integrity. Our own recording, with Oleg Kagan and Yuri Nikolayevsky, has quite simply been deleted from the catalogue (in spite of the five stars it received from critics). No doubt it's because no one bought it.

20/I
Recording
Schumann
Symphonic Studies
S.R. at the
Dubrovnik Festival

Works on this scale are bound to suffer from imperfections when recorded live, imperfections that continue to trouble your conscience like so many shameful blemishes – even when the concert itself struck you as brilliantly successful and moving.

27/I
Recording
Marlene in London
(Marlene Dietrich)

She always succeeds in creating an atmosphere. Charm and good taste personified. A crowning achievement in its way.

4/III, an evening
at the home of
Artur Rubinstein
Paris
Recordings
Chopin
Fantasia on Polish Airs
Artur Rubinstein
Mozart
Trio in E flat K 498
Cecil Aronowitz, viola
Gervase de Peyer,
clarinet
Lamar Crowson, piano

An extremely interesting and enjoyable evening at Artur Rubinstein's, where he played me some of his favourite records. In fact I've always felt at ease in his company. He has such a positive outlook on life, he's happy, uncomplicated and full of good humour and charm. I remember that each time he told us a story, he did so with such talent that we almost died laughing.

His wife, Nella, has managed to impose her own style on the house where they live – simple and elegant. This, I think, is a typically Polish feature. Our conversation was lively and witty. I've always felt relaxed with them.

Besides, the programme that he played for me was

Bizet
Excerpts from Act I
of Carmen
Gabriella Besanzoni
Donizetti
Nemorino's aria from
L'elisir d'amore
Enrico Caruso
Chopin
Mazurkas
Artur Rubinstein

made up of some really quite unique recordings. Artur is a particular fan of Gabriella Besanzoni, whom he considers the best Carmen he's ever heard and who was also, it seems, a great beauty. His recording of the mazurkas is in the good old concert tradition, with no trace of sickly flabbiness; I find it very convincing.

He's almost blind, but behaves as if it didn't bother him. Quite the opposite, it even becomes a subject for his shafts of wit.

8/III
Playback in the studios
at the Salle Wagram
Beethoven
Sonatas op. 2 no. 1
and op. 10 no. 3
S.R.
Dvořák
Concerto in G minor
S.R.
Conductor:
Carlos Kleiber

The F minor Sonata seems to me a success, the D major less so.

Dvořák's Concerto didn't go as well as I'd wanted: Carlos Kleiber and I were rather tense at the time of the recording, we concentrated too hard and the work (exceedingly tricky for the piano) suddenly lost its freshness. I'm extremely depressed by this as I like the piece a lot. But there's nothing I can do about it, and the record will be released.

18/III
Palais Garnier
Debussy
Pelléas et Mélisande
Frederica von Stade:
Mélisande
Richard Stilwell: Pelléas
Gabriel Bacquier:
Golaud
Conductor:
Lorin Maazel

Frederica von Stade *is* Mélisande! Here's a classic example of the most perfect understanding of Debussy and Maeterlinck.

Alongside her, everyone else seems pallid: the other singers, the conductor, the production, everything seems somehow false. Pelléas as a baritone? Golaud is now made the opera's central tragic figure, which is absurd. And even Maazel conducts the work correctly but without affection. The director, Jorge Lavelli, adds absolutely nothing to the piece.

April
Moscow
Rehearsal
Hindemith
2nd Trio

This is an insanely complex work that's impossible to grasp at an initial hearing. It's clearly a triumph of professionalism, but it requires an enormous amount of time before you can claim to know it properly.

Ilya Grubert, violin *Yuri Bashmet, viola* *Alexey Selezniev, cello*	On this occasion, it remained incomprehensible. Of course, you have to allow for the fact that it was merely a rehearsal, and I don't know whether the players themselves were entirely sure of what they were doing. But Herr Hindemith sometimes sets such enormous problems that he appears to go right off the rails. Having said that, I certainly wouldn't question his artistic integrity, and I remain one of his most fervent admirers.
April *Private tape* **Theofil Richter** ***Quartet in F major*** *Oleg Kagan* *Alexander Gritzevich* *Yuri Yurov* *Natasha Gutman*	This attempt to perform and record Papa's F major Quartet was undertaken by some young musicians dragged along by Oleg and Natasha, but it hasn't worked. By imposing on it a Wagnerian and Straussian character rather than that of Brahms and Grieg, they've been barking up completely the wrong tree, so that the result is utterly unconvincing. I should have listened to them from the outset and put them on the right lines.
2/v *Recording* **Hugo Wolf** ***8 Mörike Lieder*** *Dietrich Fischer-Dieskau* *S.R.*	A fairly successful recording of a concert we gave in Innsbruck, in the course of which someone in the audience dropped his stick (but this has, of course, been edited out). On this occasion it seems as though we really entered into the spirit of these songs; we'd rehearsed sufficiently and felt not only confidence but real friendship towards each other.
6/v *Recording* **Bach** ***Concerto in D major*** *Zoltán Kocsis* *Conductor:* *Albert Simon*	I specially listened to this magnificent recording by Kocsis, as I'm planning to play this work myself and wanted to hear it. I'd already heard it in its version for violin (a whole tone higher, though with my present hearing I hear it on the piano, too, in E major). It's a luminous, welcoming piece that puts you in a good mood, and I'm sure it must be a pleasure to play it.
7/v, a.m. **Bach** ***Concerto in A major***	In the morning, A major. Whenever I hear Kocsis, I'm always satisfied and feel no need to add anything. He's the sort of pianist you accept as a fact of life.

Zoltán Kocsis
Conductor:
Albert Simon

8/v **Bach** *Concerto in F minor* *Zoltán Kocsis* *Conductor:* *Albert Simon*	Not a particularly 'benevolent' concerto. It's short, but it has a real bite to it. The first time I played it was at the Fêtes Musicales in Touraine, and I played it appallingly badly. I then played it again as an encore, and that time it went very well.
9/v, a.m. **Bach** *Concerto in G minor* *Zoltán Kocsis* *Conductor:* *Albert Simon*	Clearly one associates this work with the violin, but it's good to know that it can be played on the piano. I've included it in my list of works to study.
9/v, In memory of Benjamin Britten *Recording* **Britten** *Curlew River* *with Peter Pears*	I first heard this masterpiece of Britten's at its second performance at Orford in Suffolk and fell in love with it once and for all. But it was only after I'd seen a performance at the Noh Theatre in Tokyo that I understood where Britten drew his inspiration for this mystery play. I wonder if it will ever find a wider public? I do hope so.
13/v **Theofil Richter** *Five songs* *Alla Ablaberdyeva* *S.R.*	Alla Ablaberdyeva – a pupil of Nina's – learned these songs by Papa and sang them most attractively. All who were present liked them a lot. There's a great feeling of purity to these songs, a certain sense of form (within the framework of the old Viennese school: Papa studied with Fuchs and Fischhof) and evident talent. Also lots of freshness and originality. Thank you!
24/vi, Tours Grange de Meslay **Schubert** *Quartet 'Death* *and the Maiden'* *String Quintet* *Melos Quartet with*	Schubert's D minor Quartet is considered one of his finest works, and I wouldn't disagree with this. But to me, the C major Quintet is a more enticing piece, as I'm always drawn more to major keys, even if works in the major are in fact almost always more difficult.

Klaus Storck,
second cello

25/VI Grange de Meslay **Schubert** *Sonata in A minor* *op. 143* *'Wanderer' Fantasy* *Sonata in A major* *op. post.* *Maurizio Pollini*	The beginning of the A minor Sonata was splendid and so full of insight that I was looking forward to a real feast of music, but from the second movement onwards everything became a bit samey; I'd even say that this was the case with the 'Wanderer' Fantasy and the A major Sonata. Pollini plays Schubert's works as though they'd been written by Prokofiev or by some other 20th-century composer.
26/VI Grange de Meslay **Schubert** *Die schöne Müllerin* *Peter Schreier* *Irwin Gage*	Schreier sang magnificently this evening, and his sense of Schubert's style and sentiment were altogether satisfying. Only 'Der Müller und der Bach' and the final lullaby failed to convince: there was something too human about the brook's replies, whereas everything should be unreal, strange and as though steeped in deathly cold. Nicolette Le Chevallier exclaimed in such a loud voice that everyone could hear: 'It's not Schubert. Pollini, that's the real Schubert for you!' What an idiotic and typically French way of trying to be original.
3/VII Grange de Meslay **Schubert** *Lieder* *Elisabeth Söderström* *Paul Hamburger, piano*	'Welcome to the barn': it was with this phrase that the soprano (who was appearing in Touraine for the first time) greeted the audience. It's not entirely clear why, but for her Schubert recital she wore a dress decorated on the back with a giant butterfly. Nothing she did was to the point, and she sang extremely badly. A real disaster! I'm told she burst into tears after the concert. As for the pianist, he'd do better selling sausages or hamburgers in the street. We left at the interval with Aunt Mary, who was perplexed ('Tell me, Svetik, what wasn't right'), and Nina.
9/VII Hotel Continental Lucerne *Live recording*	I've always liked the Grieg Concerto. I like it for its ruggedness, virility and coldness: a bracing north wind blows through it, and when the piano

Grieg
Concerto
S.R.
Conductor:
Paavo Berglund

enters in the second movement, you'd think you could hear a bird singing from the top of a tall pine tree. I also like it for its originality and its total absence of mawkishness.

14–15/VII (at the home of Loulou Lombard)
Mur (Switzerland)
On the radio
Ferruccio Busoni
Die Brautwahl (for symphony orchestra)
Rachmaninov
2nd Concerto
S.R.
Conductor:
Stanislaw Wislocki

Busoni's symphonic poem is full of extremely interesting music; frankly, I wasn't expecting it. But he's a real composer, on the level – say – of Cornelius, Humperdinck, Medtner or Poulenc (not that there is the least similarity between the music of any of these composers) – and he's entirely worthy of one's respect.

I listened again to my performance of Rachmaninov's 2nd Concerto with considerable pleasure; some of it has turned out quite successfully and is certainly on a par with the work itself.

In terms of its virtuosity, I also found it quite acceptable. This is what happens when you don't listen to an old recording for a long time.

27/VII
Munich
Nationaltheater
Richard Strauss
Arabella
Julia Varady
Dietrich Fischer-Dieskau
Lucia Popp
Conductor:
Wolfgang Sawallisch

Orchestra, production, singers – everything contributed to the fantastic success of this extremely popular opera by Richard Strauss. Julia Varady has come on remarkably and is now a great singer. Fischer-Dieskau is simply phenomenal. You couldn't wish for anything better. But . . .

The opera itself: I really can't say how much I dislike it – not just the subject matter (with the absurd glass of water at the end), but also the music, which is so garrulous and unoriginal.

The whole thing is terribly petit bourgeois but, as such, goes down a treat with the philistines.

30/VII
Cuvilliés-Theater
Mozart
Idomeneo
Conductor:
Wolfgang Sawallisch

A powerful musical impression – Salzburg wasn't in the same league. There's a real sense that all the details of the music and the production have been thoroughly thought through.

This was Sawallisch on a good day. The scenery,* with the Tritons suspended above the stage, is

---

* The designer was Ekkehard Grübler and the producer Peter Brenner.

impressive. And the opera itself! It yields in nothing to any other work, even *Don Giovanni*, in terms of its audacity and power. It's so innovatory.

July Salzburg *Cinema* **Mozart** *Die Zauberflöte* *Film by* *Ingmar Bergman*	This film left a negative impression on me. In the first place, the singers themselves leave a lot to be desired. Moreover, the style of the production doesn't do anything for me – it claims to be original, without actually being so. But the worst thing of all is the overture; we hear festive music of the most inspired kind, and what do we see? The faces of spectators that are unattractive and sometimes even repulsive to look at. Why? It's ghastly!
1/VIII Lucerne Kunsthaus **Mahler** *6th Symphony* *Berlin Philharmonic* *Herbert von Karajan*	Not once throughout this symphony did I feel the least thrill of excitement. The performance was completely lacking in the least sense of tragedy. Coldness, coldness and yet more coldness. The orchestra played impeccably, they couldn't have done a better job, and yet nothing . . . Then came the coda in A minor and the final *fortissimo* chord. The effect was so powerful and real that you'd have thought the roof would cave in. Success was guaranteed, and the reason for this success was the final bar.
October Moscow *Televised broadcast* **Chopin** *Polonaise-fantaisie,* *2 waltzes, 4 mazurkas,* *Study op. 25 no. 4,* *4th Scherzo* S.R.	This programme is made up of pieces by Chopin and shown under the title 'Chopiniana by Richter', which strikes me as terribly banal. But this type of platitude is commonplace here. The sound (it's best to ignore the picture) is on the whole more or less tolerable, with no obvious errors and even, here and there, a few felicitous phrases, so I've really no legal grounds for protesting. Ist es aber wirklich wunderschön? [But is it really all that wonderful?]
November (Evening in memory of Maria Callas at the home of Dr René Marteau) Paris	We listened to these phenomenal recordings in René's flat, with its splendid view over the dome of Les Invalides. Words are too feeble even to attempt to describe the impression produced by Callas's incomparable singing.

Bellini *'Casta diva'* [from *Norma*] **Verdi** *Duet and aria from* *Act I of Rigoletto*	There's only one thing one can say and that's that it verges on the miraculous and that, with her, everything is unexpected: I didn't expect such a Gilda from her, for example. Some people claim that it's her best role. Thanks to technology, one can now listen to this absolutely unique diva while lounging in an armchair and sipping whisky. It's rather bizarre.
November, at the home of René Marteau *Recording* **Dvořák** *Piano Concerto* *in G minor* *S.R. and Carlos Kleiber*	Once again, something of a disappointment. No, it shouldn't have been like this. Carlos kept splitting hairs, and I myself was very tense. Hence the absence of the charm and simplicity so characteristic of Dvořák. I remember how long I spent studying this concerto (almost three years), whereas I learned Bartók's Second Concerto within the space of two months, without experiencing any particular difficulties. That was in our tiny wooden house on the banks of the River Oka, surrounded by some of the most beautiful Russian countryside that I know.
16/XII (Awarded honorary doctorate by Strasbourg University) **Jacques-Martin Hotteterre** (1680–1761) [*recte* 1674–1763] *Suite in F minor* **Pierre Philidor** (1681–1731) *Suite in G minor* **Handel** *Sonata in D minor*	I had to submit to the ritual of dressing up, first taking several steps in one direction, then several more in another and listening to speeches in unknown languages. In these circumstances, it's hard to listen to music that in any case didn't stick in my mind, even if at the time it seemed to be accurately played. Then there were all the congratulations, requiring endless smiles appropriate to the occasion. I felt a complete idiot. What a sense of release I felt on going off afterwards and wandering through the bright streets of Strasbourg.
December (Christmas, visit from Francis Van de Velde) **Moscow** *Recording*	Evening in honour of our guest. Again the Dvořák Concerto with Kleiber (a fairly mixed pleasure, at least for me). What a shame, so much fine music, so many successful details, but, all in all, <u>it's not a success</u>. Why such injustice? For what reason? The humour

Dvořák
Piano Concerto
in G minor
S.R. and Carlos Kleiber
(Followed by slide show
of Moscow, Kosovo,
Tours and Venice)

of the moment? Insufficient preparation? Or something else?
This is the enigma of artistic success and failure. Impossible to guess in advance. We are in the hands of . . . the Fate that lurks behind the scores and the performers' music stands.

January
Televised broadcast
from La Scala, Milan
Verdi
Don Carlos
King Philip: Nesterenko
Queen Elisabeth:
Margaret Price
Don Carlos:
Plácido Domingo
Eboli: Obraztsova
Conductor:
Claudio Abbado

Musically excellent.
In the first place, <u>Abbado</u>, sure of himself, honest, on a grand scale. <u>Nesterenko</u>, very intelligent. <u>Price</u>, very pleasing, but unfortunately she's physically unsuited to the part. <u>Obraztsova</u>, as vulgar as ever, but even so very stylish.
Production* in the contemporary fashion, ruining everything and constantly disturbing the music. It becomes difficult for the listener to concentrate. When will these horrors end?!?

31/I, 118th anniversary
of Chekhov's birth
Poetry by Pushkin,
Chekhov, Pasternak and
Blok read by Dmitry
and Natasha Zuravliov
and Tamara Dudarieva
Rachmaninov
Prelude in
F sharp minor
S.R.
Bulgarian and Russian
liturgical settings
Boris Christoff
and choir

It's become a long-standing tradition with us to get together on special occasions to listen to poetry and music.
These very special and memorable evenings allow us to immerse ourselves in art.
Rachmaninov's F sharp minor Prelude is a sombre and poetical piece. Neuhaus thought it was the best of the whole collection. In it you feel the freshness of a Russian evening beside a pond from which mist rises up. Levitanian atmosphere.
A pleasure to hear Boris Christoff with a choir in these Russian liturgical settings. Great religious insight.

4/II
Musical soirée at home

I don't really know this symphony, even though I've heard it two or three times in the concert hall.

---

* The director was Luca Ronconi, the designer Luciano Damiani.

Recordings
Schumann
3rd Symphony
('Rhenish')
1) Eliahu Inbal
2) Otto Klemperer

In particular, I remember the way in which Charles Munch played the middle movement as an encore. It was quite extraordinary: under his direction, the orchestra played it as though it were a piece of chamber music.

Schumann's symphonies gain a great deal from being played in this clear and clinical way, like a string quartet. But this obviously demands two or three times as much work.

It was interesting to hear this symphony in performances by two totally different conductors. Each was convincing in his way.

Among our guests was Dmitry Krasnopevtsev. I can still see his attractive face expressing concentration and the effort of trying to understand this music.

11/II
Boris Christoff
and choir
Recording
Slav liturgical settings

Splendid! And what singing! Boris Christoff first and foremost; the power of his performance! Our guests were clearly pleased. How could it be otherwise? And the bells!!!

For my own part, I don't know why, but I always feel a tiny bit bored when listening to this kind of music. After all, it's far from being on the same level as the Bach Passions or the Glagolitic Mass.

25/III
Grand Hall of the
Conservatory
Bach
Concerto in E major
Oleg Kagan
Conductor:
Yuri Nikolayevsky

This is a concerto I adore, and I was so pleased to be able to attend this concert as the performance was as good as the work.

I've decided to play it in its version for keyboard, in D major, and also the one in G minor. I'll then have all Bach's concertos in my repertory.

10/IV
Maurice Béjart Ballet
at the Bolshoy
Stravinsky
1) The Firebird
2) Petrushka
3) The Rite of Spring

It's difficult to speak of the way in which this magnificent music was performed, when the manner in which it was staged prevented you from listening. At best, it was a source of disappointment.

It would be better to forget Monsieur Béjart's choreography once and for all. Is it an accident, or is he quite simply deaf to the music?

12/IV
*Tape of a concert
at Tours in 1977*
Schubert
6 Lieder
*Dietrich Fischer-Dieskau
and S.R.*

Working with Dieter wasn't easy. The problem is that his approach to the text is so demanding that if, for example, he has to sing consonants such as 'str' or 'pr', he insists that the pianist plays with a very slight delay. His diction is clearly phenomenal, but it very slightly alters the music's natural rhythm; you have to follow him meticulously, and it's not always all that easy.

Of course, the result is magnificent, but it required an enormous amount of work.

The way he sings *Des Totengräbers Heimweh* is fantastic. It creates the impression of something wrenched and crushed.

1/IV
Recording
Lehár
*Aria from the operetta
Giuditta*
Elisabeth Schwarzkopf

Whatever this great artist sings, she is always at her superlative best – and here, what verve and brio!

Bravo, bravissimo!

7/V
Stanislavsky–
Nemirovich-Danchenko
Theatre
Vitaly Hubarenko
Letters to Love
*Monodrama to words
by Henri Barbusse*
Galina Pisarenko

This cesspool of sentimental and melodramatic drivel of which Galya seems to be enamoured and into which she poured all her passion did none of us any favours. A question of taste, perhaps? Not at all. In agreeing to be associated with such rubbish, the artist loses the respect he should have for art and for himself. It was an absolute torment to sit through this, though we stayed till the end, of course.

But I couldn't bring myself to go and congratulate Galya, in spite of the tumultuous success she enjoyed with her audience; the enthusiasm with which this performance was greeted merely reflects the public's cheap-and-nasty, petit-bourgeois tastes.

9/V
Grand Hall of the
Conservatory (concert
in memory of
Heinrich Neuhaus)

Today Heinrich Neuhaus's son performed two of the works on which his father had left his inimitable imprint.

I recall having heard him play them at an open-air concert that he gave in the gardens at the

Haydn
Seven Last Words
Beethoven
5th Concerto
Chopin
1st Concerto
Stanislav Neuhaus
Conductor: Lev Markiz

Hermitage; I've yet to hear a better interpretation of either piece. It was a veritable *Sternstunde* that it's impossible to forget or to put into words. Stanislav was on form today and made a powerful impression; a concert worthy of the memory of the great Neuhaus.

23/VI
Festival de Touraine at the Grange de Meslay
Bach
Violin Concertos
in E major and A minor
Oleg Kagan
3rd and 6th
Brandenburg Concertos
Munich Bach Orchestra
Conductor: Karl Richter

To start with, my beloved concerto in E major, its 1st movement elegant, joyful and triumphant. The 2nd movement is one of Bach's most inspired, while the 3rd makes you think that the composer might not have spurned champagne. In my own view, the 3rd Brandenburg is the most perfect of the six. Unusual instrumentation of the 6th – everything in the lower register. Oleg played magnificently. The locals love him and have adopted him. A great success. Karl Richter is a splendid musician, but in private he seems so unsure of himself and ill at ease.

24/VI
Grange de Meslay
Bach
Orchestral Suites
nos. 2, 3 and 4
1st Brandenburg
Concerto
Munich Bach Orchestra
Conductor: Karl Richter

A cornucopia of wonders! There's nothing one can say about these works, as words are incapable of giving the least idea of their beauty and total perfection – unless, that is, one lapses into analysis, which in this case serves no useful purpose, being good only for textbooks. The Bach Orchestra under the direction of Karl Richter played well – but it's possible to play even better, and even better . . . and so on. Here, there are no longer any limits to what you can do.

Paris
Salle Wagram
Playback of recording
made at the Théâtre de
l'Athénée
Berg
Chamber Concerto

This was a good concert. As a result of poor organization, the theatre was far from full; but Nora Auric was there (she thanked me warmly for the Berg and the Hindemith – *Kammermusik* no. 2), as was Madame Pompidou accompanied by Madame Rochas (who then invited all the performers to dinner at a fashionable club near the

Oleg Kagan and S.R.
Ensemble of young
soloists from the
Moscow Conservatory
Conductor:
Yuri Nikolayevsky

Rue St Denis) and François Périer, the actor and theatre director who appeared in Jean Cocteau's film *Orphée*. The recording turned out relatively successful, but even so we decided to do a few retakes and finally recorded the whole work again in the studio under the meticulous direction of Yuri Nikolayevsky, which allowed us to produce an even more accurate and scrupulous reading of the score.

1/VII
Grange de Meslay
Mozart
Symphony in B flat
K 319
Piano Concerto
in C major K 467
Monique Haas
Salzburg Mozarteum
Orchestra
Conductor:
Leopold Hager

The Mozarteum Orchestra as conducted by Hager is clearly in a different class from the frivolous French ensemble conducted by Jean-Pierre Wallez. Here, at least, everything is as it should be. It's a serious interpretation, even though tradition and routine are not always absent (I have to say that there were times when I was bored).
Monique Haas (an elegant and attractive Parisienne whom I've known for ages, from the time of my first concerts in Prague in fact, at the end of which she came backstage to congratulate me) played superbly, but in the second movement the repeated chords in the left hand were a little too powerful, and the papers criticized her for this. I don't think she can be held responsible: the fault is entirely due to the Steinway and its ill-balanced registers. A difficult situation. The critics, once again, understood nothing.

28/VII, at the home of
Dietrich Fischer-Dieskau
Munich
Recordings
Berg
Kreuzweg [unidentified]
Hindemith
Excerpts from Act III
of Mathis der Maler
Pilar Lorengar
Donald Grobe
Dietrich Fischer-Dieskau

One of my relatively rare visits to the home of the greatest of 20th-century singers. A real treat: he showed me his paintings and played me works that I didn't know, which was extremely interesting and instructive as until now I'd only a very vague idea of what Busoni represents from a musical point of view; much the same is true of Hindemith.

Conductor:
Leopold Ludwig
Busoni
Goethe-Lieder
Dietrich Fischer-Dieskau
Jörg Demus

1/VIII
Munich
Radio studios
Live recordings
Pfitzner
Piano Concerto in E flat
1) Walter Gieseking
2) Rosa Schmidt
Conductor: Jochum

Twice in succession I listened very conscientiously to this work, with some ideas already at the back of my mind. It's a real piece, beautiful and magisterial. But I decided against playing it: there's something that disturbs me about the cadenza, which is unduly long-winded, and the final movement isn't entirely convincing. None of it is in the same league as *Palestrina*, an opera I'm infinitely fond of. What a disappointment!

16/IX
Varna
Hall of the House of
the Army
Carissimi, Verdi,
Scarlatti, Rossini
Zara Dolukhanova
Vladimir Khvostin,
piano

The delightful Zara Dolukhanova; this time too (it was the last time for me) she sang her programme most attractively, a programme based on the concert-hall tradition, which is in marked contrast to that of Lieder singers.
Unfortunately, Zara has gone in for far too many experiments in the course of her career. She's positively besotted with yoga, for example, which, in my own view, is disastrous for an artist – look at Yehudi Menuhin, Anatoly Vedernikov and Zhuraitis; then she started to sing as a soprano and ruined her voice.
Previously she had a wonderful mezzo voice and became famous; everyone regarded her as Moscow's leading singer both in the concert hall and in oratorio. She was also a great beauty (she still is) and a delightful woman (this is also still true of her). *Aber . . . alles geht vorüber* [But everything passes away].

19/XI
Recording
Chopin
Studies op. 10
nos. 1 and 2

Ránki reveals extraordinary skill in these extremely tricky studies, and brings them off flawlessly. When we pay too much attention to technical difficulties, it's unfortunately very often to the detriment of the music, which is then no longer

Dezsö Ránki
Janáček
Sinfonietta
Conductor:
Břetislav Bakala

perceived in all its truthfulness. This is almost always the case with virtuoso works, but it's not so here.

Janáček's *Sinfonietta* is a miracle; however many times you listen to it, you're still struck by its originality.

21/XI
Recording
Prokofiev
1) 1st Concerto
2) Excerpts from
Romeo and Juliet
Ravel
1) Concerto for the Left
Hand
2) Pavane
Andrei Gavrilov
Conductor:
Simon Rattle

Gavrilov plays (i) in a virtuosic manner, (ii) with power (sometimes too much), (iii) quickly (again sometimes too quickly, and as a result not always clearly), (iv) loudly (as a result the tone is not always attractive), (v) with imagination (not always justified) and (vi) with a real sense of artistry (a little studied) and in a convincing manner.

He likes to bring his imagination into play, which often results in empty effects.

All in all, a dazzling personality and in many respects close to mine. These recordings bowled me over completely.

25 & 26/XI
Recording
Mussorgsky
Boris Godunov
Talvela, Gedda etc.
Conductor:
Jerzy Semkow

It was during my adolescence in Odessa that I started to familiarize myself with this brilliant work – the finest Russian opera – by reading through the vocal score. Shortly afterwards I had the misfortune to see and hear a frightful performance at the Odessa Opera; Khilkevich's production was a complete mess and the conductor, Pokrovsky, feeble in the extreme. It's worth noting that I got to know the work in the original, rather than in the version by Rimsky-Korsakov. I was aware of this at the time and was very pleased that it was so.

The original version errs only in its instrumentation, which – not to put too fine a point on it – is sometimes defective, notably in the Coronation Scene. But the music itself (which I've often played at the piano) teems with original things and matches the words in an inspired and astounding way. I remember that Papa – a fanatical Wagnerian – always used to say that he would place this work on a par with Wagner's music dramas.

22/XII (morning)
Recording
Haydn
Symphony [no. 49]
in F minor
('La Passione')
Conductor:
Carlo Zecchi

This may not be Haydn's most inspired work, but it's certainly one that one really must listen to.
Here it is, the daily bread that's indispensable to our ear and to our musicality. Listen, listen and listen again; familiarize yourself with it, and learn to love and appreciate it. No danger of getting bored, in spite of what many people fear, but rather a sense of spiritual calm. Such is my humble advice.

22/XII (evening)
Recording
Debussy
Préludes (Book I)
Benedetti Michelangeli

Here again is this total perfection devoid not only of any atmosphere but also (in my own opinion) of the charm that is absolutely indispensable to these *Préludes*. Even so, the performance is note-perfect. He's a real perfectionist. But I think that this fanaticism and and the extreme instrumental standards he set for himself prevent his imagination from taking flight and stop him expressing any real love for the work he's performing so impeccably. It's 'inspiration' that's missing. Is this a notion that's been banished from today's dictionaries? It would be a great shame if this were so. But – one doesn't judge a master.

23/XII
Evening in memory of
Sergey Prokofiev
Haydn
Symphony in F minor
('La Passione')
Conductor:
Carlo Zecchi
Recording
Prokofiev
10 pieces from
Romeo and Juliet
Andrei Gavrilov
Prokofiev
1st Violin Sonata
David Oistrakh and S.R.
Recording

I know that Prokofiev absolutely adored Haydn: he was his favourite composer. I can say the same for myself: if not my favourite, at least one of my favourites.
And so today we listened to this serious minor-key symphony.
Andrei then played the pieces from *Romeo*, brilliantly – as always – from a virtuosic point of view – and with great assurance.
Then came the recording of the 1st Violin Sonata (with David Oistrakh and me). I was present when Oistrakh and Oborin gave the work's first public performance in the Small Hall of the Conservatory and was quite literally captivated by it: since then it has been one of my favourite works by Prokofiev, a work that has the same tragic character as the 2nd Piano Concerto. Its 1st movement is intrinsically Russian, with its almost funereal conclusion. The 2nd movement is extraordinarily

bold, with its irascible, triumphant and phenomenally original theme. The 3rd is a sort of mysterious nocturne and the finale – fiery and full of energy – includes a coda reminiscent of the 1st movement in which you'd think you could hear the wind whistling through a graveyard. The sonata is dedicated to David Oistrakh.

May
Paris
Opéra
Ravel
L'enfant et les sortilèges
Stravinsky
Oedipus rex
Conductor: Seiji Ozawa
Director: Jorge Lavelli

Everything here is contradictory and ultimately superficial. I didn't enjoy it. Ozawa has all that it takes to shine, but he abuses his gifts. Like virtually all modern directors, Lavelli attempts to surprise his audiences with gimmicks, which merely disfigure the work being performed.

June
Moscow
Recording
Schubert
Unfinished Sonata in C major [D 840]
S.R.

It was this sonata, followed by the one in B flat [D 960], that I played during my first visit to Paris. The concert took place at the Palais de Chaillot and unleashed a veritable storm of enthusiasm on the part of the Parisian audience.
I feel that since then, at least for the moment, the Parisians like me. My first visit there was in a different class from those to Vienna, London or Kostroma, where in 1943 the audience was shocked by the fact that I looked too young; my recital there was given over to works by Chopin, and although I thought it extremely successful, it left the audience completely indifferent.

---

30 June and 8 July
Marcilly-sur-Maulne
Recital
Handel
Keyboard Suites nos. 1, 4, 6, 7, 10, 11, 13 and 15
Andrei Gavrilov

On these two evenings, I turned the pages for Andrei Gavrilov for the first time; he performed the same job for me at my own concerts.* The little château where these two recitals took place is utterly enchanting. The hall isn't large but it's built in a very beautiful style, with a fireplace. All the locals turned out in force, of course, as did

---

* For a while Richter and Gavrilov shared a whole series of recitals featuring all the Handel keyboard suites, which they divided between them. (B.M.)

Hideka, a young Japanese pupil of Andrei's mother and one of his (numerous) girlfriends. The concerts passed off very well (for once) and were recorded by EMI. Andrei justified all my expectations: he played in a rigorous, stylistic way, even though in one of the Suites he indulged in an excessive *fortissimo*. But in another he remembered the film *Barry Lyndon*, which helped him to invest the Sarabande with a very real feeling of gravity.

After both concerts we had to do some retakes (effectively it meant playing everything again for the recording). Here Andrei was of great help to me: he had brought a bottle of cognac and, sitting beside me while I played, he managed to create the mood that I needed. This is a quality that he possesses in abundance (the same is true of my old friend Christian) and that he has often demonstrated, notably when he officiated as major-domo at our ball in November 1978. An amazing talent!

July (at the home of Artur Rubinstein)
Paris
Recording
Schumann
1) Kreisleriana
2) Fantasie in C major
Artur Rubinstein

This is weird! This visit has completely slipped my memory.
I remember absolutely nothing about it, though I'm sure it must have been interesting and significant. This isn't a good sign . . .

July
Playback of recordings of Japanese concerts in the 'Chant du Monde' studios
Schumann
6 Phantasiestücke
3 Novelletten
Chopin
13 Préludes
3rd and 4th Ballades
S.R.

I've been playing the *Phantasiestücke* on and off since my time in Odessa and I particularly like 'Des Abends', which looks forward to Debussy. Among the *Novelletten*, there's above all the second in D major, with its extraordinary middle section.
As for Chopin, he said it all, and there's nothing one can add. I don't recommend performing all 24 *Préludes* at once. They contain such a wealth of music of such high quality that the sheer quantity ends up preventing you from appreciating such magnificent music. Also, I don't see them as a real cycle.

The Ballades have long been part of my repertory. The third is *la noblesse en personne*, and it was with the fourth that I ended my very first recital at the Engineers' Club in Odessa. I also played it on entering the Moscow Conservatory. I played it better then than I do now. O Youth, where are you now?

August
Munich
Bavarian State Opera
Wagner
Die Meistersinger
Dietrich Fischer-Dieskau
Peter Schreier
Julia Varady, etc.
Conductor:
Wolfgang Sawallisch

I'd not expected Sawallisch to make such a decent stab at *Die Meistersinger*. The production* wasn't bad, but of no great interest.
As always, the *Kammersänger* [Fischer-Dieskau] was extraordinary, but the role isn't for him, and by the end he was running out of voice. Julia is excellent, even if her tone is sometimes a little hard. As for Schreier, it's enough to repeat the words of Elisabeth Schwarzkopf, who was also at the performance: 'Das ist ein großer Luxus, Schreier als David zu erleben' [It's a great luxury to have Schreier as David].

August
Televised broadcast
Bartók
Concerto for Orchestra
Conductor:
Erich Leinsdorf

On this occasion Erich Leinsdorf made a good impression (unlike the time we worked together in America on Brahms's 2nd Concerto).
The televised broadcast is interesting, inasmuch as it follows the score closely and, for once, doesn't ruin the music.
How I love this last work by Bartók, although I'm slightly less fond of the finale, which is a kind of 'flight to America' not unrelated to the 3rd movement of Rachmaninov's 1st Concerto. A flight from which there was no coming back.

24/IX
Moscow
Gnesin Institute
Shostakovich
String Quartets
nos. 1, 8 and 15
Borodin Quartet

Odessa. Dusk outside the entrance to the Odessa Opera. The street lamps hadn't yet been lit. I was walking along and, not looking where I was going, narrowly avoided colliding inadvertently with a young man of below average height who stared at me fixedly. His strange eyes, almost white, frightened me and I hurried on.

---

*By August Everding, with designs by Jürgen Rose.

At that distant date, the vocal score of *Katerina Izmaylova* had just appeared and after a while – thanks to the photograph that figured on the fly-leaf – I realized that it was Shostakovich whom I'd met in the twilight. Later lots of terrible things happened concerning this opera, its composer and, indirectly, me. To a certain extent, I myself was to blame for the famous article that appeared in *Pravda* under the title 'Chaos instead of Music'. It's an indisputable fact. I still remember the awful smell of glue associated with this score.

Such was my first impression based on a personal encounter with a composer to whom I was later to be bound by so many more pleasant ties. After they'd provoked a reaction of rejection in me, I finally learned to love and, I think, understand his works. For me, his Eighth Symphony, the Trio and the song cycle *From Jewish Folk Poetry* are among the most sublime and inspired works written this century.

23/X
Bolshoy Theatre
Tchaikovsky
Sleeping Beauty

I'm enormously fond of the music to this ballet. It confirms Stravinsky's opinion of Tchaikovsky and the links between the two of them.

It's undoubtedly my favourite ballet. Clearly ballet, as an art, is incapable of doing justice to the music; each time the imperfect nature of ballet surprises me. On stage there are always all kinds of irritating awkwardnesses, such as the awakening of Princess Aurora; it should come as a shock, but what do we see? A kind of limp jelly.

21/XII
In the car while driving through Poland (on the radio)
Bizet
Excerpts from L'Arlésienne (in B major and G sharp minor)

These two tunes suddenly awoke old memories of Odessa in me. I can still see the thick, magnificently bound volume of the transcription for piano four hands of *Carmen* and the incidental music to Daudet's *L'Arlésienne*. I'm playing the last act of *Carmen* with Tolya Paskarenko on an upright piano. He notices how worked up I am and spends his time ragging me (he's the elder of us) and then, with a perverse pleasure, puts an end to our music session. (Anatoly Paskarenko was a pupil of my father and made a promising start, but then went to Moscow, where he came to a bad end in every way; the idol of his parents, he was the victim of the presumption and frivolity of youth.) *L'Arlésienne* is a kind of substitute for the 2nd-act ballet in *Carmen*. How I used to love (and still do) these descending chromatic scales, above all when the major coincides with the minor, as in the trickiest of Chopin's studies, the one in A minor.

2/1
Moscow
Recording
Janáček
Taras Bulba
Conductor:
Václav Talich

I'm often overcome by an immoderate desire to share with other musicians the feelings that bind me to this ultra-expressive work, yet I'm not certain whether this sort of thing can ever be communicated and whether I shall ever achieve my goal. They always say they've enjoyed it, but I suspect that most of the time it's out of this absurd deference towards me, while in their heart of hearts they'd prefer it if I didn't make them listen to it. There's no doubt that at an initial hearing these three deaths chill the listener's blood with their almost unbearable stridency and with the composer's utterly original and highly perceptive way of recreating the mood of Gogol's novella.

6/1
Grand Hall of the
Conservatory
Medtner's centenary
Nikolay Medtner
1) Pieces for violin
Eduard Grach
2) Songs to words by
Pushkin, Tyutchev,
Goethe and Lermontov
Galina Pisarenko,
Lyudmila Simonova,
Sergey Yakovenko and
Alexei Maslennikov
Evgeni Svetlanov, piano

Svetlanov reveres Russian music, and his way of performing it bears all the hallmarks of what people call 'the Russian style'. Quite what this is, I haven't the first idea, as I think that composers in general, and Russian composers in particular, all have their own individual style. Probably something somewhere between Borodin, Mussorgsky's 'The Great Gate at Kiev' and the succulent, massive manner of Tchaikovsky? In any case, the monumental 'style' is alien to the transparency of Rimsky and the imaginative flights of fancy on the part of Scriabin. Svetlanov is highly talented, but unfortunately this side of him comes from Nikolay Golovanov, a not particularly sophisticated musician. Even so, he chose an extremely interesting programme for this concert in memory of Nikolay Medtner and, not for the first time, revealed himself as an excellent pianist. A pity he didn't play any of the composer's works for solo piano, in which he would certainly have scored a success. Medtner wrote a fair number of songs of extraordinary beauty and mastery. I think his settings of Pushkin are his finest achievement.

8/I
Bolshoy Theatre
Galina Ulanova's
70th birthday
1) The Great Ballerina
*2) Tchaikovsky
The Nutcracker*
*Vasiliev, Maximova
Conductor:
Alexander Kopilov*

How could I refuse an invitation to this detested theatre when an occasion like this is celebrated and when I'm offered a seat in the Tsar's box? In spite of my lack of enthusiasm for dancing on points, it's impossible not to be carried away by this phenomenal artist. I remember her in *Giselle*, where she was utterly divine, but I couldn't accept her performance as Juliet, in which she was simply a goddess, rather than a young woman driven to distraction by love. But let's not be judgemental. She's a great artist among the great; all praise to her. *The Nutcracker* was rather ordinary this evening, albeit *comme il faut*, but with no great revelations. The same is true of the production. A Christmas tree in a youth club or a school would have been more in place.

9/II Evening in memory
of Boris Pasternak
on the occasion
of his 90th birthday
Recordings
Scriabin
3rd Sonata
Vladimir Sofronitsky
6th Sonata
S.R.

Pasternak adored Scriabin. In one of his writings he recalls listening at an open window and hearing Scriabin write his 3rd Symphony, adding that he had somehow felt himself to be in the presence of divine inspiration.
The 3rd Sonata, once the most famous of them all, was a model of ideal interpretation in Sofronitsky's hands.
I'm especially fond of the sixth, though I've played it only twice and won't be playing it again. It's a mysterious, nocturnal work.

16/II
Moscow Chamber
Opera Theatre

It was through a recording that I first got to know this opera, but I later attended a performance in London in the small auditorium at Covent Garden;* so this is my third time, in Moscow.

---

* Presumably an error for the performance at Glyndebourne in June 1975.

Stravinsky *The Rake's Progress* Conductor: *Anatoly Levin* Director: *Boris Pokrovsky*	The work is perfection itself and inevitably recalls Mozart's *Don Giovanni* in terms of its form and inspired lightness of touch. Again, it's in a different class from Stravinsky's other works. One of the opera's highlights is the duet between father and daughter in the final act (two tonalities). Tremendous depth and tremendous simplicity.
17/II *Recording* **Suk** *Asrael* Conductor: *Václav Talich*	I've lost count of the number of times I've listened to this recording, and each time it's a miracle! Here's a true conductor for you.
31/III *Recording of a concert at the Shostakovich School* **Prokofiev** *Dance op. 32 no. 1* *Suggestion diabolique op. 4 no. 4* *Visions fugitives op. 22 nos. 3 and 4* S.R.	As so often, I now have to listen to a tape of concerts that I've recently given. I've got to find out if they're any good. It's a tiresome chore that destroys the love you may have for this music. I've always loathed technology and it repays me in kind. We're at cross purposes, and it's the music that suffers most.
5–6/IV (Easter Saturday/Sunday, after dining) *Recording* **Wagner** *Excerpts from Parsifal Prelude and Good Friday Music* Conductor: *Wilhelm Furtwängler*	What can one say about these inspired extracts from Wagner? Here he looks foward to Impressionism while remaining entirely and uniquely himself (the Good Friday Music). And what can one say about the prelude? Nothing. It's an expression of total truth.
9/IV Grand Hall of the Conservatory	This is the first time I've heard Volodya Viardo, who is currently much spoken of and discussed and who, it appears, is a rival of Gavrilov. His way of playing Prokofiev's 5th Concerto is com-

Prokofiev
5th Piano Concerto
Vladimir Viardo
Conductor:
Dmitri Kitaienko

pletely different from my own. He's undoubtedly talented; I like him and find him convincing in this concerto, which he plays not without elegance and in a way that almost reminds me of Ravel.
Kitaienko was an absolute disaster: he sleeps instead of conducting.

10/IV
Performance by the
Hungarian National
Opera at the Bolshoy
Verdi
I Lombardi
Conductor: Ferenc Nagy

The Hungarians offered us an excellent and honest performance of this opera, which I'd not heard until now. Everything about it struck me as pleasing and convincing: Verdi's music was magnificent as always (he's a veritable cornucopia), as were the singers, orchestra and production. The sets were projections of frescos by Giotto and were both interesting and unusual.
There are lots of talented artists in Hungary. I've seen and heard many things in Budapest and always been impressed. In my own view, their operetta theatre, for example, is the best in Europe. And yesterday evening, too, I attended a splendid, original and bold production of Shakespeare's *All's Well that Ends Well*.

15/IV, Melodiya Studios
Playback of recordings
of Japanese concerts
Schumann
Novelletten
nos. 2, 4 and 8
Chopin
13 Préludes
S.R.

The 2nd and 4th of the *Novelletten* really suit me, but in the 8th there's a moment of imprecision. I was finally persuaded to let it through (my weakness of character!).
I liked Chopin's 13 *Préludes* too and even thought I could detect something authentically Chopinesque about them, but it's highly unlikely that advocates of a sentimentalized Chopin will find anything to admire here.

---

21 and 22/IV
Continuation
of playback
Schubert
Moments musicaux
nos. 1, 4 and 6
Impromptu in A flat
[op. 90] *no. 4*

These works are more than inspired. How can one raise oneself up to their level??? I don't know, I really don't know.
In the case of the Ballades, I can't make up my mind. I'm sure that they're bad, like most of my recordings. It's enough for me to listen to them to put me in a bad mood.

Chopin
3rd and 4th Ballades
Debussy
Suite bergamasque
Estampes
S.R.

| 22 and 23/IV (evenings in memory of Prokofiev)
Recording
Ivan the Terrible
op. 116 (oratorio)
Conductor:
Riccardo Muti
1st Piano Concerto
S.R.
Conductor:
Kyrill Kondrashin | We began by playing the score that accompanies Eisenstein's film, as was the case with *Alexander Nevsky*. |

We began by playing the score that accompanies Eisenstein's film, as was the case with *Alexander Nevsky*.

I'd first seen this film just before the end of the war and hadn't been particularly impressed by it; essentially all that I remember is the shot in which we see Ivan's beard stand on end at the moment of his death. The part was played by Cherkassov. It was a tendentious film designed to glorify Ivan and didn't ring true.

Many years after Prokofiev's death the conductor Abram Stasevich arranged the soundtrack as an oratorio, an adaptation which, to judge by what we heard today, is extremely successful. Riccardo Muti's reading sounds convincing, a spectacular, 'terrible' performance. It's a barbaric work, with all these knout blows during the Dance of the Oprichniki and the climate of terror, but at the same time it clearly bears all the hallmarks of Prokofiev's positivistic outlook.

All our friends listened with intense interest (only Viardo said the music was rather weak, but he was really only trying to show off). For my own part, I liked it a lot.

Then, as a sort of encore, we listened to the 1st Concerto in my own interpretation with Kyrill Kondrashin. A fairly successful recording, thank God: an explosion of joy and imagination.

| 8/V
Exhibition of canvases by Shukhayev in memory of Vladimir Sofronitsky
Recording | Scriabin is made for Sofronitsky, just as Sofronitsky is made for Scriabin. |

Scriabin is made for Sofronitsky, just as Sofronitsky is made for Scriabin.

In my youth I wasn't particularly attracted to this music, which struck me at the time as salon music, and it was thanks to Sofronitsky and, of course, Neuhaus that I began to understand this composer

Scriabin
Various works for piano
Vladimir Sofronitsky

and finally to love him. It's true that I never became a hardline Scriabinian, although there were times when I was happy to be converted to his music, only for my enthusiasm to wane again for a while.

Scriabin isn't the sort of composer whom you'd regard as your daily bread, but is a heady liqueur on which you can get drunk periodically, a poetical drug, a crystal that's easily broken.

There used to be a crystal cross on his grave in the Novodevichy Cemetery. One fine day – a sad day – this cross was stolen in the very best Russian tradition.

14/V
Recording
Berg
Chamber Concerto
S.R. and Oleg Kagan
Conductor:
Yuri Nikolayevsky

This recording was the result of a lot of hard work. I've been waiting for it for a long time, and now it has finally been released. The result, one manages to convince oneself, is good. Everything is fine on the level of the performance, and the music makes sense. The only faults in the recording are due to EMI's artistic director, who recorded the work with insufficient knowledge of the score. During the mixing, he didn't always highlight the principal instruments, so that the *pianississimo* trill on the piano at the end of the 1st movement, for example, is far too loud, in spite of the markings in the score.

15/V
Recording
Monteverdi
Orfeo
Éric Tappy, etc.
Conductor:
Michel Corboz

I stood in the entrance hall to our flat, listening to this recording and not even daring to glance in the direction of our guests (it's always a temptation), who were sitting in the main room.

This recording was a fantastic revelation. I understood to what extent this work was daring for its time, almost as daring as Wagner was in the 19th century.

17/VI
Hohenems
Schubert
Winterreise

Christa Ludwig sings this inspired cycle with profundity and seriousness, if not without a certain heaviness. She transports us from June to December, and perhaps even to January. I don't suppose Schubert was feeling very light-hearted

Christa Ludwig
Erik Werba, piano

when he wrote this work, which was bound to reflect his ruined health.

I didn't like Erik Werba. He turned the pages himself, each time omitting a number of notes in the left hand. This really isn't honest.

27/VI
Tours
Grange de Meslay
Bach
3rd Partita for violin
Oleg Kagan
Hindemith
Cello Sonata
op. 25 no. 3
Natasha Gutman
Lutosławski
Bucolics
for viola and cello
Oleg Kagan and
Natasha Gutman
Ravel
Sonata
for violin and cello
Oleg Kagan and
Natasha Gutman

An unusual evening without a piano, which is the usual basis of chamber music.

Everything hovers in the air, and I feel like snatching at it, not only with my ears but also with my hands, as though my perception of things were irresistibly and excessively conditioned by the instrument that I myself play.

Bach doesn't need praising and with Oleg everything is exactly in place. He has the key of E major in his blood and bathes in it for his own delight and for ours.

Natasha's performance is staggering and does full justice to the greatness of the composer. *Bucolics* was then a most agreeable intermezzo.

As for the Ravel, I've already heard this piece on several previous occasions, each time with the same performers. A highly successful evening – and yet I felt the lack of a piano. It's certainly a failing on the part of my own very relative musicality. Perhaps it's not so much the piano as the pedal. Without it, the sense of impressionism loses something.

28 and 30/VII
Arkhangelskoye
(near Moscow)
Handel
Keyboard Suites
Andrei Gavrilov

The country mansion at Arkhangelskoye is of an austere and majestic beauty. The rooms are decorated with splendid sculptures and paintings. From the entrance gateway you can see the long symmetrical courtyard in the French style at the end of which are gardens running down to the Moskva.

The oval room in which our concerts were held – both were devoted to Handel's suites – is at the centre of the building.

The audience came from Moscow, of course (unfortunately, there were lots of official dignitaries). To look after us there was Tanya Skorobogatova (she no longer works at Arkhangelskoye, having been replaced, no doubt because she's an excellent and intelligent organizer, something that's not appreciated here). The concerts began in the late afternoon and ended at dusk. Andrei was seen in his best light on this occasion, resonating in unison with me and enjoying a great success.

The public seems to like this kind of concert: not only is there the music, but they are also surrounded by beauty. Let's not forget that Sumarokov played tennis here. And who were his guests? The cream of aristocratic society. But that's all in the past. In the room leading off to the side there's the statue of an exquisite male nude who has just been bitten by a snake.

1/VIII
Moscow
Rehearsals
Szymanowski
Songs of the Infatuated Muezzin op. 42 and a song to words by James Joyce op. 54
Galina Pisarenko and S.R., piano
Janáček
Concertino
Conductor:
Yuri Nikolayevsky
S.R., piano

We did a lot of work with Galya on the Szymanowski cycle, which she is singing in Polish (Nina Dorliac used to sing it in French). A terribly difficult and an altogether original cycle. Difficult in terms of intonation, and also by virtue of the ornamentation, which demands an extraordinarily subtle range of colours. The piano writing is on a par with that of the solo works.

The *Concertino* is a curious piece, full of humour (I've heard it said that Janáček's head was full of animals, which makes this work a close relation of *The Cunning Little Vixen*). I love the apotheosis, a sort of hymn to the forest and to nature. All in all, a musical curiosity.

We rehearsed all this for a forthcoming tour of Poland.

4/VIII
Grand Hall of the Conservatory
Rehearsal
Schnittke
3rd Violin Concerto
Oleg Kagan and soloists from the Moscow Conservatory

This concerto is dedicated to Oleg. One could say that it's predominantly in the major and fairly translucent. It left a first-rate impression on me: I found it extremely interesting and it seems to me to suit Oleg down to the ground.

Magisterial performance from both the soloist and the orchestra.

It's difficult to add anything more to this, not least because so much time has elapsed between my

Conductor: listening to the rehearsal and now.
Yuri Nikolayevsky   I'll put a + as I have a great deal of sympathy for
                           the work, and I adore Oleg. Period!

September   It's a well-established tradition of Andrei's to play
(in the car and   his own records to passers-by. He's a lucky man,
at Andrei Gavrilov's)   as it gives him such pleasure! Conversely, I suffer
Tape   untold agonies whenever I hear myself playing.
Prokofiev   There's nothing I can do about it.
3 pieces from   Of the three pieces, the one I remember best is
Romeo and Juliet   'Masks'. Stylish and with lots of verve.
Andrei Gavrilov

23/IX   A remarkable and original work in every respect.
Warsaw   I really don't know Lutosławski's music; some
Philharmonic Hall   time ago (1953?) I heard his Concerto for
Witold Lutosławski   Orchestra under Rowicki, as well as Bucolics for
Double Concerto   violin and cello.* It seems to me that he occupies
for oboe, harp and   a leading position among contemporary com-
11 instruments (1980)   posers. I met him in Warsaw, of course, and at the
Heinz Holliger   Britten Festival in Aldeburgh. He struck me as a
Ursula Holliger   deeply serious person, a man of an uncommunica-
Conductor: tive and ascetic bent who conceals within him a
Witold Lutosławski   delicate, fragile soul. The musicians gave an
                           incomparable performance of this extraordinarily
                           captivating concerto. Bravissimo!

11/IX   I shouldn't have listened to Schnittke's Concerto
Moscow University   on this occasion, as I did so immediately before
Schnittke   playing Berg's Chamber Concerto (I was hidden
3rd Violin Concerto   behind an enormous pillar). As before, I liked it
Oleg Kagan   immensely (perhaps even more), but . . .
Conductor: I completely lost my concentration during the
Yuri Nikolayevsky   Berg, and it was unbelievably awful. To make
                           matters worse, it affected all the other players.
                           Unbreakable rule: never listen to anything before
                           going on stage; it invariably leads to disaster.

---

* The Concerto for Orchestra received its first performance in Warsaw on 26 November 1954.
Bukoliki was originally scored for piano and premièred in December 1953. Lutosławski's own
arrangement for viola and cello dates from 1962.

11/IX
Following the concert
at the University
Recording
Berg
Chamber Concerto
S.R.
Oleg Kagan
Conductor:
Yuri Nikolayevsky

In an attempt to forget this frightful concert at the University and to convince myself that we (and I) don't play the Berg too badly, I made myself listen to the famous Paris recording that same evening, a recording which, having been awarded five stars by the musical press in France and Italy, was almost immediately withdrawn from the catalogue because no one was buying it. The only worthwhile and note-perfect recording was considered to be the one with Saschko Gawriloff and Barenboim under Boulez.

Fischer-Dieskau's opinion on our recording: 'I finally and for the first time understood this work.'

25/IX
Performance by the
Deutsche Oper am
Rhein at the Bolshoy*
Schoenberg
Moses und Aron
Conductor:
Grischa Barfuss†

Schoenberg ideally performed with German (almost obsessional) exactitude, a colossal achievement, and yet – was it really worth all the effort?

The music is so complex, so difficult to grasp straight away that it's almost impossible to retain a single bar, a single motif, a single harmony. Hence this strange contradiction. It has to be said that the German singers had rehearsed it all to the very limits of their abilities. (Quotation by Sasha Gabrichevsky: 'I can't bear the Germans.')

The production was every bit as good as everything else.

And suddenly, the last two sections of the work: absolutely splendid (similar in this to the final sections of Bartók's *Bluebeard's Castle*).

It makes you think.

21 and 22/X
Berlin
Apollosaal
Handel
Keyboard Suites
Andrei Gavrilov

On our way into Gavrilov's first recital – it took place in the afternoon – we saw a number of people queuing for tickets at the box office. The organizer, Frau Gonda, said that the hall was full and that these people wouldn't get in.

But when we looked round the hall just before the

---

* A bizarre memory lapse: the performance was in Warsaw, not Moscow.
† The conductor was Günther Wich. Grischa Barfuss was the company's intendant from 1964 to 1986. The present production had first been seen in 1968.

concert started, we saw that the first six rows were completely empty: they'd been bought by the Soviet Embassy, but no one had come. A total idiot from the Embassy went backstage to explain that there had been a meeting that morning but that everyone would turn up for my own concert in the evening. This cretin said this to Andrei just as he was going out on stage. Andrei turned white as a sheet. The hall – attractively Classical – smelt of rotten fish.

Munich
Playback of a recording of a concert from Salzburg
Schubert
Sonata in C major (unfinished)
Prokofiev
*Legenda,
10 Visions fugitives,
Dance, Waltz and
5 pieces from Cinderella*
S.R.

No doubt this is how I played at the concert. I find the programme quite acceptable; but when did it take place?* How much water has flowed under the bridge since then?

The first time I played Schubert's C major Sonata was at the Palais de Chaillot in Paris, and it was enormously successful with the Parisians, who were bowled over by it.

I've been playing Prokofiev's enchanting pieces for a long time. Sergey Sergeyevich criticized my interpretation of the Dance: 'You're not playing it as it should be played.' 'How should it be played then?' He didn't reply.

I like *Cinderella* far more than *Romeo* as a ballet. The young Plisetskaya was amazing as the Autumn Fairy; as for the Gavotte and Waltz, it was Ulanova!!

4/xi, Restaurant 'Roma' (beside the house where Jules Verne was born)
Nantes
Recording
Verdi
Choruses from Aida, Il trovatore, I Lombardi, etc.

A delightful evening among friends. Sometimes, when you hear something you weren't expecting in an unexpected place, the impression it produces is fresher than in the concert hall where the mere fact that you're expecting it means that your perception of things loses its immediacy.

A frisky little cat spent the whole meal running in every direction, even rummaging in Nina's bag and taking out a cigarette, before finally jumping up on to a picture, which became unhooked, so that both painting and cat fell to the ground with a crash. We laughed a lot.

---

* This concert did not take place within the framework of the Salzburg Festival.

25/XII
Bolshoy Theatre
Shostakovich
Katerina Izmaylova
Conductor: Gennady
Rozhdestvensky
Director:
Boris Pokrovsky

I've blundered again. Long ago I swore never again to set foot in the Bolshoy. Well, I broke my word and have paid dearly for it.
Sheer madness!
From a formal, musical point of view, it was perfect, but it left no lasting impression (you can't expect anything more from Rozhdestvensky, who's no better than a mechanical doll). As for the production, our friend Boris Pokrovsky surpassed himself. But even I wasn't expecting such an abomination. If I've understood him correctly, his aim was evidently to combine the two Katerinas – Leskov's and Ostrovsky's – and you can imagine the result!
Of the entire performance, only three moments had anything to do with art: the magnificent and unexpected violin solo (played by Seryozha Ghirshenko) during the nocturnal love scene, the reflector during the transportation of the convicts in the final act and the role of Sonetka, who was played by Tatiana Yerastova in a poignant and convincing manner.
Unfortunately, that's just about everything.
P.S. And the scenery. Why have the Moscow Kremlin instead of Mtsensk – and, on top of everything, blood-red in colour!

8/I
Recording
Liszt
1) Sonata in B minor
(at Carnegie Hall in
New York)
2) Funérailles
(Budapest)
3) Hungarian Fantasia
(Budapest)
S.R.
Conductor:
János Ferencsik

When I played the Liszt Sonata at Carnegie Hall, our American impresario Sol Hurok didn't invite any of the music critics from the New York press, and so this concert – which was in fact extremely successful – passed off completely unnoticed.
I was delighted that Rachmaninov's daughter, Irina Volkonskaya, came backstage to see me and to say some very flattering things about me and to castigate the famous New York critic Harold Schonberg, who had been exceedingly hostile about me. For a long time, technical shortcomings meant that this record, which is made up entirely of works by Liszt, could not be released, even though it's one of my genuinely successful recordings. I myself enjoy listening to it, which is not that often.

14/1 *Recording* **Berlioz** *Grande messe des morts op. 5* Soloist: Peter Schreier Conductor: Charles Munch	I've always thought that this was the most significant and most beautiful of all Berlioz's works; and this recording by Charles Munch is the best performance of it. Berlioz was incredibly daring, though he sometimes abuses that gift; not here, however, where all is harmony and balance. I particularly like the first and last movements, with the motif repeated in the sopranos like a pedal point. The 'Lacrymosa' and especially the Sanctus, as performed by the young Schreier, are both magnificently daring.
15/1 *Recording* **Wagner** *Lohengrin* Conductor: Eugen Jochum	Today we plunged into the limpid fountain of the musico-literary miracle that is Wagner. Everyone knows, of course, what this 'Romantic' opera represents; but if one has had the good fortune to know this opera in all its details – which are like those of the architecture of a Gothic cathedral – from one's earliest childhood, one has an enormous advantage over everyone else. In fact, I was extraordinarily lucky, and I can truthfully say that I can appreciate the greatness of this ideal work in all its essential details. P.S. I sometimes have the impression that the third act was written before the first and second, but I may be wrong. I don't know anyone I could ask.*
16/1 Playback of recordings in the Melodiya Studios **Liszt** *Funérailles* *Hungarian Fantasia* *Sonata in B minor* S.R.	This recording contains a fair number of technical shortcomings – they don't bother me in the slightest – and is interesting and, it seems to me, exceptionally successful. But the problems bound up with its technical imperfections continue to block its release. True, there's a mediocre piano in *Funérailles*, but the rest! The Fantasia almost carries you away with enthusiasm (sorry!). The Sonata is virtually without mishaps from beginning to end, and it has a verve and an atmosphere that make it an outright success. What more do you want?

* Wagner began the first complete draft of the music with Act I, although the second complete draft of Act III was made before those of the other two acts.

31/III
Grand Hall of the
Conservatory
Grieg
Peer Gynt Suite no. 1
9 Songs (orchestrated
by Svetlanov)
Galina Pisarenko
Norwegian Dances
Suite from Sigurd
Jorsalfar
Conductor:
Evgeni Svetlanov

Svetlanov is not only a talented musician, he's also a man of great intelligence and a magnificent conductor. Moreover, he's a fine pianist and he loves chamber music.

He has done a splendid job orchestrating these songs, which Galina Pisarenko sang to great acclaim. But I can't see why he needed to orchestrate them at all. It's this eternal obsession with wanting to show that everything sounds better when orchestrated, an obsession that afflicts nearly all conductors (even someone like Evgeny Mravinsky, who wanted to conduct the Liszt Sonata), and it's universally considered that *Pictures at an Exhibition* should be heard only in its orchestral arrangement.

I think this is a terrible misconception. A work should always be played in its original version, otherwise it's no longer authentic.

It's a different matter when the composer himself does the transcription, but another hand is always out of place here.

Svetlanov is a composer in his own right, but, in spite of all his efforts, he has been wasting his time here. He's also very full of himself.

Be that as it may, this evening's concert was generally most convincing. Even so, I have to say that, in spite of my love of Grieg, I've no great sympathy for the March from the *Sigurd Jorsalfar* Suite.

23 and 24/IV
(Maundy Thursday
and Good Friday)
Recording
Bach
St Matthew Passion
Fischer-Dieskau, Pears,
Schwarzkopf, Ludwig,
Gedda, Berry
Conductor:
Otto Klemperer

Magnificent tradition.

With Klemperer, nothing is simple or straightforward. It's as though he has to force himself to climb the Tower of Pisa, weighing up and considering each step, before finally seeing the starry heavens.

To return to our tradition, we should really observe it more often, but we do so only once a year. That's how the calendar dictates. But if it weren't organized along these lines, would people find the time and have the inclination to rise to such heights on more frequent occasions? People are so busy and so fond of vacuous conversation that, short of forcing them, there's no way of silencing them.

And so we must thank God for giving us a calendar and making us stick to it.

That's why those who don't fully understand the beauty of this tradition and of this music may none the less feel afterwards a sense of satisfaction at the miracle that has been enacted (even passively) and at least for a time feel at peace with themselves.

We are grateful to the great artists who appear in this recording for the riches that they have to offer us.

10/VI
Recording
Prokofiev
6th Sonata
Ivo Pogorelich

Some time ago we received a visit from a 'lady' from Tbilisi. She brought with her a photograph of Paradzhanov with Lili Brik, and a recording made by her husband, Ivo Pogorelich. On the cover of the record is his photograph, a young and pretty little face with curly hair. The 'lady' is his teacher; she claims to be Liszt's great-granddaughter. In fact, she looks rather like a costermonger.

I've listened to the recording – again, a total misunderstanding of Prokofiev. An exhibitionist temperament and a sloppy use of the pedal.

14/VI
Brahms
Study–Variations on a Theme by Paganini
Arturo Benedetti Michelangeli

I'm currently working on these study–variations and so I listened again to Michelangeli's recording. And unfortunately (yes, unfortunately) I didn't find what I was looking for.

Everything proved to be a little stilted and superficial, very much in the style of a 'study'. I fully understand that it's hard to break away completely from the technical side of this music, but even so one would like a little more distance from it.

Of course, it's easy to say this – and I've no wish to criticize a great artist.

20/VI, Tours
Grand Théâtre
Recital by
Nicolai Gedda
Bellini, Donizetti,

The theme of this year's Fêtes Musicales de Touraine is singing. The first concert was given by Nicolai Gedda. But, horror of horrors, the hall for this concert was half empty! Could it be that the French don't like singing? No, not at all, it's some-

Gounod, Bizet, Wagner, Rossini, Verdi

thing far worse. They're all sitting in front of their television sets awaiting the results of the presidential elections. Here's an intelligent and cultured country for you!?! As if it made any difference for them to be glued to their screens. For me, all it does is illustrate the way in which our age has fallen into total decay. *O tempora! O mores!* Gedda sang magnificently, of course, and the audience, although thin, did what it could to give the impression through its enthusiasm and ovations that the hall was full.

As everyone knows, Gedda is an extraordinarily likeable man. In his dressing-room after the concert, I played him some excerpts from the tenor role in Pfitzner's *Palestrina* (which I like a lot), and he was amazed to discover that I know this music by heart, whereas he himself has forgotten it completely.

28/VI
Grange de Meslay
Tom Krause
Irwin Gage, piano
Songs by Schubert, Sibelius and Schumann (Dichterliebe)

This was the first time I'd heard this singer. An excellent impression. A serious and thoughtful performance, real culture. Schubert and Schumann in the noblest tradition; but as for the Sibelius, I really can't see anything in it, it's completely alien to me and as insipid as the Finnish lakes.

The singer himself has a slightly strange appearance, he's very tall and his face has something childishly inexpressive and yet likeable about it.

It's often like this with singers – a feeling that 'it's always the same', perhaps it's because they're not sufficiently trained as actors (they think first and foremost of their voices and of the individual notes), but perhaps I'm quibbling.

Irwin Gage is an excellent pianist, but he too has an odd face.

Forgive me.

2/VII
Grange de Meslay
Christoph Eschenbach and Justus Frantz

How well they played this evening, especially in the Mozart! I think that Eschenbach, who invariably leads the way, holds the key to understanding this music and its extraordinary charm, a charm that springs to life beneath his fingers.

Mozart
Sonata for two pianos
K 448
Schubert
Fantasie in F minor
[D 940]
Brahms
Sonata for two pianos
op. 34b

The Schubert and Brahms, too, were a real treat, although in the case of the Brahms I prefer the version for piano quintet, which I've played on numerous occasions.

3/VII
Grange de Meslay
Recital by
Barbara Hendricks
Stafan Scheja, piano
Songs by Schubert
and Brahms and
Negro spirituals

Here she is, the new star, the young rival of Jessye Norman.

The impression that she produces is excellent – voice, cultivated singing, charm, artistry. Her programme has been put together with a good deal of taste, and of course she ends with Negro spirituals (a type of music for which, it's true, I feel no affinity). Great success with the local audience, who have already been extremely spoilt with a large number of very fine programmes and superb artists such as Fischer-Dieskau, Schwarzkopf, David Oistrakh, Benjamin Britten and Benedetti Michelangeli – all in the course of the last seventeen years.

I got to know Hendricks's husband (and impresario) during one of my visits to Paris. An extremely handsome young man, bursting with vitality, he joined me and Alexander Slobodianik for dinner at a famous night-club in the Rue Mazarine lit by multicoloured neon tubes. We ended the evening at an extremely louche cabaret; above us was a kind of hammock in which the smuttiest imaginable movements were performed. Nothing to do with this evening's concert; just as an aside.

4/VII
Grange de Meslay
Cathy Berberian
Massimiliano Damerini,
piano
Monteverdi, Berio,

This year Elisabeth Schwarzkopf gave some masterclasses in Tours that were attended by a woman of a certain age with blond white hair and a slightly disturbing appearance. She followed closely the lessons which Schwarzkopf, with her extraordinary energy, turned into a kind of theatrical per-

Debussy, Stravinsky,
Kurt Weill,
impersonations of a
pupil of Régine Crespin
and an English oratorio
singer, African songs
(with a fan instead of a
drum), Azerbaijani song,
Offenbach and
Gershwin

formance. This woman was Cathy Berberian, a personality in her own right, an artist of the rarest kind and a splendid singer to boot. Everything she did bore the hallmarks of authenticity. Whether it was early music (Monteverdi) or contemporary works (Berio, Kurt Weill and Stravinsky), everything rang true. And as for Debussy, I don't think anyone could sing him better. She has a way with Sprechgesang that won me over completely.

She's a mistress of metamorphosis, a female chameleon. At the time of her concert, she was suffering from a dreadful cold, but it didn't stop her from singing for a moment. Mastery and total freedom.

And the wit that she brought to her impersonations! And the way the danced the Azerbaijani song, as well as the Offenbach and Gershwin! What a phenomenal talent!

At the end, there were flowers; I gave her an orchid that she held with great delicacy while performing an encore.

Not very long after this I learned she had died. What a tremendous loss to art.*

July
Munich
Opera House
Richard Strauss
Der Rosenkavalier
Gwyneth Jones, Brigitte
Fassbaender, Lucia
Popp, Kurt Moll, etc.
Conductor:
Carlos Kleiber

Here, we're dealing with the cream of the Munich Opera – both Richard Strauss *and* Kleiber. Impossible not to fall under their spell and feel a sense of heady intoxication. The lightness and freedom with which Carlos conducts this opera are quite simply amazing – the ultimate in conducting. The production* is totally satisfactory (for the present, contemporary producers are clearly afraid of tampering with this work).

Gwyneth Jones is excellent, though she's no Schwarzkopf. Fassbaender is remarkable in the role of Octavian. Her disguise as a boy is extraordinary and she looks like Fischer-Dieskau. All the others are in perfect harmony, vocally and visually, with the rest. It's only a pity that the dissonant

---

* Cathy Berberian died in Rome on 6 March 1983 at the age of fifty-four.
† Otto Schenk's production, with designs by Jürgen Rose, was first seen in 1972.

retouchings that Strauss made to the orchestration are barely perceptible.

July–August, at the home of Lisa Leonskaja Vienna
Recording of my recital in Tours on 20/VI
Weber
Sonata no. 1 in C major
Liszt
Eight Études d'exécution transcendante
S.R.

I had to live through this fiasco all over again. The Weber just about works and one can more or less accept it (Lisa even made a copy of it for herself), but the Liszt remains a catastrophe. I simply went too far and ruined everything.
I should really have thought about this beforehand and not risked such an undertaking.

August, at the home of Lisa Leonskaja
Recording
Richard Strauss
Sinfonia domestica
Conductor:
Herbert von Karajan

I'm not entirely sure what Strauss wanted here, but for me this sort of performance of one of my favourite works is simply unacceptable. After all, 'domestica' suggests a certain chamber atmosphere, a kind of reserved and agreeable warmth. So what are these exaggerated *fortissimos* and this misguided monumentality doing here?

23 and 25/VIII
Zvenigorod
Bach
6 Cello Suites
Natasha Gutman

These two concerts were what you might call experimental and took place in two tiny houses rented for the summer by the Kagans and Chemberdzhys in a little village on the heights of Zvenigorod.
There were a mere handful of listeners, crowded together and sitting or more or less reclining on couches or in the few available armchairs. An extremely intimate and brilliantly single-minded atmosphere.
Natasha plays Bach with her eyes closed, obliterating herself completely, her inspired face revealing a supreme inner beauty. She delves deep into the very essence of the music.
All around is the everyday life of the countryside, a kitchen with odd bits of washing up piled high, battered washbasins, colourful towels and Oleg's mother – Sinaida Mikhailovna Kagan – busying herself with her chores.

31/VIII
Moscow
Pushkin Museum
(Moscow–Paris
1900–1930 Exhibition)
Shostakovich
Quartet no. 1 op. 49
Prelude and Scherzo
for string octet op. 11
Prokofiev
Overture on Hebrew
Themes
Ravel
Quartet in F major
Borodin Quartet
and a second quartet
Lyudmila Berlinskaya,
piano
Ivan Mozgovenko,
clarinet

The Borodin Quartet is the best quartet in our country, incredibly well-oiled and very experienced. They play all Shostakovich's quartets and 'almost' the whole of the string quartet repertory. They're virtually always on form.

Unfortunately, they don't really get on together, which is the fate of virtually all groups whose members get on each other's nerves as a result of the vast amount of time spent working together. There was once a Beethoven Quartet: the viola player wouldn't speak to the second violin and communicated all his intentions through the intermediary of the first violin or else they wrote each other notes. The Borodin Quartet hasn't reached that point yet, but *attenzione.*

Miloshka Berlinskaya (the daughter of the cellist) today played the modest piano part in the Prokofiev Overture, but not long ago she created an excellent impression in the piano part in Britten's opera *The Turn of the Screw*, emerging with considerable credit from the great difficulties of this music.

I was most impressed by this concert at the Pushkin Museum. It was not without interest.

9/I
Grand Hall of the
Conservatory
Schoenberg
Phantasy
for violin and piano
Schnittke
1st Violin Sonata
Lutosławski
Recitative e arioso
Shostakovich
Polka from the ballet
The Golden Age
Brahms–Heifetz
Wie Melodien zieht es mir
Oleg Kagan and
Vladimir Skanavi

Successful and compelling performances of extraordinarily complex works. Schoenberg's Phantasy finally made sense to me (no doubt I've matured in the interim); it was high time.

Schnittke's Sonata, in which one detects the influence of Shostakovich, is splendidly written and made a deep impression.

The encores comprised pieces by Lutosławski and Shostakovich and were perfectly in keeping with the rest of the programme, but Milord Heifetz shows incredible cheek with his sickly and salonesque transcription of one of Brahms's most beautiful songs.

A brilliant performance by Oleg Kagan and Vladimir Skanavi.

18/I
Recording
Suk
Asrael
Conductor:
Václav Talich

A splendid symphony that's written in heart's blood. (Comparable to Tchaikovsky's 6th and Myaskovsky's 6th.)
An inspired performance. How wonderful that this recording exists!

29/I
Concert at home
Beethoven
Violin Sonatas
nos. 7, 8 and 10
Oleg Kagan and
Vassili Lobanov

Beethoven's violin sonatas are <u>self-evidently</u> brilliant, but there's no comparison with the piano sonatas, which are far more inspired, far fresher and more direct.
In fact, I even think they are the best things that Beethoven ever wrote.

17/II
Musical evening
Schumann
Three Phantasiestücke
op. 73
Brahms
Trio in A minor for
piano, clarinet and cello
Andrei Gavrilov
Anatoly Kamyshev
Ivan Monighetti

Today Andrei Gavrilov reigns over us, in the company of his partners.
Everything is impetuous, hot-blooded, a little untidy, but sincere, effective and fairly boisterous. How lucky he is to be almost always satisfied with himself. I think it's a sign of good health, but it would be even better if he were just a tiny bit more modest.

14/IV
Recording
Haydn
Seven Last Words
Amadeus Quartet

With what extreme economy of means Haydn wrote this work! He must certainly have observed Lent when composing it!

29/IV, In memory
of Theofil Richter
(1872–1941) on the
110th anniversary
of his birth
Schumann
Symphonic Studies
S.R.

I first heard the Symphonic Studies played by Papa, and they accompanied my childhood while he worked on them in the barely lit room in our flat in Odessa.
At the Odessa Opera Papa played the organ part in the Cathedral Scene in *Faust*. It's a very special and a very remarkable scene; the organ part is really quite original both in its austerity and by virtue of the fact that it remains entirely accessible to the listener.

Gounod *Act IV Scene 2* [recte 3] *of Faust* *Mirella Freni* *Nicolai Ghiaurov* *Conductor:* *Georges Prêtre* **Brahms** *2nd Violin Sonata* *David Oistrakh and* *S.R.*	The Brahms Sonata is a fairly successful recording with Oistrakh.

30/IV, In memory of Theofil Richter *Recordings* **Beethoven** *Sonata op. 7* *S.R.* **Gounod** *Act IV Scene 2* [recte 3] *of Faust* *Victoria de los Angeles* *Boris Christoff* *Conductor:* *André Cluytens* **Wagner** *Prelude to Act III* *of Tannhäuser* *Prelude to Parsifal* *Conductor:* *Otto Klemperer*	In the second movement (in C major) of his E flat major Sonata, Beethoven seems to be communing with Our Lord and affirming His existence. The performance of the Cathedral Scene from *Faust* is even better in this second recording than it was in the first one. And what can one say about Wagner???

2/VII, Tours Meslay *Recital by* *Jessye Norman* *Philip Moll, piano* **Songs by Schubert,** **Mahler and Brahms and** **Negro spirituals**	This concert was something of an event. It took place amid thunder and lightning, so that there was a power cut and we had to use candles to light the hall; suddenly there was a real atmosphere. Jessye is enormous (I always think of her under a canopy), a phenomenon that's half threatening, half triumphant. And the music! Only she can sing Schubert's *Die Allmacht* as she did. It was a fantastic concert, with the music rivalling Nature, which made threatening noises outside.

Magnificence and light-heartedness.

To end, there were some spirituals. They're not for me, but on the other hand, it's her world, and she feels at home in it. Then there was thunderous applause that rang out at the same time as the last claps of thunder outside, and we emerged into the hall's water-logged courtyard. It smelt of rain and freshness; there was a real sense of liberation.

3/VII
Grange de Meslay
Alain Bancquart
Voix
Stravinsky
1) Ave Maria
2) Credo
3) Mass for choir and double wind quintet
Groupe Vocal de France conducted by John Alldis

Extremely interesting concert. Unfortunately I've forgotten the piece by Bancquart, but I still remember the ones by Stravinsky.

The Mass draws on the Russian *a cappella* choral tradition. Once is unfortunately not enough for this type of music if you're to assimilate all its splendid qualities, which are of an intellectual order.

August, at the home of Éric Anther, France
Recording
Liszt
Pensée des morts
Andante lagrimoso
Ave Maria
S.R.
at the Grange de Meslay

I can't complain at the standard of performance in any of these three works. I remember the Grange half-lit and how Fischer-Dieskau, too, liked to sing Brahms and Wolf in semi-darkness.

24/IX
Moscow
Rehearsal at home
Shostakovich
Seven Romances on Verses by Alexander Blok op. 127
Galina Pisarenko, Kopelman, Berlinsky and Lobanov

I've often heard this cycle on poems by Blok, but I've never liked it, unlike the Michelangelo or Jewish cycles. It seems to me that the qualities of the poet and of the musician are on such totally different levels that there can be no real match between them.

25/IX *Recording* **Britten** *Piano Concerto* S.R. *Conducted by* *the composer*	What a shame that this recording of this delightful early work is not more successful! Britten was no more than a shadow of himself – he was ill – and there was only a single rehearsal, then the recording immediately afterwards. That's why it's not turned out properly. How sad!
4/XII *Recording* **Handel** *Suites nos. 2, 3 and 5* S.R.	My recordings of Handel's Suites aren't the alpha and omega of Handel performance, even if all the notes are there, and there are no mistakes as such. It seems to me that in a certain sense Handel is harder to play than Bach (probably because there's a little less real music here).
7/XII Rehearsal at home **Mozart** *Violin Sonatas* K 380, 403 and 454 Oleg Kagan and S.R.	Rehearsal for a concert for the December Nights. Although we've often played these sonatas together before, we're still trying to find something in them, which still evades us. Perhaps we'd do better to sight-read them, rather than trying to split hairs. But that, too, is risky. One should <u>enjoy</u> playing. There you have it! But what if that doesn't happen?
20/XII Concert at the Pushkin Museum **Mozart** *Sonatas for four hands* *and two pianos* K 521, 497 and 448 Christoph Eschenbach and Justus Frantz **Mozart** At home, after the concert *'Dissonance' Quartet* K 465 Viktor Tretyakov, Oleg Kagan, Yuri Bashmet and Natasha Gutman	Once again a superb concert by these two musicians. Their ensemble playing is well-oiled, they make real music and understand one another marvellously well. I think Eschenbach holds the key to understanding Mozart's music. There are moments at which he's quite simply irresistible and his way of playing casts a very real spell on the listener. Back home, a new treat awaited us. Mozart's C major Quartet. Impossible to say who was happier, those who were playing or those who were listening. Eschenbach and Frantz are very uncomplicated and sympathetic. But I like Eschenbach infinitely more, on a musical and personal level. He's both a superb pianist and a very serious conductor. That's why there's a tendency to ignore him or to criticize him in the West.

24/XII
Concert
at the Pushkin Museum
Mozart
Violin Sonata K 380
Duos for violin and
viola K 423 and 424
Vladimir Spivakov,
Yuri Bashmet and
Boris Bechterev

I have to say that this concert gave the impression of two adversaries locked in a life-or-death struggle, with the emphasis on death. Impossible to decide at the time who would emerge victorious. Yuri makes no secret of his feelings and is desperately keen to win (and to have his own chamber orchestra). As for his rival, all sorts of rumours are currently circulating about him, the ones directed at Yuri verging on the criminal.

The concert was none the less of a high standard, and the audience (especially the ladies) were completely infatuated with Spivakov.

26/XII
Concert
at the Pushkin Museum
Mozart
Three Sonatas and
Rondo in A minor
Eliso Virsaladze

Virsaladze plays Mozart magnificently, but her Schumann is in another class entirely.

It's all perfectly well done, it sounds good, but I feel a certain lack of spontaneity, a slightly mannered approach. But there's no question that she has a conception and a musicality that are out of the ordinary. She's an artist of considerable stature, perhaps the leading female pianist of our day. She's an essentially honest and genuinely modest musician. She's also of noble 'blood', which isn't unimportant for an artist. She impresses me deeply in every respect.

But what is it about Mozart? Is there a pianist alive who really manages to play him well?

Casadesus, whom I heard in Odessa in the F major Sonata K 332 – it must be about a century ago – left an unforgettable impression, a miracle such as one rarely witnesses.

And then there was Neuhaus, who played the A minor Rondo in so touching a manner that it almost reduced you to tears.

It's odd, but Haydn – who seems after all to be fairly close to Mozart in terms of genius – is infinitely less difficult to play (he's almost easy in fact).

So what's Mozart's secret?

8/1, at the home
of Oleg Kagan
Recordings
Purcell
Harpsichord works
Gustav Leonhardt
Debussy
Prélude à l'après-midi
d'un faune
Conductor:
Ernest Ansermet
Stravinsky
Capriccio
The composer
at the piano
Conductor: Ansermet
Liszt
Polonaise in E major
Sergey Rachmaninov
Johann Strauß
The Blue Danube
Josef Lhévinne
(in an unbelievably
difficult transcription)
Hugo Wolf
Abschied
Dietrich Fischer-Dieskau
and S.R.

Oleg had drawn up his own programme of works to listen to, and extremely interesting and varied it proved to be.

Purcell: a first course full of nobility and elegance.

Debussy: a magnificent interpretation by Ansermet. Incomparably beautiful.

Stravinsky: a performance by the composer. So when shall I finally play this prodigious work myself? I've already made two attempts to learn it, but so far without success.

Liszt: I don't like Rachmaninov's interpretation, I've a completely different conception of this work.

Johann Strauß: brio, virtuosity, circus music. A live performance; fantastic success for Lhévinne.

Wolf: no comment.

12/1
Recording
Handel
Keyboard Suites
No. 11
Andrei Gavrilov
Nos. 14 and 16
S.R.
Liszt
Polonaise in E major
S.R. in Prague

Listening repeatedly to recordings.

Handel: fairly plain and academic, but not dry.

Liszt in Prague: a delightful period when I got to know Julius Katchen and his wife Arlette. I remember hearing him give a superb concert. For one reason or another, Arlette particularly liked my way of playing the Liszt Polonaise, and she asked for this recording as a memento (the record hadn't been officially released).

Where are these friends today?* And all these people who gave me so many tokens of their

*Katchen died in Paris on 29 April 1969 at the age of forty-two.

Chopin *8 Studies* *opp. 10 and 25* *S.R. in Bucharest*	affection in Prague? I never see them. Chopin in Bucharest: I think this was all right in the concert hall, but it's not suitable for a recording. This is a situation with which I've long been all too familiar.
21/i *Televised broadcast* **Dvořák** *Piano Quintet* *Borodin Quartet* *and S.R.*	I don't need to dwell on the remarkable qualities of this work. Brahms had good reasons for valuing this composer. It's true that he didn't like Bruckner, but there he was greatly mistaken.
24/i *Recording* **Chopin** *1st Ballade, 8 Studies* *Polonaise and Andante* *spianato* *Conductor:* *Kyrill Kondrashin* *S.R.*	I don't know where these recordings were made, though I've played the works themselves innumerable times. Nor do I know why I put this record on, but it was no doubt at the request of all the friends around me, who – oddly enough – continue to want to hear me. A phrase that's been circulating at the Moscow Conservatory for twenty-five years: 'When will Richter finally go out of fashion?'
28/i *Recording* **Dvořák** *Piano Concerto* *S.R.* *Conductor:* *Kyrill Kondrashin* (London)	My London recording of the Dvořák Concerto has lots of shortcomings – and not only in the piano part. I don't know the reason for all this: could it be London, where I always feel very ill at ease; or the indifference and conservatism of the English; or the critics, who decided that this piece by Dvořák – like Chopin's Polonaise and Andante spianato – is third-rate music?
29/i *Recording* **Beethoven** *Sonata op. 111* *S.R.*	I'm sure I must sometimes have played this sonata reasonably well. But of all the recordings that have been made of it, not one of them is any good. It's almost always like this with recordings. I find it very depressing.
31/i *Recording* **Debussy** *Jeux*	I'd not heard this piece before and understood very little. Perhaps it's due to my lack of attention? Or perhaps it's Boulez?

Conductor: *Pierre Boulez*	
11/11 *Recording* **Bizet** *L'Arlésienne* *Suites nos. 1 and 2* *Conductor:* *Roger Desormière*	It's bound to be good when the conductor's called Desormière. One of the true greats! And especially when it's (good) French music!
End of February Vienna Konzerthaus *Stephane Grappelli,* *jazz violin*	A concert of pure enjoyment. Initially, I didn't even want to go. Grappelli is a great artist in his way, original and unwilling to take himself seriously. It's all extremely light-hearted and entertaining. Brilliant jazz music, which – needless to say – I immediately forgot.
March Vienna State Opera **Verdi** *Rigoletto* *Gilda: Gruberová* *Rigoletto: Bruson* *Conductor:* *Riccardo Muti*	A first night at the Vienna Opera.* I don't think I've ever seen or heard such an abomination, even if Muti more or less respected Verdi's tempos (which no doubt explains why the audience booed him). (Sorry, I almost forgot the storm scene, which was taken at an inadmissibly rapid tempo.) As for the singers, all of whom are undoubtedly blessed with fine voices, they sang with so little expression and feeling (especially Gruberová) that the work (which is so inspired!) lost all its significance, while the high notes were received with storms of enthusiasm. We saw no trace of the opera's emotional aspect. Bruson is the most ordinary of Rigolettos, of whom I've already seen literally hundreds. The Duke is simply a cretin. And the production – impossible to imagine anything more outdated or more routine. In the second scene, the moonlight was so bright on the left that Rigoletto couldn't possibly have been mistaken, even with a blindfold on; and suddenly another wan moon appeared on

* This was the first performance in Vienna of the new critical edition of the opera in a production by Sandro Sequi, with designs by Pantelis Dessyllas.

the right. And everything else was on a par with this. A real nightmare!

But the worst part of it all was the audience! They drowned out the music with their shouting and screaming, behaving like a bunch of lunatics and evidently enjoying themselves in the process.

All that was missing was a machine-gun.

Muti greeted the applause triumphantly, and Maazel proudly showed me his office (he's now director of the Vienna Opera).

How it all disgusts me!

Congratulations!

29/III
Paris
Recording
Rimsky-Korsakov
Concerto
in C sharp minor
Glazunov
1st Concerto
S.R.
Conductor:
Kyrill Kondrashin

Re-encounter with my 'antediluvian' recordings that are now considered to be 'technically' imperfect. But what about those by Slezak, Nezhdanova and Shalyapin??

Rimsky

Here there's a shortcoming: incorrect accents in the final octaves in D flat. The rest isn't too bad.

Glazunov

A very difficult work. 'Why do you play this concerto?' I'm often asked.

First, because I like it, of course, and secondly because it's very Glazunovian, a unified whole and it has a style very much its own (a bit like *Anna Karenina* in the 1st movement and almost balletic in the 2nd). It's magnificently structured (unlike the Violin Concerto, which I don't like). So much for its eclecticism.

Unfortunately, Kondrashin doesn't play the theme in the second movement in a sufficiently penetrating manner. Even so, it's an extremely pleasing recording on the whole.

31/III
Recording of a concert
at Aldeburgh
Rachmaninov
Études-tableaux
in F sharp minor
op. 39 no. 3 and

The *Étude-tableau* in F sharp minor is one of my favourites. These fiery escarpments, these waterfalls with shards of ice seem almost to have been caught in a single inspired breath. And the way he suddenly applies the brakes in the final bars – this phenomenal study looks forward to the whole of Prokofiev's art of piano writing, but this is true of

in B minor *op. 39 no. 4* S.R.	all these *Études-tableaux* (Prokofiev would be furious if he heard me say this). A batty old lady once said to me on hearing the B minor Study: 'I can just see the French aristocracy leaving the country (in carriages, of course) before the *great* revolution. I can imagine their state of mind.'
2/IV *Recording* **Wagner** *Act III of Parsifal* *Parsifal: Peter Hofmann* *Gurnemanz: Kurt Moll* *Amfortas: José van Dam* *Conductor:* *Herbert von Karajan*	An exceptionally successful release from Karajan. Here he reveals some remarkable insights. Time itself seems to be conducting the music. Everything is so profound and at the same time so clear from the prelude and Good Friday Music to the final beguiling notes on the harp that seem to bar the way to the uninitiated lay person. The three soloists share in this mystery through the profundity of their singing. What grandeur Karajan is capable of achieving! It's enough for him to will it so. What humanity and depth! Thank you for this third act! This was the real Wagner.
27/IV Bavarian Radio *Live recording* **Rachmaninov** *Études-tableaux op. 33* *no. 5 and op. 39 no. 9* *Vladimir Horowitz* *Six Études-tableaux* *op. 39* *Olaf Dreßler*	In this recording, Horowitz is already old and clearly off form. His playing is intolerably mannered, messy, superficial, botched and banal. I can't take it. The Carnegie Hall audience gave him an ovation. Olaf Dreßler has recorded all the *Études-tableaux*. I prefer not to discuss them.
5/V, at the home of Lisa Leonskaja on the eve of my departure Vienna *Recording* **Chopin** *13 Préludes* S.R.	Spent the morning at Lisa's. Got to know Andreas Lucewicz, who has just arrived and who is going to drive me to the border with Belorussia. By way of wishing me a safe journey, they put on this record; it would have been better if they hadn't as there was something almost official about their action that isn't really appropriate to this music.

I didn't really concentrate while listening but was more interested in the way the others listened. This often happens to me, which is why it's better for me to listen on my own in an adjacent room. Anyway, I know this recording intimately and there could be no question of my being pleasantly surprised by it. Fifteen minutes later we said goodbye next to the car and set off with my new friend across Slovakia and Poland where, due to the impossibility of finding any petrol, we broke down; we ended up being towed by an old man.

10/v
Moscow
Recording
Debussy
La mer
Conductor:
Roger Desormière

How many times I've played this record (at least a hundred) and each time I feel as though it's the first time! It's extraordinarily successful. The mere fact that technology has managed to capture this degree of inspiration is in itself a miracle! I don't know a finer recording. As for the interpretation, there's nothing one can say. It's unique.
<u>Roger Desormière</u>!!

11/v
Recording
Britten
Act I Scene 1
of Albert Herring
Conductor:
Benjamin Britten

I've started work on *Herring*, which we're performing next December. At the moment I'm simply listening for my own pleasure. There's no denying the quality of this recording. As long as Ben is in charge, you're certain of the highest standards. I'd say the same was true of Peter Pears.
The decision to transpose the story from a corner of France to England is really quite interesting. The details are fabulous, but in fact everything about it is extraordinarily amusing and lighthearted.
There it is, the greatest comic opera of the century. Peek-a-boo!

12/v, afternoon
Britten
Act II of Albert Herring
Conducted by
the composer

Continuing to mix business and pleasure.
The horn establishes the mood of celebration right from the very outset and when it returns, unusually harmonized, it continues to reverberate in our memories.
The use of harmonic ideas à la *Tristan* is an extraordinarily witty conceit. And the intervention

of Lady Billows billowing up like a balloon . . .
And then the nocturne-like music in the Herring
household . . . But what's the point of listing them
all!!!

12/v, in the evening Rehearsal at home **Britten** *Act I Scene 1* *of Albert Herring* *Vladimir Ziva* *at the piano*	First attempts at production, under the initially passive direction of Yuri Borisov (this is natural at the start of such an enterprise). The artists from the Chamber Opera Theatre (Sokolenko, Lemesheva) are hugely talented, as is Emma Sarkisian from the Nemirovich Theatre. They're all giving of their best, though it's not easy. Very friendly and pleasant atmosphere. The young Ziva at the piano is proving to be a very fine musician and very sure of himself. For once, everything's going very well. But the main thing is that it should be interesting. As of today, my flat has been turned into a rehearsal studio with its own rules. Everything for *Albert Herring*!
14/v *Recording* **Britten** ***Albert Herring, Act I*** *Peter Pears* *Conducted by* *the composer*	I've again been listening to this piece, this time in the company of Oleg Kagan and Natasha Gutman. It was their first exposure to this music. The idea of staging this opera at the December Nights festival at the Pushkin Museum was young Yuri Borisov's, a producer at Boris Pokrovsky's Chamber Opera Theatre. He is, as it were, the inspiration behind this event and has brought his friend from Leningrad, the conductor Vladimir Ziva, who struck us as a very young child. What emerged from all this is another matter.
29/v Gorky Orchestral rehearsal at the Kremlin Theatre **Ravel** *Tzigane* *Oleg Kagan* *Conductor:* *Israel Gusman*	I went to Gorky to give an airing to Ravel's Concerto for the Left Hand under Gusman's direction. Oleg Kagan also took part in the concert, playing *Tzigane*, which I listened to from the side of the stage. Each time I hear this masterpiece, I enjoy it enormously, if only fleetingly – the work is so short. Oleg plays it magnificently.

4/VI
Moscow
Rehearsal at home
Handel
Air from Samson
Purcell
Air from King Arthur
Brahms
Sapphische Ode
Alto: Erik Kurmangaliev
(a pupil of Nina's who
came to visit us for the
first time today, but who
showed absolutely no
emotion)
S.R., piano
Debussy
Fantaisie
for piano and orchestra
Ravel
Concerto for the Left
Hand
S.R.
At the second piano:
Vladimir Skanavi

Party atmosphere. More like a concert than a rehearsal. Lots of guests.
To begin with, an odd character with a very individual voice sings three austere works. Then it's my turn on two pianos with Dima Skanavi. It looks like the evening was a success and that everyone was satisfied. Afterwards we moved on to the food.

5/VI, farewell party
on the eve of my
departure on tour
Rehearsal at home
Debussy
Fantaisie
Ravel
Concerto for the Left
Hand
S.R. and
Vladimir Skanavi

Repeat of yesterday evening, but without Kurmangaliev.
Hand-picked guests and an attractive programme. Nina thinks it's not appropriate to invite students (Ziva, Borisov) when the rector of the Conservatory is present. I disagree entirely.
Everything passed off as it should, and in two days I'll be playing the same programme at Gorky, unless I've already played it.
YES, I'VE ALREADY PLAYED IT!

June
In Andreas Lucewicz's
car somewhere between
Brest-Litovsk and

After all sorts of musical discussions in the course of our journey (which lasted 17 hours, what with all the problems of border crossings, visas and so on), Andreas played me a recording by Collard,

	who struck me as a first-rate pianist.
Helmstadt	Unfortunately, I later changed my mind about
Schumann	him.
3rd Sonata	
Jean-Philippe Collard	

Between 15/vi and 9/vii — Yes, that's a lot of Tchaikovsky and Rachmaninov, but it's a real pleasure to play them. In this way you can find out all about the Russian soul, in the very best sense of the word.

Paris and Tours
Recordings made by
Éric Anther
Tchaikovsky
Piano pieces
(recorded live at
Rolandseck, Tours
and Paris)
Rachmaninov
Études-tableaux
opp. 33 and 39
(ditto)
S.R.

But it's essential to overcome all the difficulties, so that they don't trouble the artist in any way; of course, this is true in all cases – sorry about the truism – otherwise the music won't reach the listener. It's difficult to master this music, which, conversely, is easy to listen to. Often, in fact, the listener has the impression that it's neither particularly hard nor particularly serious.

Sometimes I hear such stupid remarks in this context – remarks proferred by musicians both at home and abroad – that I don't even want to quote them here.

25/vi, Tours
Grand Théâtre
Ravel
Rapsodie espagnole
Orchestre de Paris
conducted by
Daniel Barenboim

Frankly, this performance left no great impression on me, though I was so looking forward to it. But perhaps I wasn't listening properly, as I'd just played Debussy's *Fantaisie* and Ravel's Concerto for the Left Hand.

26/vi
Grange de Meslay
Recital by Paul Tortelier
and Maria de la Pau
Sonatas by Saint-Saëns,
Fauré and Debussy
Variations on May
Music Save Peace
by Tortelier
Debussy *Prélude* and
Prelude from Bach's
1st Suite

Monsieur Tortelier, I may say straight away, isn't my hero, but he's clearly a personality, a larger-than-life artist, and it goes without saying that he has perfect mastery over his instrument. I particularly liked the Saint-Saëns Sonata and would be happy to include it in my repertory, even if the idiotic French annoy me when all they can say about it is 'Quelle barbe!' [How boring].

In fact, Fauré's Second Sonata seemed just like lukewarm water lacking in any flavour, whereas the Debussy is such a miracle as to reduce me to total silence.

But Mademoiselle Maria de la Pau (Tortelier's daughter) left no impression at all in Debussy's *Prélude*, 'Ce qu'a vu le vent d'ouest'. It was simply bad.

28/VI
Grange de Meslay
Homage to French jazz
Martial Solal Trio

Improvisation, freedom, emancipation within the rules that govern this kind of music – these were the qualities that prevailed this evening at the Grange de Meslay.

Martial Solal left me literally stunned. I can see that it's an affair of the moment, but such freedom is so rarely obtainable, and on this occasion it was present in abundance.

Part of the audience seemed reserved and slightly shocked. For my own part, I couldn't restrain myself but clapped and shouted with the best of them.

2/VII
Grange de Meslay
Rameau
Pigmalion
Les Arts Florissants
under the direction of
William Christie

Rameau's opera is a wonderful piece and was very well performed. The style of the period is superbly caught, and it's clear that the artists enjoyed working on it.

Dominique Visse in the role of Pygmalion is quite simply phenomenal and looks as though he has stepped straight out of the period: very feminine, with long curly hair and a voice on the border between tenor and alto. He lives for this period and its style, and I'll always think of him as a part of Rameau himself.

11/VII–20/VII
Recordings made by
Éric Anther at the Salle
Gaveau in Paris
Vienna
Szymanowski
2nd and 3rd Sonatas,
'Shéhérazade' and
'Tantris the Clown'
[from *Masks*],
Mazurkas
S.R.

I've been listening to 'my' Szymanowski again. There are so many of his works that I play that you'll easily understand the seductive appeal that he has for me. It's real!

The genuinely musical public is gradually – albeit very slowly – beginning to understand him and, as a result, to acknowledge him (but there are so few musicians among them).

I dream of learning two more pieces from *Metopes*, but at the same time I'm afraid of them: 'The Island of the Sirens' (unbelievably difficult) and 'Calypso'. But when shall I be able to do so?

Myths
S.R. *and Oleg Kagan*
Songs
Galina Pisarenko
and S.R.

There's so much good music!?!!

Moscow
Britten
August–September
Rehearsals for
Albert Herring and
The Turn of the Screw
13, 14, 16/XII
Dress rehearsal and
two performances
Orchestra conducted
by Vladimir Ziva

We worked on these operas – both the music and the staging – in a state of perpetual excitement. Musically, virtually everything passed off more or less without a hitch, except that Ziva sometimes took things exaggeratedly quickly; I made a remark to this effect and it appears not to have pleased him.

With the director, Yuri Borisov, by contrast, things went very badly. He'd no idea what to do and we virtually came to a complete standstill.

And so I appealed to Boris Pokrovsky and asked him for his advice, which he was more than happy to give. At this, I realized (and I wasn't alone in this) that Yuri had been playing a double game and doing everything in his power to prevent me from seeing Pokrovsky. He also said some terrible things about the latter, and no doubt said similar things to him about me. We were getting nowhere; sets and costumes were a disaster.

One day, realizing that we'd never make it, Borisov suddenly announced: 'We'll dispense with the staging and give a concert performance.' He was withdrawing from the production.

It was then that I took things into my own hands. All right, I said to myself, 'a concert performance'. I lost no time in concocting a surprise. The audience would think they were attending a concert performance, but they'd be shown a performance they weren't expecting, a sort of improvised charade. Having got Pokrovsky's permission, I decided to tackle the production myself.

Just as a completely idiotic and ridiculous presenter starts to announce the names of the performers, the orchestra breaks in and interrupts him, while Emma Sarkissian runs through the hall, trips and measures her length, dropping the parcels that she

was carrying. There follows the scene of the meeting at the home of Lady Billows (Sokolenko is
sensational), the election of the Queen of the May
(with varied lighting to underline the state of mind
of each of the characters) and the scene in the
Herring household (Naparin is perfect as Albert).
The children (especially Maxim Ivashkin) are
magnificent, and so enthusiastic! The arrival of
Lady Billows through the rows of seats; her aria
with its harp accompaniment; and Mrs Herring's
dressing down of her son. During the interval, we
served free *pirozhki* and sweets in honour of the
May festival.

Then, to mark the end of the interval, a horn call,
issuing first from the upper floor, then getting
gradually closer.

Start of Act Two.

To the sound of the *Tristan* chord, violent pink
light. The speeches in front of the table, which has
now been laid for tea, are superbly executed
(Lemesheva as the head teacher is the archetypal
Englishwoman). As Nancy, Trofimova is delightful, as is little Shalaeva, who cycles through the
hall (the bicycle plays an important part here).

The introduction to Act III takes place in the dark,
with the characters searching for Herring in the
audience with torches in their hands (this effect
worked well). There was a minor incident here,
when Shalaeva tripped over an old woman who
had installed herself in the middle of the aisle.

Then the scenes of mourning and, to end, Albert's
appearance now that he has shaken off the traces,
then Lady Billows's anger – she faints and is
dragged off to a seat in the front row.

When Albert throws away the crown at the end,
he throws it at her out of derision. The children
wave flags, as does the audience, who have been
given their flags in advance. And with this the
adventure reaches its climax and end.

I have to say that Natasha Gutman helped me
enormously; she was a sort of assistant director,
cueing the actors' entrances, operating the lighting

and sound effects and keeping an eye on the children. Without her, I'd have been lost.

Yuri Borisov didn't come to see the show. But that's no longer of any interest to me.

October (dinner with
Éric Anther)
Vienna
Doppeladler Restaurant
Liszt
The two concertos
Walter Lang, piano

I'm in a foul mood, a sort of double depression. I'm sitting at the marble bar, the walls are an old-fashioned dark brown (but I used to like this little restaurant, which no longer exists and whose owner also ran the Turkish baths near the Seilerstätte). From the loudspeakers above the bar come the intermittent strains of Liszt's concertos, and I have the impression that the pianist plays them infinitely better than I do.

That's why I asked his name.

At the home
of Jörg Demus
Recording
Haydn
Concerto in D major
Jörg Demus

How fast he plays (exactly twice the tempo). I don't think the music gains anything. Oh, this professorial reading and this conservatory routine! Bah!

26/XII, Christmas tree
Recording
Mozart
Sonata for four hands
K 521
S.R. and
Benjamin Britten
Concerto in E flat K 482
S.R.
Conductor:
Riccardo Muti

Our guests for our traditional Christmas party are gathered in our flat on the sixteenth floor of Bolshaya Bronnaya Ulitsa.

As a treat – music: a discipline in its own way.

And music by Mozart, angelic and brilliant: the Sonata for four hands recorded at a concert with Britten in Aldeburgh. If I remember correctly, there were no more than three rehearsals!

Then my 'new' recording of the Mozart Concerto, with a cadenza by Britten in the opening movement, under the direction of Muti, my Italian protégé who is now a star among the stars.

Britten's cadenza is debatable.

Britten's cadenza is splendid! And oddly enough it turns out that I play it better than the concerto itself. If he had heard me say that, Ben would certainly have smiled and said nothing. He was so sympathetic!

31/XII, New Year's Eve
Britten
*1) Introduction and
Rondo alla burlesca
2) Mazurka elegiaca
op. 23/2 for two pianos
Alexander Slobonianik
and S.R.
3) Cello Sonata
Natasha Gutman
and S.R.*

An odd New Year, totally improvised and with lots of foreign visitors: Lisa Wilson from London and other musicians from Europe who didn't utter a word all evening. And our faithful Midori, without whom I don't take a single step in Japan.

Equally odd – and risky – was our joint performance with Slobodianik (the first such performance until now), but, thank goodness, we didn't go off the rails.

Then came Britten's Sonata with Natasha, a tricky piece (from the point of view of ensemble).

Finally, supper in the main room with the two pianos. I can't say that there was much sense of order. Wine, spirits, salads and all sorts of good things. Then the dirty dishes piled up in Nina's kitchen, and the washing-up.

There was no real sense of harmony this evening at Bolshaya Bronnaya Ulitsa.

11/IV
Recording
Mozart and Beethoven
*Piano Quintets
Rudolf Serkin and
Philadelphia Wind
Ensemble*

A magnificent ensemble assembled round Rudolf Serkin. Their Mozart is convincing in a way that their Beethoven isn't. This is due essentially to the terribly slow tempo that they adopt in the second movement. The result is something so painful and unnatural that you feel like running a mile. I don't understand how such musicians didn't take the trouble to read and follow the composer's instructions. Or is this the result of another of these idiotic traditions?

You have the impression of a film played at the wrong speed. The music suffers, and so do you.

10/V
Paris
USSR Embassy
*Elena Obraztsova
(taking part in a concert
by S.R.)*
**Massenet, Bizet,
Rachmaninov, Mascagni**

An amiable, uncomplicated (or at least pretending to be uncomplicated) woman rigged out in a hilarious hair-do had expressed the desire to take part in the recital I was to give.

She sang in a slightly heavy-handed way and in a beautiful operatic voice, but I doubt whether there was a single substantial thought in her head the whole time that she was singing.

20/V
In the car between
Munich and Vienna
Recording
Bach
Goldberg Variations
Alexis Weissenberg

Weissenberg (who says he's a fervent admirer of mine) has completed a colossal undertaking and one can only congratulate him on it. His work bears all the hallmarks of honesty, conscientiousness and the love that he feels for this work.
If only his fingers didn't press ahead so much at the end of the fast variations, as this really spoils Bach's music. But I actually believe that it does not come easily to him.

25/V
In Italy, on the road
from Bergamo to
Bolzano
Debussy
Suite bergamasque
Alexis Weissenberg

I find this performance of the *Suite bergamasque* is like that of most (if not all) pianists: a good, thoroughly pianistic reading, but you don't feel that it's Debussy (it could be Chopin or Rachmaninov). Not the slightest trace of impressionism.
I remember a Canadian reviewer of a concert at which I'd played this work saying that I'd played in such an 'ethereal' way that one could scarcely hear me.

31/V
Deutschlandsberg
Live recording
Brahms
*Variations on a
Hungarian Song
op. 21 no. 2*
S.R.

I learned these variations fairly recently and really like them, but I don't think I'll learn any other works by Brahms (except the B major Trio and the D major Variations op. 21 no. 1).
The atmosphere at the concerts in Deutschlandsberg is always so congenial. The reasons for this are the medium-sized hall, Frau Faulend-Klauser, the non-official ambience, the small town and so on. By day, the town is no longer so attractive.

15–18/VI
Paris
*Indian music
for string instruments*
Surashringar and
Subrahar

I had to summon up all my patience to listen to this music. I can see that it's interesting (for the mind) and that there's something in it, but everything about it distracts me, in particular my own thoughts (assuming I manage to have any).
I can appreciate the sophistication of the playing, but that's no good: it's as though I weren't there. (Europe? And yet I love the Orient.)

22/VI, Grange de Meslay
Opening of Fêtes
Musicales de Touraine

The F major Quartet seemed really quite ordinary, making me doubt the qualities of the famous Amadeus Quartet, but as if to make up for this,

Beethoven
*Quartets op. 18 no. 1
and op. 131*
Amadeus Quartet

the op. 131 left an extremely powerful impression. In spite of his age, the first violin is remarkable for his genuine artistry and carries the whole group with him.

An enjoyable and worthy opening to the Fêtes Musicales.

23/VI
Grange de Meslay
Beethoven
Quartets nos. 2, 3 and 4
Orlando Quartet

I once played all these early quartets in arrangements for four hands, so they're old friends. I like the second one – the one in G major – best of all. A pity that the first movement was taken too fast, so that it lost its charm.

On the whole, the concert impressed me favourably; how lucky we are that all Beethoven's quartets are being played this year.

24/VI
Grange de Meslay
Beethoven
*Violin Sonatas
nos. 6, 10 and 7*
*Régis Pasquier and
Jean-Philippe Collard*

Very disappointing.

Jean-Philippe Collard struck me as really quite ordinary today, an uninteresting, uninterested musician. I still recall his playing of Schumann's 3rd Sonata and was expecting something quite different.

The concert went well, but there was too much of a sense of routine about it. The violinist is decent, no more, cleanly though he played.

And why do I feel such antipathy towards the 7th Sonata? There's no doubt that it's a superb piece.

30/VI
Grange de Meslay
Beethoven
*Quartets
nos. 6, 8 and 10*
Via Nova Quartet

I didn't really listen to this concert, as I was slightly drunk (was it the champagne I drank at the bar in Meslay, the whisky I had with Francis Van de Velde or something else?). Be that as it may, it wasn't under the best of auspices that they launched into the final movement of the 6th Quartet, which is headed 'La Malinconia'.

Life in the Touraine has recently become a little more stressful and not as enjoyable as before.

1/VII
Grange de Meslay
Beethoven
Quartets nos. 12 and 13

A massive programme solidly and ponderously played by large fat Germans. Not bad, but very German.

After a concert like this, what better than to go to

and Große Fuge *Brandis Quartet*	a restaurant and order sausages, sauerkraut und so weiter?
2/VII, at the home of Patrick Lefèvre *Playback of a recording* *of a concert at Meslay* **Beethoven** *'Archduke' Trio* *Kopelman, Berlinsky* *and S.R.* **Brahms** *2nd Piano Quartet* *Kopelman, Shebalin,* *Berlinsky and S.R.*	I played the 'Archduke' only once with Kopelman and Berlinsky. For once it didn't go too badly – and at Meslay! I know that as a result my own regular trio was jealous. I can't begin to understand this phenomenon; I regard jealousy in all its forms as a real sin and can state categorically that, as for myself, I'm innocent of this vice.
4/VII, at the home of Éric Anther Paris **Prokofiev** *8th Sonata* *1) Andrei Gavrilov* *2) S.R.*	With the 8th Sonata I fell into a trap. I was given Gavrilov's recording and told that it was mine (I believed it and was very dissatisfied with the performance), whereas with my own, I was told it was Gavrilov (again I believed them and immediately thought: 'This is in a completely different class!') A dangerous game to play. The others laughed a lot.
22/VII In the car crossing through Germany **Beethoven** *Sonata in C minor* *op. 10 no. 1* *Artur Schnabel*	I was literally astounded by this remarkable interpretation. The sonata is suddenly brought to life to the point where it's almost palpable. It was splendid.
14/VIII Moscow Moscow Chamber Opera Theatre **Stravinsky** *1) Concertino for string* *quartet* *2) Two Poems of* *Konstantin Balmont*	An extremely unpleasant evening. I spent the whole time consumed with rage. It began modestly enough and more or less seriously, but after that things rapidly went downhill and left a nasty aftertaste, a crassly contemporary taste of glue, which the general public clearly likes but which is most certainly not suited to a composer who was distinguished, above all, by his extreme rigour and purity, which is why all these tricks at the limits of

3) Deux poèmes de
Paul Verlaine
4) Pribaoutki
5) Rag-time for
11 instruments
6) Histoire du soldat
Conductor:
Anatoly Levin

'naturalism' had such a perfectly repugnant effect. The showcasing of young and talented artists!
Histoire du soldat was staged by a youth of 23 barely out of school and lacking in taste and talent but not short of 'ideas' of his own. Thank you very much.
I remember only one thing: the way in which the devil appears, tearing and passing through the skin of a large drum on which was painted a picture of Stravinsky, thereby signalling the start of the nonsense that was to follow.
After this performance, all I wanted to do was have a shower.
And where was the audience in all this? Wild enthusiasm.

23/VIII, in Yuri
Bashmet's car between
Yaroslavl and Moscow
Johann Strauß
Frühlingsstimmen and
Perpetuum mobile
Conductor:
Herbert von Karajan
Haydn
Violin Concerto
in C major
Josef Suk

Yuri Bashmet, Ninoshka and me.
A magnificent sunny day, Russia, the forest, Rostov, Pereslavl–Zalessky and the musical pleasures of Johann Strauß, together with Karajan.
(Swallows, gunshots and authentically Viennese gaiety.)
Then, following a *déjeuner sur l'herbe* and attempts on Yuri's part to take some impromptu photographs, more music. If it really was Suk who was playing, he's a superb violinist, and Haydn's C major Concerto sounded like a real celebration.
We gradually approach Moscow and start to notice what people are doing to destroy their country's natural beauty.

19/IX
Recording
Schoenberg
Piano Concerto
Anatoly Vedernikov
Conductor:
Igor Blazhkov

This is the first time I've heard this work. It's a successful recording and, in its way, the work is clearly accomplished. Vedernikov plays it with the requisite clarity and precision, as does the orchestra. You really need to listen repeatedly to works of this kind if you want to understand them, but the spirit isn't always willing. Boulez once told me that this concerto is easy to play. Hmm!?

20/IX in the morning
Recording

Beethoven in the early morning.
I'm making myself listen to chamber music; I often

Beethoven *Quartet no. 13 op. 130* *Budapest Quartet*	have difficulty with it. I don't know why, but it's not easy for me to retain this music, and I soon tire. What's to be done?
20/IX, in the evening *Ariola recording* **Tchaikovsky** *14 Morceaux*	I don't think I chose too badly when I selected these pieces – which no one plays – for my recording. All of them have the Russian charm of a - country house of the last century and are musically utterly enchanting. Lots of people don't agree with me. Routine, again.
11/X Grand Hall of the Conservatory *Recital by Peter Schreier* *Walter Olbertz, piano* **Songs by Mendelssohn,** **Schumann and Schubert**	I don't remember all the details of this concert, but as always Schreier was on top form, a model of simplicity and nobility. A splendid programme that was out of the ordinary. What a pity that I can't remember the Lieder repertory. It's the same with chamber music for strings and with . . . poetry (I'm incredibly untalented in this respect). I particularly love the way in which Schreier always sets out from the music and subordinates the words to it. This is the exact opposite of Fischer-Dieskau who, for his part, sets out from the text. For me, this is a strange approach and I lose some of my freedom of performance when I accompany him. But what riches composers have left us in the world of vocal music!!
14/X, evening in memory of Heinrich Neuhaus (20th anniversary of his death) **Wagner** *Tristan und Isolde* *René Kollo* *Margaret Price* *Brigitte Fassbaender* *Dietrich Fischer-Dieskau* *Kurt Moll* *Conductor:* *Carlos Kleiber*	This recording with Carlos Kleiber is a great musical event. Everything about it is utterly inspired, and I'd say without the least hesitation that as a result the music expands like a natural phenomenon, producing an effect that is literally extraordinary. The singers are the best you can dream of, and the conductor is the greatest of all. Even so, I still think that Furtwängler's recording is ever so slightly superior, but this is arguable. With the passage of time (which is passing *presto agitato*), the number of Neuhaus's friends and pupils who attend these reunions continues to decrease.

3/XI
Bolshoy Theatre
Performance by the
Tbilisi Opera
Richard Strauss
Salome
Conductor:
Dzansug Kakhidze

Yes, *Salome* IN GERMAN! In a performance by the Tbilisi Opera! Everyone sings well. True, the conductor, Kakhidze, isn't in complete command of Strauss's style, and while his orchestra plays accurately enough, there's a certain dryness that's somewhat reminiscent of Prokofiev.

Space doesn't allow me to list all the pretentious inanities in the production.

For reasons that escape me, Salome seduces Jokanaan from behind. Jokanaan is dressed in white, like Christ. The whole stage is covered in linen left out to dry as on the balconies of Tbilisi. No matter, the provinces have made an effort.

10/XII
December Nights at the
Pushkin Museum
Bartók
Elegy no. 1
Allegro barbaro
Zoltán Kocsis
4th Quartet
Takács Quartet

Once again the Takács Quartet exceeded all my hopes today. This was the second time I'd heard this concert and it was again a total delight.

I think Kocsis is one of the most serious young musicians of our day; he's clearly more serious than Gavrilov (in spite of the latter's diabolical talent); and perhaps more original than Ránki. Above all, however, it's clear that he's infinitely more interesting than Pollini or Ashkenazy. He's sure of himself, obstinate and wilful, but this doesn't stop him from playing well. (He should simply have put his transcriptions to one side.)

21/XII
Televised broadcast
Ravel
4th movement of
Trio in A minor
Oleg Kagan, Natasha
Gutman and S.R.

'They're showing the trio on television,' Ninoshka called out. 'Come and listen.' Without stopping to finish our tea, we all adjourned to her rooms, where there's the most incredible jumble of objects in no kind of order whatsoever: a grand piano, two television sets, a record player, cupboards full of scores and books, a worn-out piece of Louis XV furniture and then, of course, scores on the piano and window sill, and magazines and newspapers. It turned out they were already showing the final movement of the Ravel Trio in a broadcast from the Grand Hall of the Conservatory, and so it was very soon over.

8/I In Yuri Bashmet's car on our way to the Bolshoy **Rachmaninov** *Two Études-tableaux* *op. 39* S.R.	Yuri played me this recording on our way to a performance of *Swan Lake*, believing, of course, that it would give me pleasure. It was kind of him, but I'm not Gavrilov, who each time (!) he takes someone in his luxury car inflicts his own recording of the Tchaikovsky Concerto on them (excellent though it is). I'm sure he does it even when he has no 'audience'. He's a lucky boy.
22/III Vienna *Tape* **Beethoven** *Sonatas nos. 4 and 24* *Roger Woodward* **Brahms** *1st Concerto* *Roger Woodward* *Conductor: Kurt Masur*	First movement of Beethoven's 4th Sonata: too fast and too loud, 'fingers of steel'. Didn't like it. The F sharp major Sonata, too, is too aggressive. Brahms: robust, virile and convincing. P.S. This is the first time I've encountered this pianist, who is said to have a 'dubious reputation', but who is clearly talented.
23/III *Tape* **Xenakis** *Mists* *Roger Woodward*	This is the first time I've heard any music by Xenakis; it's completely bowled me over, even though I'm not sure whether I've really understood it (or not understood it). Intuition? But can one always trust it?
24/III *Tape* **Xenakis** *1) Mists* *2) Eonta* *Roger Woodward* *Conductor: Eliahu Inbal*	I can now see that Woodward plays this music convincingly. And I like it even more, especially *Eonta*, with its unexpected and extraordinarily interesting orchestral interjections.
25/III *Tape* **Xenakis** *Synaphaï* *Roger Woodward* *Conductor: Eliahu Inbal*	I can say the same about *Synaphaï*. It seems to me that this, in fact, is what I'd call real 'new' music.

28/III *Tape* **Mozart** *Concerto K 503* *Roger Woodward* *Conductor:* *Witold Rowicki*	A satisfying recording from every point of view (it was recorded during the Chopin Competition). But I was exhausted and my eyes kept closing in spite of all my efforts to stay awake, so I can't form a definitive opinion.
7/V Moscow At home in Bolshaya Bronnaya Ulitsa **Bach** *Sonata in A minor and Partita in E major for unaccompanied violin* *Oleg Kagan*	Oleg has set himself the truly heroic task of playing all Bach's works for solo violin. He's persevering through sheer force of will and endless hours of work. This desire for perfection and this integrity in his work (I really can't understand how one can play this on this instrument) are bearing fruit. Not overnight, of course, but slowly and surely. If one thinks of all the worries that he has to contend with and that have nothing to do with music and if one thinks of the time spent trying to sort them all out, one can only marvel at the endurance of this marvellous musician and man.
13/V *Recording* **Jean Barraqué** *Sonata for Piano* *Roger Woodward*	Composers are often very critical of each other. Vassya Lobanov listened to this piece with me, and I noticed how condescending he was. According to him, Barraqué has nothing particularly significant to offer. According to me – well, unfortunately, I've no opinion at all, nor any desire to listen to this sonata ten times in a row in an attempt to understand it.
28/V Bolshoy Theatre Visit by the Warsaw Opera **Szymanowski** *King Roger* *Conductor:* *Agnieszka Kreiner* *Staged by the conductor* *Robert Satanowski*	Everything about this unexpected and magnificent performance by the Warsaw Opera is to my liking. I'm thinking not so much of the musical side of things – the orchestra sounds authentically Szymanowskian and the singers are just right (with Barbara Zagórzanka as Roxana) – but of the production, lighting and ballet: you couldn't wish for anything better. All credit to the director with the redoubtable name of Satanowski. There was enthusiastic applause at the end. Natasha Zhuravliova and I exchanged knowing glances that summed up all we felt.

29/v Concert at home **Bach** *Cello Suites* *nos. 4, 5 and 6* *Natasha Gutman*	This concert was both a feast of music and an object lesson for the performer and for the audience. Natasha played sublimely and with total concentration. I find it difficult to listen to these works, but afterwards I feel an extraordinary sense of inner jubilation, as though I've just done my duty by them. Thank you, Natasha.
4/vi Open rehearsal at home **Stravinsky** *1) Movements* *2) Capriccio* S.R. *Orchestral part played* *on a 2nd piano by* *Vassili Lobanov* *3) Concerto* *for two pianos* *Vassili Lobanov* *and S.R.*	It's really rather unseemly to boast of one's own achievements, but this went very well, to the amazement and delight of our audience, which was made up of friends (they'd not heard these works before). This was our final rehearsal before leaving for Tours, where Boulez, the Boilles, the Van de Veldes and a whole assortment of characters from Molière and Racine are awaiting us.
14/vi In Yuri Bashmet's car radio on the road between Warsaw and Dresden **Beethoven** *Excerpts from Act I* *of Fidelio* **Wagner** *Act I Scene 3* *of Die Walküre* *Sieglinde:* *Jessye Norman*	A period of peregrinations across Europe with Bashmet; endless hours spent in his car, mainly at night. Once, when we'd lost our way in some provincial backwater, I turned on the radio in search of some entertainment. To begin with, there were some barely comprehensible excerpts from *Fidelio*. Then came Jessye Norman in Act I of *Die Walküre*, deeply expressive, powerful and utterly Wagnerian. I don't know why, but I had difficulty getting into this work (no doubt because of the terrible tiredness induced by the journey). What a strange injustice on the part of nature that a singer gifted with such a voice is condemned to look like this (her physical appearance is larger than life).
29/vi, Tours Grange de Meslay	The complete version of this work left me a little tired. I don't know whether it was because of the way it was played or whether I myself was to blame.

Stravinsky
Pulcinella (complete)
Conductor:
Pierre Boulez

No doubt I should listen to it twice in order for it to become clear: for the present, the only impression I gained was that of a mass of music lacking in any connecting thread.

Boulez, too, looked rather tired. He's had to carry out a lot of work for this year's festival.

30/VI
Grange de Meslay
Ligeti
Chamber Concerto
Berio
Corale
Boulez
Éclat/Multiples
Conductor:
Pierre Boulez

This was a really interesting concert and splendidly conducted by Boulez. I was hearing all these works for the first time.

Ligeti: highly original, with these 'thousands of insects', but I wasn't exactly overwhelmed. Conversely, I really liked the Berio, a new and interesting piece magnificently played by Maryvonne Le Dizès-Richard as the solo violinist. Boulez: the composer himself conducted; here he showed his very particular gifts as a conductor. I thought the work a bit too long, and of course it's formalistic. At any rate that's how it was conceived.

7/VII
Grange de Meslay
Messiaen
Poèmes pour Mi
Franco Donatoni
Cadeau
Schoenberg
Three Pieces (op. post.)
Chamber Symphony
op. 9
Conductor:
Pierre Boulez

Messiaen. Sung and played with extreme expressivity by the soprano Phyllis Bryn-Julson and by a hugely talented pianist, Pierre-Laurent Aimard. A beautiful piece masterfully structured, but not my cup of tea. I'd already heard the *Turangalîla* Symphony at the Paris Opéra with the amazing Yvonne Loriod and also a concert that she and Messiaen gave at the second Fêtes Musicales de Touraine. It was all on a very high level, but no . . . I don't want to . . .

Donatoni. A charming work, full of orchestral verve and humour, and the composer is a most amiable fellow. I got to know him after the concert, during a reception at the town hall.

Schoenberg. I've got used to this work (the op. 9 Chamber Symphony), though I used not to like it. This sort of Viennese 'depravity' has its own charm and seductiveness, whereas the work's complexities now don't seem as complex as all that.

Splendidly conducted by Boulez.

Fréjus In the car with Éric Anther **Hindemith** *1st Piano Sonata* *Glenn Gould*	I listened to only the first three movements, which I didn't like. It's too studied, with too many slow tempi. In fact, I find it pretentious.
20/IX Moscow *Recording* **Debussy** *Images oubliées* *Zoltán Kocsis*	What a surprise, unknown Debussy! And, of course, a marvel! Kocsis is really quite splendid, he's the first person to have made up his mind to play these pieces. I'd like to hear them played live – not in a mechanical recording.
29/IX *Recordings of concerts* *at Meslay* **Stravinsky** *Movements* *Capriccio* *S.R.* **Bartók** *Sonata for two pianos* *and percussion* *S.R. and* *Vassili Lobanov*	Boulez conducted the Stravinsky quite well. His orchestra isn't of the best and the way the musicians behave is typically 'Parisian'. I think their much-loved conductor could place greater demands on them, but he too, after all, is 'Parisian'. On listening to the tape, I didn't find the Bartók as catastrophic as I'd feared. The disaster that struck in the first movement passes virtually unnoticed (even Boulez, who was in the audience, didn't realize). The rest is quite respectable, though I still wish it could have been better.
13/XI *Recordings* **Jean Barraqué** *Piano Sonata* *Roger Woodward* **Stravinsky** *Concerto for two pianos* *Vassili Lobanov* *and S.R.* *(recorded at a concert* *at Meslay)*	Musically, Barraqué is a great stumbling block. Natasha Gutman listened to it with me and reacted very positively to Roger Woodward's performance – and on this point it's impossible to disagree with her. But the work itself? I find it difficult to believe – and I'm not alone in this – that it really holds the road. But what if, fifty years from now, it's thought to be a work of genius? Who knows? There've already been similar examples. <u>Stravinsky</u>. Each time I hear this work, I can't believe my ears – there are so many fine things in it.

27/XI
Recording
Schumann
Dichterliebe
Nina Dorliac and S.R.

This old recording has just been reissued, and I think it's Nina Dorliac's finest and most inspired (it's a live recording, of course). You can sense in it the very essence of this great artist. Remarkable.

4/XII
Bolshoy Theatre
Verdi
La traviata
Violetta: Julia Varady
Conductor:
Algis Zhuraitis

Julia Varady's Moscow début. She was sublime in this difficult role, which isn't exactly tailored to her voice. Both as an artist and as a singer, she's totally reliable and utterly convincing; and she's head and shoulders above the others on stage. It was an utter delight.

Now for Zhuraitis. He's become a sort of monster, or rather an anti-monster of music. He has absolutely no idea about rhythm and knows only how to beat time. A kind of lifeless capon. Quick passages he takes at twice the speed they should be, slow passages twice as slow.

It's appalling, and I can imagine how hard it must be to sing under his direction.

There were also all the traditional cuts, so that all that was left was a pot-pourri of the opera.

11/XII
Televised broadcast of the 1984 December Nights Festival at the Pushkin Museum
Britten
Lachrymae (2nd part)
Yuri Bashmet and S.R.
Cello Sonata (4th and 5th movements)
Natasha Gutman and S.R.
Stravinsky
Movements (1959)
S.R.
Conductor:
Yuri Nikolayevsky
Shostakovich
Trio op. 67

As always with these broadcasts, only excerpts are given (this was the case with Britten today), which I find appalling.

The Stravinsky, by contrast, was shown complete, and it strikes me as fairly successful, from Nikolayevsky's point of view as well as from my own. The Shostakovich Trio also seemed quite good. It's one of his best works, and it was played with suitably tragic and oppressive humour.

But – how I suffered while watching it! Our contorted faces (Oleg's, my own and, on this occasion, even Natasha's) were such an obstacle to our appreciation of the music that I cursed the day when television was invented. It's so unwarranted. Far better just to listen to the music.

Oleg Kagan, Natasha *Gutman and S.R.*	
16/XII December Nights at the Pushkin Museum **Schumann** *Lieder* *Robert Holl* *Konrad Richter, piano*	A magnificent singer singing magnificent music and, beside him at the piano, a professional killer, an undertaker's assistant who rains mortal blows on the listener (in this case, me). I can't begin to understand what aberration has led these two men to make music together.
27/XII December Nights at the Pushkin Museum **Chopin** *recital by* *Murray Perahia*	What happened? A terrible attack of nerves? Lack of confidence in his own abilities? Or circumstances of which I'm unaware (it's rumoured that an idiotic female interpreter-cum-guide pushed him to the limit)? But the fact remains that this famous pianist played virtually everything badly and that his Chopin left me cold. When I asked him why he didn't do the repeat of the exposition in the B minor Sonata, he seemed surprised and exclaimed 'But no one does it', adding that the same is true of Schubert's sonatas?!?!? He seemed unhappy.
6/II *Live recording* **Schnittke** *Viola Concerto* *Yuri Bashmet* *Conductor: Lucas Vis*	'Tragic confusion' characterizes this new work by Schnittke, which was written specially for Bashmet and designed to add to his laurels. I can't say that I liked it, it's a very unhealthy piece (it's true that the composer was himself very ill while writing it) and laboured. But it was a real event for the young musicians, and I agree with that. I don't know who else, in this day and age, could concoct a piece on such a high professional level, but – but there remains a 'but'.
20/V In the car between Vienna and Mantua *Tape* **Hindemith** *1st Piano Sonata* *Glenn Gould*	I've been listening again to this recording, which strikes me as highly controversial, but on this occasion I played it through to the end. The first four movements continue to make the same negative impression as before, but the fifth is phenomenally well played. I think the reason for this is that it's an insanely

virtuosic and difficult movement. It goes so quickly that you don't have time to start monkeying around with it; suddenly you hear Hindemith and not Gould.

7/v Vienna On the car radio **Chopin** *Two Nocturnes* *Maurizio Pollini*	This Chopin has well-developed biceps. In the first place, everything is *forte* and in the second place there's no poetry or delicacy (even if everything's impeccably precise) and absolutely no sense of improvisation. Of heroism, yes, there's more than enough, but there was a 'Polish tendency' at the time that Pollini won his prize in the Warsaw competition. Chopin just *had* to be presented as a patriot and revolutionary. Bad.
13–14/VI At night, in the car on the road from Vienna to Copenhagen **Telemann** *Trio Sonata for two violins and continuo from Tafelmusik* *Performed by –* *Germans*	*Tafelmusik*: yes, you can gorge yourself on this music, peer out at the night through the car windows and exchange inconsequential phrases with a not very interesting companion. Even so, this music can stand on its own two feet (and I say that without intending any offence) in its noble perfection.
18/VIII Cheboksary **Liszt** *Sonata in B minor* S.R.	This recording, which I've been waiting for for so long, has finally appeared, and our whole company assembled in my room (disgustingly filthy) to listen to it. An outright success. On the table the remains of dinner, bottles of kefir, crumbs of black bread and everything else to match. A journey into the land of the Soviets.
8/XI Chita In the main square *On the radio* *(with echo)* **Chopin** *Polonaise in A major* *(Who's playing?)*	Celebrations to mark the 'Revolution'. I'm wandering through the vast public squares in Chita. From every direction come the strains of Chopin's A major Polonaise, producing a sort of collage effect as a result of the echo. Someone's playing in a very vulgar, militaristic manner. How unpleasant!

4/XII
Kustanay
At the Palace of the
Pioneers following my
recital.
Recording
Liszt
1) Funérailles
2) Hungarian Fantasy
3) Sonata in B minor
S.R.

Once the audience had left and the hall was empty,
I remained behind with Volodya Tchaikovsky and
we listened to my Liszt recording on the Palace of
Pioneers' loudspeakers with the music at full blast.
I received his full and entire approval (even without any sentimentalism), although I was expecting
nothing less.
It would be no bad thing if Volodya lost a little
weight.

15/XII
Moscow
December Nights
at the Pushkin Museum
Tchaikovsky
Sonata in G major
op. 37
Album pour enfants
op. 39
Mikhail Pletnev

This young man is extraordinarily talented.
I very much liked the sonata – although it has
nothing whatever in common with my own interpretation (only the 3rd and 4th movements were
less to my liking). And I was completely won over
by the *Album pour enfants*.
But why does Pletnev look so unhappy? You'd
think it was sheer torment for him to play.

26/XII
Prokofiev School
of Music
Tchaikovsky
Serenade for Strings
Goskino Orchestra
Conductor:
Yuri Nikolayevsky

Yuri Nikolayevsky's problems with his public and
musicians are assuming epic proportions. There's
something psychotic at work here. And it's all due
to external reasons and his frantic love of work. It
appals me. I value him and love working with
him. And to think that orchestras – which have
always detested work – are boycotting this marvellous musician.

January
Vienna
Brahms
3rd Sonata in F minor
Annie Fischer

Annie Fischer is a great artist imbued with a spirit
of greatness and with genuine profundity.
Brahms's F minor Sonata is one of her finest
achievements. As for a handful of wrong notes,
who gives a damn (sorry)!

February
At the Girardinis'
Mantua

Shostakovich's 8th in Haitink's interpretation does
nothing for me: it's well oiled and he makes a
beautiful sound, but what's that got to do with it?
There's only one conductor who can conduct this

Shostakovich *8th Symphony* Conductor: *Bernard Haitink*	symphony, and that's Evgeny Alexandrovich Mravinsky.
April Wiesen *Tapes of concerts* *(Amsterdam, Heide,* *Prague)* **Beethoven** *Diabelli Variations* S.R.	Checking up to find where the Diabelli Variations were best. It's difficult to decide, given the incredible breadth and length of the piece. But the producer is anxious to know my decision; he's waiting to release the recording. A difficult situation.
En route from Vienna Wels-Schusterberg *Tape of Amsterdam* *concert* **Beethoven** *Diabelli Variations* S.R.	Otmar Drugovich is driving. I'm very fond of him. He was very keen to hear the Amsterdam recording and I let him. It's clearly the best; this is the one I'll allow to be issued.
April Vienna (Hotel Ambassador) **Beethoven** *Diabelli Variations* *(Amsterdam)* **Liszt** *Pensée des morts* *Andante lagrimoso* *Ave Maria* **Franck** *Prélude, choral et fugue* *(Polling* [Bavaria]*)* S.R.	Once again these Diabelli Variations, which I've already listened to so many times. And my endless and annoying doubts. <u>Liszt</u>: listened to it for pleasure. It can be released, but no one will do so at present, as it's not long enough for a single record (always these technical questions). <u>Franck</u>: I don't remember how I played . . . The work is unique for its combination of palpable severity and beauty.
11/v Moscow *Old recording of a con-* *cert in the Grand Hall* *of the Conservatory*	This recording must date from 1949. There's no doubt that it's not entirely worthless, but with some dubious notes. <u>As always</u>!

Liszt
Mephisto Waltz
S.R.

Liszt *Gnomenreigen* S.R. *Old recording*	This seems fine; I must have played it as an encore; it's the <u>right</u> speed. Only I can't manage to picture these gnomes. It's more like elves playing in a state of joyful drunkenness.
21/V *Recording* **Rachmaninov** *2nd Piano Concerto* S.R. *Conductor:* *Stanislaw Wislocki*	I now feel that this is a really good recording; Wislocki's 'docile' accompaniment doesn't prevent you from hearing it as a unified whole. Although my reading of this concerto may seem unusual, it doesn't strike me as unnatural. After all, I've merely imitated the composer's manner of performing it.
3/V Grand Hall of the Conservatory **Debussy** *Pelléas et Mélisande* *(concert performance)* *Young French singers* *Conductor:* *Manuel Rosenthal*	Oh, what a wretch this Rosenthal is! He managed to conduct *Pelléas* (without cuts) twenty minutes faster than he should have done. Throttling him wouldn't be a sufficient punishment for him. A criminal in matters of art has dared to lay his hand on this masterpiece. The French singers were no better than decent students, but, to cap it all, Rosenthal – who is guilty of shamefully cheating the audience – is regarded as the finest interpreter of this opera!
18/VII *Recording* **Beethoven** *'Pastoral' Sonata op. 28* *'Les adieux' Sonata* *op. 81a* *Ivan Moravec*	Moravec gave me this recording ages ago, but only now have I found the time and inclination to listen to it. I've no desire to pick holes in his interpretation and, when all's said and done, there's really nothing to pick holes in. These two sonatas aren't a part of my repertory, so I can listen to them purely for my own enjoyment (an enjoyment guaranteed, of course, by the composer). Moravec is an altogether admirable and professional pianist. He understands what he's playing.

Televised broadcast *from Glinka Hall in* *Leningrad* **Szymanowski** *Songs of the Infatuated Muezzin* *Galina Pisarenko and S.R.*	Galya gives an account of our working sessions on the 'Muezzin', which she does with great charm and freedom; of course, it's another panegyric about me. She creates a stunning impression in her red dress, and Glinka Hall has an atmosphere all to itself. But the actual recording doesn't give a clear enough idea of these songs. This is due in part to Galya but even more to my own accompaniment.
29/VII *Recording* **Bruckner** *5th Symphony in B flat* *Conductor:* *Franz Konwitschny*	I listened, but with some difficulty. Because of my impaired hearing, the modulations, tonalities and harmonies were impossible to tell apart. But it's also clearly due to the record player, which doesn't reproduce the right pitch. Of course, it's a remarkable symphony, but I feel more at home with the others.
30/VII *Recording* **Beethoven** *4th Symphony* *Conductor:* *Wilhelm Furtwängler*	It's perfectly clear that this is the finest version of this symphony! Does anyone want to argue?
19/VIII *Recording* **Debussy** *1) L'île joyeuse* *2) Masques* *3) Estampes* *Jean-Philippe Collard*	I don't find Jean-Philippe Collard particularly inspiring, but I was interested to hear *Masques*, which I'd not heard before. (I should add in passing that he's made a very fine recording of Schumann's Third Sonata.)
24/VIII Zvenigorod **Beethoven** *Piano Trios nos. 1 and 3* *Violin Sonata ('Spring')* *Piano Trio op. 70 no. 1* *Oleg Kagan, Natasha Gutman and Vassili Lobanov*	I must say that they gave a magnificent performance of the 1st and 3rd trios. If it's been recorded, it can be released at once. But the 'Spring' Sonata couldn't have been more different, a complete disaster! Again, they'd not worked on it sufficiently conscientiously or it was inadequately prepared through lack of time, in which case it would have been better not to have played it at all. Oleg, Oleg – The

D major Trio was serious and excellent, perhaps not free enough, unless it was me: I was hearing the piece for the first time and wasn't really free myself and had some difficulty listening to it.

30/VIII, Nikolina Gora *Tape of Mantua concert* **Brahms** *1st Sonata in C major* S.R.	This won't do at all, whole bundles of wrong notes. In the uninspiring presence of Mr Mitchum and his pipe, Emi Moresco* had persuaded me that all was for the best and that the record should come out as soon as possible. Also, it was 42°. What can you expect in the circumstances?
31/VIII *Tape of Mantua concert* **Brahms** *2nd Sonata* *in F sharp minor* *Variations on a Theme* *by Paganini* S.R.	This is a real calamity!! Also, I suddenly had to stop right in the middle of the final movement from the first book of the Variations, not because my fingers were jammed but because of the infernal heat in the hall.
4/IX Moscow *Recording* **Mahler** *3rd Symphony* *in D minor* *Conductor: Kurt Adler*	Magnificent recording of a magnificent work. In a certain way, it's a benchmark performance. This symphony was my first encounter with Mahler when I played it with Dima Guzakov in an arrangement for four hands at the students' circle that I'd founded. It was fifty years ago.
13/IX Small Hall of the Conservatory **Liszt** *20 Lieder* *Galina Pisarenko* *Alexander Bakhchiev,* *piano*	What a wonderful evening! A programme chosen with taste, Galya on excellent form, her voice perfectly suited to these songs, Bakhchiev's accompaniment sophisticated and tactful, everything came together to ensure that this concert was crowned with success. I'm thinking of working with Galya on a Grieg programme, though totally different qualities will be needed here, of course: pride and a cold Norwegian ardour. It's odd that most people regard Grieg as a mawkish,

* Richter's Italian agent.

sentimental composer (think of what's generally done to the A minor Concerto), whereas in my own view he's essentially an austere individual, like the landscapes and nature of the North. We'll see whether this will work with Galya.

2/x
Recording
Debussy
12 Études
Anatoly Vedernikov

I've often listened to this recording, which I regard as one of this pianist's greatest achievements. It's terrible to realize that such records don't enjoy the reputation that they deserve.

---

7 and 8/x
Recordings
Handel
Keyboard Suites nos. 1,
4, 6 and 7
Andrei Gavrilov
Keyboard Suites nos. 2,
3, 5 and 8
S.R.
Chopin
Andante spianato and
Polonaise
S.R. (live recording
from London)
Conductor:
Kyrill Kondrashin

Interesting to listen once again to this 'historic' recording. I know the general public didn't really take to it, so that the people who sell these things clearly didn't make any profit (will it suffer the same fate as Berg's Chamber Concerto?). And why? Audiences (in every country) prefer to buy Bach – out of habit – and because, in doing so, they think they are showing 'greater musicality'. They undervalue Handel or else they ignore him completely. During their own lifetimes, it was exactly the opposite. Handel travelled everywhere in a carriage and was treated like royalty, while Bach humbly played the organ at the Thomas-kirche.

Now for Gavrilov and Richter. As soon as I started to listen, Gavrilov struck me as infinitely more interesting (in spite of a certain irreproachability to Richter's playing). Everything about his playing is fresher, more alive, freer. There's nothing studied about it. Only occasionally does he allow himself to be carried away by the *fortissimo* passages, and here he has a tendency to bang.

Oddly, the friends who were listening with me and to whom I didn't say who was playing what often thought that Gavrilov was me and vice versa. If I'd not known, I too could have mixed the two of us up. Clearly there's a reciprocal influence at work here. Be that as it may, these Suites are veritable miracles, laminated in gold but with virtually no patina.

Chopin: I liked this, though I don't know if it's

because of my love of the work or whether it really *is* good.

Mrs Chemberdzhy was ecstatic.

17/x **Beethoven** *Sonata op. 106* *('Hammerklavier')* *Emil Gilels*	To my great shame, I don't recall the first thing about this performance. I don't understand.

25/x *Recording* **Brahms** *Piano Quartet* *in A major* *S.R. and members of* *the Borodin Quartet*	One of the few successful records I've made. And on the cover a portrait of the young Brahms, who is already very impressive!

11/xi, At home. An evening in memory of Anna Pavlovna Richter *1) Slide show with old photographs of the Moskalyov family* **2) Sviatoslav Richter** *1st Sonata in C major* *(written when I was ten)* *S.R.* *Bela's Arioso* *('Compliment') from Bela, unfinished opera to words by Lermontov (written when I was twelve)* *Galina Pisarenko* **3) Theofil Richter** *Romance on lines by Afanasy Fet, 'Do Not Leave Me'* *Oleg Kagan, violin* **4) Anna Richter** *Svetik Examining Stones*	A family get-together; a bit sentimental; only I, Nina, Ira Naumova and Volodya Tchaikovsky knew Mother. But in the end it was a very pleasant evening. It's always a pleasure to see old snapshots, as long as there aren't too many and there's an interesting commentary to go with them. My childhood works are no more than a curiosity, of course; but Galya gave a lovely performance of the monologue from *Bela*. Papa's Romance was played by Oleg on the violin. All who were present were also touched by the miniature written by Mother. My recording of neither the 'Abegg' Variations nor of *Waldscenen* is a disaster. I always feel slightly embarrassed at these celebrations, but I find that there's a certain individual pleasure to be had from the fact that it's all bound up with my past, a past to which I clearly can't be indifferent.

S.R., *piano*
5) Schumann
'Abegg' Variations
6) Schumann
Waldscenen
S.R. *(recordings)*

13/XI
Video, *Vladimir
Horowitz: The Last
Romantic*
1) **Bach–Busoni**
*Chorale Prelude
in G minor*
(Remarkable in its way)
2) **Mozart**
Sonata in C major
K 330
(Good)
3) **Schubert**
Impromptu in A flat
(Vulgar)
4) **Chopin**
Mazurka in A minor
(Very discerning)
5) **Chopin**
1st Scherzo
(Dreadful)
6) **Liszt**
Consolation in D flat
(Yes . . .)
7) **Schumann**
Novellette in F major
(. . .)
8) **Rachmaninov**
Prelude op. 32 no. 12
(No, no)
9) *Scriabin
Study in C sharp minor
(– – –)*

Phenomenal
and off-putting
and excellent (in the 'conservatory' sense)
and fantastic tone, and thoroughly contradictory.
Such talent! And such a trivial mind . . .
Such a sympathetic person, so artistic and yet so
limited (listen to his little laughs and look at him).
And what an enormous influence on the tastes of
young pianists (<u>not musicians</u>).
It's all so strange . . .
And the wicked Wanda,* said to be 'understanding'
and ready to help, always at his side, on the alert.
I don't know what else to say.

---

* Horowitz's wife.

10) Chopin
Polonaise in A flat
(Where's the nobility?)
11) Moszkowski
Study in F major
(Splendid)

22/XI *Tape from Tours* **Berio** *Corale* Maryvonne Le Dizès- Richard, violin Conductor: Pierre Boulez	I like this work, and I like the way in which this sympathetic woman plays it. I've been told that it's virtually unplayable – well, she emerged with flying colours. Bravo!
24/XI *Recording* **Suk** *Asrael* Conductor: Václav Talich	I've listened to this music so often, yet it's still just like the first time. It still touches me, overwhelms me and terrifies me. It's absolutely unique in the way it enters into the world of tragedy (and Talich!!). 'Asrael', the angel of death.
24/XII, Christmas *Recording of a recital* *in Tokyo* **Brahms** ***Variations on a Theme*** ***by Paganini*** *S.R.*	I've again been listening to a work in which it's hard to achieve perfection, even well-nigh impossible. Nina asks me: 'In that case, why do you play it? And so often?' In the first place, it's a masterpiece; secondly, it's a formidable form of self-discipline; and, in the third place, I like it. Ultimately, there must be a certain amount of professional *amour propre* in my desire to rise to this challenge.
20/II Hamburg Opera **Mascagni** *Cavalleria rusticana* Santuzza: Julia Varady Conductor: *an idiot of an Italian*	I came specially to Hamburg to see Julia Varady, with whom I'm due to give a recital of Tchaikovsky's songs in Tours. After endless discussions, we agreed on a date when we could rehearse together, but it all came to nothing through lack of time. Both as a singer and as an actress, she was absolutely sublime as Santuzza. Also, I love *Cavalleria rusticana*.

Munich
New Philharmonic Hall
Scriabin
2nd Sonata
(Sonata-fantasy)
Chopin
2nd Sonata
in B flat minor
Nocturne op. 55 no. 2
Ivo Pogorelich

Pogorelich, in the flesh.
Bizarre, and one doesn't know why . . .
You have the impression that he doesn't understand what he's playing. It's not affectation, but
rather something physical.
Curious imbalance between the right hand and the
left, which is sometimes barely audible. And I'm
not even talking about the insane and unnatural
ritardandos in the Scriabin.
He turns the first movement of the Chopin Sonata
into a kind of high-flying pianistic study, with an
overtly *forte* second subject; he takes the Funeral
March very quickly and plays the middle section
as though it were Bach (but with a beautiful tone).
The final movement is drowned by the pedal. As
for the end of the Nocturne, it's simply risible.
What a strange character!

12/IV
Moscow
Televised broadcast
of a concert marking
Heinrich Neuhaus's
centenary
Chopin
Scherzo in B flat minor
Evgeni Malinin
Scriabin
Prométhée
Conductor:
Evgeni Svetlanov
S.R., piano

I was astonished that Genya Malinin adopted such
a frivolous attitude to this concert. What's this?
The 2nd Scherzo, already played millions of times –
so why play it in such an uninteresting way?
Where are the whipcracks in the 5th bar? I was
shot down by the Salzburg press for these, but
look at the score! And sentiment instead of passion in the 2nd subject. No, Genya, it would have
been better not to have done this.
In *Prométhée*, we were together, and everything
passed off without a hitch, but – what do you
mean by deviating from Scriabin's tempo markings? And these gigantic ritardandos in the *prestis-
simo* finale?
Svetlanov seemed satisfied.

23/IV
Recording of a recital in
Cologne on 10/II/88
Liszt
2nd Mephisto Waltz
7 Études d'exécution
transcendante
S.R.

Here's another of my recordings made at a concert
that seemed at the time to be fairly successful.
How wrong can you get!
True, it has a certain atmosphere and everyone
(except me) thinks this is the prime quality. But the
blurred notes, the exaggerations, the absence of
real concentration and this quality that seems to
be inherent in my playing – a sort of superfluous

heaviness – it all makes me very sad (if not worse). I'd so much like to play better.

31/v In the car between Kassel and Heidelberg **Beethoven** *4th Concerto* *Emil Gilels*	Gilels has a very serious and Beethovenian approach to this concerto. In terms of technique and sonority, it's impeccable. Only one thing disappoints me: the exaggeratedly slow tempo of the first movement, which results in a certain shapelessness, a certain inertia.
6/vi, Hotel Penta Heidelberg *Chopiniana* video with Sviatoslav Richter **Chopin recital** *S.R.* **Scriabin** *Prométhée* *Conductor:* *Evgeni Svetlanov* *S.R., piano* *Video*	I listened to this while sipping whisky, as I've been very depressed these last two days. But this *Chopiniana* (what a ghastly title) is really quite decent as a recording; there's even a certain atmosphere to it, and no fluffs. So I don't feel too dissatisfied after all. *Prométhée* isn't a disaster either, but the problem with Svetlanov is his 'Russian' style of interpretation, which I don't like at all (this insistence on monumentality). In Scriabin, it's a bit like plonking the domes of the Donskoy Monastery on top of Chartres Cathedral.
12/vi Paris Adonis Restaurant *Sutherland and Callas* *'Casta diva', Linda di* *Chamounix, Juliet, Il* *barbiere di Siviglia etc.* *(Marvellous!!)*	Following my UNESCO recital in memory of Artur Rubinstein, I went off to a restaurant that used to be called 'Le Jardin d'Albran' but which is now the 'Adonis'. With me were Signora Borromeo and Dr Marteau. A delightful black with a pigtail served us, and the food was wonderful. As the owner (the black fellow) was a music lover, we were surrounded by the divine sounds of operatic arias emanating from the restaurant's loudspeakers. Sutherland and Callas – impossible to say which was better.
15/vi, Rue des Lombards **Rimsky-Korsakov** *The Snow Maiden* *(beginning of prologue)* *Irina Arkhipova* *Conductor: Vladimir* *Fedoseyev (execrable)*	A nightmare! You'd think it was inferior, tasteless music. These are the 'artistic results' that you get when a work's conducted by someone who used to conduct a balalaika orchestra. Not even Arkhipova emerges unscathed. As for the Chorus of Birds, it's simply unacceptable! It's terrible to have to listen to works you love played like this.

19/VI, Tours Grange de Meslay *Martial Solal Trio*	Brilliant, virtuosic, a real treat . . . And it's all improvised. The double-bass solos soon became tedious; the percussion solos (the percussionist is also a painter who has exhibited alongside Musset and with photographs of Pierre Loti) were full of bravura and very noisy; and then Solal – phenomenal. The so-called 'new style' in jazz is in fact much more old-fashioned than what I heard this evening.
23/VI Grange de Meslay **Rossini** *Petite messe solennelle* *Conductor:* *Claude Panterne*	I've never felt any great affection for Rossini (apart from the overture to *La scala di seta* and the tarantella for voice),* but this evening we heard a magnificent performance, especially from Élisabeth Vidal (soprano) and Donald Litaker (tenor), an extremely comic-looking individual, with a moustache; all that was missing was a straw boater. It was clear that the conductor had worked with care and great devotion. The two pianists – Noël Lee and Christian Ivaldi (especially Ivaldi) – were excellent (their solo 'entr'actes' were extremely interesting). The work itself is extremely likeable. The audience went wild, but the applause was directed in the main at Nathalie Stutzmann who, in my own view, was by no means the most interesting singer.
6 and 7/VII Flensburg and Neumünster **Bruckner** *6th Symphony* *Conductor:* *Christoph Eschenbach*	I'd never heard this symphony before, so I listened to it with particular interest. Eschenbach conducted it with great seriousness and sensitivity. I went to both concerts and am not complaining. Clearly you need time to come to terms with Bruckner and twice isn't enough, especially as my hearing has got worse and I can never manage to work out what key each passage is in. I used to have perfect pitch. It's very depressing.
1/IX Island of Hokkaido	I made a special effort to listen to the *Burlesques*, as I'm studying them with a view to including

* *La danza* from the *Soirées musicales* of 1835.

Bartók *Three Burlesques* *Dezsö Ránki*	them in a programme of 20th-century music that I'm planning to give. Ránki plays them to perfection, with great evenness and very little pedal. I'm almost envious.

19/IX *En route* to Takasaki Janáček *Taras Bulba* *Conductor:* *Václav Neumann* Beethoven *1st Concerto* *S.R.* *Conductor:* *Christoph Eschenbach*	Again, the seduction of Janáček. *Taras Bulba* is a unique work. How well he succeeded in creating the atmosphere of this terrible time of disorder and tyranny. And it's so sincere that you can't help but be amazed. The Beethoven was recorded at Neumünster. It's not bad, and I wasn't dissatisfied even after the concert. Best of all is the cadenza. Of Beethoven's five concertos, this is the one I prefer. Together with the Schumann, it's one of my favourite concertos.

November Yokohama In the car on the way to Kamakura Britten *Rondo alla burlesca* *Mazurka elegiaca* Stravinsky *Concerto for two pianos* *Vassili Lobanov* *and S.R.*	A grey and rainy day. I'd just landed with Natasha Zhuravliova and we were scarcely in the car before we put on this tape of a concert recorded in Tours; we listened to it against the background of the noise of these giants' causeways on which we were driving. I don't think it's a disaster, especially the Stravinsky Concerto with its pealing bells, French-style gardens, Venetian lace and its fugue by way of a starter. The Britten isn't too bad either.

8/X Tokyo *Live recording* Liszt *Polonaise in E major* *Nuages gris* *Consolation in E major* *Hungarian Rhapsody* *no. 17* *Scherzo and March* *S.R.* *(Horror of horrors!!)*	One's mind boggles at a recording like this, and you can easily lose all confidence in yourself. With the exception of *Nuages gris*, it's absolutely appalling. But I'm not disappointed, as I felt during the concert that I was going to pieces and was under no illusions.

26/IX
Sony Studios, Tokyo
*Recordings of concerts
in Tokyo and Nagasaki
in 1986*
Haydn
Sonata in E flat no. 62
Schumann
*Three Studies on
Paganini's 4th, 5th and
6th Caprices*
Brahms
*Variations on a Theme
by Paganini*
S.R.

Having decided to entrust the editing to Sony, we settled down in their studios (located in a vast building that houses an extremely busy and noisy shop) and listened to the recordings for two and a half hours, by which point we were completely exhausted.

The Sony representative was very unctuous and promised to carry out all my instructions. But when I got back to Moscow I realized that these were only promises and that nothing had changed. This is an example of Japanese precision and conscientiousness, all wrapped up in Japanese smiles. It's true that it's happened only once. An exception, but disappointing.

November, Moscow
Beethoven
Diabelli Variations
Tatyana Nikolayeva
Beethoven
*Scherzo from Sonata
op. 31 no. 3*
Chopin
*Nocturne in F major
and Waltz in A flat*
Chopin–Liszt
*Two paraphrases of
Chants polonais*
Josef Hofmann
Bartók
Suite 'Out of Doors'
Dezsö Ránki

Three pianists.
The Lady. She understands virtually nothing of what she's playing. Such tempi are harmful to your health; the rest is boring and prosaic.
Hofmann. His playing is stunning, with absolutely no smudging. A pity that in the Beethoven there are none of the *sforzatos* that I'm so fond of.
Ránki. I very much liked both the work and his interpretation of it.

November
Video
(Vienna Opera)
Rossini
Il viaggio a Reims
Montserrat Caballé,

Rossini, Abbado, a first night at the Vienna Opera (a madhouse). A curious, brilliant and entertaining piece. Original and amusing production,[*] though not lacking in instances of bad taste. Non-stop roulades from the singers, so that I sometimes can't understand what they're singing. This must

---

[*] By Luca Ronconi.

Cappuccilli,* etc.
Conductor:
Claudio Abbado

be the fault of the conductor, who takes things too quickly, and of the Italian tradition, which consists in singing everything quickly with a dash of southern temperament. Interesting on the whole, but the ultimate impression is of a lack of integrity and precision. It's all done to please the public, which admittedly almost brought the house down with its applause.

28/XI
Rehearsal at home
Theofil Richter
Quartet in F major
Borodin Quartet

The Borodins have fallen in love with Papa's quartet and decided to include it in their repertory; I was very touched by this, as it was clearly a sincere and objective response on their part. I like this work for its charm and lack of artifice, two qualities intrinsic to all Papa's works.

1/XII
Bach
Partita in D major
Brahms
Intermezzo in A major
op. 118 no. 2
James Ambrose
(a pianist from Boston)

This young pianist sent me this recording and asked me what I thought of it. It's going to be difficult to reply.
Bach (a brilliant partita): solid fingerwork and good tone. Phrasing exaggeratedly expressive; naturally, he doesn't do the repeats; the Allemande is too slow; but he clearly loves the piece and, on the whole, there's a natural flow to it.
Brahms: too much tone (a feeling of uniformity), and why is everything *affettuoso*?

12/XII
Vienna
Live recording of concert at the Pushkin Museum on 6/XII
Franck
Piano Quintet
Borodin Quartet
and S.R.

This is a recording that you can listen to.
As for the work +++++!!!

---

* Piero Cappuccilli was not involved in this production. Probably an error for Ferruccio Furlanetto.

16/XII
Vienna Volksoper
Eugen d'Albert
Tiefland

This famous opera by the pianist–composer is an excellent work, and it's only right and proper that it hasn't been forgotten.

The advent of Eberhard Waechter to run the Volksoper has transformed this theatre. You now feel that there's a real ensemble and that everything's properly rehearsed. And success has followed as surely as night follows day: the house was full.

A delightful evening.

18/XII
State Opera
Massenet
Manon
Gruberová
Conductor:
Adam Fischer

As always at the State Opera, everything hinges on the 'stars', Gruberová, in this case, who was brilliant in her role as the 'rococotte', if insufficiently spontaneous at the beginning.

On the whole, Ponnelle's production is a success (you can see four rooms in the casino at once, all lit by candles).

I know this opera virtually by heart and was pleased to hear it and see it today.

25/XII
Volksoper
Lehár
Das Land des Lächelns

Another pleasant evening at the Volksoper. The operetta (which I didn't know) is delightful; it dates from the thirties,* so it's later than Puccini, Richard Strauss and their kind. Of course, this Chinese 'smile' wins little sympathy and you can't believe in it either, but there are plenty of similar examples in history and in the present day.

The tenor couldn't have been better, a freely produced and fresh-sounding voice. The other singers were equally outstanding. Everything was in good taste. An attractive and exotic production.

---

5 and 6/I
Recording
Beethoven
Sonata no. 26
Chopin
4th Scherzo

What a surprise! I've known Lucewicz since Rolandseck, which was some years ago; he's often driven me around Europe and I've always felt a certain sympathy for him, but nothing more.

And now here's a recording of his that has won me over completely. His Beethoven in particular is

---

* It was premièred in Berlin on 10 October 1929.

Schumann *Novellette no. 2* *Andreas Lucewicz*	better than that of many 'stars': total understanding, a fine temperament and perfect technical mastery. This is also true of the 4th Scherzo, which shows signs of my own influence. The *Novellette* is admirable.
7/1 Santa Margherita *Recording* **Puccini** *Il tabarro* Conductor: *Erich Leinsdorf*	A real masterpiece by Puccini. It's no longer a melodrama but an excellent adaptation of Maupassant's short story, with all its temperament and passions.* It's one of my favourite works – there's no comparison with *Gianni Schicchi* or *Suor Angelica*. There's a real sense of Paris here, with all its dangers and seductions! Unfortunately, Leinsdorf isn't on the same level.
25/1 Genoa Teatro Margherita **Puccini** *Turandot* *Ghena Dimitrova*	Theatre packed and atmosphere electric. I didn't particularly like the 1st act, but as from the 2nd, things took off and it got better and better. Ghena Dimitrova is an outstanding Turandot. Production and scenery are a great success, as are the costumes. A real triumph of the Italian variety (there's no equivalent with us). The applause for the artists went on and on and was very warm, no doubt as it used to be long ago.
29/1 Venice Teatro La Fenice **Wolf-Ferrari** *I quatro rusteghi*	A performance at La Fenice during the carnival is bound to be an event. It begins with the appearance of traditional masks in the audience, with large black copes edged with white lace and the usual ritual greetings. This was the first time I'd heard this opera (until now I'd known only *I gioielli della Madonna*). A brilliant performance and a great success. A real treat.
28/11 Wells [or Wels?] *Video recording of*	Neither good nor bad. As always, hard to know why. Mozart – an age-old problem, I really can't get to

---

* *Il tabarro* is based on Didier Gold's play *La houppelande*.

London recital **Mozart** *Two sonatas* S.R.	grips with him and am afraid that I'm not convincing when I play him.
10/III *En route* from Nantes to Rouen *Recording of an old concert in Paris* **Schubert** *Sonata in B major* **Prokofiev** *5 pieces from Cinderella* S.R.	In the hubbub of the car and the company of two 'impresarios', who turn out to be fanatical admirers and connoisseurs of my records. In the hubbub of the car it's clearly impossible to hear properly, but it's still possible to tell that the quality of the tape isn't bad. I'd approved it at the time; now I find something new and fairly successful in it. In the hubbub of the car on the roads through France.
12/III Rouen *Television* **Brahms** *Intermezzo op. 119 no. 2* *Vladimir Ashkenazy*	Total disappointment. Expression = zero. Nothing happens. And this is Volodya Ashkenazy! Is he from another planet?
16/III London Coliseum Opera* **Britten** *The Turn of the Screw*	I went to this performance on the day I arrived in London. Musically and in terms of the production, it was a great success. All the performers were admirable. But I can't help thinking of my own 'production' at the Pushkin Museum, which is bound to be closer to me; the effect of the ghosts singing through a megaphone while the other singers on stage stood stock-still was, I think, more interesting. But it was a fine performance!
23/III Covent Garden **Mozart** *Così fan tutte*	A really fine performance. The conductor (whose name I unfortunately forgot to note down)† is as hunchbacked as Quasimodo, but what a marvellous musician! The tempi were both free and

---

* English National Opera at the Coliseum. The production was by Jonathan Miller and the cast included Elizabeth Byrne, Menai Davies, Eileen Hulse, Gillian Sullivan and Robert Tear.
† Jeffrey Tate. The cast was Margaret Marshall, Susanne Mentzer, Anne Howells, Hans Peter Blochwitz, Andreas Schmidt and Claudio Desderi.

precise; as for the singers, everything was clear and perfectly in place. Johannes Schaaf's production isn't lacking in talent, though it's sometimes in dubious taste.

Paris *Television* **Jessye Norman sings** *La* ***Marseillaise*** **in the Place** **de la Concorde**	This is clearly a star turn. Wrapped in her tricolour flag, she is magnificent. The effect is enthralling. She sings as one imagines Melpomene would have done. But what's this tempo for the *Marseillaise*? Almost an *andante*. Who could march to this?
Bonn **Hoffmeister** ***Viola Concerto*** *Yuri Bashmet*	Likeable music, stylistically close to Mozart and Haydn; an extremely attractive finale that you can remember right away. Yuri Bashmet plays in his usual manner, but I don't find his interpretation particularly convincing. He always makes too much contrast between *forte* and *pianissimo*, something that never fails to excite the audience's enthusiasm but invariably leaves me cold.
Schnittke ***Trio (arranged for*** ***chamber orchestra)*** *Yuri Bashmet*	Schnittke is clearly an important phenomenon in contemporary Russian music, but to be quite frank he doesn't stir my soul. In his own language, he simply repeats what Shostakovich has already said before him, and this in itself isn't particularly thrilling. Compared with the original, the Trio necessarily loses something in Bashmet's arrangement.
Portofino *Recording* **Mozart** ***Concerto*** [no. 9 in E flat major] *K 271* *S.R.* *Conductor:* *Lorin Maazel*	Neither good nor bad. Neither quite air-borne, nor quite expressive, nor quite Mozartian. Soloist and conductor are always together, but you feel that rhythmically their contact isn't one hundred per cent.
Mozart ***Concertos*** [no. 22 in E flat major] *K 482 and*	In spite of a few imperfections, this is an authentically Mozartian interpretation, and the two performers are in perfect accord.

[no. 27 in B flat major] K *595* *S.R.* *Conductor:* *Benjamin Britten*	In the Concerto no. 27 (it was the first time I'd played it), I made a terrible mistake: instead of playing the first phrase, I played the second one twice. I had a terrible attack of nerves. But the rest is interesting. Britten conducts magnificently.
Liszt **Christus** *Conductor: Antal Dorati*	Yes! Liszt is inspired and incredibly bold. I'm not speaking only of the music but also of the religious conception. He took a risk by moving away from what's normally allowed, and he triumphed. (This is true above all of the second part of the oratorio.) It's a challenge that he issued to himself on a human level. The piece is far from straightforward and you have to listen to it several times. The first time it tends rather to fill you with trepidation and remains inaccessible.
8/I San Remo *Recordings* **Brahms** *2nd Concerto* *S.R.* *Conductor: Mario Rossi* **Prokofiev** *5th Concerto* *S.R.* *Conductor:* *Kyrill Kondrashin*	<u>Brahms</u>: terrible. This recording should never have been released. Everything's bad, orchestra, conductor and soloist. It may be possible to listen to it once, but no more. <u>Prokofiev</u>: unexpected, brilliant, arresting. A single shortcoming: the technicians, in their infinite wisdom, have decided to boost the volume in the lyrical passage in the fourth movement and in doing so have ruined the music.
9/I **Bartók** *2nd Concerto* *(recorded at Royan)* *S.R.; Conductor: Iwaki* **Bartók** *2nd Concerto* *(recorded in Moscow)* *S.R.* *Conductor: Svetlanov*	The Royan recording is a disaster. It's completely unintelligible. Perhaps the concert itself was a success, but in the recording all you can hear is the surrounding noise and nothing else! How could they have allowed this to be released? There's something about this concerto that reminds me of a commercial jingle and on this occasion it left me cold, as did its jovial ending.

10/I **Beethoven** *Sonata no. 11 in B flat* *'Eroica' Variations* S.R. *(London)* **Weber** *3rd Sonata in D minor* S.R. *(Milan)* **Liszt** *Sonata in B minor* S.R. *(Aldeburgh)* **Ravel** *Concerto for the* *Left Hand* S.R. *Conductor:* *Riccardo Muti* (Genoa)	The two Beethoven works are astonishingly successful. Weber: it's not easy to listen to this after the Beethoven – it's a bit old-fashioned. Mediocre recording. A pity. Liszt: powerful and convincing impression (the few wrong notes don't bother me). I don't know, no doubt good. Oleg Kagan says that if it wasn't so trite, he would have thrown himself to his knees. Poor Oleg – Ravel: the orchestral opening is terribly unclear and imprecise. After that, it becomes more convincing – first and foremost the music itself.
11/I **Schumann** *Toccata in C major* S.R.	No, this is a real horror, this tempo; in the first place, it strikes me as impossible to play this work at such a speed. And secondly the music loses something, and it's this that is so awful. Did I really play like this? Or have the technicians manipulated it and speeded it up? It would be a crime if they have.
13/I Jouques Notre Dame de Fidélité *Compline* *(the nuns' final service* *before nightfall)*	In near-total darkness it's deeply impressive. The same endlessly repeated chants and the homophony produce a hypnotic effect, resulting in a feeling of great strength and great purity. The abbess gives her blessing to the nuns before they retire for the night, and you can watch the ceremony from a distance, from behind the screen of homophony. (And in Latin.)
24/I	Vespers at five o'clock. Gregorian chant, the *Magnificat*, etc. struck my ear today as almost cloying and cajoling. As we left the church, magnificent colours of the setting sun over Provence.

Munich
Bartók
2nd Piano Concerto
S.R.
Conductor:
János Ferencsik
(recorded in Budapest
in 1958)

Bartók's 2nd Concerto again; it's beginning to get on my nerves. (Macht mich nervös!)
The recording is undoubtedly a success. It was the first time I'd played it, and I remember the shock I had when Zoltán Kodály walked into my dressing-room just before I went out on stage.
However, there's a serious blemish: a split high C on the trumpet in the second movement (but it appears that this can be corrected when it's edited). We had eight rehearsals: the orchestra and Ferencsik are excellent.

Vienna
Beethoven
Sonata op. 106
('Hammerklavier')
S.R. *(London)*

I can't work out whether this recording should be issued or not.
The concert went well (there was even an old gentleman who leapt up and down in his enthusiasm), there are virtually no wrong notes and everything is clear.
I think I'll risk it and give my permission. Even so, there's something (what?) that doesn't entirely satisfy me about this interpretation.
I don't like myself.

12/VI
Volksoper
Johann Strauß
The Gypsy Baron

I saw and heard *The Gypsy Baron* during a tour by the Kharkov Operetta to Odessa.
I loved Safi's song (there's an amazing recording by Elisabeth Schwarzkopf) and, indeed, the performance as a whole.
This time I felt no such enthusiasm (though I'm sure the present performance was infinitely better), but nor was I disappointed.
It's just that times have changed.

Moscow
Recording
Franz Schreker
Der ferne Klang

This work was a revelation to me when I was fifteen and I was given a copy of the full score and I literally immersed myself in this music, which is steeped in passion and the pleasures of the flesh. It accompanied my whole life, I know each note by heart, and it has turned me into a different man from the one I should otherwise have been. I dream of it incessantly and, of course, I understand it fully.

Now I have a recording of it. It's very mediocre and in no way lives up to my expectations. It's always the same shortcomings: the orchestra, on which the entire work rests, isn't sufficiently audible, the tempi are too fast and the balance is poor. But it's the first time I've heard the work.
Where am I? This can't be me.

Tchaikovsky *Barcarolle** *(A young pianist)* ***Waltz of the Flowers*** ***from The Nutcracker*** *Conductor: Temirkanov*	By chance, on television. The young pianist plays the Barcarolle in a sentimental and insufficiently serious way (either too fast or too slow, I no longer remember which). The waltz from *The Nutcracker*. Nothing to quibble over, but there's neither poetry nor the mysterious character that you ought to hear when the theme enters in the horns. Temirkanov is a vicious man.
Liszt *Recording of a recital* *at Ulm* ***Polonaise, Scherzo,*** ***Nuages gris,*** ***Consolation no. 6,*** ***Hungarian Rhapsody*** ***no. 17, Mephisto Polka,*** ***2nd Mephisto Waltz*** S.R.	I'd already listened to this recording, so my reaction is still the same, if not worse. There's still something unsuccessful about my performance of the Polonaise, which is a pity as it's a dazzling piece. The little Scherzo isn't a success on account of the leaps, *Nuages gris* because the tremolandos aren't sufficiently even. *Consolation* isn't as easy as it initially appears. The Rhapsody fares better, in spite of its brutality. The Mephisto Polka is horribly difficult, on top of which you have to play it with elegance. The 2nd Mephisto Waltz isn't so convoluted; even so I don't manage to play it with enough feeling. Zero, zero, zero –
Bolshoy Theatre **Rimsky-Korsakov** ***The Golden Cockerel*** *The Tsarina:* *Elena Brilova* *Conductor:* *Evgeni Svetlanov*	This was the third time I'd attended a performance of this marvellous 'fairy-tale' opera (Odessa, Saratov and Moscow). I know it very well and adore both the music and the words. The musical performance under Svetlanov is precise and wholly satisfying (even more). But the director and designer have done everything in

* From *The Seasons* op. 37b.

their power to diminish the work: always the same idiocies and the same sense of arbitrariness.

Elena Brilova plays the Tsarina and gets through this extraordinarily difficult role marvellously well. As for the other singers, it would be better to pass a veil over them.

Television
A film about
Kyrill Kondrashin

(A conductor who has fled the Soviet Union. I often performed with him.)

The mere fact that a film about Kondrashin has been shown on television in this country is in itself a positive development. Who would have imagined that it would ever be possible?

It transpires that the high point in Kyrill's life was conducting Mahler's First Symphony. The film isn't badly made, but it suffers from the inclusion of a number of tendentious elements (the scenes shot in a police station, and the telephone box from which he's said to have rung up to announce that he was staying in Holland).

19/VIII
Televised broadcast
from the Bolshoy
Vladimir Vasiliev's
jubilee

God, how I hate jubilees!

And I don't much care for the ballet either. It's such an inconsistent art: when the music's good, it can't hold a candle to it; only when it's mediocre is it just about acceptable.

Vladimir Vasiliev is clearly an immensely talented dancer, as is Katya Maximova, but it gave me no pleasure to watch them.

We stayed to the end. Nina Dorliac was in raptures. Interminable ovations. Only the director of the Bolshoy Ballet didn't deign to grace the performance with his presence (Grigorevich, in case you've forgotten).

Liszt
Study in F minor
Evgeny Kissin

He's knowledgeable and plays well, but he never throws himself headlong into the sea. Perhaps he'll never do so.

27/VIII
Moscow
Compact discs

This is the second time I've listened to these recordings; the first time was with Oleg at San Remo.

Mozart *1) Sonata in C major* *[K 545]* *2) Variations on* *La belle Françoise* *3) Sonata in G major* **Weber** *3rd Sonata* **Mendelssohn** *Variations sérieuses* **Liszt** *Sonata in B minor* *S.R.*	The Mozart Sonata in C is more or less acceptable and doesn't put me to shame. The Variations could have been more elegant, but – even so. The G major Sonata has been a pleasure to listen to. Weber: my listeners liked it, though I thought less highly of it (I'm speaking of the interpretation). It's a highly original work and I like it a lot. Mendelssohn: excellent in terms of both mood and technique. Liszt! Great disappointment this time, unfortunately. This is what comes of listening to something twice. Or is it simply impossible to play this work well?
11/IX *Tape of Oleg Kagan's* *last interview in* *Germany* **Fragments of a sonata** **(with S.R.) and a** **Mozart quintet**	Terribly painful impression. Oleg had great difficulty speaking; he was struggling for breath and for the right German words. Why did he have to be tormented in this way? I fully understand his insistence on giving this concert (it was his last), but this interview exhausted him; also, there must have been so many people and so much prosaic bustle around him . . . And no one to protect him.
17/IX **Szymanowski** *1st Violin Concerto* *Wanda Wilkomirska* *Conductor:* *Witold Rowicki*	This is the concerto that Oleg wanted and promised me to play, but which he'll never play. Today we accompanied him to the cemetery at Vagankovsky. Das ist der Lauf der Welt [That's the way of the world].
10/X *Recording* **Prokofiev** *2nd Cello Concerto* *Mstislav Rostropovich* *Conductor: S.R.* *(First performance in* *the Grand Hall of the* *Conservatory in 1952)*	This is in fact the work now called the Symphony–Concerto for cello and orchestra, the third movement of which has suffered a great deal from the revisions inspired by the (almost great) cellist to whom the work is dedicated. I'll never forgive him for this.

13/x *Recording* **Chopin** *Studies op. 25* *nos. 1 and 5* *Vladimir Horowitz*	What can one say against this? Yet there's nothing that one feels like saying in its favour either. A pianist! Phenomenal fingers . . . But what about the music?
16/x **Prokofiev** *Cello Concerto* *(first version)* *Mstislav Rostropovich* *Conductor: S.R.*	This was the first time that Natasha Gutman had heard this antediluvian recording of my one and only appearance as a conductor. She feels exactly as I do about the damage done to the work by the revisions to the finale and she, too, would like to try to restore the original. It's complicated, as no one knows where to dig up the score.
29/x Bonn Opera **Bruno Maderna** *Satyricon* *(chamber opera)*	This was quite a surprise, from a musical point of view as well as from that of the production (which proved to be most original and interesting). Clearly, the music isn't of the highest quality, nor did it have to be. Is the *Satyricon* after all really great literature?
31/x Bonn Opera **Berlioz** *La damnation de Faust* *Conductor: Serge Baudo*	In my own view, this work loses something when it's staged. The result is always a bit lame, and I was disappointed, in spite of a first-rate performance. It's true to say that I can't really relate to Berlioz – I feel he's a great man and a great artist, but that he never really found himself in the world of music. The only exception is the *Requiem*.
1/xi Rolandseck *Recording* **Brahms** *1st Violin Sonata* Grieg *2nd Violin Sonata* Ravel *Violin Sonata* *Oleg Kagan and S.R.*	This was an extremely successful concert and it really should come out on record. It was the last time we appeared together. I'm afraid that, as always, things will drag on (for two or three years), and I'd like to avoid that.

11/XI Bonn **Prokofiev** *Sonata for* *unaccompanied violin* *Five Melodies* *Two violin sonatas* Gidon Kremer and Martha Argerich	I didn't like this at all. But it's hardly surprising, as these people go out on stage and play without any rehearsal; what can they expect? It's nothing less than scandalous (especially the violin). I can't begin to understand how people can adopt this approach to art. The outcome – a tumultuous success.
12/XI *Recording of a recital* *in Bologna* **Schubert** *Sonata in G major* S.R.	This is my favourite sonata by Schubert. But this recording left no impression on me.
22/XI – 23/XI *Recording of December* *Nights at the Pushkin* *Museum* **Schumann** *Trio in D minor* Oleg Kagan, Natasha Gutman and S.R. **Schubert** *Sonata (Duo)* *in A major* *for violin and piano* Oleg Kagan and S.R.	The Schumann Trio is magnificent! And yet I don't remember it. Why is that? It must be a physical shortcoming on my part: I can't remember the quartet repertory, for example, or half of Mozart's music. I loved the Schubert Duo. It could be issued on record.
Rolandseck Station **Schubert** *Schwanengesang* Brigitte Fassbaender	The artiste comes out on stage. She looks very Russian. She sings splendidly in every way (voice, understanding, taste). We dined together after the concert and had a very interesting conversation. She has stopped singing in *opera* (*besser zu früh, als zu spät* [better too soon than too late]). In the near future she's reckoning on directing Schreker's *Der ferne Klang* somewhere or other.*

* For Opera North in Leeds in January 1992.

New compact disc
Prokofiev
6th and 9th Sonatas
Five pieces from
Cinderella
S.R.

In the 6th Sonata the first movement is clearly not a success, but the rest is fine.

The 9th and the pieces from *Cinderella* are really quite acceptable, but for one reason or another the overall impression is of a certain sluggishness.

It all fills me with feelings of sadness, I don't know why.

February
Recording of a concert
at Yamaha's in Vienna
Prokofiev
2nd Sonata
Stravinsky
Piano-rag-music
Shostakovich
2 Preludes and Fugues
Webern
Variations op. 27
Szymanowski
Metopes nos. 1 and 2
Bartók
3 Burlesques
Hindemith
Suite '1922'
S.R.

This seems more or less successful.

The concert took place half an hour after I'd fallen heavily on the stairs and sprained both ankles. 'That's all I need,' I screamed, then limped to the taxi and dragged myself out on stage. Elisabeth Schwarzkopf was waiting for me in my dressing-room.

12/V
Dijon, Rolandseck,
Vienna until May, then
Moscow
Bach
Concertos in D major
and G minor
Zoltán Kocsis
Conductor:
Albert Simon
Concerto in G minor
Andrei Gavrilov
Conductor:
Yuri Nikolayevsky

I really don't know what I can have been thinking about when I heard Zoltán Kocsis in these same works a few years ago. It's simply appalling. Such a fast tempo (you'd think it was *Gnomenreigen*) is impossible in Bach; and in the (exaggeratedly) slow movements, such narcissism . . .

Same thing with Gavrilov.

They race through these works as though they were sports competitions, and in the second movements they have forty winks.

21/VI
Château des Artannes
Schumann
Recording
Dichterliebe
Nina Dorliac and S.R.

I'm very fond of this recording, the best – in my view – that this singer has made.
It's only a shame that the accompaniment was recorded in such a distant acoustic, so much so that it's sometimes barely audible.

28/VI
Grange de Meslay
Bach
6th Suite for unaccompanied cello
Natasha Gutman

Natasha played especially well this evening. I was terribly tired, but the music brought me to life again.

Haseldorf
Prokofiev
Legenda,
Visions fugitives etc.
S.R.

It's really not worth wasting any paper on writing down the impressions left by your own recordings. It's virtually always the same, and it's tedious to reread it –

Ischia
Max Reger
Requiem
Dietrich Fischer-Dieskau
Conductor:
Gerd Albrecht

A strange work in which Reger alludes to the First World War.
As a whole it reminds you of Berlioz or Busoni: it's mournful and bombastic.
And Fischer-Dieskau is no longer quite the singer he was.
O Seele, verlaß uns nicht [O soul, do not abandon us].

Reger
Vier Tondichtungen
nach Arnold Böcklin
Conductor:
Gerd Albrecht

I didn't know this. I wasn't expecting such sumptuous orchestration on Reger's part. Serious, full-toned music, but repetitive, slightly too cerebral and lacking in freshness.

13/XI
Ingolstadt
Recording of a recital at Wildbad Kreuth
Mozart
Fantasia in C minor
S.R.

A little too studied to begin with; it later becomes more spontaneous.
I find it quite Mozartian, *pace* Mme Schwarzkopf, who was present at the concert.

24/XII, Christmas
Moscow
Recording
Mozart
Concerto in G major
S.R.
Conductor:
Eugene Ormandy
Britten
Cadenza for Mozart's
Concerto in E flat K 482
S.R.

Having found this recording of Mozart's G major Concerto with Ormandy not too bad, I gave my permission for it to be released. I've now changed my mind; I listened to it with some difficulty. Of course, my guests who listened to it with me (especially Eliso Virsaladze) fell over each other praising it – all except Mitya, who quite rightly compared our interpretation with 'a kind of flour'. Far from playing ideally well on this particular day, the Philadelphia Orchestra was itself partly to blame.

By contrast, Britten's cadenza for the Concerto no. 22 is full of life. It brought a little glamour to our Christmas party in Moscow. The tree, too, was lit.

26/XII
Recording
Wagner
Lohengrin
Scene between Elsa
and Ortrud in Act II
Elisabeth Schwarzkopf
+++
Christa Ludwig +++
Conductor: ?

This will always be the best, and one can only marvel that it exists at all, surpassing everything else and utterly perfect in every note. But who takes the trouble to understand this and to acknowledge it?

The scene of reconciliation between these two symbolic women is fraught with danger. I find that the postlude in G major is almost always drawn out by conductors in the manner of Isolde's *Liebestod*, whereas it should be played *fliegender*, more humbly and more naturally.

29/I
Bordighera
Stradivarius compact
disc recorded at Tours
Bach
2nd Sonata in C major
4th Sonata in D major
5th Sonata in D minor
S.R.

Sonata in C major: unfortunately, there's a slight mishap in the left hand in the Prelude. The Fugue is clearer than in the Castelfranco recording. On the whole, not too bad.

Sonata in D major: the first movement could have been better, but the second movement and the Fugue are fine.

Sonata in D minor: you can sense the hard work that's gone into this. The first movement is boring, the second very laboured, the third boring, the fourth much better.

Ultimately, it's more of a document than a true interpretation, which is understandable, as I'd not

---

* Heinz Wallberg.

played these pieces for 35 years. This is what happens when you record them all at once after such a lengthy period of time, it sounds as if you're sight-reading them. What's to be done?

31/I *Stradivarius compact* *disc recorded at Tours* **Bach** ***Capriccio, 4 Duos,*** ***Italian Concerto*** S.R.	Here I play like a student – diligently, but with no artistry. It's an attempt to play in the style of Bach. But yes, I *am* still a student. I don't think it can be otherwise. Perhaps the student will one day play well. The Capriccio: not at all what's needed . . . The Duos: cautious and diligent. The *Italian Concerto*. First movement: not at all what's needed. Second movement: not too bad. Third movement: ditto. On the whole, an extremely dubious record. And to think that I agreed to this compromise, given the circumstances in Tours!
21/II Jouques Notre Dame de Fidélité **Bach** ***3rd, 5th and 6th Suites*** ***for unaccompanied*** ***cello*** *Natasha Gutman*	It was in a solemn and religious setting that Bach's 'dancelike' music was heard this evening. On this occasion Natasha wasn't on form, she's visibly affected by the hectic life that she's leading (for entirely noble reasons, it's true, and in memory of Oleg). I can't approve of this. Moreover, she has constant pains in her hands. She really must find another modus vivendi, otherwise I don't know how she'll survive. Even so, I was impressed by the 3rd Suite. The rest was played with difficulty. The nuns listened and watched from behind the iron screen.
28/II Arles **Britten** ***First Suite for*** ***unaccompanied cello*** *Natasha Gutman*	I listened from the wings, from a makeshift dressing-room, as I was taking part in the concert myself. It was the first time I'd followed the work with a score. It's one of the most interesting I know and, of course, frighteningly difficult. Natasha mastered it without any problems. But – there are lots of things I disagree with. It seems to me that in the (canto) passage that's repeated three times, the tempo is too quick and there's not enough sense of severity and abstraction (an

abstraction entirely in place in this work but which Natasha does everything to avoid).

The Fugue, Serenade and March are also taken very quickly. Music like this needs to be spoon-fed to the audience, otherwise they won't be able to understand it. The finale is completely lacking in clarity as a result of the speed at which she takes it. Well, all this is easy enough to say; perhaps I should try playing the work myself . . .

London
Covent Garden
Richard Strauss
Salome
Salome: Maria Ewing
Conductor: excellent
with lots of tempera-
ment. But who?*

I wasn't expecting a Salome like this. The singer is so gifted that she almost frightens you. She keeps us in a state of incredible suspense, sings sublimely, is spectacularly beautiful and dances superbly (in total harmony with the music). She *is* Salome.

Everything was on a par with this (in spite of some tempi that were occasionally too fast – in keeping with tradition – and sets that weren't entirely convincing). Dazzling impression.

Schliersee Bauerntheater
Concert of pupils from
Nina Dorliac's
masterclass
Elena Brilova,
Magdalena Schäfer, etc.

Concert of young singers in this extraordinarily sympathetic theatre. I didn't recognize Elena Brilova to begin with, but when she sang the Queen of Night at the end, it was fabulous! I can now understand why they're fighting over her in Europe.

Freiburg
Poulenc
Concerto for two pianos
François-René Duchâble
Jean-Philippe Collard
Conductor:
James Conlon

I was particularly keen to hear this charming work with Lisa Leonskaja; I want to play it, and Lisa doesn't seem to be against the idea. When? I still don't know.

What we heard had an entirely contemporary roughness to it; perhaps it would be better to round off the angles a little. I once heard the recording made by the composer himself with Jacques Février. As far as I recall, it was really rather feeble.

Milan
Recording of a concert
at Zug

At Zug the critics tore me to pieces, saying that my concert gave rise to sad thoughts (i.e., it was time for me to stop playing).

---

* Edward Downes. The production was by Peter Hall, with designs by John Bury.

Mozart
Fantasia and Sonata in C minor
S.R.

I can't say that this recording supports them in their opinion.

Saillon
Televised broadcast
Concert by Marlene Dietrich at the Café de Paris in London

The 'Astarte' of our age, '*Die blonde Venus*', the sublime film actress (*Morocco*, etc.) in one of her last appearances before she collapsed with a glass of champagne in her hand.
How does she manage to produce such a powerful musical impression in the absence of any music? After all, in her famous '*Ich bin von Kopf bis Fuß*', it's impossible to recall even the main motif.
Unfortunately, she's visibly aged (her mouth gives it away).
But what does it matter, the miracle remains.

27/X
Nijmegen
*Televised broadcast from Covent Garden
Georg Solti's jubilee*
Verdi
Act IV of Otello
Desdemona:
Kiri Te Kanawa
Otello:
Plácido Domingo
Conductor: Solti

Ninoshka: 'Slava, come quickly, there's going to be Plácido Domingo in *Otello*' – and she drags me over to the television even though I was practising at the Clavinova.
I go into the next room, all the more reluctantly in that it's to hear the opening of Act IV, which is in F sharp minor, a key I don't particularly care for. Kiri Te Kanawa is beautiful, but she's not Desdemona, rather a kind of Catherine Deneuve. She has a rather tedious scene that ends in F sharp minor and that she makes artificially touching with an expected *fortissimo* (but not, in fact, as unexpected as all that) on the final A sharp.*
There follows the austere Ave Maria in the major, then it's the turn of Plácido Domingo, overcome with grief and wild-eyed. With the exception of a rather mawkish episode in E major, he maintains a tragic tone to the end and proves extremely convincing.
In *Otello* I much prefer the 1st and 3rd acts, the 4th strikes me as far weaker, but what does it matter, it's still Verdi! I almost hate this brilliant tragedy!

---

* The A sharp is marked *forte* in the score.

1/XI
Pinneberg
*Televised broadcast
from the Berlin State
Opera*
Wagner
Parsifal (Acts II and III)
*Parsifal: Poul Elming
Kundry: Waltraud Meier
Conductor:
Daniel Barenboim
Director: Harry Kupfer*

Television again! Barenboim, Kupfer (SOS, *molto pericoloso!*).

Let me say right away that Barenboim is clearly devilishly talented and that, joking apart, he emerges from *Parsifal* with some credit. But he's so keen to seem thoughtful and profound that he almost becomes boring (note his beautiful but not particularly inspired face in the prelude to Act III). Secondly, the beginning proves to be interesting, in spite of a bad Klingsor watching Parsifal through a giant magnifying glass. Our hero then loses his way among two dozen TV sets, the home of the Flowermaidens (Kupfer brilliant as ever).

The scene between Parsifal and Kundry surpasses all our expectations; here the performers – especially Waltraud Meier – scale the highest peaks.

The third act takes place in a contemporary setting made entirely of glass and is completely impossible. Gurnemanz looks like a sort of moronic Knecht Ruprecht, Amfortas is repugnant, almost naked, with a suppurating wound like something out of a medical textbook.

As for the ending, it's so feeble as to be a veritable disaster.

And this is *Parsifal*?!?!?!?!

11/XI
Berlin
Philharmonie
Bach
First Suite in C major
*Conductor:
Peter Schreier*

In the first half of this concert, I played two concertos by Bach. Schreier, of course, sings better than he conducts, but it's always a pleasure to be with him. Even so, he hasn't succeeded in avoiding criticism on the part of my friends and of Nina.

In the second half there was this Suite. We were sitting fairly high up, and I particularly liked the work's festive, *galant* character. One can just as well condemn as approve of this method of doing the repeats by using only half as much sound.

23/XI
En route from Smolensk
to Moscow
Tape

In spite of the noise of the car, I listened to this recording with pleasure and astonishment.

The orchestra (presumably Barshai's) plays very well, in fact, and the soloist isn't bad either. When was it recorded? I need to clarify this point and

Mozart
Piano Concerto K 450
S.R.
Conductor:
Rudolf Barshai

perhaps give my permission for this record to be released.

11/XII
Vienna
State Opera
Richard Strauss
Capriccio

'From the boat (train) to the ball (opera)!'
We arrived here today from Moscow and went straight to the Opera for the simple reason that Lena Brilova was taking what, after all, is the modest role of the Italian Singer. We sit in a first-tier box on the prompt side. From there we can see the whole of the orchestra, which plays the introduction superbly in the purest Classical style. The curtain goes up, everyone sings well, the production is totally honest and in excellent taste.*
Walter Berry is excellent in the role of the impresario. In spite of the static character of the action, the performance is full of life and fire. A very fine performance, which isn't always the case in Vienna. But – and it's a big 'but' – this superbly professional music, full or freshness and originality, is it ultimately anything more than empty verbiage? I fear that this is indeed the case.
The result is that the meaning behind Clemens Krauss's splendid libretto (which is the more essential, music or words?) consists in handing the victory to the words!

24/XII, Midnight Mass
at the Cathedral
Asolo
Music by Gabrieli, Bach
and Monteverdi

The cathedral is packed. Impossible to squeeze through anywhere. The altar is decorated with Christmas plants with red leaves that in Italy replace the Christmas tree. Between the Latin texts we hear liturgical music. An old officiant spends some time struggling to light the long candles and finally manages to do so.
Buon Natale.

31/XII–1/I, Hotel Shelley
Lerici

We spend the New Year with just the three of us (Nina Dorliac, Milena Borromeo and me) listening

---

* Rudolf Hartmann's production was first seen in 1960.

Bach
Toccata in D major
S.R.

to firecrackers going off, in a room with a terrace overlooking the sea where Shelley drowned. Between two rounds of fireworks I play Bach's Toccata on the Clavinova and very much enjoy doing so.

24/1, Villa Igea
Palermo
*Recording of a concert
at Benevento*
Bach
Sonata in D minor
Beethoven
Sonata op. 54
Chopin
*Polonaise in D minor
op. post.
Three posthumous
studies*
Scriabin
Sonata-fantasy no. 2
Debussy
L'île joyeuse
S.R.

At Benevento I gave a recital in a ruined theatre (but currently being restored) for students at the local school of music. It was like playing in the open air in an ice-cold draught. It was an interesting experience and I enjoyed playing, even if I kept wondering how I was going to avoid catching a cold. I think I managed to create a decent atmosphere.

Bach: almost as it should be.

Beethoven: only the second movement. The slow passages are tortuous and not sufficiently expressive. I don't like what I'm doing.

Chopin: the Polonaise more or less good (the eternal 'more or less'). But not the studies.

Scriabin: it has atmosphere but not enough clarity, and there's too much pedal.

Debussy: yes . . . (. . . ? . . .)

It saddens me to have to cause problems for whoever made this recording.

12/II
Teatro Politeama
Stravinsky
Oedipus rex
Conductor: Kurt Martin

Having attended so many opera performances, I had no great illusions about what I was going to see, but I none the less felt a glimmer of vague hope. It started: from the very beginning I was exasperated by the chorus, then by the inappropriate style of singing adopted by the Oedipus, who has in fact an attractive voice. The orchestra doesn't appear to come from the same place and sounds like a sort of milky jelly. In fact, they're simply playing badly, unlike the excellent chorus. But now Jocasta appears; she sings her scene with lots of conviction; her singing, the way she moves and her costume are all splendid. Better to ignore the Tiresias, a sort of Father Christmas who has climbed down from his tree.

And of course there had to be a visual counterpart

to all this: four young men, virtually naked, explain the subject of the tragedy by means of dance. It looked like an advert for swimming costumes. What a shame . . .

Honegger *Antigone* *Conductor: Kurt Martin*	I didn't like Honegger's *Antigone* at all, even though it was infinitely better played than *Oedipus rex*. The music races past at a permanent *prestissimo accelerando*. You'd think you were at a cross-country riding competition. (Where's Sophocles in all this?) The singers had clearly worked hard and made a conscientious effort to enter into the spirit of the competition. But what's the reason for this headlong flight? The French language? I came away with the impression of something physically and aesthetically unclean.
14/II *Video* New Year's Day Concert from Vienna **Selected works by** **Johann Strauß** *Vienna Philharmonic* *conducted by* *Carlos Kleiber*	I was very tired and this overdose of optimism, gaiety and Viennese frivolity finished me off completely. A dazzling spectacle: marvellous music impeccably played beneath the gilt panelling and countless chandeliers of the Musikverein and, above all, the king of the evening, who casts a spell on you the moment he enters. One scarcely dares mention his way of conducting, simple, natural, extraordinarily elegant . . . It was all quite splendid, and the Viennese audience went wild. You can understand them, for who else is there nowadays who is so in tune with this music? And who can cast such a powerful spell on the listener with Johann Strauß's triple-time rhythms? P.S. But today's the 14th of February, not New Year's Eve. It's extremely hard to resonate in a major tonality for two whole hours. Unfortunately, I'm not in good form. P.P.S. In this orgy of brilliant works, it was *Frühlingsstimmen* that I liked best of all.

16/II
Teatro Golden
Recital by Eliso
Virsaladze
Schumann
Arabeske and Phantasie
Chopin
24 Préludes, Berceuse
and Mazurka

Can one imagine a more beautiful Schumann than the one offered to us this evening by Eliso Virsaladze? Not since Neuhaus have I heard Schumann like it.

The recital was a real revelation. Virsaladze plays even better than before.

The Chopin isn't quite that. She is still looking but trying too hard to understand, whereas in this case it's enough to believe and to play as God inspires you, in other words, to improvise. To judge by the *Berceuse*, she'll get there in the end.

Her technique is staggeringly good (Préludes): a sort of yardstick by which to judge other pianists.

23/II
Teatro Golden
Recital by Gustav
Leonhardt (harpsichord)
Frescobaldi,
Michelangelo Rossi,
Johann Kaspar Kerll

Yes, hard to endure, in spite of the quality of the performances. In such a large auditorium, the harpsichord can hardly be heard and there are times when you can't follow the music. If it had been a simple drawing room, I'm sure I'd have enjoyed it. The harpsichord was very beautiful to look at and played by a master of unfailing reliability, but its tone wasn't particularly interesting and it soon went out of tune. It had to be retuned during the interval; we didn't stay for the second half.

I'm sure I'd be more appreciative of these beautiful early works if I knew them better. Of course, one has to play them, but perhaps not for a whole evening on a barely audible instrument.

This is a real shame, especially for someone who, it seems to me, is an altogether remarkable interpreter.

25/II
Teatro Metropolitan
Recital by Dezsö Ránki
Haydn
Sonata in C minor
Schubert
Sonata in C minor
Debussy
Estampes

Long live the younger generation! To judge by this evening's concert, its representatives are much more irreproachable professionally than the pianists of the past.

I was much taken by the <u>Haydn</u>, even though the 1st movement wasn't *moderato* and the interpretation was very different from my own. But one senses a real desire to recreate the 18th-century style and the result is most convincing.

Ravel
Sonatine
Liszt
1st Mephisto Waltz and Csárdás as an encore

The wretch didn't do all the repeats.
Schubert: broadly structured; interesting to listen to. Sometimes a certain lack of clarity as a result of too much pedal.
The final movement – horribly difficult – was brilliantly performed. But it lacked something.
Debussy and Ravel: this isn't right at all. He plays them in a Romantic, brilliant way. He doesn't feel them on their deepest level.
Mephisto Waltz: phenomenal in every respect. Technically amazing.
Csárdás: dazzling impression.
In sum, a very slightly docile artist who tries to do everything well but who maintains a certain distance towards the music.
Milena rushed off to his dressing-room afterwards. The boy (he's forty-two) was all on his own, weary and slightly lost.

26/11
Teatro Politeama Garibaldi
Donizetti
Lucia di Lammermoor
Lucia: Mariella Devia
Edgardo: Ramon Vargas
Raimondo:
Michele Pertusi
Conductor:
Stefano Ranzani
Director: Filippo Crivelli

I already knew *Don Pasquale*, *L'elisir d'amore* and *La favorita* but I'd never heard *Lucia*. I know that Donizetti always prefers the major to the minor, even in the most tragic passages, and so I was amazed by the orchestral introduction, as dark as the Scottish clouds, and in a minor key. But as soon as the curtain rose, everything returned to the major.
The opera is a unified whole and extremely attractive. Donizetti gives his singers a chance to display all their vocal potential and mastery. I even believe this was his main objective (listen, for example, to the duet for Lucia and Edgardo at the end of Act I, Lucia's Mad Scene and the finale with the aria for the dying Edgardo). But he's also capable of other flights of imaginative fancy such as the harp solo that precedes Lucia's first entrance.
I very much liked this performance (though not straight away). It harks back to the good old Italian tradition. The traditional production, too, is entirely acceptable. In the incredible Mad Scene, the soprano reveals a quite staggering coloratura technique. Excellent, too, is Ramon Vargas. He

sings very intelligently and with a perfect sense of moderation. We were delighted by both the chorus and the orchestra.

Tremendous success with the first-night audience in Palermo. And rightly so.

13/IV
Video from Munich
Johann Strauß
Die Fledermaus
Conductor:
Carlos Kleiber

Impossible to imagine a better performance of this extraordinary operetta.

It's all here: music, theatre, the <u>Viennese atmosphere</u>!

Who's responsible for this? First and foremost, of course, Carlos, but also the marvellous singers and Otto Schenk, the director.

Subarashii [marvellous]!!!

20/IV
Vienna
State Opera
Verdi
Un ballo in maschera
Conductor:
Jan Latham-Koenig

Whatever it may claim, the Vienna State Opera isn't always as good as its reputation. On this occasion, an excellent conductor (with temperament and taste), a superb Renato (Leo Nucci) and a good Oscar (Elizabeth Norberg-Schulz); the rest of the cast (including Zampieri's Amelia) is first-rate, too, but something is missing.

I think this opera is one of Verdi's really great successes, but that he spoilt things by virtue of the undeniable fact that it contains an unfortunate mixture of art and politics (essentially in the libretto). The role of Oscar – half secretary, half spy to the king – has always irritated me, for example. Similarly the 'Ha, ha, ha' of the chorus of conspirators in the night-time scene with Ulrica. The staging is traditional, but tasteless and over-decorative.*

6/V, At Lisa Leonskaja's
Tape
Gershwin
Concerto in F
Philippe Entremont
Conductor:
Eugene Ormandy

Ouch!!!

Can one really play this concerto like this?

Fast, fast, confused, with no sense of rhythm . . .

I'm amazed and dismayed, not only by the pianist (Entrecôte), but also by Ormandy. It put me in a bad mood.

---

* Gianfranco De Bosio's production was first seen in 1986. The sets were by Emanuele Luzzati.

16/v
Musikverein
Mozart
Symphony in B flat
K 319
Richard Strauss
Ein Heldenleben
Conductor:
Carlos Kleiber

The gilt, and the packed and simmering hall of the Vienna Musikverein.

The hero of the day enters, as handsome and as elegant as we know him to be and takes his place on the podium.

The Mozart Symphony (which I didn't know) is played brilliantly and straightforwardly. The only thing that annoys me is that Kleiber omits the repeats.

In the second half, it's the young Strauss's prodigiously daring work that grabs you by the throat in an orgy of energy, inspiration and mastery. Here's the real Strauss, a Titanesque figure! How much imagination he had in his youth! And what dazzling ideas (the violin solo, the portrait of his wife, the bunch of critics, the decisive combat and the culmination with all its quotations from his own works)! But I'm disturbed by the ending, which is calm (even though some chromatic passages portend other storms) and almost – forgive me – petit bourgeois.

30/v
Schwetzingen
Rehearsal at the Rococo
theatre
Ravel
Ma mère l'oye
Stuttgart Orchestra
Conductor:
Christoph Eschenbach

After a very good rehearsal of the Gershwin Concerto and Saint-Saëns's 5th with Eschenbach, I stayed to hear the Ravel. No point in singing the latter's praises, there's no need. I just want to say how much pleasure he gives me. These exquisite miniatures are of a sophisticated *bon goût*, and how well it all sounds in the orchestra!

Eschenbach is a splendid musician, right up with the best of them. I sat in the stalls, which were empty, and in the dark. The music was soon over. Nothing lasts very long with Ravel, which is why one is always so sad to take one's leave of him.

4/vi, Hôtel Majestic
Paris
Tape
Tchaikovsky
The Sleeping Beauty
Conductor: Gergiev

I had to listen to a tape to decide which section would be played in Tours. We searched and settled on one of my favourite passages from this ballet, the Pas de Six from the Prologue.

I most emphatically do not like this conductor, whom everyone praises to the skies and whose reputation is literally second to none in the world of Russian music.

Under his direction the orchestra plays impeccably, but without the least expression. No emotion; no love for the work.

Appalling!

20/VI, Tours
Grange de Meslay
Mauricio Kagel
1) Die Windrose
2) . . . den 24.XII.1931
Ensemble Schoenberg
Conducted by
the composer

Yes, here's a composer over whom you can really get excited!

His music leaves a powerful impression; it's both new and perfectly accessible. It's adventure music. As for the performance, the composer and the magnificent Ensemble Schoenberg left nothing to be desired. *Die Windrose* is a piece that you could call poetic. It immediately touched us, while the second work on the programme, with a fearfully difficult part that's sung and declaimed by a superb artist, is a sort of historical survey of all that is most extreme about our age.

At the end, the pealing of Christmas bells attests to the work's extraordinary originality. Great musical events still exist.

25/VI
Grange de Meslay
La nuit des fous
Micrologus (Italy)
(Everything is played
on authentically old
instruments or sung a
cappella; *to begin with,*
it's monks, then carnival
masks. The Prior reads
a text in splendid
French. Large altar
candles light the stage
and create the illusion
that we're in the 13th
or 14th century.)

A very special evening. Darkness in the Grange; candles are lit one by one. Here we are transported back into a distant past, a real Middle Ages, to the sound of archaic *a cappella* chanting and period instruments. To begin with, everything is very austere, but later comes the effervescent exhilaration of the carnival. All the actors wear masks (mostly animal faces) and dance in an unbridled way, while squealing like savages and forming colourful processions that wind their way through the Grange, making the audience feel that they are joining in the general enjoyment and playing their part in a spectacle reminiscent of canvases by Brueghel.

An unforgettable evening. A staging that shows what the Italians are capable of. I've never seen or heard anything like it.

27/VI
Grange de Meslay

I think the French adore Satie. I don't know if it's because of the music or because of its allusive contents, contents that escape me completely. The

**Anne Queffélec
plays Satie
*(Scarlatti as an encore)***

performance by this young and brilliant pianist suffered a great deal from the interminable commentaries that are meant to accompany these pieces but which lasted longer than the music. Having listened carefully to it all, I've decided that this will last me for the whole of the rest of my life (Shakespeare, first act of *King Lear* and *Much Ado about Nothing*).

And suddenly at the end, by way of an encore, a sonata by Scarlatti, inspired!

Let's forget Satie . . .

**16 and 17 July
Moscow
Rehearsals at home
Grieg
2nd Violin Sonata
Piano Sonata in E minor
Vadim Repin, violin
Sasha Valentinov, piano
*(or Melnikov)****

First rehearsal. Repin and Sasha came to play me this sonata and are happy to do so. Sasha isn't satisfied with his accompanying role and sometimes has a tendency to push himself forward. But, even so, everything is very spirited and in excellent taste. By contrast, I don't like the E minor Sonata at all; Sasha's performance is pretentious, mannered and lacking in rhythmic muscle. I immediately detected the influence of his teacher. I told the young pianist what I thought and, at the second rehearsal the next day, he miraculously played it exactly as it should be played, <u>simply magnificently</u> (thank God!).

I think he's a hugely talented artist. Their concert at Tarusa, I'm told, was a great success. Unfortunately, I wasn't able to go. I was completely worn out and had to stay in bed at my hotel, surrounded by a forest of birches.

**I/VIII
Wagner
Das Rheingold
Conductor:
Wilhelm Furtwängler†**

It's very difficult for me to write about this, as this constitutes one of the most striking impressions of my entire life as a musician and the culmination of my relationship with Wagner.

I've finally heard this work in the full force of its brilliant inspiration. Here I can put my finger on

---

* The pianist's name is indeed Melnikov, but for reasons that are unclear Richter could not bear this name (it means 'miller' in Russian) and often asked him to change it. The unfortunate Sasha was already internationally known as Melnikov and evidently unwilling to yield to Richter's demands (B.M.).

† The 1953 Rome recording.

the gulf that separates Wagner from all other great musicians, writers and so on.

Why? Because the interpretation is on a par with the work itself. Everything is subordinate to <u>Furt-wängler</u>, and Furtwängler is connected to Wagner by a direct link. I'm convinced that it's impossible to wish for anything better. This is true happiness! I can understand why Wagner is so inaccessible to the vast majority of listeners – they fail to lift themselves up to the same height. Unfortunately, they are too lazy, too mean-spirited, lacking in the necessary imagination. Between Wagner and them there lies a (gigantic) gulf.

Whenever I play these records at home, I've established a tradition of providing written explanations of everything that happens and pinning these to a desk that everyone can see. This stimulates the listener's imagination, allowing them to see the action unfold in their mind's eye according to an ideal image, rather than some contemporary production that is either absurd or arrogant or both. I know only too well what one normally sees at the opera; it's almost always disappointing, if not tragic, sometimes even a veritable betrayal of the work.

And so we began the *Ring* today. It's pure, it's alive, it's true.

3/VIII
Wagner
Die Walküre
Conductor:
Wilhelm Furtwängler

My first encounter with *Die Walküre* goes back many years. I was twelve, and it was at Lupyan-ovka, near Odessa. I was spending the summer at the home of some Germans; the master of the house was an old man, a former sailor, whom I didn't like at all.

His wife, Frau Lupyan, was an extraordinarily jolly woman. The neighbouring house was occupied by the Sirenko sisters, Russians, but the Lupyans' home was always full of Germans. It was here that I played the vocal score of *Die Walküre*, much to the annoyance of the master of the house, who understood nothing about this music. He said that Wagner was 'Ein technisches Geklimpel' [technical tinkling].

I remember another evening when (again to Herr Lupyan's great annoyance) I played for the Sirenko sisters, who were always eager to hear music. It was the terrifying passage in D minor that culminates in a thunderclap on the *fortissimo* pedal point. At that very moment, the door flew open and this repulsive old man came in, sat down at the piano and, to his own accompaniment, started to sing the most frightful sea shanties. He clearly hated his neighbours. At this time I was completely under Wagner's spell and spent whole days with him (not that this has changed since then).

My second encounter was a catastrophe. In 1939, the pact with Germany, signed by Molotov and Ribbentrop. The Bolshoy in Moscow. Nebolsin conducted; Eisenstein directed. This was the real cause of the war with Germany, Neuhaus said jokingly.

The third time was at Bayreuth, under the serious and faultless direction of Pierre Boulez, in a production by Chéreau (? –) and with Peter Hofmann as Siegmund ++. This time things were infinitely better.

This tragic opera is the one that audiences like most, whereas I myself think that the *Ring* gets better and better as it goes on. *Das Rheingold* +, *Die Walküre* ++, *Siegfried* +++, *Götterdämmerung* ++++. Unlike many people, I think Wagner's libretto is inspired, gripping and Shakespearian in its sweep.

Stravinsky wrote that no one understands it, not even Wagner himself.

– He simply never read it. –

4/VIII
Wagner
Siegfried
Conductor:
Wilhelm Furtwängler

Here again is this sombre prelude that I've known since my childhood, in fact since I was nine. A vocal score of the whole *Ring*, elegantly bound in black, had been sent to Papa from Vienna, it's *Siegfried* that he liked best – I tried to play it, but, not really knowing how to read music, I managed no more than the first few pages; I didn't understand the words either and was convinced that

'Mime' was a woman. *Siegfried* is so different from the two previous 'evenings'. Everything is much more detailed here, all these capricious changes of mood on the hero's part, angry one moment, lyrical the next, always spontaneous and childlike; same thing with Mime, whose music almost looks forward to that of the 20th century (Prokofiev, say).

The characters are drawn with such psychological clarity that you'd think it was chamber music or Lieder.

And what enchantment in all these inner transformations: Siegfried and the bear; Siegfried hating Mime; Siegfried forging the sword; Siegfried reclining in the shade of a forest of fir trees and talking with the Woodbird (Rita Streich++); Siegfried meeting his father (in reality his grandfather) and making fun of him; and finally Siegfried discovering Brünnhilde asleep and ending by recovering his sight.

I have to say that it's not easy to grasp all this by listening to a recording. You have to see Siegfried in the flesh; he's a close friend whom you love.

The opera culminates in a fugato in C major, a homage to Classicism.

To listen to this work in this tremendous interpretation has been a real treat for me. I know every note of the music, which rose up again within me, just as it did the first time.

What a conductor and, in all its variety, what an edifice!

But (and it's a big but), you should never watch people listening in these circumstances. You immediately notice that such and such a person (not all of them, of course) are not in a receptive frame of mind and that their attention keeps wandering through tiredness or lack of musicality and that their heads start to nod. The struggle to stay awake is etched into their features, they grimace terribly or simply fall quietly asleep.

Must make a note not to invite these people again. Never again!

5/VIII **Wagner** *Götterdämmerung* *Conductor:* *Wilhelm Furtwängler*	What can you say about this music? You can only throw yourself on your knees and offer up your thanks. For me personally, this is the supreme masterpiece.
12/VIII **Haydn** *The Seasons* *Conductor: Karl Böhm*	An inspired and consummate work teeming with ideas. What a constant stream of *trouvailles* there is in Haydn (the G, F, E flat and D of the beginning!!!) and what freshness! He really is our contemporary, and there were good reasons why Prokofiev liked him so much. He's a kind of musical horn of plenty. I associate him in my mind with the landscapes of Rubens. Everything is earthbound, but the earth is resplendent in its beauty . . . I listened to the work on my own, with the score. The last time I heard it in the concert hall was a long time ago, under Maazel. I was very impressed. I'm more familiar with *The Creation*, which I've played on the piano and which I listened to in the Markevich recording when we lived in Nezhdanovoy Ulitsa. I also heard a performance at Aldeburgh, under the magnificent direction of Britten, with Heather Harper as the soprano. I'm immensely fond of these two works, which are so beautiful and so easy to listen to. But I don't have to prove how much I love Joseph Haydn: seventeen of his sonatas feature in my repertory.
24/VIII Oslo Oslo Konserthus **Ravel** *Cinq mélodies populaires grecques* **Schoenberg** *Cabaret Songs* *Encores: Richard Strauss, Bizet and Negro spirituals*	Enormous hall and, of course, packed. We arrived for the second half of the concert. Entrance of the black queen in a stunning dress. The audience was spellbound. Her singing scales the highest peaks of vocal artistry: her *pianissimo* is as staggering as her *fortissimo*. She can do anything, and she does it all so well, including unnecessary gestures. She's beautiful, she's a symbol, she's a unique phenomenon. Ravel: magnificently sung, but it doesn't produce much of an impression on me; it's not one of his

Jessye Norman
Philip Moll, piano

best works, scarcely original and somewhat primitive.

Schoenberg: virtuoso performance, but there are lots of trivial things in these songs, which teeter on the brink of music-hall turns, there's a lack of originality in their complexity that makes them very unsympathetic to me.

As an encore, a song in E flat by Richard Strauss. Splendid. Then the Habanera from *Carmen*. This sends the audience into ecstasies. She sounds convincing, in spite of an impossibly slow tempo that's more suited to a funeral march.

Finally the spirituals. Yes, yes, but not for me. I don't like this kind of music.

You normally find this degree of enthusiasm only in stadiums. Something else that strikes me: everything is very American and designed to create an effect.

The following day Jessye Norman came to the concert that I was giving with Lisa Leonskaja. She came majestically down the narrow stairs that led to my dressing-room. After we'd complimented each other, I suggested that she should wear a tiara on stage; it would suit her. We laughed – she's very sympathetic.

21/IX
Vienna
Konzerthaus
Shostakovich
*Chamber Symphony
op. 34a
(Rudolf Barshai's
transcription of the
4th String Quartet)*
*Conductor:
Rudolf Barshai*

In the first half of this concert I played two concertos by Bach with Barshai. I'd not played with him for more than twenty years, since he fled the Soviet Union. Honesty, professionalism. Genuine Bach. Barshai is a true master . . .

The Shostakovich was hugely successful with the Viennese public. The work is splendid and bleak, with a barb of bitter humour at the end. It's not a work that fills you with feelings of joy. Excellent transcription by Barshai.

23/ix
En route from Jesolo
to Padua
Recordings

We drove into Jesolo for lunch. The town was deserted in November. There was a pale sun and the sea was very rough; the waves threatened to engulf us as we walked out towards them on a

Saint-Saëns
5th Concerto
S.R.
Conductor:
Christoph Eschenbach
*(Recording of a concert
at Schwetzingen)*
Gershwin
*3rd movement
from Concerto in F
(arranged for cabaret
orchestra)
Soloist: The composer*

wooden jetty. Milena was frightened. While we were eating, Raoul and I kept an eye on the car to prevent it from being stolen. We set off again after a solid lunch to the sound of Saint-Saëns's music, followed by Gershwin. I like the Saint-Saëns recording, apart from a slight mishap in the third movement.

Once again Eschenbach struck me as very convincing. I'd already played Saint-Saëns's 5th with Markevich's son in Vienna. We had three rehearsals and achieved a decent(?) result at the concert. But Eschenbach achieved better results at our very first rehearsal together. I enjoy performing with him.

Gershwin: difficult to say anything against this, as it's got the composer himself at the piano, but this arrangement (whose? I don't know) isn't one that I care for very much (or rather, I don't like it at all). Also, it's taken terribly quickly; I can't deny the virtuosity, but it's still a bit flashy. But after all – it's the composer.

We soon reached Padua, where Yuri Bashmet and Pavel Vernikov were waiting for us, and we made an immediate start on Bach's 3rd and 7th Concertos and Mozart's 25th, which we'll be performing together throughout Italy.

12/XI, Hotel Josefshof
Vienna
Recording
Krenek
Jonny spielt auf
Conductor:
Lothar Zagrosek

Uli Fischer's brother – Baby – a master pâtissier, gave me this recording as a present (it's part of a series called *Entartete Musik* – 'Degenerate Music') and, for good measure, he also made us some delicious pastries.

I'd not heard this work since I left Odessa, though I still remember every last detail of it. Listening to it today was far from being a disappointment.

Quite the opposite, I realized what a miracle this piece is and that Krenek was a remarkable composer. Shortly afterwards, I was delighted to discover that Eschenbach thinks so too.

What a pleasure to discover, after all these years, that my adolescent love of this work was justified; it was in 1930 or 1931 at the Odessa Opera. The conductor was Samuel Stolerman, the director

Greshnev (a daring production). The role of Max was taken by Chishko, that of Anita by Zhukov-skaya, Jonny by Illin, Daniello by Snibrovsky and Yvonne by Slivak.

You could see a glacier through your opera glass-es, then a train entered. It was all so new and so interesting for the time! But the important thing was the music, and <u>this hasn't aged at all</u> –

28/XI
Moscow
Richard Strauss
Aus Italien
Conductor:
Riccardo Muti

I've long been very fond of this work. My affec-tion for it goes back to Odessa, when I was given a pocket edition of the score (yellow in colour) that I often used to read through, but without understanding very much: my imagination was stimulated by the titles of the different episodes and so I invented make-believe stories to go with them. When I gave my first concerts with a young con-ductor who was then at the start of his career – Riccardo Muti – I advised him, with some force, to tackle this work (that virtually no one plays); he did so. One day, following a rehearsal, he even conducted it just for me. I recently bumped into him – much changed and no longer so young – in the foyer of the Hotel Imperial in Vienna; I was delighted to discover that he had just sent me his recording. It's this that I'm listening to today.

In my own view, the most beautiful movement is 'The Roman Countryside'; it conjures up the place to perfection. 'The Ruins' is a very lively episode with no hint of nostalgia. The writing and orches-tration in 'On the Beach at Sorrento', with the backlash of waves, is completely different from Debussy's approach and really rather saccharine. The fourth movement is a model of brilliant orchestration. Strauss certainly knows what he's doing – a delightful work.

7/XII
Tape
The Hungarian pianist
Balázs Szokolay

In Budapest there is always an endless stream of visitors coming to see me in my dressing-room. Pavel F. isn't sufficiently vigilant and can't get rid of them. Among them there's always a bland young man (a pianist and the son of a composer)

Scarlatti
Three sonatas
Haydn
Fantasia in C major

who, needless to say, gets on my nerves. He follows me everywhere, even to my hotel and the restaurant. Pavel F. has even said that he would happily have killed him.

He gave me a tape of his recordings and I've finally found time to listen to it. It's left me completely perplexed. I was simply bowled over by the accuracy and technical brio of his playing of the three Scarlatti sonatas, to say nothing of the beauty of the works themselves. The Haydn Fantasia was a complete surprise; I immediately decided to include it in my repertory.

Nina Dorliac, who had been listening from her flat,* came in and asked: 'What's that horror that you're listening to? Who's that frightful pianist with this dreadful tone?'

I don't know what to say.

19/XII
Recording
Krenek
Jonny spielt auf
Conductor:
Lothar Zagrosek

Initially this opera (operetta) was wildly successful throughout the entire world, but in 1932 it was banned by the authorities (on racial grounds, as it deals with the love of a black man for a white woman) and since then it has been completely forgotten. Today, more than fifty years later, attempts are being made to restore it to the repertory.

It was with great satisfaction and pleasure that I listened to it again. It's so interesting and so gripping . . .

I really must get to know other operas by this composer.

25/XII
Recordings
Bach
Sonata in C major
S.R. (Stradivarius)
Concerto in C major
for two pianos

Yesterday evening was Christmas. We'd planned to listen to some records, but with all the conversations going on around the candlelit tree, the spirit was no longer willing. So it was only today that we got round to doing so.

In spite of the uncertainties surrounding the quality of this Stradivarius recording, this very difficult Reincken-based sonata seems to have produced an

---

* Nina Dorliac and Sviatoslav Richter lived in a large flat in Moscow separated into adjoining apartments (B.M.).

S.R. and
Anatoly Vedernikov
Conductor:
Rudolf Barshai

excellent impression on all concerned. The concerto, which is the only recorded testimony to my musical activities with Anatoly Vedernikov, is undoubtedly a success (except perhaps that the orchestra sometimes sounds a bit crude). It's so homogeneous that it's practically impossible to tell who's playing the first piano and who's playing the second.

22/I
Tokyo
Following a
performance of *Fall
into the Abyss* at the
Noh Theatre,
Der Jasager,
an opera by Kurt Weill
to words by
Bertolt Brecht

The Noh Theatre is something quite special, it's strange and even alien to a European spectator, but utterly remarkable in its beauty and within its own conventions.
On this occasion, as on previous ones, I left the theatre deeply impressed by this very special rhythm and by the mixture of singing and speaking. The costumes reflect other criteria about beauty, and I find it difficult to speak of them.
In its way, it's unique.
But in the second half they gave this frightful opera by Weill that deserves only to be thrown in the dustbin. It's an insult to art. The Japanese made every effort, but it was a waste of time, the result was nothing but a mass of crude effects.

24/II
Okayama
Recordings
Bach
2nd English Suite
S.R.
*(Stradivarius recording
from Budapest, Philips
recording from
Rolandseck)*

Not bad at all, either in Budapest or in Rolandseck. At all events, that's the impression I get from listening to these recordings; what others may say, I don't know.
I remember a long time ago, following a concert in Budapest, Annie Fischer told me straight out that she hadn't liked it, and she was no doubt absolutely right at the time. It's so much better when people have the courage to tell you the truth, while looking you straight in the eye. I'm not always capable of that.
This Suite is extremely difficult, but something is finally beginning to emerge.

26/II
Kyoto Recording

Curiously, these two toccatas left a favourable impression on me. Probably because it's so long since I've played them that I'd forgotten them. As

Bach
*Toccatas in D minor
and G major*
S.R. *(Philips recording)*

a result, I seemed to be listening not to myself but to some other pianist. There you are!

1/III
Recording
Grieg
22 Lyric Pieces
S.R.

I've played these Lyric Pieces so often this year, and with so much pleasure, that it's difficult to listen to this recording; I simply don't feel like it. I did so, however, out of professional concern, but without pleasure and without sensing Grieg's freshness.

Everything is more or less in place, but it's not really interesting. I can imagine the number of disagreeable discussions that I'll again have to contend with in connection with this recording. A sad situation.

2/III
*Tape of a concert
in Kyoto*
Grieg
*Wedding Day at
Troldhaugen*
S.R.

I've got my doubts about this, as I keep catching on notes in this little piece (15 or 16 times). So I've decided to listen to the recording that was made during my last recital in Kyoto, which, as far as I remember, was relatively successful. I liked the recording and didn't detect a single wrong note. But who knows whether my ears are deceiving me? At my age, anything's possible.

3/v
Hamburg
State Opera
Prokofiev
Cinderella
*Ballet by John Neumeier
The order of the musical
numbers has been
turned on its head; the
choreographer–director
has treated the score just
as he likes. To give him
his due, I have to admit
that the character
dances are choreo-
graphed with talent.*

There are good reasons why this *Cinderella* is advertised as a ballet by Neumeier. It's all of a piece, apart from the music, which is obscenely misused.

Far from blushing, Herr Neumeier triumphs and invites us to applaud him on the ruins of Prokofiev's marvellous score.

When shall we see an end to this arbitrary approach to direction – which has now become common currency?

The music isn't the only thing that's sacrificed, so is the story. There's no longer any question here of Cinderella losing her slipper. No, she's content to sit on a tree. Moreover, according to the choreographer's programme notes, Cinderella 'is Cordelia, Hamlet and Anne Frank'!

What appals me is that not a single voice is raised in protest. Nowadays vast sums of money are squandered on rubbish like this, which is conscientiously played, danced and sung by magnificent artists; wonderful works of art are exposed to the vandalism of directors destitute of talent and of rights.

I think it's better if I stop going to the opera and theatre.

7/v
Berlin
Philharmonie
Schumann
2nd Symphony
Conductor: Kurt Masur

In the first half of this concert, I played Mozart's E flat Concerto K 271, not too badly, it seems. Masur conducted superbly. Schumann's symphony was played with real fervour and precision, and I know how difficult this is. I was deeply impressed by both the work and the performance: the composer's intentions were carried out to the letter.

September
In the train between
Kassel and Munich
*Recording of a concert
from Wildbad Kreuth*
Max Reger
*12 Variations and
Fugue on a Theme of
Beethoven for two
pianos op. 86*
*Andreas Lucewicz
and S.R.*

I've been planning to play these variations by Reger for a long time. With Gavrilov it came to nothing; likewise, for even more compelling reasons, with Alexander Slobodianik . . .

My decision to play with Andreas Lucewicz gave rise to protests on the part on Nina Dorliac and reservations on the part of Natasha Gutman. Our work together has shown me that I was right. And now we've finally played the piece at the festival organized by Oleg Kagan. For once, it was really a great success, and all the calumnies about Andreas's allegedly disagreeable and harsh tone have been swept aside.

Even so, it seems a bit premature to authorize the release of this recording, even though Nina is in favour. I'm certain that at other concerts we'll be able to do even better.

25/xi
Abano Terme
Hugo Wolf
Der Corregidor
Act 1

I didn't enjoy this. It struck me as second-rate music lacking in any interest. Whenever you try to apply Wagnerian principles to comic opera, there's always something that goes wrong. It's exactly the same problem with Cornelius's *Der Barbier von Bagdad*. Everything is much more interesting and

Conductor: *Gerd Albrecht* *Lukas:* *Dietrich Fischer-Dieskau*	alive in Humperdinck's fairy tale for children. I couldn't even bring myself to listen to the remaining acts, although here it is the recording itself that is to blame, coupled with my record player and my hearing.

Abano Terme *Recording from* *Philips collection* **Brahms** *Variations on a Theme* *by Paganini* S.R.	It would have been better if this recording had never seen the light of day . . . Philips's undertaking, consisting of releasing a number of my recordings (said to be authorized by me – with a reproduction of my signature on the front of the box), recordings that I've never listened to, is a more than dubious exercise – it's a disgrace. How did it happen? It's a mystery. To me . . . Be that as it may, the Brahms is an amateurish recording, not at all professional: in loud passages, the volume is turned down by the technicians and so on. Also, the performance itself is far from satisfactory; the second book is a bit better.

December Ascolo *Video* **Richard Strauss** *Der Rosenkavalier* *Gwyneth Jones,* *Brigitte Fassbaender,* *Lucia Popp,* *Manfred Jungwirth,* *Benno Kusche,* *Francisco Araiza* *Producer: Otto Schenk* *Conductor:* *Carlos Kleiber*	The <u>first time</u> I saw this opera on stage was in Vienna. I was in a box to the right of the stage or to the left, depending on where you're standing (I always get confused in this respect), looking right down on the orchestra. Hilde Zadek was the Marschallin, Irmgard Seefried Octavian. The <u>second time</u>, unforgettable, was at Salzburg, with Karajan (sketching in Strauss's rubatos). Among the cast were Elisabeth Schwarzkopf, Sena Jurinac, Anneliese Rothenberger. The <u>third</u>, in London, with Lisa Della Casa. Mediocre. The <u>fourth</u>, in Munich, with the same cast as in the present film and with Carlos Kleiber conducting. I found Gwyneth Jones very affecting both as a singer and as an actress; Fassbaender is very convincing (what a shame that she's now retired from the stage). I didn't like Lucia Popp. An excellent production, but Schenk, too, wants to retire and, as a result, the critics are complaining that he's old hat.

Kleiber conducts the show with the greatest of ease. He achieves exactly what he wants and with him everything comes off to perfection. It's amazing.

December
Milan
La Scala
Wagner
Die Walküre
Siegmund:
Plácido Domingo
Sieglinde:
Waltraud Meier, etc.
Conductor:
Riccardo Muti

The talented Riccardo Muti has taken the risk of staging *Die Walküre* at La Scala. It all went very well, and at the end of the second act I went to his dressing-room to congratulate him. There were so many people there, who'd all come to bow and scrape to him. An unnatural, official ambience, typically theatrical. But it's of no importance.
Total success. Musically and vocally, everything was on the right level, serious and honest. Domingo clearly isn't a Wagnerian hero, but he's a great artist; the others* had demonstrably worked hard, and it's difficult to pick holes.
Yet I felt almost completely remote from it all, especially from the production, which didn't really reflect the music, even though it was serious and thoughtful. It's not what Wagner wanted. It was interesting, but irrelevant.

April
(somewhere on the road)
Haydn
Sonata in F major no. 44
S.R.
(Recording of a concert at Wildbad Kreuth in 1994)

So many of my recordings have been released recently that it's impossible to keep track of them all . . .
I'm not at all pleased. Such a glut of recordings devalues them all. And now K. & M. have leapt on the bandwagon in turn and are trying to record me wherever possible. It may not even be bad, but what's the point of so many recordings?!!
And what about me? Where am I going to find time to listen to them all?

Pinneberg
Portrait of Maria Callas
A film by Tony Palmer
(Maria's last words, as
Jacques, Christian and
I were setting off down-

This documentary film on this great artist revolts me. It's more about Callas's life than her art. The result is something vain and prosaic. We meet her husband Meneghini, Onassis and even Winston Churchill. On the other hand, the accounts of Di Stefano (looking much older), Visconti and

---

* Brünnhilde was sung by Gabriele Schnaut, Wotan by Monte Pederson. The director and designer was André Engel.

stairs after the only visit that I paid her in her flat in Paris, were: 'Don't forget me and never break the thread that binds us together . . .') – Amen –

Zeffirelli are welcome, and interesting.

At the end, we see Vasso Devetzi getting out of an aeroplane holding an urn containing the singer's ashes. Difficult to imagine anything in worse taste. The succession of shots and the structure of the film are totally inconsequential; it's just a series of tasteless sequences in which the heroine is surrounded by journalists and photographers. Callas is filmed in a uniform manner, concentrating above all on her affectations, and always wearing the same unbecoming dress. The sequences in which she sings are few and far between and hacked up into little pieces. Only Tosca's prayer is given in its entirety.

The film has been made by people with no talent who are unworthy of their subject.

Somewhere
Recording of a concert at the Vienna Konzerthaus in 1993
Saint-Saëns
Concerto in G minor
S.R.
Conductor:
Oleg Caetani

This was the first time I'd played this concerto, a work which, in my own view, is extremely difficult and risky from a virtuosic standpoint and full of charm from a musical standpoint . . .

I'd been afraid of it, but, having listened to this recording, I found that it 'wasn't too bad for an old man' (to quote Vladimir Horowitz after he'd played Chopin's 1st Scherzo – badly) or for a first time.

Caetani clearly isn't a very interesting conductor, and rhythmically he's rather formal.

There are no plans to release this recording.

28/VI
Paris
Autumn Journey
Portrait of Dietrich Fischer-Dieskau
A film by Bruno Monsaingeon

Everyone who sees this film will fully understand just what this great artist has achieved in his life – something that's clearly quite phenomenal and almost beyond belief.

The director is Bruno Monsaingeon, who has done a tremendous amount of work of the most monstrous difficulty and managed to bring together archival footage from different periods to give an idea of the scope of Fischer-Dieskau's activities, mainly in the field of opera, but also as a Lieder singer.

We see excerpts from prodigious performances of

operas by Mozart (Don Giovanni), Verdi (Posa), Wagner (Wolfram and Hans Sachs) and Richard Strauss (*Arabella*). Fischer-Dieskau's utterly brilliant impersonation of Verdi's Falstaff occupies pride of place in the film. It would be difficult to list everything.

How many magnificent and superbly lit shots in which we see a close-up of the singer's inspired face in the very act of singing!

Let me say straight away that the film deals exhaustively with every possible topic: from the advice he gives Julia Varady while accompanying her in Amelia's aria at the piano to a scintillating production of *Le nozze di Figaro*; and from the final scene of *Don Giovanni* to the duet for Lear and Cordelia (Varady) in Reimann's opera.

Fischer-Dieskau speaks at length about his way of singing, his artistic training, the particular problems of singing Wagner, where you have to be perfectly integrated into the orchestral fabric, and especially Schubert and Bach, with numerous examples to support him.

We see a number of the conductors with whom he has appeared (Furtwängler, Solti and Böhm), pianists (Pollini, Brendel, Gerald Moore and Barenboim). He's also seen conducting – extremely convincingly – a rehearsal of a Schubert symphony, as well as painting and teaching.

It's all extremely valuable and fascinating and does full justice to his personality.

Personally, there's only one thing that I have a little difficulty in swallowing; it seems almost impossible to hear and see so much music at a single stretch. However willing I may be, I can't manage to take it all in. I think the fault is Bruno Monsaingeon's.

Bruno, keep a sense of proportion!

October
Paris
Rudolph Nureyev
Biographical film

I really liked the whole of the section devoted to his childhood in Bashkiria, his early career in Leningrad, with contributions from his teacher and from Dudinskaya (who has gone to seed and got a lot fatter since giving up dancing); his flight to the West and his successes; and also the episodes with Margot Fonteyn, who is charming. I'm not a great fan of Nureyev or of ballet in general, but I have to admit that in the second part of the film, after an awful *Dame aux camélias* to the music of Liszt's B minor Sonata, he proves to be a highly talented choreographer. His ballets have a musical authenticity that you encounter very rarely. I really loved the Adagio from *The Nutcracker*, *Apollon musagète* and Schoenberg's *Pierrot lunaire*. All in all, an interesting biography.

Tape of a concert in Tokyo
Mozart
Concerto in B flat K 456
S.R.
Conductor:
Rudolf Barshai

This is good, especially the second and third movements. It can be released, and I'll send Rudolf Barshai a postcard to this effect. It has always been possible to make music seriously with him. But unfortunately it isn't easy to find dates that suit us both.

2/XI
David Oistrakh: Artist of the People?
A film by Bruno Monsaingeon

I liked this film by Monsaingeon even more than his film about Fischer-Dieskau. It's not overloaded and you sense the director's immense tenderness towards his subject.

From the very outset you're struck by the violin's golden tone in the hands of this great artist. Even in your dreams you couldn't imagine a more beautiful sound, there's nothing like it in the world. You hear lots of music in this film: excerpts from the Tchaikovsky Concerto, ideally interpreted (each note, even in the fastest passages, is perfectly articulated and audible, everything is utterly honest, he never has to bluff his way through); the insanely difficult cadenza in Shostakovich's 2nd Concerto; and some short violin pieces. All in all, a great variety of music. However everything is impeccably organized, with Oistrakh himself providing the sense of unity.

We see a very young Oistrakh studying with Stolyarsky in Odessa (the Opera and the harbour), before and after the Brussels Competition; we also see his wife, Tamara Rotariova (who, be it added in passing, studied the piano with my father), and his son Igor, who has changed a lot with age and who speaks about his father.

Gidon Kremer, Oistakh's pupil, takes more of the credit for himself; I didn't particularly like what he says.

Gennady Rozhdestvensky's contribution is very carefully weighed and goes into great detail. A pity that he has a face that's so disagreeable to look at . . .

But the person who speaks in the most scintillating way is Yehudi Menuhin, who's so sincere and warm in expressing his friendship for this great musician.

Rostropovich, too, offers his mite to the film, speaking and playing with his usual exuberance.

Also included in the film is a photograph of the first performance of Shostakovich's Violin Sonata, in which you can see the composer, Oistrakh and me. I remember that when we'd finished playing we dragged Dmitry Dmitriyevich out on to the stage to take a bow and that he kept whispering: 'I don't want to cause a scene. I don't want to cause a scene.' He was afraid of falling.

All the documents are grouped together to produce a magnificent and rigorous composition not lacking in imagination – it must have been a real headache to trace them and put them in some kind of order, given their rarity. But the essential point is the miracle of David Oistrakh and his music. He'll always remain the foremost violinist in the world. Incomparable. How happy I am to have been able to make music with him!

P.S. There are, of course, allusions in the film to the difficulties faced by artists under the Soviet regime, to the dangers that they ran and to the constraints to which they were subjected (Party membership etc.). The truth is the truth, but ultimately it's of secondary importance, I think, when you find yourself face to face with such a giant of music. Let's be grateful to the director who made this splendid film.

11/XI
*Recording of a concert
in 1978 in the Grand
Hall of the Moscow
Conservatory*
Hindemith
*The four violin sonatas
Oleg Kagan and S.R.*

A surprise, this tape, and a delight!
From the very first notes, I'm hooked by this music, which I'd completely forgotten. And what freshness and virtuosity in the performance! What a magnificent violinist Oleg was! I think I can allow this recording to be released . . .
It was only the fourth time we'd played these works. We never played them again. Why? Simply because there were other concerts and other programmes; then Oleg left us.

Appendices

Appendices

A Don Juan of Music, or Richter in Figures

Beginning in 1940, Richter kept a detailed record of the programme, place and circumstances of each of his public appearances. These manuscript notes end in 1995 and are contained in eighteen substantial exercise books, which he entrusted to me and which have enabled me to draw up the following tables, a task in which I have been helped by Antoine and Alexis Joly and Thérèse Salviat. They have been devised in such a way as to give an idea of the scope of Richter's repertory and the number of concerts that he gave throughout the world. In the course of a career lasting fifty-five years he gave more than 27,000 performances at around 3,600 concerts in a thousand different places. There were years during which Richter gave over one hundred concerts a year, performing over two hundred different works, some twenty of which were new to his repertory. Many pianists would be content with these figures spread over a whole lifetime, but as Richter himself said, he had an insatiable appetite. In attempting to establish his repertory as precisely as possible, I arrived at a figure of 833 works (a work being anything from a Prelude and Fugue by Bach or a Chopin waltz to a Mozart concerto and Beethoven's 'Diabelli' Variations). Each of these works was performed at least once in his career and, except towards the end of his life, was played from memory. The total does not include around six hundred songs, but, even so, it far exceeds the famous 'mille e tre' mentioned by Leporello in the context of his master's conquests.

Between 1930 and 1937 Richter kept no immediate record of his already active performance schedule, which was still essentially domestic in character. He later attempted an approximate reconstruction of these events, a reconstruction that fills several pages of his notebooks and that is reproduced below.

Repertoire

Bach: Prelude and Fugue in E flat minor (*The Well-Tempered Clavier*, Part 1).
Mozart: Sonata in E flat major K 282.
Beethoven: Sonata in C minor op. 13 ('Pathétique').
Schumann: Concerto in A minor (accompanied by 2nd piano).
Paganini–Schumann: Caprice no. 5 in B minor.
Liszt: Sonata in B minor.
Wagner–Liszt: 'Death of Isolde'.
Grieg: Sonata in E minor. 4 Lyric Pieces.
Mozart–Grieg: Sonata in F major for two pianos K 533.
Chopin: Polonaise in C sharp minor op. 26; Polonaise in A major op. 40; Polonaise-fantaisie op. 61; Nocturne in B flat minor op. 9; Nocturne in G minor op. 15; Nocturne in G major op. 37; Nocturne in E flat major op. 55; Studies op. 10 nos. 1, 3, 4, 6, 10; Study op. 25 no. 5; Preludes op. 28 in A minor, D major, F sharp minor, C sharp minor, B major, F sharp major, D flat major, A flat major, E flat major and B flat major; Prelude in C sharp minor op. post.; Barcarolle op. 60; Scherzo in C sharp minor op. 39; Scherzo in E major op. 54; Ballade in F minor op. 52; Variations brillantes in B flat major op. 12; Waltz in A flat op. 34; Waltz in D flat op. 70; Mazurkas op. 24 no. 3, op. 17, op. 30, in F major and in F minor op. 68.
Debussy: Suite bergamasque; Preludes: 'Cloches à travers les feuilles', 'Le vent dans la plaine', 'Les sons et les parfums', 'Les collines d'Anacapri', 'La cathédrale engloutie'.
Ravel: 'La vallée des cloches'.
Albéniz: 'Navarra'.
Glazunov: Suite on the Name 'Sasha'; Nocturne in D flat op. 37.
Lyadov: Study in A minor and Canzonetta op. 48.
Rachmaninov: Barcarolle op. 10; Romance in F minor op. 10; Preludes in B flat major and G minor op. 23.
Scriabin: Preludes in A minor, E major, C sharp minor and B major op. 11.
Richter: Own works.

Accompaniment of songs by Tchaikovsky, Rimsky-Korsakov and Richard Strauss. Small family concerts, at home or for friends, in Odessa and Zhitomir.

Between 1932 and 1937, accompanying singers in excerpts from operas, in clubs, retirement homes and factories in Odessa and the surrounding area; and a handful of solo appearances in the following repertory: Chopin's Polonaise in A major; 'Death of Isolde' by Wagner–Liszt; 'Ride of the Valkyries' by Wagner; Coronation Scene from Mussorgsky's *Boris Godunov*; Polovtsian Dances from Borodin's *Prince Igor*; Adagio in E flat from Tchaikovsky's *The Sleeping Beauty*; various numbers from Glazunov's ballet *Raymonda*.

In 1932 or 1934 [*recte* 1934], on the occasion of the death of Hindenburg, concert at the German Consulate: Funeral March from Beethoven's Sonata op. 26 and 'Funeral March on the Death of Siegfried' from Wagner's *Götterdämmerung*.
In the course of the three seasons 1934–7, piano solo in Act III of Glazunov's ballet *Raymonda*.
During these same three years, concerts on collective farms and in barracks at Abomelikovo, Vygod, Novoekaterinovka, Voznesensk, Ochakov, Tiraspol and Znamenka.

MY FIRST REAL PUBLIC RECITAL: ODESSA, CENTRAL ENGINEERS' CLUB, 19 MARCH 1934
<u>Chopin programme</u>
Part 1: Prelude in C sharp minor op. post., Preludes in D major, F sharp major, E flat major, B major and F sharp minor op. 28. Nocturne in G minor op. 15. Polonaise-fantaisie op. 61.
Part 2: Scherzo in E major op. 54. Nocturne in E flat major op. 55. Mazurka in C major op. 24. Studies in C major op. 10 no. 1 and in A flat op. 10 no. 10. Ballade in F minor op. 52.
Encore: Study in C sharp minor op. 10 no. 4.

So isolated was this début recital both geographically and chronologically that I have not included it in my general account of Richter's concerts or in the tables below. The same is true of the tour that he undertook to the front line in 1943, when he performed in the trenches and in military hospitals in Arkhangelsk, Molotovsk and Murmansk but did not note down the exact date or the details of the programme. For the rest, I have tried to deal with the mass of material placed at my disposal in the most exhaustive, precise and informative manner possible.

Clearly, it is entertaining to note that the four composers who figured most frequently in Richter's programmes were Shostakovich (4,641 times), Rachmaninov (2,683), Debussy (2,444) and Beethoven (2,327), with Prokofiev (1,797) and Schumann (1,734) narrowly beating Bach (1,664) and

Brahms (1,375) into seventh and eighth place. No less entertaining is it to note that the single most performed piece, whether as part of the programme proper or as an encore, was Rachmaninov's Prelude in G sharp minor op. 32 no. 12 (319 performances); and that the total number of Richter's concerts in Moscow (851) was fourteen times greater than the number for Paris (60), the western capital in which he performed most often (two or three times more often than in London or New York). These are no more than a few brief and particularly striking observations intended to suggest ways in which the reader may decode the information contained in the following tables. I leave it to readers to draw whatever conclusions they like and, refraining from adding any comments of my own, leave them to form their own opinions.

Also included is a brief chronology that draws attention to some of the non-musical events that marked Richter's career. Between his first and last recitals, he gave 3,590 concerts, making it one of the most packed, diverse and significant careers in the whole history of musical interpretation.

	30s	40s	50s	60s	70s	80s	90s	total	details of premières
Alyabyev									
Song	o	o	2	o				2	1956
Bach									
Songs and cantata arias	o	1	2	o				3	1945
4 Duetti BWV 802–5					o	o	21	21	1991, 8/v Moscow
English Suite no. 1 BWV 806	o	o	2	o	o	o	28	30	1951
English Suite no. 3 BWV 808	o	5	o	o	o	o	29	34	1948
English Suite no. 4 BWV 809					o	o	27	27	1991, 1/I Pisa
English Suite no. 6 BWV 811					o	o	27	27	1991
French Suite no. 2 BWV 813	o	o	3	14	o	o	21	38	1953, 6/XII Moscow
French Suite no. 4 BWV 815					o	o	25	25	1990, 14/II Murcia
French Suite no. 6 BWV 817	o	o	2	o	o	o	23	25	1951
French Overture BWV 831					o	o	17	17	1991, 23/I Serenno
Minuet in G major BWV 843					o	o	6	6	1991, 1/I Pisa
The Well-Tempered Clavier I:									
Prelude and Fugue no. 1 BWV 846	1	16	14	25				56	1937
Prelude and Fugue no. 2 BWV 847	o	16	13	23				52	1943
Prelude and Fugue no. 3 BWV 848	o	11	13	21				45	1945
Prelude and Fugue no. 4 BWV 849	o	16	13	21				50	1943
Prelude and Fugue no. 5 BWV 850	o	10	13	21				44	1946
Prelude and Fugue no. 6 BWV 851	o	9	13	21				43	1945
Prelude and Fugue no. 7 BWV 852	2	9	12	20				43	1937
Prelude and Fugue no. 8 BWV 853	o	11	13	21				45	1946
Prelude and Fugue no. 9 BWV 854	o	9	2	8				19	1946
Prelude and Fugue no. 10 BWV 855	o	7	4	9				20	1946
Prelude and Fugue no. 11 BWV 856	o	13	4	8				25	1943
Prelude and Fugue no. 12 BWV 857	o	15	2	9	1	o	o	27	1943
Prelude and Fugue no. 13 BWV 858	o	8	1	14	1	o	o	24	1946
Prelude and Fugue no. 14 BWV 859	o	7	1	14				22	1946
Prelude and Fugue no. 15 BWV 860	o	7	1	13				21	1945
Prelude and Fugue no. 16 BWV 861	o	7	1	13	1	o	o	22	1945
Prelude and Fugue no. 17 BWV 862	o	6	4	16				26	1946
Prelude and Fugue no. 18 BWV 863	o	5	4	16				25	1946
Prelude and Fugue no. 19 BWV 864	o	11	4	17				32	1943
Prelude and Fugue no. 20 BWV 865	o	11	4	19				34	1943
Prelude and Fugue no. 21 BWV 866	o	5	4	12				21	1946
Prelude and Fugue no. 22 BWV 867	o	7	4	11	1	o	o	23	1946
Prelude and Fugue no. 23 BWV 868	o	13	5	9				27	1946
Prelude and Fugue no. 24 BWV 869	o	14	5	10				29	1945
The Well-Tempered Clavier II:									
Prelude and Fugue no. 1 BWV 870	o	2	o	o	9	o	o	11	1944
Prelude and Fugue no. 2 BWV 871	o	2	o	o	10	o	o	12	1944
Prelude and Fugue no. 3 BWV 872	o	1	o	o	9	o	o	10	1944
Prelude and Fugue no. 4 BWV 873	o	1	o	o	9	o	o	10	1944
Prelude and Fugue no. 5 BWV 874	o	3	o	o	9	o	o	12	1944
Prelude and Fugue no. 6 BWV 875	o	3	o	o	9	o	o	12	1944
Prelude and Fugue no. 7 BWV 876	o	1	o	o	9	o	o	10	1944
Prelude and Fugue no. 8 BWV 877	1	1	o	o	9	o	o	11	1938

	30s	40s	50s	60s	70s	80s	90s	total	details of premières
Prelude and Fugue no. 9 BWV 878	o	2	o	o	13	o	o	15	1944
Prelude and Fugue no. 10 BWV 879	o	2	o	o	12	o	o	14	1944
Prelude and Fugue no. 11 BWV 880	o	1	o	o	12	o	o	13	1944
Prelude and Fugue no. 12 BWV 881	o	1	o	o	12	o	o	13	1944
Prelude and Fugue no. 13 BWV 882	o	3	o	o	12	o	o	15	1944
Prelude and Fugue no. 14 BWV 883	o	3	o	o	13	o	o	16	1944
Prelude and Fugue no. 15 BWV 884	o	1	o	o	12	o	o	13	1944
Prelude and Fugue no. 16 BWV 885	o	1	o	o	12	o	o	13	1944
Prelude and Fugue no. 17 BWV 886	o	2	o	o	9	o	o	11	1944
Prelude and Fugue no. 18 BWV 887	o	2	o	o	9	o	o	11	1944
Prelude and Fugue no. 19 BWV 888	o	1	o	o	9	o	o	10	1944
Prelude and Fugue no. 20 BWV 889	o	1	o	o	9	o	o	10	1944
Prelude and Fugue no. 21 BWV 890	o	1	o	o	9	o	o	10	1944
Prelude and Fugue no. 22 BWV 891	o	3	o	o	9	o	o	12	1944
Prelude and Fugue no. 23 BWV 892	o	3	o	o	9	o	o	12	1944
Prelude and Fugue no. 24 BWV 893	o	1	o	o	9	o	o	10	1944
Fantasia and Fugue in A minor BWV 904	o	3	o	o	o	o	3	6	1948
Fantasia in C minor BWV 906	o	2	o	o	o	o	33	35	1948
Toccata in D major BWV 912					o	o	12	12	1992
Toccata in D minor BWV 913					o	o	11	11	1991, 30/x Bremen
Toccata in G major BWV 916					o	o	33	33	1991, 30/x Bremen
Toccata in G minor BWV 917					o	o	19	19	1992, 17/III San Sebastián
Prelude (Fantasia) in C minor BWV 921	o	1	o	o	o	o	11	12	1949
Fantasia and Fugue in A minor BWV 944					o	o	3	3	1992, 19/VII Pinneberg
Sonata in D major BWV 963	o	2	o	o	o	o	38	40	1948
Sonata in D minor BWV 964	o	o	4	o	o	o	9	13	1951
Sonata in C major BWV 966					o	o	17	17	1991, 8/v Moscow
Adagio in G major BWV 968					o	o	10	10	1993
Italian Concerto BWV 971	o	3	o	o	o	o	17	20	1948
Capriccio sopra la lontananza del fratello dilettissimo BWV 992	o	4	o	o	o	o	1	5	1948
Capriccio in E major BWV 993					o	o	13	13	1991, 8/v Moscow
Prelude, Fugue and Allegro BWV 998					o	o	11	11	1993
Violin Sonata no. 2 in A major BWV 1015	o	o	1	o				1	1952
Violin Sonata no. 3 in E major BWV 1016	o	o	1	o				1	1952
Violin Sonata no. 4 in C minor BWV 1017	o	o	1	o				1	1952
Violin Sonata in G major BWV 1021	o	o	1	o				1	1952
Gamba Sonata in G major BWV 1027	o	o	1	o				1	1955, 27/III Moscow
Gamba Sonata in D major BWV 1028	o	o	2	o				2	1952
Gamba Sonata in G minor BWV 1029	o	o	2	o				2	1952
Flute Sonata in E minor BWV 1034	o	o	1	o				1	1953, 6/XII Moscow
Brandenburg Concerto no. 5 BWV 1050					10	o	o	10	1978, 21/III Dubna

	30s	40s	50s	60s	70s	80s	90s	total	details of premières
Concerto in D minor BWV 1052	o	1	14	o	8	o	o	23	1941
Concerto in E major BWV 1053	o	o	o	3				3	1969, 20/v Moscow
Concerto in D major BWV 1054					o	o	10	10	1991, 18/v Moscow
Concerto in A major BWV 1055	o	o	o	3				3	1969, 29/vi Parçay-Meslay
Concerto in F minor BWV 1056	o	o	o	5				5	1964, 28/vi Parçay-Meslay
Concerto in F major BWV 1057					10	o	o	10	1978, 21/iii Dubna
Concerto in G minor BWV 1058					o	o	10	10	1991, 18/v Moscow
Concerto in C minor for 2 keyboards BWV 1060					o	o	1	1	1993, 23/xi London
Concerto in C major for 2 keyboards BWV 1061	2	1	2	o				5	1938
Concerto in A minor for 4 keyboards BWV 1065	o	1	o	o				1	1941
Balakirev									
Songs	o	1	3	o				4	1949
Bartók									
Concerto no. 2	o	o	4	3				7	1958, 6/x Budapest
Sonata for two pianos and percussion	o	o	1	o	o	2	o	3	1956, 2/x Moscow
Violin Sonata no. 1					3	o	o	3	1972, 29/iii Moscow
Burlesque no. 1 op. 8c/1					o	15	o	15	1988, 23/x Kyoto
Burlesque no. 2 op. 8c/2					o	15	o	15	1988
Burlesque no. 3 op. 8c/3					o	15	o	15	1988
15 Hungarian Peasant Songs	o	o	5	o	19	o	o	24	1956, 6/x Moscow
Beethoven									
Choral Fantasia op. 80	o	1	3	o				4	1949
Piano Concerto no. 1 in C major op. 15	o	4	11	10	o	3	1	29	1944
Piano Concerto no. 3 in C minor op. 37	o	2	13	6	10	o	o	31	1949
Rondo in B♭ major WoO 6	o	o	o	2	1	o	o	3	1962, 8/v Moscow
Triple Concerto op. 56					3	o	o	3	1970
Cello Sonata no. 1 op. 5/1	o	o	3	1				4	1951
Cello Sonata no. 2 op. 5/2	o	o	5	1				6	1951
Cello Sonata no. 3 op. 69	o	o	5	2				7	1950
Cello Sonata no. 4 op. 102/1	o	o	4	1				5	1950
Cello Sonata no. 5 op. 102/2	o	o	4	1				5	1952
Piano Trio ('Archduke') op. 97					o	2	2	4	1984, 23/vi Tours
Quintet for piano and wind op. 16					o	2	5	7	1984, 30/vi Tours
Variations on 'Bei Männern' WoO 46	o	o	2	o				2	1951
Violin Sonata no. 1 op. 12/1	o	1	o	o	4	o	o	5	1970, 6/v Moscow
Violin Sonata no. 2 op. 12/2	o	o	o	o	10	o	o	10	1975, 14/x Moscow
Violin Sonata no. 3 op. 12/3					2	o	o	2	1970, 6/v Moscow
Violin Sonata no. 4 op. 23					13	o	o	13	1975, 14/x Moscow
Violin Sonata no. 5 ('Spring') op. 24					15	o	o	15	1974, 5/vii Parçay-Meslay

	30s	40s	50s	60s	70s	80s	90s	total	details of premières
Violin Sonata no. 6 op. 30/1	o	o	o	4	2	o	o	6	1969, 3/V Moscow
Violin Sonata no. 10 op. 96					3	o	o	3	1970
Andante in F major WoO 57					25	o	o	25	1977, 3/III Paris
Bagatelle op. 33/3	o	1	16	o				17	1948
Bagatelle op. 33/5	o	1	15	o				16	1948
Bagatelle op. 119/2	o	1	16	2				19	1948
Bagatelle op. 119/7	o	1	15	2				18	1948
Bagatelle op. 119/9	o	1	16	2				19	1948
Bagatelle op. 126/1	o	1	14	2	84	o	o	101	1948
Bagatelle op. 126/4	o	1	5	o	48	o	o	54	1948
Bagatelle op. 126/6	o	1	16	o	54	o	o	71	1948
'Diabelli' Variations op. 120	o	o	3	o	12	17	o	32	1951
'Eroica' Variations op. 35	o	3	3	27	18	o	o	51	1949
Rondo op. 51/1	o	o	6	o	o	34	o	40	1951
Rondo op. 51/2	o	o	6	o	o	34	1	41	1951
Sonata no. 1 in F minor op. 2/1					57	o	o	57	1975, 10/VII Gourdon
Sonata no. 3 in C major op. 2/3	o	5	o	31	78	o	o	114	1947
Sonata no. 4 in E♭ major op. 7					37	o	o	37	1974
Sonata no. 6 in F major op. 10/2		1			o	43	o	44	1944
Sonata no. 7 in D major op. 10/3	o	6	18	38	20	34	o	116	1949
Sonata no. 8 ('Pathétique') in C minor op. 13	o	19	22	o	o	1	18	60	1942
Sonata no. 9 in E major op. 14/1	o	4	1	32	18	o	7	62	1944
Sonata no. 10 in G major op. 14/2	o	5	o	26	o	o	7	38	1947
Sonata no. 11 in B♭ major op. 22	2	11	3	26	14	o	11	67	1937
Sonata no. 12 in A♭ major op. 26	o	14	11	42	40	o	16	123	1947
Sonata no. 17 ('Tempest') in D minor op. 31/2	o	18	11	51	o	33	12	125	1941
Sonata no. 18 in E♭ major op. 31/3	o	1	9	58	o	25	16	109	1941
Sonata no. 19 in G minor op. 49/1	o	o	2	7	o	o	9	18	1952
Sonata no. 20 in G major op. 49/2	o	o	2	6	o	o	9	17	1952
Sonata no. 22 in F major op. 54	o	4	5	32	o	o	22	63	1944
Sonata no. 23 ('Appassionata') in F minor op. 57	o	19	17	32	o	o	6	74	1943
Sonata no. 27 in E minor op. 90	o	4	1	30	24	o	o	59	1944
Sonata no. 28 in A major op. 101	1	5	1	32	24	39	o	102	1937
Sonata no. 29 ('Hammerklavier') in B♭ major op. 106					22	o	o	22	1974, 13/IV Moscow
Sonata no. 30 in E major op. 109	o	o	1	24	22	o	20	67	1952
Sonata no. 31 in A♭ major op. 110	4	1	11	40	23	o	38	117	1937
Sonata no. 32 in C minor op. 111	o	o	7	21	52	o	15	95	1952
6 Variations op. 34	o	o	10	o	20	o	o	30	1950
6 Variations op. 76	o	o	8	o	20	o	o	28	1950
6 Lieder	o	5	13	o				18	1947
Berg									
Chamber Concerto					29	7	o	36	1972, 9/IV Moscow

	30s	40s	50s	60s	70s	80s	90s	total	details of premières
Bizet									
6 Songs	o	2	7	o				9	1947
Borodin									
In the Monastery	o	o	1	o	1	o	o	2	1952
Mazurka in C major	o	o	1	o				1	1952
Serenade	o	o	1	o				1	1952
Brahms									
Concerto no.2 in B♭ major op. 83	1	1	18	20	1	o	o	41	1939
Piano Quartet no. 2 in A major op. 26	o	o	2	o	o	7	o	9	1952
Piano Quartet no. 3 in C minor op. 60	o	o	2	o				2	1951
Piano Quintet in F minor op. 34	o	1	4	o				5	1941
Cello Sonata no. 1 in E minor op. 38	o	o	6	2				8	1950
Cello Sonata no. 2 in F major op. 99	o	o	5	1				6	1952
Clarinet Sonata no. 1 in F minor op. 120/1					6	o	o	6	1977, 18/II Moscow
Scherzo in C minor for violin and piano WoO 2	o	o	o	6	1	o	o	7	1967, 2/VII Parçay-Meslay
Violin Sonata no. 1 in G major op. 78					o	12	o	12	1985, 12/II Berlin
Violin Sonata no. 2 in A major op. 100					3	o	o	3	1972, 29/III Moscow
Violin Sonata no. 3 in D minor op. 108	o	o	o	10	4	o	o	14	1967, 2/VII Parçay-Meslay
Ballade in D minor op. 10/1	o	1	1	18	o	o	25	45	1946
Ballade in D major op. 10/2	o	1	1	39	o	o	26	67	1946
Capriccio in C major op. 76/8	o	o	o	32	o	o	22	54	1964, 14/IV Leningrad
Rhapsody in G minor op. 79/2	o	o	o	20	o	o	22	42	1964
Capriccio in G minor op. 116/3	o	o	o	23	25	o	22	70	1964, 14/IV Leningrad
Intermezzo in E minor op. 116/5	o	o	o	29	26	o	21	76	1964, 14/IV Leningrad
Intermezzo in E major op. 116/6	o	o	o	22	28	o	26	76	1964, 14/IV Leningrad
Capriccio in D minor op. 116/7	o	o	o	22	25	o	20	67	1964, 14/IV Leningrad
Intermezzo in B♭ minor op. 117/2	o	2	6	1	8	o	3	20	1947
Intermezzo in A minor op. 118/1	o	2	10	53	37	o	11	113	1941
Ballade in G minor op. 118/3	o	3	9	62	13	o	2	89	1941
Intermezzo in E♭ minor op. 118/6	o	2	3	46	o	o	3	54	1941
Intermezzo in B minor op. 119/1	o	6	6	40	o	o	4	56	1941
Intermezzo in E minor op. 119/2	o	4	5	41	1	o	1	52	1945
Intermezzo in C major op. 119/3	o	5	6	47	6	o	2	66	1941
Rhapsody in E♭ major op. 119/4	o	5	5	53	o	o	8	71	1941
Sonata no. 1 in C major op. 1					o	32	o	32	1986, 7/III Nitra
Sonata no. 2 in F♯ minor op. 2	o	o	3	o	o	50	o	53	1959, 8/I Moscow
Variations on an Original Theme op. 21/1					o	9	o	9	1988, 4/VI Rolandseck

	30s	40s	50s	60s	70s	80s	90s	total	details of premières
Variations on a Hungarian Song op. 21/2					o	40	o	40	1983, 27/xi Tula
Variations and Fugue on a Theme by Handel op. 24					o	31	o	31	1988, 23/vii Vinnitsa
Variations on a Theme by Paganini op. 35					o	56	o	56	1986, 7/iii Nitra
11 Lieder	o	4	13	o				17	1946
4 Serious Songs op. 121					o	1	o	1	1982, 4/vii Parçay-Meslay
Die schöne Magelone op. 33	o	o	o	2	1	o	o	3	1965, 20/vi Aldeburgh
Britten									
Concerto in D major op. 13	o	o	o	5	5	o	o	10	1967, 18/vi Snape
Cello Sonata op. 65	o	o	o	2	o	8	5	15	1961, 26/xii Moscow
Lachrymae op. 48 for viola and piano					o	14	o	14	1984, 6/xii Moscow
Introduction and Rondo alla burlesca (2 pianos)	o	o	o	1	o	9	o	10	1967, 20/vi Snape
Mazurka elegiaca (2 pianos)	o	o	o	1	o	9	o	10	1967, 20/vi Snape
Chausson									
2 Songs	o	o	1	o				1	1957, 23/iv Leningrad
Cherubini									
Arias	o	o	1	o				1	1954
Chopin									
Concerto no. 2 in F minor op. 21	o	o	o	5				5	1966, 25/xi Genoa
Cello Sonata in G minor op. 65	o	o	o	3	o	4	o	7	1961, 26/xii Moscow
Rondo in C major for two pianos op. 73	o	1	o	o				1	1942
Andante spianato and Polonaise op. 22	o	o	o	3				3	1961, 27/vi Sochi
Ballade no. 1 in G minor op. 23	o	o	o	39	3	27	11	80	1960, 31/i Yaroslav
Ballade no. 2 in F major op. 38	o	o	1	12	15	26	11	65	1950
Ballade no. 3 in A♭ major op. 47	o	29	19	27	34	22	13	144	1943
Ballade no. 4 in F minor op. 52	2	24	7	26	29	22	13	123	1937
Barcarolle in F♯ major op. 60	1	16	o	60	19	o	o	96	1939
Étude no. 1 in C major op. 10/1	2	29	50	85	o	54	4	224	1937
Étude no. 2 in A minor op. 10/2	o	o	7	8	o	55	4	74	1951
Étude no. 3 in E major op. 10/3	1	32	45	44	5	52	4	183	1939
Étude no. 4 in C♯ minor op. 10/4	o	1	28	36	36	69	4	174	1945
Étude no. 6 in E♭ minor op. 10/6	o	1	7	11	5	44	4	72	1943
Étude no. 10 in A♭ major op. 10/10	o	19	29	69	47	48	4	216	1943
Étude no. 11 in E♭ major op. 10/11	o	4	5	11	o	45	4	69	1943
Étude no. 12 in C minor op. 10/12	o	41	36	48	o	59	4	188	1942
Étude no. 17 in E minor op. 25/5	o	o	9	5	o	69	o	83	1950
Étude no. 18 in G♯ minor op. 25/6	o	o	8	6	o	56	o	70	1951
Étude no. 19 in C♯ minor op. 25/7	o	o	3	5	40	22	o	70	1951
Étude no. 20 in D♭ major op. 25/8	o	o	5	5	o	55	2	67	1951
Étude no. 23 in A minor op. 25/11	o	o	3	7	o	50	o	60	1951

	30s	40s	50s	60s	70s	80s	90s	total	details of premières
Étude no. 24 in C minor op. 25/12	o	14	10	7	o	32	1	64	1943
Étude no. 25 in F minor op. post. no. 1						o	o	9	9	1990
Étude no. 26 in A♭ major op. post. no. 2	o	1	o	o	o	6	9	16	1946
Étude no. 27 in D♭ major op. post. no. 3						o	7	9	16	1986
Impromptu no. 2 in F♯ major op. 36					o	o	7	7	1990, 31/I La Roque d'Anthéron
Impromptu no. 3 in G♭ major op. 51					o	o	7	7	1990, 31/I La Roque d'Anthéron
Introduction and Variations in B♭ major op. 12	o	13	o	16				29	1943
Mazurka no. 1 in F♯ minor op. 6/1	o	2	o	o				2	1949
Mazurka no. 4 in E♭ minor op. 6/4	o	3	o	o				3	1946
Mazurka no. 5 in B♭ major op. 7/1	o	9	o	o				9	1944
Mazurka no. 9 in C major op. 7/5	o	7	o	o				7	1945
Mazurka no. 13 in A minor op. 17/4	o	1	2	13				16	1945
Mazurka no. 14 in G minor op. 24/1	o	24	11	1				36	1943
Mazurka no. 15 in C major op. 24/2	o	21	3	28				52	1945
Mazurka no. 16 in A♭ major op. 24/3	o	26	5	2				33	1946
Mazurka no. 17 in B♭ minor op. 24/4	o	13	4	1				18	1946
Mazurka no. 20 in D♭ major op. 30/3	o	23	6	19				48	1943
Mazurka no. 23 in D major op. 33/2	o	2	o	o				2	1945
Mazurka no. 24 in C major op. 33/3	o	1	o	o				1	1946
Mazurka no. 34 in C major op. 56/2		1						1	1949
Mazurka no. 41 in C♯ minor op. 63/3	o	6	o	o	40	o	o	46	1949
Mazurka no. 44 in C major op. 67/3	o	3	o	o	40	o	o	43	1945
Mazurka no. 48 in F major op. 68/3	o	5	o	5	40	o	o	50	1943
Mazurka no. 49 in F minor op. 68/4	o	2	o	5				7	1943
Mazurka no. 58 in A minor op. post.					40	o	o	40	1976
Nocturne no. 1 in B♭ minor op. 9/1	o	10	5	17	10	o	o	42	1946
Nocturne no. 3 in B major op. 9/3					5	o	o	5	1975, 12/I Moscow
Nocturne no. 4 in F major op. 15/1	o	23	16	39	32	o	o	110	1943
Nocturne no. 5 in F♯ major op. 15/2	o	o	o	3	15	o	o	18	1969, 21/XI Lvov
Nocturne no. 6 in G minor op. 15/3	o	4	1	3	10	o	o	18	1949
Nocturne no. 12 in G major op. 37/2	o	6	1	o				7	1949
Nocturne no. 15 in F minor op. 55/1	o	12	1	o	12	o	o	25	1943
Nocturne no. 16 in E♭ major op. 55/2	o	6	o	o	12	o	o	18	1943
Nocturne no. 18 in E major op. 62/2	o	6	1	4	19	o	o	30	1942
Nocturne no. 19 in E minor op. 72/1	o	o	2	3	19	o	o	24	1950
Polonaise no. 1 in C♯ minor op. 26/1	o	10	3	14	o	1	35	63	1943
Polonaise no. 3 in A major op. 40/1	o	9	4	o	o	o	35	48	1943
Polonaise no. 4 in C minor op. 40/2	o	10	4	o	o	o	35	49	1943
Polonaise no. 7 in A♭ major ('Polonaise-fantaisie') op. 61	o	14	6	34	54	9	53	170	1943
Polonaise no. 8 in D minor op. 71/1	o	o	1	o				1	1950

	30s	40s	50s	60s	70s	80s	90s	total	details of premières
Prelude no. 2 in A minor op. 28/2	o	2	5	5	30	o	o	42	1944
Prelude no. 4 in E minor op. 28/4	o	o	o	3				3	1967
Prelude no. 5 in D major op. 28/5	o	5	5	6	34	o	o	50	1944
Prelude no. 6 in B minor op. 28/6	o	1	5	9	30	o	o	45	1944
Prelude no. 7 in A major op. 28/7	o	1	4	3	32	o	o	40	1944
Prelude no. 8 in F♯ minor op. 28/8	o	o	1	2	30	o	o	33	1950
Prelude no. 9 in E major op. 28/9	o	2	1	1	30	o	o	34	1945
Prelude no. 10 in C♯ minor op. 28/10	o	5	5	11	30	o	o	51	1944
Prelude no. 11 in B major op. 28/11	o	5	5	13	30	o	o	53	1944
Prelude no. 13 in F♯ major op. 28/13	o	5	5	13	30	o	o	53	1944
Prelude no. 15 in D♭ major op. 28/15	o	6	5	13	30	o	o	54	1944
Prelude no. 17 in A♭ major op. 28/17	o	7	5	13	30	o	1	56	1944
Prelude no. 19 in E♭ major op. 28/19	o	2	4	13	30	o	o	49	1944
Prelude no. 21 in B♭ major op. 28/21	o	1	1	15	34	o	o	51	1944
Prelude no. 23 in F major op. 28/23	o	1	1	14	30	o	o	46	1944
Prelude no. 24 in D minor op. 28/24	o	1	1	14	30	o	o	46	1944
Prelude no. 25 in C♯ minor op. 45	o	2	o	11				13	1946
Rondo 'à la Mazur' in F major op. 5	o	o	o	24				24	1967, 24/VIII Salzburg
Scherzo no. 1 in B minor op. 20	o	o	2	43	10	o	o	55	1950
Scherzo no. 2 in B♭ minor op. 31	o	28	25	57	30	o	o	140	1943
Scherzo no. 3 in C♯ minor op. 39	o	10	2	57	11	o	o	80	1944
Scherzo no. 4 in E major op. 54	1	19	17	60	52	o	o	149	1939
Waltz no. 2 in A♭ major op. 34/1	o	8	1	o	22	o	o	31	1942
Waltz no. 3 in A minor op. 34/2	o	7	1	o	22	o	o	30	1942
Waltz no. 4 in F major op. 34/3	o	4	1	o	62	o	o	67	1942
Waltz no. 10 in B minor op. 69/2	o	1	o	o	3	o	o	4	1942
Waltz no. 13 in D♭ major op. 70/3	o	10	o	o	40	o	o	50	1942
Waltz no. 14 in E minor op. post.	o	9	o	o				9	1949
5 Songs	o	4	3	o				7	1946
Copland									
Piano Quartet	o	o	o	2				2	1961, Leningrad
Dargomizhsky									
9 Songs	o	o	12	o				12	1950
Debussy									
Fantaisie for piano and orchestra					o	1	o	1	1983, 25/VI Tours
Cello Sonata	o	o	o	4	o	2	o	6	1961, 26/XII Moscow
En blanc et noir for two pianos	o	2	o	1	o	21	o	24	1940
Estampes: Pagodes	o	o	o	23	40	o	o	63	1962
Estampes: La soirée dans Grenade	o	o	o	24	40	o	o	64	1962
Estampes: Jardins sous la pluie	o	o	o	32	42	o	o	74	1962, 23/V Florence
Étude no. 1: Pour les cinq doigts					o	o	18	18	1990
Étude no. 2: Pour les tierces					o	o	18	18	1990
Étude no. 3: Pour les quartes					o	o	18	18	1990
Étude no. 4: Pour les sixtes					o	o	18	18	1990

	30s	40s	50s	60s	70s	80s	90s	total	details of premières
Étude no. 8: Pour les agréments					o	o	18	18	1990
Étude no. 10: Pour les sonorités opposées					o	o	18	18	1990
Étude no. 12: Pour les accords					o	o	18	18	1990
Hommage à Haydn	o	o	o	3	45	o	o	48	1967
Images: Reflets dans l'eau	o	10	o	6	45	21	o	82	1942
Images: Hommage à Rameau	o	5	o	4	25	2	o	36	1944
Images: Mouvement	o	3	o	5	39	20	o	67	1947
Images: Cloches à travers les feuilles	1	11	34	35	14	3	o	98	1938
L'isle joyeuse	o	13	4	25	40	12	32	126	1943
La plus que lente	o	1	o	o	24	o	1	26	1947
Préludes: Danseuses de Delphes	o	2	2	15	o	12	o	31	1947
Préludes: Voiles	o	2	7	25	o	32	o	66	1947
Préludes: Le vent dans la plaine	2	5	15	24	11	36	o	93	1938
Préludes: 'Les sons et les parfums'	2	1	13	11	3	26	3	59	1938
Préludes: Les collines d'Anacapri	2	8	36	32	o	36	o	114	1938
Préludes: Des pas sur la neige	o	1	1	31	16	27	o	76	1947
Préludes: Ce qu'a vu le vent d'ouest	o	o	6	27	o	30	o	63	1952
Préludes: La sérénade interrompue	o	1	3	52	o	25	o	81	1947
Préludes: La cathédrale engloutie	o	2	4	16	o	31	o	53	1947
Préludes: La danse de Puck	o	1	13	27	16	40	o	97	1947
Préludes: Brouillards	o	1	1	21	o	o	1	24	1940
Préludes: Feuilles mortes	o	2	1	28	o	o	9	40	1940
Préludes: La Puerto del Vino	o	1	2	24	o	o	1	28	1940
Préludes: 'Les fées sont d'exquises danseuses'	o	2	5	37	16	13	9	82	1940
Préludes: Bruyères	o	4	1	52	61	o	5	123	1940
Préludes: Général Lavine	o	3	2	60				65	1940
Préludes: La terrasse des audiences	o	o	3	25	o	3	o	31	1956, 16/II Moscow
Préludes: Ondine	o	2	8	20	9	o	o	39	1947
Préludes: Hommage à S. Pickwick Esq.	o	o	7	31	o	o	18	56	1954, 23/V
Préludes: Canope	o	4	o	46	o	o	20	70	1945
Préludes: Les tierces alternées	o	o	o	41	o	o	18	59	1966, 14/XII Brno
Préludes: Feux d'artifice	o	o	o	47	o	o	18	65	1966, 14/XII Brno
Suite bergamasque	o	4	o	42	38	o	o	84	1944
Aquarelles [unidentified]	o	4	18	o				22	1945
Chansons de Bilitis	o	1	3	o				4	1945
Chevaux de bois from Ariettes oubliées	o	1	12	o				13	1945
Fêtes galantes	o	o	o	1				1	1967, 20/VI Snape
Mandoline	o	2	16	o				18	1945
Noël des enfants qui n'ont plus de maison	o	1	22	o				23	1945
Songs [unidentified]	o	o	2	o				2	1955
Trois ariettes oubliées	o	1	13	o				14	1945
Delibes									
3 Songs	o	7	5	o				12	1946
Dvořák									
Concerto in G minor op. 33	o	o	o	9	2	14	o	25	1960, 21/X Philadelphia

	30s	40s	50s	60s	70s	80s	90s	total	details of premières
Piano Quintet in A major op. 5					o	21	o	21	1982, 31/I Moscow
Piano Quintet in A major op. 81					o	21	o	21	1982, 31/I Moscow
5 Songs	o	o	2	o				2	1952
Falla									
3 Songs	o	1	5	o				6	1947
Canciones populares españolas	o	2	6	o				8	1946
Franck									
Les Djinns	o	o	2	o				2	1952
Piano Quintet in F minor	o	3	4	o	o	8	o	15	1946
Piano Trio in F♯ minor op. 1/1					o	8	o	8	1983, 28/v Gorky
Violin Sonata in A major	o	o	o	6	1	o	o	7	1967, 2/VII Parçay-Meslay
Prélude, choral et fugue	o	4	13	10	o	11	9	47	1946
Gershwin									
Concerto in F					o	o	4	4	1993, 30/v Schwetzingen
Glazunov									
Concerto no. 1 in F minor op. 92	o	1	6	o				7	1949
Nocturne op. 37	o	o	2	o				2	1952
Suite on the name 'Sasha' op. 2	o	3	o	o				3	1942
2 romances	o	1	3	o				4	1949
Glinka									
20 Songs	o	12	22	o				34	1945
Grieg									
Concerto in A minor op. 16	o	o	1	13	6	o	o	20	1955, 16/VIII Kislovodsk
Cello Sonata in A minor op. 36	o	o	4	3	o	1	o	8	1951
Violin Sonata in G major op. 13					o	3	o	3	1984, 26/x Pushchino
Arrangement of Mozart keyboard sonatas for two pianos					o	o	7	7	1992, 8/VIII Haseldorf
Lyric Pieces op. 12/1					o	o	37	37	1993, 5/VII Baden-Baden
Lyric Pieces op. 12/2					o	o	37	37	1993
Lyric Pieces op. 12/3					o	o	37	37	1993
Lyric Pieces op. 12/4					o	o	37	37	1993
Lyric Pieces op. 12/8							37	37	1994
Lyric Pieces op. 38/12					o	o	37	37	1993
Lyric Pieces op. 38/16					o	o	37	37	1993
Lyric Pieces op. 43/17					o	o	37	37	1993
Lyric Pieces op. 43/22					o	o	37	37	1993
Lyric Pieces op. 47/23					o	o	37	37	1993
Lyric Pieces op. 47/27					o	o	9	9	1994
Lyric Pieces op. 54/31					o	o	46	46	1993
Lyric Pieces op. 54/33					o	o	9	9	1994
Lyric Pieces op. 54/34					o	o	46	46	1993
Lyric Pieces op. 54/35					o	o	37	37	1993
Lyric Pieces op. 57/39					o	o	36	36	1993

	30s	40s	50s	60s	70s	80s	90s	total	details of premières
Lyric Pieces op. 57/40					o	o	36	36	1993
Lyric Pieces op. 57/41					o	o	36	36	1993
Lyric Pieces op. 62/43					o	o	9	9	1994
Lyric Pieces op. 62/46					o	o	45	45	1993
Lyric Pieces op. 65/53					o	o	36	36	1993
Lyric Pieces op. 68/57					o	o	36	36	1993
Lyric Pieces op. 71/62					o	o	45	45	1993
Lyric Pieces op. 71/63					o	o	45	45	1993
Lyric Pieces op. 71/65					o	o	36	36	1993
Lyric Pieces op. 71/66					o	o	36	36	1993
Lyric Pieces op. 71/69					o	o	9	9	1994
Sonata in E minor op. 7	o	2	o	o				2	1944
6 Songs	o	1	5	o				6	1947
18 Songs	o	o	o	o	o	o	2	2	1993, 28/VII Moscow
Handel									
Suite no. 2					6	5	o	11	1978, 17/IV Moscow
Suite no. 3					7	5	o	12	1978, 24/VIII Volos
Suite no. 5	o	o	o	13	3	5	o	21	1962, 19/V Florence
Suite no. 8					3	5	o	8	1979, 14/III Tokyo
Suite no. 9					1	6	o	7	1979, 8/VII Marcilly-sur-Maulne
Suite no. 12					1	6	o	7	1979, 8/VII Marcilly-sur-Maulne
Suite no. 14					1	6	o	7	1979, 8/VII Marcilly-sur-Maulne
Suite no. 16					1	6	o	7	1979, 8/VII Marcilly-sur-Maulne
Arias	o	o	2	o				2	1955, 11/IV Leningrad
Haydn									
Concerto in D major Hob. XVIII:11					o	2	o	2	1983, 8/XII Minsk
Andante with variations Hob. XVII:12					o	o	28	28	1992, 22/II Jouques
Sonata no. 11 in Bb major Hob. XVI:2	o	o	o	o	o	4	o	4	1985, 6/V Moscow
Sonata no. 31 in Ab major Hob. XVI:46	o	o	o	o	o	10	25	35	1986, 16/V Milan
Sonata no. 32 in G minor Hob. XVI:44	o	o	o	11	o	16	o	27	1960
Sonata no. 33 in C minor Hob. XVI:20	o	3	2	5	o	o	7	17	1947
Sonata no. 37 in E major Hob. XVI:22	o	o	o	4				4	1961, 17/IV Moscow
Sonata no. 39 in D major Hob. XVI:24					o	36	o	36	1984, 27/III Tokyo
Sonata no. 43 in Eb major Hob. XVI:28	o	o	o	11				11	1966, 16/VII Spoleto
Sonata no. 44 in F major Hob. XVI:29	o	o	o	1	o	o	13	14	1961, 8/VII London
Sonata no. 45 in A major Hob. XVI:30	o	5	5	o				10	1945
Sonata no. 47 in B minor Hob. XVI:32					o	22	o	22	1984, 27/III Tokyo
Sonata no. 48 in C major Hob. XVI:35	o	o	o	24				24	1960, 23/IX Moscow
Sonata no. 54 in G major Hob. XVI:40					o	12	o	12	1986, 21/X Nagano
Sonata no. 55 in Bb major Hob. XVI:41					o	18	6	24	1986
Sonata no. 56 in D major Hob. XVI:42					o	o	12	12	1995
Sonata no. 57 in F major Hob. XVI:47					o	o	6	6	1995
Sonata no. 58 in C major Hob. XVI:48	o	o	o	16	o	39	o	55	1966, 9/VII Fontainebleau

	30s	40s	50s	60s	70s	80s	90s	total	details of premières
Sonata no. 59 in E♭ major Hob. XVI:49	o	4	o	2				6	1946
Sonata no. 61 in D major Hob. XVI:51					o	o	2	2	1995
Sonata no. 62 in E♭ major Hob. XVI:52	o	3	14	47	o	37	2	103	1946
Hindemith									
Kammermusik no. 2 op. 36/1					16	8	o	24	1977, 8/XII Dresden
Bassoon Sonata (1938)					3	o	o	3	1978, 17/IV Moscow
Trumpet Sonata (1939)					3	o	o	3	1978, 17/IV Moscow
Viola Sonata in E♭ major op. 11/4					o	18	o	18	1984, 5/X Zhukovsky
Violin Sonata in E♭ major op. 11/1					15	o	o	15	1977, 11/X Leningrad
Violin Sonata in D major op. 11/2					4	o	o	4	1978
Violin Sonata in E major (1935)					4	o	o	4	1978, 25/IV Yurmala
Violin Sonata in C major (1939)					19	o	o	19	1976, 10/V Moscow
Ludus tonalis					o	7	o	7	1985, 7/IV Budapest
Sonata no. 1 in A major	o	o	o	15				15	1962, 19/V Florence
Sonata no. 2 in G major					o	15	o	15	1985, 7/IV Budapest
Suite '1922' op. 26					o	14	o	14	1988, 23/X Kyoto
Janáček									
Concertino					o	5	o	5	1980, 2/VIII Moscow
Liszt									
Concerto no. 1 in E♭ major	o	4	9	3				16	1949
Concerto no. 2 in A major	o	o	5	7				12	1955, 14/III Moscow
Fantasia on Hungarian Folk Themes	o	o	1	3				4	1955, 27/VIII Kislovodsk
Concerto pathétique for two pianos	o	1	2	o				3	1942
Années de pèlerinage: Au bord d'une source	o	2	12	o				14	1948
Années de pèlerinage: Vallée d'Obermann	o	1	13	o				14	1948
Années de pèlerinage: Sposalizio	o	1	7	o				8	1948
Années de pèlerinage: Sonetto 123 del Petrarca	o	5	30	o				35	1944
Années de pèlerinage: Les jeux d'eaux à la Villa d'Este	o	8	10	o				18	1945
Ave Maria (Die Glocken von Rom) in E major					o	11	o	11	1982, 4/VII Parçay-Meslay
Concert Study no. 3: Un sospiro	o	8	4	o	o	5	o	17	1947
Consolation no. 6	o	o	3	o	o	43	o	46	1957, 29/IV Moscow
Erlkönig (transcription of Schubert song)	o	6	o	o				6	1947
Étude d'exécution transcendante no. 1: Preludio	o	13	34	o	o	13	o	60	1943
Étude d'exécution transcendante no. 2 in A minor	o	3	34	o	o	13	o	50	1949
Étude d'exécution transcendante no. 3: Paysage	1	13	42	o	o	13	o	69	1938
Étude d'exécution transcendante no. 5: Feux follets	2	18	60	o	o	16	o	96	1938
Étude d'exécution transcendante no. 7: Eroica	o	16	23	o	o	15	o	54	1943

	30s	40s	50s	60s	70s	80s	90s	total	details of premières
Étude d'exécution transcendante no. 8: Wilde Jagd	o	4	21	o	o	13	o	38	1945
Étude d'exécution transcendante no. 10 in F minor	o	3	25	o	o	14	o	42	1949
Étude d'exécution transcendante no. 11: Harmonies du soir	3	8	43	o	o	25	o	79	1938
Gnomenreigen	o	10	8	o	o	4	o	22	1947
Harmonies poétiques et religieuses: Pensée des morts	o	o	4	o	o	11	o	15	1957, 29/IV Moscow
Harmonies poétiques et religieuses: Funérailles	o	10	7	o				17	1943
Harmonies poétiques et religieuses: Andante lagrimoso					1	12	o	13	1975, 10/X Moscow
Hungarian Rhapsody no. 17	o	o	6	1	o	43	o	50	1957, 29/IV Moscow
Isoldens Liebestod (Wagner transcription)	1	1	o	o				2	1938
Konzertstück in F♯ major					o	14	o	14	1988, 24/II
Liebestraum no. 2 in E♭ major	o	6	4	o				10	1945
Liebestraum no. 3 in A♭ major	o	6	4	o				10	1945
La lugubre gondola	o	o	2	o				2	1950
Mephisto Polka					o	14	o	14	1988, 24/II
Mephisto Waltz no. 1	o	10	21	o				31	1947
Mephisto Waltz no. 2					o	14	o	14	1988, 24/II
Nuages gris	o	o	4	o	o	53	o	57	1954, 14/X Moscow
Polonaise no. 2 in E major	o	6	24	o	o	43	o	73	1947
Scherzo and March	o	o	2	o	o	15	o	17	1957, 29/IV Moscow
Scherzo in G minor					o	37	o	37	1988, 24/II
Sonata in B minor	2	16	8	47				73	1938
Valse oubliée no. 1	o	24	29	o				53	1944
Valse oubliée no. 2	o	9	15	o				24	1947
Valse oubliée no. 3	o	9	5	o				14	1947
Venezia e Napoli	o	15	15	o				30	1943
10 Songs	o	11	20	o				31	1947
Lyadov									
Canzonetta in B♭ major op. 48/2	o	o	1	o				1	1952
Étude in A major op. 48/1	o	2	1	o				3	1947
A Musical Snuffbox op. 32	o	7	3	o				10	1947
Medtner									
Violin Sonata in B minor no. 1 op. 21					o	1	o	1	1981, 27/XII Moscow
Sonata reminiscenza op. 38/1	o	2	o	o	o	1	o	3	1947
12 Songs to words by Pushkin	o	o	o	o	o	2	o	2	1981, 27/XII Moscow
2 Songs op. 36	o	o	3	o				3	1958, 21/I Moscow
Mendelssohn									
Cello Sonata no. 2 in D major op. 58	o	o	o	1				1	1969, 3/VII Parçay-Meslay
Songs without Words op. 19/1					28	o	o	28	1972, 12/II Kiev
Songs without Words op. 19/2					28	o	o	28	1972
Songs without Words op. 19/3					28	o	o	28	1972
Songs without Words op. 19/5					29	o	o	29	1972
Songs without Words op. 19/6					29	o	o	29	1972

	30s	40s	50s	60s	70s	80s	90s	total	details of premières
Variations sérieuses op. 54	o	8	12	26				46	1946
Mozart									
Concerto no. 1 in F major K 37					o	o	2	2	1994, 22/II Osaka
Concerto no. 5 in D major K 175					o	o	2	2	1994, 22/II Osaka
Concerto no. 6 in Bb flat major K 238					o	o	1	1	1994, 18/IV Seoul
Concerto no. 9 in Eb major K 271	o	o	o	4	o	o	2	6	1966, 29/XI Salzburg
Concerto no. 14 in Eb major K 449	o	o	o	2	4	o	o	6	1967, 1/VI Moscow
Concerto no. 15 in Bb major K 450	o	o	o	10				10	1968, 27/I Salzburg
Concerto no. 17 in G major K 453	o	o	o	11	2	o	o	13	1968, 9/IV Moscow
Concerto no. 18 in Bb major K 456	o	o	o	o	2	o	2	4	1977, 9/I Moscow
Concerto no. 20 in D minor K 466	o	1	10	o				11	1943
Concerto no. 22 in Eb major K 482	o	o	o	9	4	o	o	13	1966, 31/VII Aix-en-Provence
Concerto no. 24 in C minor K 491					12	o	o	12	1971, 22/VI Moscow
Concerto no. 25 in C major K 503					o	o	1	1	1992, 1/XII Moscow
Concerto no. 27 in Bb major K 595	o	o	o	9	7	o	4	20	1965, 16/VI Blythburgh
Piano Quartet in G minor K 478					o	2	o	2	1982, 25/XII Moscow
Piano Quartet in Eb major K 493					o	2	o	2	1982, 29/XII Moscow
Sonata in D major for two keyboards K 448	o	o	o	1				1	1967, 20/VI Snape
Sonata in C major for keyboard duet K 521	o	o	o	1				1	1966, 19/VI Aldeburgh
Violin Sonata no. 21 in E minor K 304					8	8	o	16	1974, 14/X Naples
Violin Sonata no. 22 in A major K 305					14	8	o	22	1974, 14/X Naples
Violin Sonata no. 23 in D major K 306					20	8	o	28	1974, 14/IV Moscow
Violin Sonata in Bb major K 372 (inc.)					20	o	o	20	1974, 14/IV Moscow
Violin Sonata no. 24 in F major K 376					7	2	o	9	1975, 2/V Tbilisi
Violin Sonata no. 26 in Bb major K 378					8	2	o	10	1974, 14/IV Moscow
Violin Sonata no. 27 in G major K 379					8	2	o	10	1974, 14/IV Moscow
Violin Sonata no. 28 in Eb major K 380					9	2	o	11	1975, 6/V Kislovodsk
Violin Sonata no. 29 in A major K 402 (inc.)					9	o	o	9	1974, 14/X Naples
Violin Sonata no. 30 in C major K 403 (inc.)					6	2	o	8	1975, 20/V Moscow
Violin Sonata no. 31 in C major K 404 (inc.)					24	8	o	32	1974, 14/IV Moscow
Violin Sonata no. 32 in Bb major K 454					6	2	o	8	1975, 20/V Moscow
Fantasia in C minor K 475	o	o	o	11	o	o	26	37	1965, 9/IX Ljubljana
Minuet in D major K 355	o	o	o	2				2	1968, 25/I Salzburg
Prelude and Fugue in C major K 394	o	o	o	2				2	1968, 25/I Salzburg
Rondo in A minor K 511	o	2	6	1				9	1945
Sonata no. 2 in F major K 280	o	o	o	33				33	1961, 29/XI Moscow
Sonata no. 4 in Eb major K 282	o	o	7	o	o	14	o	21	1953, 14/II Yerevan
Sonata no. 5 in G major K 283	o	o	o	24	o	o	5	29	1965, 14/XI Riga
Sonata no. 7 in C major K 309	o	o	o	20				20	1967, 29/XII Istanbul
Sonata no. 8 in A minor K 310	o	19	44	7	o	16	o	86	1941

	30s	40s	50s	60s	70s	80s	90s	total	details of premières
Sonata no. 13 in B♭ major K 333	o	o	o	12	o	o	7	19	1966, 28/I Salzburg
Sonata no. 14 in C minor K 457	o	o	o	14	o	o	20	34	1965, 9/IX Ljubljana
Sonata no. 15 in F major K 533/494	o	3	4	o	o	11	5	23	1944
Sonata no. 16 in C major K 545	o	1	16	o	o	14	5	36	1941
Sonata no. 17 in B♭ major K 570					o	o	7	7	1990, 29/I Aix-en-Provence
Variations on 'La belle Françoise' K 353	o	o	o	12				12	1968, 25/I Salzburg
8 Lieder	o	7	22	o				29	1946
Mussorgsky									
Pictures at an Exhibition	o	5	55	27	17	o	o	104	1949
The Nursery	o	o	29	o				29	1953, 30/I Tbilisi
Songs and Dances of Death	o	1	1	o				2	1949
Songs	o	5	3	o				8	1949
Myaskovsky									
Sonata no. 2 op. 81 for cello and piano	o	o	2	o				2	1953, 3/XII Moscow
Sonata no. 3 in C minor op. 19	o	1	9	o	12	o	o	22	1947
4 Songs	o	o	4	o				4	1952
7 Romances	o	1	7	o				8	1947
Poulenc									
'Aubade': concerto chorégraphique	o	o	2	2				4	1957, 11/VI Moscow
Concerto pour 2 pianos					o	o	3	3	1993, 18/VI Caen
Prokofiev									
Concerto no. 1 in D♭ major op. 10	o	8	7	o				15	1943
Concerto no. 5 in G minor op. 55	o	2	8	5	2	o	o	17	1941
Symphony-Concerto in E minor for cello and orchestra op. 125	o	o	1	o				1	1952
Overture on Hebrew Themes op. 34	o	2	2	1	o	3	o	8	1943
Cello Sonata in C major op. 119	o	2	6	1	o	o	10	19	1949
Flute Sonata in D major op. 94	o	6	2	1	o	6	o	15	1943
Violin Sonata no. 1 in F minor op. 80					3	o	o	3	1972, 29/III Moscow
4 Pieces: Dance op. 32/1	o	2	16	9	18	9	o	54	1945
4 Pieces: Waltz op. 32/4	o	2	16	8	17	3	o	46	1945
Landscape op. 59/2	o	1	1	40	34	4	o	80	1940
Legend op. 12/6	o	o	o	4	17	8	o	29	1960, 23/IX Moscow
Pastoral Sonatina op. 59/3	o	1	o	12	o	4	o	17	1940
Pensées op. 62/3	o	2	o	12	o	4	o	18	1945
3 Pieces from Cinderella: Gavotte op. 95/2	o	7	33	9	21	14	o	84	1947
10 Pieces from Cinderella: Autumn Fairy op. 97/3	o	o	7	2	21	6	o	36	1950
10 Pieces from Cinderella: Oriental Dance op. 97/6	o	o	7	2	21	6	o	36	1950
6 Pieces from Cinderella: Quarrel op. 102/3	o	o	7	o	21	6	o	34	1950
6 Pieces from Cinderella: Waltz op. 102/4	o	o	6	o	21	6	o	33	1950
Rondo op. 52/2	o	2	2	o	o	4	o	8	1940
Sonata no. 2 in D minor op. 14	1	3	13	55	o	8	15	95	1939

	30s	40s	50s	60s	70s	80s	90s	total	details of premières
Sonata no. 4 in C minor op. 29	o	8	2	17	o	6	12	45	1943
Sonata no. 6 in A major op. 82	o	9	9	67	o	12	o	97	1940
Sonata no. 7 in B♭ major op. 83	o	13	28	o	24	o	o	65	1943
Sonata no. 8 in B♭ major op. 84	o	9	12	33	15	o	o	69	1945
Sonata no. 9 in C major op. 103	o	o	12	o	8	5	o	25	1951
Suggestion diabolique op. 4/4	o	o	o	9	o	2	o	11	1961
Visions fugitives op. 22/3	o	3	6	31	17	8	o	65	1945
Visions fugitives op. 22/4	o	3	4	32	17	8	o	64	1945
Visions fugitives op. 22/5	o	4	5	33	17	8	o	67	1945
Visions fugitives op. 22/6	o	3	5	33	17	8	o	66	1940
Visions fugitives op. 22/8	o	3	5	33	17	8	o	66	1945
Visions fugitives op. 22/9	o	3	5	32	17	8	o	65	1945
Visions fugitives op. 22/11	o	4	6	32	17	8	o	67	1940
Visions fugitives op. 22/14	o	3	6	30	17	8	o	64	1945
Visions fugitives op. 22/15	o	3	4	30	17	8	o	62	1945
Visions fugitives op. 22/18	o	3	4	29	17	8	o	61	1945
Visions fugitives op. 22/20	o	3	6	7	17	8	o	41	1945
Waltz from War and Peace op. 96/1	o	o	o	54	43	13	o	110	1961, 8/VII London
5 Akhmatova Songs op. 27	o	2	2	o				4	1945
Russian Folksongs op. 104	o	o	15	o				15	1951
The Ugly Duckling op. 18	o	5	15	o				20	1947
Rachmaninov									
Concerto no. 1 in F♯ minor op. 1	o	8	7	o				15	1947
Concerto no. 2 in C minor op. 18	o	9	11	o				20	1943
Suite no. 2 for two pianos op. 17	o	1	1	o				2	1942
Barcarolle in G minor op. 10/3	o	5	4	o	o	8	o	17	1942
Études-tableaux op. 33/3	o	9	6	o	o	69	o	84	1946
Études-tableaux op. 33/4					o	68	o	68	1983, 24/V Klin
Études-tableaux op. 33/5	o	1	o	9	o	73	o	83	1946
Études-tableaux op. 33/6	o	o	2	o	2	o	o	4	1953
Études-tableaux op. 39/1	o	8	7	20	o	68	o	103	1942
Études-tableaux op. 39/2	o	9	6	21	o	72	o	108	1945
Études-tableaux op. 39/3	o	5	14	55	o	74	o	148	1945
Études-tableaux op. 39/4	o	4	6	20	o	74	o	104	1945
Études-tableaux op. 39/7	o	3	8	2				13	1942
Études-tableaux op. 39/9	o	8	8	41	2	65	o	124	1945
Liebesfreud (arrangement of Kreisler)	o	4	1	o				5	1946
Mélodie in E major op. 3/3	o	15	o	o	2	1	o	18	1942
Mélodie in E major op. 3/3 (revised version)	o	o	o	o	o	5	o	5	1982, 4/I Moscow
Moment musical op. 16/6	o	7	o	o	2	1	o	10	1946
Polichinelle in F♯ minor op. 3/4	o	6	o	o	2	1	o	9	1946
Polka in A♭ major [unidentified]	o	13	o	o	2	1	o	16	1942
Prelude op. 23/1	o	15	33	54	14	o	o	116	1942
Prelude op. 23/2	1	29	61	52	14	o	o	157	1939
Prelude op. 23/4	1	22	39	51	14	o	o	127	1939
Prelude op. 23/5	1	27	76	51	14	o	o	169	1939

	30s	40s	50s	60s	70s	80s	90s	total	details of premières
Prelude op. 23/7	0	17	31	51	26	0	0	125	1942
Prelude op. 23/8	0	17	17	50	19	0	0	103	1943
Prelude op. 32/1	0	9	17	50	17	0	0	93	1942
Prelude op. 32/2	0	6	18	51	16	0	0	91	1942
Prelude op. 32/6	0	12	14	51	14	0	0	91	1946
Prelude op. 32/7	0	16	23	54	14	0	0	107	1942
Prelude op. 32/9	0	3	15	33	14	0	0	65	1943
Prelude op. 32/10	0	26	39	55	15	0	0	135	1942
Prelude op. 32/12	0	41	117	92	61	8	0	319	1942
Romance op. 10/6	0	4	1	0	2	1	0	8	1942
10 Songs	0	2	3	0				5	1945
3 Romances	0	4	5	0				9	1947
9 Romances	0	4	2	0				6	1945
Ravel									
Concerto for the Left Hand	0	0	4	5	0	3	0	12	1951
Piano Trio in A minor					0	6	0	6	1983, 3/VII Parçay-Meslay
Violin Sonata in G major	0	0	0	0	0	3	0	3	1986, 15/IX Khabarovsk
Gaspard de la nuit: Le gibet	0	0	2	7				9	1954, 26/III Budapest
Jeux d'eau	0	3	21	14				38	1944
Miroirs: Noctuelles	0	0	1	18	0	0	25	44	1959, 2/XI Prague
Miroirs: Oiseaux tristes	0	0	1	43	0	0	25	69	1959, 2/XI Prague
Miroirs: Une barque sur l'océan	0	0	0	38	0	0	25	63	1964, 23/VI Parçay-Meslay
Miroirs: Alborada del gracioso	1	3	22	27	0	0	25	78	1939
Miroirs: La vallée des cloches	0	5	8	27	0	1	38	79	1943
Pavane pour une infante défunte	0	1	4	8				13	1944
Valses nobles et sentimentales	1	2	2	16	0	0	25	46	1939
5 Mélodies populaires grecques	0	0	10	0				10	1956, 27/VI Moscow
Vocalise en forme de habanera	0	0	9	0				9	1954, 3/V Moscow
Reger									
Piano Quintet in C minor op. 64	0	0	0	2				2	1960, 28/V
Variations and Fugue for two pianos op. 86					0	0	6	6	1995, 13/III Vienna
Rimsky-Korsakov									
Concerto in C♯ minor op. 30	0	5	4	0				9	1949
8 Mélodies	0	5	5	0				10	1947
Saint-Saëns									
Concerto no. 2 in G minor op. 22					0	0	4	4	1993, 19/V Vienna
Concerto no. 5 in F major op. 103	0	0	9	0	0	0	6	15	1952
Cello Sonata no. 1 in C minor op. 32					0	0	9	9	1991, 30/XI Smolensk
Variations on a Theme of Beethoven for two pianos op. 35	0	1	0	0				1	1942

	30s	40s	50s	60s	70s	80s	90s	total	details of premières
Schubert									
Piano Quintet in A major ('The Trout') D 667	o	2	o	o	o	5	o	7	1944
Sonata (Duo) in A major for piano and violin D 574	o	o	o	6		1		7	1967, 2/VII Parçay-Meslay
Andantino varié in B minor for piano duet D 823/2	o	o	o	1				1	1965, 22/VI Aldeburgh
Divertissement à l'hongroise for piano duet D 818					3	o	o	3	1977, 20/VI Hohenems
Divertissement in E minor for piano duet D 823					3	o	o	3	1977, 20/VI Hohenems
Fantasie in F minor for piano duet D 940	o	o	o	1				1	1965, 22/VI Aldeburgh
4 Ländler for piano duet D 814					1	o	o	1	1977, 1/VII Parçay-Meslay
Marche caractéristique no. 1 for piano duet D 886/1					3	o	o	3	1977, 20/VI Hohenems
March in G major ('Kindermarsch') for piano duet D 928					3	o	o	3	1977, 20/VI Hohenems
Sonata in Bb major for piano duet D 617					3	o	o	3	1977, 20/VI Hohenems
Sonata in C major ('Grand Duo') for piano duet D 812	o	o	o	1				1	1965, 22/VI Aldeburgh
Variations on a French song in E minor for piano duet D 624					3	o	o	3	1977, 20/VI Hohenems
Variations on an Original Theme in Ab major for piano duet D 813	o	o	o	1				1	1964, 20/VI Aldeburgh
Allegretto in C minor D 915	o	o	o	7	5	o	o	12	1961, 22/x Paris
12 Deutsche op. 171: no. 8 in Ab minor D 790/8					1	o	o	1	1978
12 Deutsche op. 171: no. 11 in Ab major D 790/11					1	o	o	1	1978, 18/x Moscow
Écossaise in Ab major no. 1 [unidentified]	o	o	1	o	1	o	o	2	1953, 3/v Moscow
Écossaise in Ab major no. 2 [unidentified]					1	o	o	1	1978
Écossaise in Ab major no. 3 [unidentified]	o	o	o	o	1	o	o	1	1978, 18/x Moscow
Écossaise in Eb major no. 6 [unidentified]	o	o	1	o	1	o	o	2	1957
Écossaise in A minor op. 67/1 D 734/17	o	o	1	o	1	o	o	2	1953
Écossaise in A major op. 67/2 D 734/18	o	o	1	o	1	o	o	2	1953
Impromptu in Eb major op. 90/2 D 899/2	o	2	22	o	11	o	o	35	1945
Impromptu in Gb major op. 90/3 D 899/3	o	3	16	21	6	o	o	46	1945
Impromptu in Ab major op. 90/4 D 899/4	o	6	25	25	20	o	o	76	1945

	30s	40s	50s	60s	70s	80s	90s	total	details of premières
Impromptu in A♭ major op. 142/2 D 935/2	0	2	6	6				14	1945
Klavierstück in A major D 604	0	0	0	5	4	0	0	9	1966, 28/VI Parçay-Meslay
3 Klavierstücke: no. 1 in E♭ minor D 946/1	0	0	0	18				18	1961, 22/X Paris
3 Klavierstücke: no. 2 in E♭ major D 946/2	0	0	0	20				20	1963, 1/III Vienna
3 Klavierstücke: no. 3 in C major D 946/3	0	0	0	23				23	1963, 9/II Brussels
4 Ländler op. post. 1 [unidentified]	0	0	4	3	7	0	0	14	1953, 3/V Moscow
4 Ländler op. post. 3 [unidentified]	0	0	4	2	7	0	0	13	1953
4 Ländler op. post. 4 [unidentified]	0	0	4	2	7	0	0	13	1953
4 Ländler op. post. 5 [unidentified]	0	0	4	2	7	0	0	13	1953
March in E major D 606	0	0	2	3				5	1958, 31/I Moscow
Moment musical in C major op. 94/1 D 780/1	0	3	24	1	21	0	0	49	1946
Moment musical in F minor op. 94/3 D 780/3	0	2	5	2	20	0	0	29	1946
Moment musical in A♭ major op. 94/6 D 780/6	0	1	4	2	7	0	0	14	1949
Scherzo in D♭ major D 593/2	0	0	0	4	4	0	0	8	1966, 9/VII Fontainebleau
Sonata in E major D 459	0	0	0	0	2	5	0	7	1978, 2/VII Tours
Sonata in E minor D 566	0	0	2	13	12	0	0	27	1953, 3/V Moscow
Sonata in B major op. 147 D 575	0	0	0	31	12	0	0	43	1965, 11/IV Washington
Sonata in F minor D 625					62	0	0	62	1978, 11/VI Moscow
Sonata in A major op. 120 D 664	0	0	18	11	36	0	0	65	1953, 31/X Moscow
Sonata in A minor op. 143 D 784	0	0	18	10	9	0	0	37	1957, 8/IV Moscow
Sonata in C major D 840 (inc.)	0	0	0	2	22	1	0	25	1961, 22/X Paris
Sonata in A minor op. 42 D 845	0	0	17	0				17	1953, 18/X Leningrad
Sonata in D major op. 53 D 850	0	5	7	0				12	1946
Sonata in G major op. 78 D 894	0	3	2	0	4	9	0	18	1948
Sonata in C minor D 958	0	0	9	0	54	0	0	63	1950
Sonata in B♭ major D 960	0	1	5	16	20	0	0	42	1949
13 Variations on a Theme of Anselm Hüttenbrenner D 576	0	0	0	19	8	0	0	27	1969, 15/VII Saint Tropez
12 Waltzes op. 18 D 145	0	0	3	11				14	1951
'Wanderer' Fantasy D 760	2	14	8	23	0	0	11	58	1938
Die schöne Müllerin D 795	0	1	3	0				4	1948
Winterreise D 911	0	6	1	0	0	3	0	10	1947
9 songs from Schwanengesang D 957	0	2	1	0				3	1945
9 songs to poems by Goethe	0	12	17	0				29	1945
23 Lieder	0	0	0	0	8	0	0	8	1977, 2/VII Tours
Schumann									
Concerto in A minor op. 54	0	12	11	0	11	0	0	34	1941
Introduction and Allegro appassionato op. 92	0	1	2	1				4	1949

	30s	40s	50s	60s	70s	80s	90s	total	details of premières
Andante and variations for 2 pianos, 2 cellos and horn					16	o	o	16	1978, 11/VI Moscow
Bilder aus Osten for piano duet op. 66	o	o	o	1	o	3	o	4	1966, 21/VI Aldeburgh
Märchenbilder for viola and piano op. 113					o	4	o	4	1985, 11/XII Moscow
3 Phantasiestücke for clarinet and piano op. 73	o	o	o	1	o	2	o	3	1969, 3/VII Parçay-Meslay
Piano Quintet op. 44	o	4	2	3	o	3	2	14	1942
Piano Trio no. 1 op. 63					o	5	o	5	1985, 11/XII Moscow
'Abegg' Variations op. 1	o	o	1	9				10	1955, 20/VI Moscow
Blumenstück in D♭ major op. 19					o	17	o	17	1985, 13/XII Moscow
Bunte Blätter op. 99	o	o	9	19	17	o	o	45	1951
Fantasie in C major op. 17	o	9	11	4	25	12	o	61	1940
Faschingsschwank aus Wien op. 26	o	o	10	23	38	o	o	71	1950
Fugue in D minor op. 72/1	o	o	9	o	o	16	o	25	1956, 18/IX Moscow
Fugue in D minor op. 72/2	o	o	9	o	o	16	o	25	1956
Fugue in F minor op. 72/3	o	o	9	o	o	16	o	25	1956
Fugue in F major op. 72/4	o	o	9	o	o	16	o	25	1956
Humoreske in B♭ major op. 20	o	o	15	o				15	1955, 20/VI Moscow
Konzert-Etüden nach Capricen von Paganini op. 10/4					o	68	o	68	1985, 11/XII Moscow
Konzert-Etüden nach Capricen von Paganini op. 10/5					o	68	o	68	1985, 11/XII Moscow
Konzert-Etüden nach Capricen von Paganini op. 10/6					o	68	o	68	1985, 11/XII Moscow
March in G minor op. 76/2	o	o	9	o	o	18	o	27	1956, 18/IX Moscow
Nachtstücke op. 23					o	21	o	21	1986, 24/IV Brescia
Novellette op. 21/1	o	o	12	53	11	14	1	91	1952
Novellette op. 21/2	o	o	8	58	2	8	o	76	1952
Novellette op. 21/4	o	o	9	21	2	o	o	32	1952
Novellette op. 21/8	o	o	9	36	3	o	o	48	1952
Papillons op. 2	o	7	3	9				19	1948
Phantasiestück op. 12/1	o	16	22	19	38	o	o	95	1943
Phantasiestück op. 12/2	o	15	26	30	50	5	o	126	1943
Phantasiestück op. 12/3	o	12	18	19	35	o	o	84	1943
Phantasiestück op. 12/5	o	10	20	19	49	o	o	98	1943
Phantasiestück op. 12/7	o	10	18	19	43	o	o	90	1943
Phantasiestück op. 12/8	o	14	20	19	43	o	o	96	1943
Sonata no. 2 in G minor op. 22	o	5	8	35				48	1949
Symphonic Studies op. 13	o	8	8	33	35	1	o	85	1944
Toccata in C major op. 7	1	2	24	o	o	18	o	45	1938
Waldscenen op. 82	o	4	9	o				13	1940
Dichterliebe op. 48	o	5	5	o				10	1946
Frauenliebe und -leben op. 42	o	1	o	o				1	1945
10 Lieder	o	7	15	o				22	1946
Scriabin									
Prométhée op. 60					2	1	o	3	1972, 3/IV Moscow
Énigme op. 52/2	o	o	1	o				1	1956

	30s	40s	50s	60s	70s	80s	90s	total	details of premières
Étude op. 8/5	o	2	4	o				6	1946
Étude op. 8/11	o	4	4	o				8	1947
Étude op. 42/2	o	2	4	o	19	o	o	25	1946
Étude op. 42/3	o	o	4	o	14	o	o	18	1952
Étude op. 42/4	o	2	5	o	14	o	o	21	1946
Étude op. 42/5	o	o	4	o	19	o	o	23	1952
Étude op. 42/6	o	2	4	o	19	o	o	25	1947
Étude op. 42/8	o	2	4	o	19	o	o	25	1947
Étude op. 65/1	o	3	4	o				7	1946
Étude op. 65/2	o	4	4	o				8	1946
Étude op. 65/3	o	4	5	o				9	1946
Fantaisie in B minor op. 28	o	10	o	o	o	o	22	32	1942
Flamme sombre op. 73/2					o	o	25	25	1992
Guirlande op. 73/1					o	o	24	24	1992
Ironies op. 56/2	o	4	o	o	o	o	1	5	1944
Mazurka in E minor op. 25/3	o	1	3	o				4	1949
Mazurka in D♭ major op. 40/1					o	o	18	18	1992, 21/IV Gardone Riviera
Mazurka in F♯ major op. 40/2					o	o	18	18	1992
3 Pieces op. 2	o	7	4	o				11	1944
Poème op. 32/1	o	9	o	o	o	o	5	14	1944
Poème op. 52/1	o	3	1	o	5	o	o	9	1945
Poème-nocturne op. 61					o	o	39	39	1992, 21/IV Gardone Riviera
Prélude op. 11/1	o	2	o	o				2	1949
Prélude op. 11/2	o	12	1	o	3	o	o	16	1940
Prélude op. 11/3	o	11	1	o	3	o	o	15	1940
Prélude op. 11/4	o	2	o	o				2	1949
Prélude op. 11/5	o	11	1	o	3	o	o	15	1943
Prélude op. 11/9	o	13	1	o	3	o	4	21	1940
Prélude op. 11/10	o	12	1	o	3	o	3	19	1940
Prélude op. 11/11	o	11	1	o	3	o	o	15	1942
Prélude op. 11/12					3	o	o	3	1972
Prélude op. 11/15	o	6	1	o	3	o	1	11	1942
Prélude op. 11/16	o	7	1	o	3	o	o	11	1942
Prélude op. 11/17	o	5	1	o	3	o	o	9	1940
Prélude op. 11/18	o	6	1	o	3	o	o	10	1940
Prélude op. 11/24	o	2	1	o	3	o	o	6	1943
Prélude op. 13/1	o	2	1	o	3	o	o	6	1945
Prélude op. 13/4	o	1	1	o	3	o	o	5	1945
Prélude op. 37/1	o	1	1	o	14	o	o	16	1949
Prélude op. 37/2	o	1	1	o	15	o	o	17	1949
Prélude op. 37/3	o	1	1	o	3	o	o	5	1949
Prélude op. 37/4	o	1	1	o	3	o	o	5	1949
Prélude op. 39/3	o	5	1	o	15	o	o	21	1949
Prélude op. 39/4	o	5	1	o	15	o	o	21	1949
Prélude op. 51/2	o	2	2	o	3	o	o	7	1945
Prélude op. 59/2	o	2	1	o	3	o	o	6	1944

	30s	40s	50s	60s	70s	80s	90s	total	details of premières
Prélude op. 74/1	0	1	2	0	3	0	1	7	1949
Prélude op. 74/3	0	1	2	0	3	0	0	6	1949
Prélude op. 74/4	0	1	2	0	3	0	0	6	1949
Sonata no. 2 in G# minor op. 19	1	12	2	0	17	0	3	35	1938
Sonata no. 5 in F# major op. 53	0	7	8	34	22	0	0	71	1947
Sonata no. 6 in G major op. 62	0	1	1	0				2	1944
Sonata no. 7 in F# major op. 64	1	4	3	14	0	0	9	31	1938
Sonata no. 9 in F major op. 68	0	8	1	7	4	0	0	20	1943
Vers la flamme op. 72	0	9	3	0	0	0	29	41	1940
Shostakovich									
Piano Quintet in G minor op. 57	0	1	2	6	0	9	0	18	1947
Piano Trio no. 2 in E minor op. 67					0	6	0	6	1984, 8/XII Moscow
Viola Sonata op. 147					0	30	0	30	1980, 2/VIII Moscow
Violin Sonata op. 134	0	0	0	4	1	9	0	14	1969, 3/V Moscow
Prelude op. 34/6					0	1	0	1	1985, 3/VIII La Roque d'Anthéron
Prelude op. 34/12					0	1	0	1	1985, 3/VIII La Roque d'Anthéron
Prelude op. 34/23					0	1	0	1	1985, 28/VI Parçay-Meslay
Prelude and Fugue in A minor op. 87/2	0	0	14	0				14	1956, 5/XI Moscow
Prelude and Fugue in G major op. 87/3	0	0	17	0				17	1956, 12/II Moscow
Prelude and Fugue in E minor op. 87/4	0	0	13	19				32	1954, 24/XI Warsaw
Prelude and Fugue in B minor op. 87/6	0	0	13	0				13	1956
Prelude and Fugue in A major op. 87/7	0	0	14	0				14	1954
Prelude and Fugue in F# minor op. 87/8	0	0	0	5				5	1963
Prelude and Fugue in G# minor op. 87/12	0	0	1	19				20	1954
Prelude and Fugue in Eb minor op. 87/14	0	0	0	5				5	1963, 29/IV Budapest
Prelude and Fugue in Db major op. 87/15	0	0	24	13				37	1956
Prelude and Fugue in Ab major op. 87/17	0	0	1	13				14	1954
Prelude and Fugue in F minor op. 87/18	0	0	12	0				12	1956, 15/IX Moscow
Prelude and Fugue in Eb major op. 87/19					0	11	0	11	1988
Prelude and Fugue in C minor op. 87/20					0	12	0	12	1988
Prelude and Fugue in Bb major op. 87/21					12	0	0	12	1973
Prelude and Fugue in G minor op. 87/22					12	0	0	12	1973, 8/VI Parçay-Meslay

	30s	40s	50s	60s	70s	80s	90s	total	details of premières
Prelude and Fugue in F major op. 87/23	0	0	12	19				31	1956
From Jewish Folk Poetry op. 79	0	0	5	0				5	1958, 21/I Moscow
Song [unidentified]	0	0	3	0				3	1952
Sibelius									
2 Songs	0	0	1	0				1	1953, 5/VI Leningrad
Smetana									
Song	0	0	2	0				2	1952
Strauss									
Burleske	0	0	0	2				2	1961, 9/IX Bucharest
Stravinsky									
Capriccio (1929)					0	1	0	1	1985, 29/VI Parçay-Meslay
Movements (1959)					0	3	0	3	1984, 31/XII Moscow
Concerto for two pianos (1935)					0	10	0	10	1985, 5/VI Moscow
Piano-Rag-Music					0	8	0	8	1988, 6/X Tokyo
Szymanowski									
Mythes for violin and piano: La fontaine d'Aréthuse op. 30/1					0	6	0	6	1982
Narcisse op. 30/2					0	6	0	6	1982, 25/X Molodechno
Dryades et Pan op. 30/3					0	6	0	6	1982
Masques: Shéhérazade op. 34/1	0	1	0	0	20	4	0	25	1946
Masques: Tantris the Clown op. 34/2	0	1	0	0	20	4	0	25	1946
Mazurka op. 50/1	0	1	1	0	0	7	0	9	1945
Mazurka op. 50/3	0	0	1	0	0	7	0	8	1954, 15/XI Warsaw
Mazurka op. 50/12	0	0	1	0	0	4	0	5	1954
Mazurka op. 50/13	0	0	1	0	0	3	0	4	1954
Mazurka op. 50/16	0	0	1	0	0	3	0	4	1954
Mazurka op. 50/17	0	0	1	0	0	7	0	8	1954
Mazurka op. 50/18	0	0	1	0	0	7	0	8	1954
Metopes: Île de la sirène op. 29/1					0	14	0	14	1988, 23/X Kyoto
Metopes: Calypso op. 29/2					0	14	0	14	1988, 23/X Kyoto
Sonata no. 2 in A major op. 21	1	7	9	0	0	36	0	53	1939
Sonata no. 3 op. 36					0	13	0	13	1982, 15/X Moscow
Songs of the Infatuated Muezzin op. 42					0	13	0	13	1980, 2/VIII Moscow
7 Songs to words by James Joyce op. 54					0	10	0	10	1982, 15/X Moscow
Taneyev									
Song	0	0	1	0				1	1958, 21/I Moscow
Tchaikovsky									
Concerto no. 1 in B♭ minor op. 23	0	15	27	10				52	1940
Piano Trio in A minor op. 50	0	1	0	0	0	6	0	7	1945
Capriccioso in B♭ major op. 19/6	0	3	0	0	0	20	0	23	1947
Chanson triste in G minor op. 40/2	0	0	1	0	2	21	0	24	1952
L'espiègle in E major op. 72/12	0	0	1	1	2	21	0	25	1952

	30s	40s	50s	60s	70s	80s	90s	total	details of premières
Humoresque in E minor op. 10/2	o	4	1	o	o	20	o	25	1947
Méditation in D major op. 72/5	o	1	2	o	o	20	o	23	1949
Menuetto scherzoso in E♭ major op. 51/3	o	o	1	o	2	21	o	24	1952
Nocturne in F major op. 10/1	o	3	o	o	o	20	o	23	1947
Un poco di Chopin in C♯ minor op. 72/15	o	o	1	o	2	19	o	22	1952
Rêverie du soir in G minor op. 19/1	o	o	1	o	2	21	o	24	1952
Romance in F minor op. 5	o	4	1	o	o	20	o	25	1947
Romance in F major op. 51/5	o	o	1	o	2	21	o	24	1952
Les saisons op. 37b: Janvier	o	9	10	6	o	21	o	46	1944
Les saisons op. 37b: Mai	o	9	12	9	1	21	o	52	1944
Les saisons op. 37b: Juin	o	9	12	6	o	21	o	48	1944
Les saisons op. 37b: Novembre	o	9	15	9	o	21	o	54	1944
Sonata in G major op. 37	o	10	15	o				25	1942
Valse in A♭ major op. 40/8	o	1	o	o	o	20	o	21	1947
Valse de salon in A♭ major op. 51/1	o	o	1	o	3	21	o	25	1952
Valse-scherzo in A major op. 7	o	6	1	o	o	20	o	27	1947
9 Songs	o	14	16	o				30	1945
21 Songs	o	3	1	o				4	1946
Wagner									
Schmachtend					34	18	1	53	1975, 12/I Moscow
3 Lieder	o	1	o	o				1	1949
Weber									
Sonata no. 1 op. 24					o	2	o	2	1981, 17/VI Moscow
Sonata no. 3 op. 49	o	5	6	17	o	o	7	35	1948
Webern									
Variations op. 27					o	19	o	19	1985, 11/VI Minsk
Weckerlin									
5 Pastorales	o	16	25	o				41	1945
Wolf									
20 Lieder (Mörike and Eichendorff)	o	2	4	o				6	1946
21 Lieder on poems by Goethe					4	o	o	4	1977, 24/VII Munich
25 Mörike Lieder	o	o	4	1	6	o	o	11	1967, 28/VI Parçay-Meslay
6 sacred songs	o	o	o	o	o	1	o	1	1982, 4/VII Parçay-Meslay

Highlights of Richter's Career

18 May, Yerevan: Chopin and Liszt recital on radio

1945   7 March, 26 July, 20 Oct., 3 Nov.: radio broadcasts of works by Beethoven, Schubert, Rachmaninov and Chopin

1946   21 Jan., Moscow: radio broadcast of Franck's Quintet; 9 Oct., Leningrad: radio broadcast of a Chopin recital; 26 Oct., Moscow: radio broadcast of a Schubert recital with Nina Dorliac

1947   23 Jan., Moscow: radio broadcast of Schumann and Wolf

1948   10 Feb., radio broadcast of Schumann Concerto; 15 June, Tallinn Radio broadcast, Glinka, Tchaikovsky, Rachmaninov; 23 June, Vilnius Radio broadcast, Mozart and Schubert recital

1949   27 Sept., Moscow: playthrough of Prokofiev's Cello Sonata for secretariat of Composers' Union

29 Dec., Moscow: reception and concert to mark Stalin's 70th birthday in St George's Hall at the Kremlin; Richter plays two Rachmaninov preludes; other performers include Oistrakh, Plisetskaya and Kozlovsky

1950   23 March, Moscow: concert for Party Central Committee; Richter plays a Liszt study and two Rachmaninov preludes

22 April, Moscow: concert to mark 80th anniversary of Lenin's birth

5 May, Teplice: Richter's first foreign concert

1952   9 June, Moscow: televised broadcast of two pieces from Tchaikovsky's *The Seasons*

15 Oct., Moscow: concert to mark 19th Party Congress in St George's Hall in the Kremlin; Richter plays Chopin's Scherzo no. 2; other performers include Gilels and Igor Oistrakh

1953   8/9 March: Stalin's funeral in the Hall of Columns in Moscow; performers include Tatyana Nikolayeva and David Oistrakh and the conductors Alexander Melik-Pashayev and Alexander Gauk; Richter plays Bach and Beethoven

13 May, Leningrad: together with Rostropovich, Richter plays all Beethoven's Cello Sonatas at a single concert

24 May, Moscow: Richter performs Mendelssohn's *Variations sérieuses* on television

1954   4 March, Budapest: Richter's first concert in Hungary; he plays Tchaikovsky's Concerto no. 1

9 June, Prague: Richter's only concert with one of his favourite conductors, Václav Talich; he plays Bach's D minor Concerto

25 Aug., Moscow: radio broadcast of Prokofiev's *The Ugly Duckling* with Nina Dorliac

1957   9 May, Moscow: Schubert and Liszt recital in the Grand Hall of the Conservatory; Glenn Gould attends the concert and the two pianists meet

1959 25 March, Moscow: funeral of Olga Knipper-Chekhova; Richter plays Liszt's *La lugubre gondola*

1960 10 March, Moscow: concert in memory of Mikhail Bulgakov; Richter plays a Beethoven sonata and a Chopin study

10 May, Helsinki: Richter's first concert in the West, at which he plays four Beethoven sonatas

15 Oct., Chicago: Richter's first concert in the United States; Brahms's Concerto no. 2

19 Oct., New York: first of eight concerts at Carnegie Hall; five Beethoven sonatas, a Schubert impromptu, one of Schumann's *Phantasiestücke* and two Chopin studies as encores

18 Dec., New York: Richter plays Liszt's Concerto no. 2 and Tchaikovsky's Concerto no. 1 under the direction of Leonard Bernstein at Carnegie Hall

1961 14 April, Moscow: Richter plays a Rachmaninov prelude at the reception in honour of the cosmonaut Yuri Gagarin in St George's Hall at the Kremlin

8 July, London: Richter's first concert in Great Britain, at the Royal Festival Hall; he plays a Haydn sonata and thirteen works by Prokofiev – the Second and Eighth Sonatas and eleven *Visions fugitives*

16 Oct., Paris: Richter's first concert in France, at the Palais de Chaillot; he plays Brahms's Second Concerto

28 Oct., Nice: concert to mark Picasso's 80th birthday; Richter plays Prokofiev's Sixth Sonata

1962 19 May, Florence: Richter's first concert in Italy; he plays Handel's Fifth Suite, Hindemith's First Sonata and various pieces by Prokofiev, including the Sixth Sonata and eleven *Visions fugitives*, with Rachmaninov and Debussy as encores

1 June: Richter's first concert in Vienna; he plays Schumann's *Faschingsschwank aus Wien* and Second Sonata, Chopin's *Polonaise-fantaisie*, Debussy's *Estampes* and Scriabin's Fifth Sonata

3 Oct., Milan: plays Brahms's Second Concerto at La Scala under Sergiu Celibidache

1964 20 June, Aldeburgh: meets Britten; they give their first concerts together

23 June, official opening of first Fêtes Musicales de Touraine, a festival created by Richter at the Grange de Meslay near Tours; he plays sonatas by Prokofiev and Scriabin and Ravel's *Valses nobles et sentimentales* and *Miroirs*

1965 20 June, Aldeburgh: first recital with Fischer-Dieskau; they perform Brahms's *Die schöne Magelone*

10 Oct., Moscow: concert in memory of Heinrich Neuhaus; Richter plays five Beethoven sonatas

1966   3 Feb., Cannes: Richter takes part in gala concert for the Musée Fernand Léger, performing a Beethoven sonata and works by Chopin and Debussy; other performers include Maya Plisetskaya and Jean Vilar

1967   2 July, Grange de Meslay: first joint recital with David Oistrakh; they play sonatas by Schubert, Brahms and Franck

1969   5 March, Paris: Richter performs Ravel's Concerto for the Left Hand under Lorin Maazel, then, clearly dissatisfied with his performance, repeats it as an encore
3 May, Moscow: world première of Shostakovich's Violin Sonata with David Oistrakh

1970   18 Jan.–17 April: 23-concert tour of the United States, after which Richter declines to return to America
3 Sept.–26 Oct.: first tour of Japan (19 concerts)
24 Nov., Moscow: Richter plays Rachmaninov's Prelude in B minor at the funeral of the pianist Maria Yudina

1972   9 April, Moscow: first concert with Oleg Kagan; they play Berg's Chamber Concerto

1975   27 Oct., Moscow: Beethoven recital with Oleg Kagan in memory of David Oistrakh

1986   20 July: start of 91-concert tour by car from Leningrad to Vladivostok and back; last concert in Moscow on 31 Nov.

1991   1 Jan.–26 Feb.: tour of Italy, Spain and France at which Richter plays only works by Bach, each programme dedicated 'To the memory of Oleg Kagan, musician and friend'
27 April, Moscow: concert in memory of Boris Pasternak on the centenary of his birth; Richter plays Bach's Third English Suite, Mozart's Fantasia and Sonata in C minor and Beethoven's Sonata op. 111
21 May, Moscow: concert in memory of Andrey Sakharov

1992   23 Dec., Monastery of Jouques, Abbey of Notre-Dame de Fidélité; Richter notes that he played Ravel's *La vallée des cloches* at the baptism of his friend B. E. E. A.
15 May: Richter hears of the death of Marlene Dietrich and sends 500 roses to her funeral in Berlin, dedicating a Munich recital 'to the memory of the great German artist, Marlene Dietrich'

1995   30 March, Lübeck: Richter's last concert, at which he plays Haydn's Sonatas nos. 55, 56 and 57 and Reger's Variations and Fugue on a Theme of Beethoven op. 86

Partners

Singers

Nina Dorliac, *soprano*
Dietrich Fischer-Dieskau, *baritone*
Peter Pears, *tenor*

Galina Pisarenko, *soprano*
Peter Schreier, *tenor*

Conductors

Hermann Abendroth
Oleg Agarkov
Alfred Alessandrescu
Karel Ancerl
Nikolay Anosov
Vladimir Ashkenazy
Mikhail Bachtaze
Mladen Bačic
Břetislav Bakala
Daniel Barenboim
Rudolf Barshai
Mircea Basarab
Paavo Berglund
Anisim Berlinsky

Leonard Bernstein
Pierre Boulez
Radosveta Boyadjieva
Lev Braghinsky
Benjamin Britten
Oleg Caetani
Sergiu Celibidache
Myung-Whun Chung
Odissely Dimitriedi
Victor Dubrovsky
Karl Eliasberg
Christoph Eschenbach
Solomon Feldman
János Ferencsik

Rafael Frühbeck de Burgos
Chingiz Gadzhibekov
Alexander Gauk
Ashraf Gasanov
George Georgescu
Lev Ginzburg
Dzhemal Gokieli
Nikolai Golovanov
Israel Gusman
Anton Heiller
Konstantin Iliev
Konstantin Ivanov
Hiroyuki Iwaki
Arvid Jansons
Mikhail Kanerstein
Herbert von Karajan
Vitali Kataev
Arnold Katz
Kharadjanian
G. Kiladze
Carlos Kleiber
Paul Kletzki
Alexander Klimov
Nikolai Kolesa
Vilmos Komor
Kyrill Kondrashin
András Kórodi
Jaroslav Krombholc
Mikhail Lefterov
Erich Leinsdorf
Ferdinand Leitner
Bogo Letskovic
Peter Maag
Lorin Maazel
Mikhail Maloutsian
Kurt Masur
Lovro von Matačić
Karl Melles
Vladimir Moshinsky
Evgeny Mravinsky
Charles Munch
Karl Münchinger

Riccardo Muti
Niazi
Leonid Nikolaiev
Yuri Nikolayevsky
David Oistrakh
Alexander Orlov
Eugene Ormandy
Jean-François Paillard
Isaac Pain
Vakhtang Paliachvili
Bernhard Paumgartner
Antonio Pedrotti
Demian Pelekhatny
Fernando Previtali
Sergey Prokofiev
Nikolay Rabinovich
Rouslan Raichev
Natan Rakhlin
Sviatoslav Richter
János Rolla
Mario Rossi
Witold Rowicki
Gennady Rozhdestvensky
Paul Sacher
Kurt Sanderling
Peter Schreier
Claudio Scimone
Ilya Shaposhnikov
Constantin Silvestri
Konstantin Simeonoff
Václav Smetáček
Stasevich
Grigory Stoliarov
Karol Stria
Evgeni Svetlanov
Václav Talich
Yuri Temirkanov
Benjamin Tolba
Stepan Turchak
Daniil Tyulin
Yuri Tziriuk
Leonids Vigners

Stanislaw Wislocki
Bogdan Wodicko
Nikolay Yukhnovsky
Zhivozhin Zaravkovich

Igor Zhadrov
Mikhail Zhukov
Algis Zhuraitis

Instrumentalists
Andris Arnitsans, *bassoon*
Lev Berezovsky, *cello*
Valentin Berlinsky, *cello*
Pierre Fournier, *cello*
Natalia Gutman, *cello*
Mstislav Rostropovich, *cello*
Daniil Shafran, *cello*
Sergey Shirinsky, *cello*
Anatoly Kamyshev, *clarinet*
Nikolay Kharkovsky, *flute*
Alexander Korneyev, *flute*
Konstantin Mikhailov, *flute*
Jean-Pierre Rampal, *flute*
Marina Vorozhtsova, *flute*
Ludmilla Berlinsky, *piano*
Benjamin Britten, *piano*

Emil Gilels, *piano*
Anton Ginsburg, *piano*
Zoltán Kocsis, *piano*
Elisabeth Leonskaja, *piano*
Vassili Lobanov, *piano*
Andreas Lucewicz, *piano*
Anatoly Vedernikov, *piano*
Vladimir Zykov, *trumpet*
Yuri Bashmet, *viola*
Galina Barinova, *violin*
Oleg Kagan, *violin*
Mikhail Kopelman, *violin*
David Oistrakh, *violin*
Viktor Tretyakov, *violin*
Dmitry Tsyganov, *violin*

Beethoven Quartet
Bolshoy Theatre Quartet
Borodin Quartet
Gabt Quartet
Georgian State Quartet

Komitas Quartet
Moscow Philharmonic Quartet
Tátrai Quartet
Moraguès Quintet

Index

Figures in italics indicate picture captions.

The translator wishes to acknowledge the help of Milena Borromeo and Alberto Notarbartolo in preparing this index. Above all, he would like to thank Bruno Monsaingeon for working through the translation in meticulous detail.